GRANTA BOOKS

THE GRANTA BOOK OF THE FAMILY

The Granta Book
of the Family

GRANTA BOOKS
LONDON
in association with
PENGUIN BOOKS

GRANTA BOOKS
2/3 Hanover Yard, Noel Road, London N1 8BE

Published in association with the Penguin Group
Penguin Books Ltd, 27 Wrights Lane, London W8 5TZ, England
Viking Penguin, a division of Penguin Books USA Inc.,
375 Hudson Street, New York NY 10014, USA
Penguin Books Australia Ltd, Ringwood, Victoria, Australia
Penguin Books Canada Ltd, 10 Alcorn Avenue,
Toronto, Ontario, Canada M4V 3B2
Penguin Books (NZ) Ltd, 182–190 Wairau Road,
Auckland 10, New Zealand

Penguin Books Ltd, Registered Offices: Harmondsworth, Middlesex,
England

First published in Great Britain by Granta Books 1995
This edition published by Granta Books 1996

1 3 5 7 9 10 8 6 4 2

Printed in Great Britain by Clays Ltd, St Ives plc

A CIP catalogue record for this book is available from the British Library

CONTENTS

Raymond Carver

Where he was: Memories of my Father

My dad's name was Clevie Raymond Carver. His family called him Raymond, and friends called him C.R. I was named Raymond Clevie Carver, Jr. I hated the 'Junior' part. When I was little, my dad called me 'Frog', which was OK. But later, like everybody else in the family, he began calling me 'Junior'. He went on calling me this until I was thirteen or fourteen and announced that I wouldn't answer to that name any longer. So he began calling me 'Doc'. From then until his death on 17 June 1967, he called me 'Doc' or else 'Son'.

When he died, my mother telephoned my wife with the news. I was away from my family at the time, between lives, trying to enrol in the School of Library Science at the University of Iowa. When my wife answered the phone, my mother blurted out, 'Raymond's dead!' For a moment, my wife thought my mother was telling her that I was dead. Then my mother made it clear which Raymond she was talking about, and my wife said, 'Thank God. I thought you meant *my* Raymond.'

My dad walked, hitched rides and rode in empty boxcars when he went from Arkansas to Washington State in 1934, looking for work. I don't know whether or not he was pursuing a dream when he went out to Washington. I doubt it. I don't think he dreamed much. I believe he was simply looking for steady work at decent pay. Steady work was meaningful work. He picked apples for a time and then landed a construction labourer's job on the Grand Coulee Dam. After he'd put aside a little money, he bought a car and drove back to Arkansas to help his folks, my grandparents, pack up for the move west. He said later that they were about to starve down there; and this wasn't meant as a figure of speech. It was during that short while in Arkansas, in a town called Leola, that my mother met my dad on the sidewalk as he came out of a tavern.

'He was drunk,' she said. 'I don't know why I let him talk to me. His eyes were glittery. I wish I'd had a crystal ball.' They'd met once, a year or so before, at a dance. He'd had girlfriends before her, my mother told me. 'Your dad always had a girlfriend, even after we married. He was my first and last. I never had another man. But I didn't miss anything.'

They were married by a justice of the peace on the day they left for Washington, this big, tall country girl and an ex-farm-

2

hand-turned-construction worker. My mother spent her wedding night with my dad and his folks, all of them camped beside the road in Arkansas.

In Omak, Washington, my dad and mother lived in a little place not much bigger than a cabin. My grandparents lived next door. My dad was still working on the dam and later, with the huge turbines producing electricity and the water backed up for a hundred miles into Canada, he stood in the crowd and heard Franklin D. Roosevelt dedicate the dam. 'He never mentioned those guys who died building that dam,' my dad said. Some of his friends had died there, men from Arkansas, Oklahoma and Missouri.

He then took a job in a sawmill in Clatskanie, Oregon, a little town alongside the Columbia river. I was born there, and my mother has a picture of my dad standing in front of the gate to the mill, proudly holding me up to face the camera. My bonnet is on crooked and about to come untied. His hat is pushed back on his forehead, and he's wearing a big grin. Was he going in to work, or just finishing his shift? It doesn't matter. In either case, he had a job and a family. These were his salad days.

In 1941 we moved to Yakima, Washington, where my dad went to work as a saw-filer, a skilled trade he'd learned at the mill in Clatskanie. When war broke out, he was given a deferment because his work was considered necessary to the war effort. Finished lumber was in demand by the armed services, and he kept his saws so sharp they could shave the hair off your arm.

After my dad had moved us to Yakima, he moved his folks into the same neighbourhood. By the mid-1940s, the rest of my dad's family—his brother, his sister and her husband, as well as uncles, cousins, nephews and most of their extended family and friends—had come out from Arkansas. All because my dad came out first. The men went to work at Boise Cascade, where my dad worked, and the women packed apples in the canneries. And in just a little while, it seemed—according to my mother—everybody was better off than my dad.

'Your dad couldn't keep money,' my mother said. 'Money burned a hole in his pocket. He was always doing for others.'

The first house I clearly remember living in, at 1515 South

15th Street, in Yakima, had an outdoor toilet. On Hallowe'en night, or just any night for the hell of it, neighbouring kids, kids in their early teens, would carry our toilet away and leave it next to the road. My dad would have to get somebody to help him bring it home. Or these kids would take the toilet and stand it in somebody else's backyard. Once they actually set it on fire. But ours wasn't the only house that had an outdoor toilet. When I was old enough to know what I was doing, I threw rocks at the other toilets when I'd see someone go inside. This was called bombing the toilets. After a while, though, everyone changed to indoor plumbing until, suddenly, our toilet was the last one in the neighbourhood. I remember the shame I felt when my third-grade teacher, Mr Wise, drove me home from school one day. I asked him to stop at the house just before ours, claiming I lived there.

I had one bad spanking from my dad when I was little. He took off his belt and laid it on me when he caught me walking down a railroad trestle. As he was whipping me, he said, 'This hurts me worse than it does you.' Even at the time, as small and dumb as I was, I knew this wasn't true. It had the sound of something his father might have said to him under the same circumstances.

I can recall what happened one night when my dad came home late to find that my mother had locked all the doors on him. He was drunk, and we could feel the house shudder as he rattled the door. When he'd managed to force open a window, she hit him between the eyes with a colander and knocked him out. We could see him down there on the grass. For years afterwards, I used to pick up this colander—it was heavy as a rolling-pin—and imagine what it would feel like to be hit in the face with something like that.

It was during this period that I remember my dad taking me into the bedroom, sitting me down on the bed and telling me that I might have to go live with my Aunt LaVon for a while. I couldn't understand what I'd done that meant I'd have to go away from home to live. But this, too—whatever prompted it— must have blown over, more or less anyway, because we stayed together, and I didn't have to go live with her or anyone else.

For a time in the late forties we didn't have a car. We had to walk everywhere we wanted to go, or else take the bus that stopped near where they used to carry our toilet. I don't know why we didn't have a car, some sort of car, but we didn't. Still, it was all right with me that we didn't. I didn't miss it. I mean, we didn't have a car and that's all there was to it. Back then I didn't miss what I didn't have. 'We couldn't afford a car,' my mother said, when I asked her. 'It was your dad. He drank it up.'

If we wanted to fish, my dad and I would walk to some ponds that were only a couple of miles away, or to the Yakima river, only a little farther away than the ponds. With or without a car, we went fishing nearly every weekend. But once in a while my dad wouldn't want to get out of bed. 'He feels bad,' my mother would say. 'No wonder. You better leave him alone.'

I remember her pouring his whiskey down the sink. Sometimes she'd pour it all out and sometimes, if she was afraid of getting caught, she'd only pour half of it out and then add water to the rest. I tasted some of his whiskey once for myself. It was terrible stuff, and I didn't see how anybody could drink it.

When we finally did get a car, in 1949 or 1950, it was a 1938 Ford. But it threw a rod the first week we had it, and my dad had to have the motor rebuilt.

'We drove the oldest car in town,' my mother said. 'We could have had a Cadillac for all he spent on car repairs.' One time she found someone else's lipstick on the floorboards, along with a lacy handkerchief. 'See this?' she said to me. 'Some floozie left this in the car.'

Once I saw her take a pan of warm water into the bedroom where my dad was sleeping. She took his hand from under the covers and held it in the water. I stood in the doorway and watched. I wanted to know what was going on. This would make him talk in his sleep, she told me. There were things she needed to know, things she was sure he was keeping from her.

Every year or so, when I was little, we would take the North Coast Limited across the Cascade Mountains from Yakima to Seattle and stay in the Vance Hotel and eat, I remember, at a place called the Dinner Bell Café. Once we went to Ivar's Acres of Clams and drank glasses of warm clam broth.

Both my grandparents died in 1955. In 1956, the year I was to graduate from high school, my dad quit his job at the mill in Yakima and took a job in Chester, a little sawmill town in northern California. The reasons given at the time for his taking the job had to do with a higher hourly wage and the vague promise that he might, in a few years' time, succeed to the job of head filer in this new mill. But I think, in the main, that my dad had grown restless and simply wanted to try his luck elsewhere. Things had gotten a little too predictable for him in Yakima. Also, there were the deaths, within six months of each other, of my grandparents.

But just a few days after my graduation, when my mother and I were packed to move to Chester, my dad pencilled a letter to say he'd been sick for a while. He didn't want us to worry, he said, but he'd cut himself on a saw. Maybe he'd got a tiny sliver of steel in his blood. Anyway, something had happened and he'd had to miss work, he said. In the same mail was an unsigned postcard from somebody down there telling my mother that my dad was about to die and that he was drinking 'raw whiskey'.

When we arrived in Chester my dad was living in a trailer that belonged to the company. I didn't recognize him immediately. I guess for a moment I didn't want to recognize him. He was skinny and pale and looked bewildered. His pants wouldn't stay up. He didn't look like my dad. My mother began to cry. My dad put his arm around her and patted her shoulder vaguely like he didn't know what this was all about, either. The three of us took up life together in the trailer, and we looked after him as best we could. But my dad was sick, and he couldn't get any better. I worked with him in the mill that summer and part of the fall. We'd get up in the mornings and eat eggs and toast while we listened to the radio, and then go out the door with our lunch pails. We'd pass through the gates together at eight in the morning, and I wouldn't see him again until quitting time. In November I went back to Yakima to be closer to my girlfriend, the girl I'd made up my mind I was going to marry.

He worked at the mill in Chester until the following February, when he collapsed on the job and was taken to hospital. My mother asked me to come down there and help. I caught a bus from Yakima to Chester, intending to drive them back to Yakima. But now, in addition to being physically sick, my dad was in the midst of a nervous breakdown, though none of us knew to call it that at the time. During the entire trip back to

Yakima, he didn't speak, not even when asked a direct question. ('How do you feel, Raymond?' 'You OK, Dad?') He'd communicate, if he communicated at all, by moving his head or else turning his palms up as if to say he didn't know or care. The only time he said anything on the trip, and for nearly a month afterwards, was when I was speeding down a gravel road in Oregon and the car muffler came loose. 'You were going too fast,' he said.

Back in Yakima a doctor saw to it that my dad went to a psychiatrist. My mother and dad had to go on relief, as it was called, and the County paid for the psychiatrist. The psychiatrist asked my dad, 'Who is the President?' He'd had a question put to him that he could answer. 'Ike,' my dad said. Nevertheless, they put him on the fifth floor of Valley Memorial Hospital and began giving him electric shock treatments. I was married by then and about to start my own family. My dad was still locked up when my wife went into the same hospital, just one floor down, to have our first baby.

After she had delivered, I went upstairs to give my dad the news. They let me in through a steel door and showed me where I could find him. He was sitting on a couch with a blanket over his lap. *Hey*, I thought. *What in hell is happening to my dad?* I sat down next to him and told him he was a grandfather. He waited a minute and said, 'I feel like a grandfather.' That's all he said. He didn't smile or move. He was in a big room with a lot of other people. Then I hugged him, and he began to cry.

Somehow he got out of there. But now came the years when he couldn't work and just sat around the house trying to figure what next and what he'd done wrong in his life that he'd wound up like this. My mother went from job to crummy job. Much later she referred to that time he was in the hospital, and those years just afterwards, as 'when Raymond was sick.' The work 'sick' was never the same for me again.

In 1964, through the help of a friend, he was lucky enough to be hired at a mill in Klamath, California. He moved down there by himself to see if he could hack it. He lived not far from the mill in a one-room cabin, not much different from the place he and my mother had started living in when they went west. He scrawled letters to my mother, and if I called, she'd read them

aloud to me over the phone. In the letters, he said it was touch
and go. Every day he went to work he felt like it was the most
important day of his life. But every day, he told her, made the
next day that much easier. He said for her to tell me he said
hello. If he couldn't sleep at night, he said, he thought about me
and the good times we used to have. Finally, after a couple of
months, he regained some of his confidence. He could do the
work and didn't think he had to worry that he'd let anybody
down ever again. When he was sure, he sent for my mother.

He'd been off work for six years and had lost everything in
that time: home, car, furniture and appliances, including the big
freezer that had been my mother's pride and joy. He'd lost his
good name too—Raymond Carver was someone who couldn't
pay his bills—and his self-respect was gone. He'd even lost his
virility. My mother told my wife, 'All during that time Raymond
was sick we slept together in the same bed, but we didn't have
relations. He wanted to a few times, but nothing happened. I
didn't miss it, but I think he wanted to, you know.'

During those years I was trying to raise my own family and
earn a living. But, with one thing and another, we found
ourselves having to move a lot. I couldn't keep track of what was
going on in my dad's life. But I did have a chance one Christmas
to tell him I wanted to be a writer. I might as well have told him
I wanted to become a plastic surgeon. 'What are you going to
write about?' he wanted to know. Then, as if to help me out, he
said, 'Write about the stuff you know about. Write about some
of those fishing trips we took.' I said I would, but I knew I
wouldn't. 'Send me what you write,' he said. I said I'd do that,
but then I didn't. I wasn't writing anything about fishing, and I
didn't think he'd particularly care about, or even necessarily
understand, what I was writing in those days. Besides, he wasn't
a reader. Not the sort, anyway, I imagined I was writing for.

Then he died. I was a long way off, in Iowa City, with things
still to say to him. I didn't have the chance to tell him goodbye,
or that I thought he was doing great at his new job. That I was
proud of him for making a comeback.

My mother said he came in from work that night and ate a big
supper. Then he sat at the table by himself and finished what was
left of a bottle of whiskey, a bottle she found hidden in the bottom

of the garbage under some coffee grounds a day or so later. Then he got up and went to bed, where my mother joined him a little later. But in the night she had to get up and make a bed for herself on the couch. 'He was snoring so loud I couldn't sleep,' she said. The next morning when she looked in on him, he was on his back with his mouth open, his cheeks caved in. *Grey-looking*, she said. She knew he was dead—she didn't need a doctor to tell her that. But she called one, anyway, and then she called my wife.

Among the pictures my mother kept of my dad and herself during those early days in Washington was a photograph of him standing in front of a car, holding a beer and a stringer of fish. In the photograph he is wearing his hat back on his forehead and has this awkward grin on his face. I asked her for it and she gave it to me, along with some others. I put it up on my wall, and each time we moved, I took the picture along and put it up on another wall. I looked at it carefully from time to time, trying to figure out some things about my dad, and maybe myself in the process. But I couldn't. My dad just kept moving farther and farther away from me and back into time. Finally, in the course of another move, I lost the photograph. It was then I tried to recall it, and at the same time make an attempt to say something about my dad, and how I thought that in some important ways we might be alike. I wrote the poem when I was living in an apartment house in an urban area south of San Francisco and at a time when I found myself, like dad, having trouble with alcohol. The poem was a way of trying to connect up with him.

PHOTOGRAPH OF MY FATHER IN HIS TWENTY-SECOND YEAR

October. Here in this dank, unfamiliar kitchen
I study my father's embarrassed young man's face.
Sheepish grin, he holds in one hand a string
of spiny yellow perch, in the other
a bottle of Carlsberg beer.

In jeans and flannel shirt, he leans
against the front fender of a 1934 Ford.
He would like to pose brave and hearty for his posterity,
wear his old hat cocked over his ear.
All his life my father wanted to be bold.

9

But the eyes give him away, and the hands
that limply offer the string of dead perch
and the bottle of beer. Father, I love you,
yet how can I say thank you,
        I who can't hold my liquor either
and don't even know the places to fish.

The poem is true in its particulars, except that my dad died in
June and not October, as the first word of the poem says. I wanted
a word with more than one syllable to it to make it linger a little.
But more than that, I wanted a month appropriate to what I felt
at the time I wrote the poem—a month of short days and failing
light, smoke in the air, things perishing. June was summer nights
and days, graduations, my wedding anniversary, the birthday of
one of my children. June wasn't a month your father died in.

After the service at the funeral home, after we had moved
outside, a woman I didn't know came over to me and said,
'He's happier where he is now.' I stared at this woman until she
moved away. I still remember the little knob of a hat she was
wearing. Then one of my dad's cousins—I didn't know the man's
name—reached out and took my hand. 'We all miss him,' he said,
and I knew he wasn't saying it to be polite.

I began to weep for the first time since receiving the news. I
hadn't been able to before. I hadn't had the time, for one thing.
Now, suddenly, I couldn't stop. I held my wife and wept while
she said and did what she could to comfort me there in the
middle of that summer afternoon.

I listened to people say consoling things to my mother, and I
was glad that my dad's family had turned up, had come to where
he was. I thought I'd remember everything that was said and
done that day and maybe find a way to tell it sometime. But I
didn't. I forgot it all, or nearly. What I do remember is that I
heard our name used a lot that afternoon, my dad's name and
mine. But I knew they were talking about my dad. *Raymond*,
these people kept saying in their beautiful voices out of my
childhood. *Raymond*.

SAUL BELLOW

MEMOIRS OF A
BOOTLEGGER'S SON

'*Gott meiner,*' said my father to my mother. 'Again no money? But I gave you twelve dollars at the beginning of the week. What have you done with it?'

'I don't know. It went away.'

'So quickly . . . by Thursday? Impossible.'

'It couldn't be helped. Some of it I used to pay old bills. We've owed money to Herskovitz for I don't know how long.'

'But did you have to pay him this week?'

'He's right in the block. For two months now I've been coming home the long way around. I gave him three dollars.'

'How could you! Haven't you any sense? And what did you do with the rest? Joshua,' he said, turning to me furiously. 'Take a pencil and write these things down. I have to know where it all went. I bought eggs and butter on Tuesday.'

'Seventy-five cents to the milkman,' said Ma, earnest and frightened. She must have believed she had done something wrong.

'Write it,' he said.

I had taken a piece of Ma's checkered stationery and placed the figures carefully within the tiny boxes. I was shaken, too, and eager to escape condemnation.

'Willie had a tooth out. It cost fifty cents.'

'Fifty?' he said.

'Yes, it's usually a dollar an extraction. I sent him up alone and told him to say it was all he had. And after he was done, I waited for him downstairs. I was ashamed to show my face to Dr Zadkin.'

'Did it have to come out?'

'There was nothing left of it but the walls. Do you want to look at it? The child was in pain . . . Then there was fifty cents to have the boys' hair cut.'

'I'm going to buy a pair of clippers and do it myself,' Pa said. He was always resolving to do this.

'Fifty cents for the gas meter. Twenty cents for a coal shovel. Twenty-five cents to the insurance man. Twenty cents for a flat-iron handle. Forty cents to the tinsmith for relining my copper pot. Leather mittens for Bentchka cost me thirty cents. I haven't even started on the bigger things yet, such as meat.'

'We have meat far too often,' Pa said. 'We don't need it. I

prefer milk soups anyway.'

'Don't expect me to stint on the stomach,' my mother said with determination. 'If I do nothing else, I'm going to feed the children.'

'They don't look starved,' said Pa. 'Especially this one. I never look at him but what he's chewing.'

My appetite was large and I seemed never to have had enough. I ate all the leftovers. I chewed down apple parings, gristle, cold vegetables, chicken bones.

'If I knew how to do things more cheaply,' said Ma, as though she now consented to take the blame.

'You don't bargain enough,' my father said to her harshly. His accusation always was that she did not accept her condition and was not what the wife of a poor man ought to be. And yet she was. She was whatever would please him. She made over our clothes. On the table there often appeared the thick Russian linens she had brought, but on our beds were sheets that she had made of flour sacks.

'Like your sister Julia?' said my mother.

'Yes, Julia. That's why they're rich. It was she that made him so.'

I had been with Aunt Julia to the farmer's market and knew how she worked. 'How much'a der han?' she would say when she seized a rooster. 'Oh, *trop cher*,' she'd cry at the Canadian farmer, and she'd say to me in Yiddish, 'Thieves, every last man of them. But I will beat them down.' And in her Russian shawl, with her sharp nose jutting, she would shuffle to another wagon, and she always did as she promised.

'A wife *can* make the difference,' said Pa. 'I am as able as Jomin, and stronger.'

'They have grown children.'

'Yes, that's so,' said Pa. 'Whereas I have no one to turn to.'

He would often repeat this, and particularly to me. 'You can turn to me,' he'd say. 'But to whom can I turn? Everything comes from me and nothing to me. How long can I bear it? Is this what the life of a man is supposed to be? Are you supposed to be loaded until your back is broken? Oh my God, I think I begin to see. Those are lucky who die when their childhood is over and never live to know the misery of fighting in the world.'

When he flew into a rage, he forgot himself altogether and lost his sense of shame.

'Aren't you taking money for your brother?' he once shouted at Ma. 'Aren't you saving to send him . . . ?'

He meant her brother Mordecai in St Petersburg. Her brother Aaron had recently died. The Bolsheviks had come to his house and slashed open the beds and the furniture in their search for jewels and gold. They had taken everything from him and he was dead.

'No, no,' Ma cried, and it was obvious to me that she was not telling the truth. 'How can you say it?'

She greatly loved these two brothers. On the day she received the news of Aaron's death, when she had been doing a Monday wash, she sat sobbing by the tub. Except to mourn, Jews were forbidden to sit on the floor. She hung over the tub, and her arms, in grey sleeves, trailed in the water. I came up behind her to draw her from the water. My arms felt the beating of her heart through her bosom. It was racing, furious, sick and swift.

'Let me be, Joshua. Leave me alone, my son,' she said.

'Aha! You do save money for him, and for your mother,' said my father.

'And if I do?' said Ma. 'Think, Jacob. Did they do nothing for you?'

'And did they do nothing *to* me?' Pa was beside himself.

'If I do put aside a little money now and then, it's less than you spend on your tobacco.'

'And do you know how much money I'd have now if it weren't for you and the children?' he roared at her. 'I'd be worth ten thousand dollars. Ten thousand, do you hear? And be a free man. Do you hear what I say?' he glared with a strained throat. In his rage his face wore an expression that resembled hunger. His eyes grew huge, like those of a famished man. 'I say I might have had ten thousand dollars.'

'Why don't you leave then?' My mother wept.

'That's what I will do!'

He hurried out. It was night. He was gone for about an hour, and then I saw his cigarette glow on the front step, and he said to me, meekly, that he had only gone to buy a package of Honeysuckles.

'Will you please save the package for me, Papa?' said Willie, and Pa said to him, 'Of course, my boy. I'll remember this time and not throw it away.'

Pa was a mercurial man, and very unlucky. He had the energy to be a millionaire but nothing came of it except poverty. From Aunt Julia, I knew the story of the dowry. In less than a year, Pa had lost the ten thousand roubles and went to Ma's brothers to ask for more. One of them, Uncle Mordecai, was very rich. He had run away to South Africa as a boy and made a fortune among the Kaffirs and later he sold cattle to the Russians during the Japanese war. When they lost they didn't settle their debt, but he made a fortune nevertheless. He came back to Russia after this, and until the War led the life of a rich man. According to Ma, he was princely, dashing, brave and open-handed. By Pa's account, he drank too much and spent his money on women and neglected his respectable wife. Pa would sometimes frown at me and say that I reminded him of Mordecai. He saw the faults of my mother's family embodied in me. In my own mind I came to accept this, and was not ashamed of it even when Pa would say, 'There's insanity in your mother's line. Her Uncle Poppe was a firebug, and he was very dangerous. He used to set the curtains afire. These things are inherited. There's no taint like that on my family.'

'Not if you don't count hard hearts and bad tempers,' Ma would occasionally, but too rarely, answer. Only occasionally, because she loved him. When he was away she'd say to the children, 'If you told Mordecai that you needed something, he put his hand in his pocket and gave you what was in it, without looking.'

In Petersburg, Pa had made a handsome living. He dealt in produce and travelled widely. He was the largest importer of Egyptian onions and Spanish fruit. And it was evident that he and Ma had been people of fashion. She still owned black taffeta petticoats and ostrich feathers, now out of fashion, and some jewellery, while Pa had a Prince Albert in the trunk, and a stove-pipe hat, a brocaded vest and a fox-lined overcoat. Ma's fur coat was made over for Zelda and she wore it for four years at the Baron Byng school, complainingly. 'Over there, we had everything we needed,' Ma said. There were photos of Zelda in silk dresses, and of me in velvet pants, with long hair, like Rasputin. But every minute of this prosperity was stolen. Bribes made it possible. Then Pa was seized by the police for illegal residence. My uncles got him out of prison, and we escaped to Canada.

Within a year, the money he had brought from Russia was almost gone. The last of it he put into a partnership with three other men who owned a bakery. He had to drive a wagon, and he wasn't used to rough labour then. He had never before harnessed a horse. Over there, only coachmen and teamsters knew how to harness. Pa had to learn to do it by lantern light in the cold Canadian nights, with freezing hands which he would try to warm by the lantern-glass or against the horse's belly. His route lay in Lachine and Wilson's Pier, along the St Lawrence, by the Lachine Canal, around Monkey Park and the Dominion Bridge Company. Across the river, in Caughnawaga, the Indians lived in their old cottages. At this time Pa smelled of bread and his hair was somewhat floury. His partners were quarrelsome and rough, they swore obscenely and held Pa for a dude, and as the misery of his sudden fall was too much to hide they gave him a hard time. Why should it be so terrible to have become one of them? Ma said they gave him all the worst things to do.

The bakery was a shanty. The rats took refuge from the winter there, and were drowned in the oil and fished out suffocated from the jelly. The dogs and cats could not police them, they were so numerous. The thick ice did not float leisurely, it ran in the swift current. In March and even April the snow still lay heavy. When it melted, the drains couldn't carry off the water. There were grey lagoons in the hollows of old ice; they were sullen or flashing according to the colour of the sky.

The partners had fist fights. Pa was no judge of the strength of others, and as he was very proud and reckless he usually got the worst of it. He came home with horrible bruises on his face and his voice broke as he told how it happened. Eliahu Giskin was the one with whom he had most trouble. Huge and stout, Eliahu had a shaved head and a tartar moustache. He drove one of the skinny, rusty wagons of the firm. The very rust was fading deeper, into mauve, and on it was spelled in a circle of blind letters *Pâtisserie de Choix Giskin*. He was a bawling and clutching kind of man. He bullied the horse so that it put forth the best speed for him. Scared of him, it turned its head sidewards from the whip and galloped with heavy, hairy ankles through the streets. On the ground, Giskin himself was awkward and moved with hampered steps because of the size of his belly and his enormous boots. Pa also walked in a certain peculiar smart way; he put more weight on the left heel than on the right and marched as he went. He almost limped. It was an old Jewish way of walking, with his hands held at his back.

He and Giskin had their worst fight one day in the yard of the bakery when my mother and I were there. Exactly why they were fighting I couldn't tell you. They grappled and Pa's shirt was torn from him. It was a Russian style of fighting. Each tried to carry the other down and there was no idea of self-defence, but just one desperate body squeezing the other. Pa was burned up with violence, and he was a strong muscular man in his young days. Giskin clawed and scratched his white back as they clinched while Pa struck him with his elbow and fists. They fell on the rutted ground. A baker and one of the helpers ran out from the shack and pulled them apart.

'How can this go on?' said Ma at home where she helped him to undress and washed the dirt from him.

Pa admitted that it couldn't. He might kill Giskin or Giskin him, he said. And Ma insisted that he should withdraw from the partnership, and he did so although he did not know what to turn to next.

He tried the junk business, at which my Uncle Jomin had grown rich, and with the string of jingling junk bells stretched across the wagon he drove along the St Lawrence shore and up and down the shanty streets, the little brick streets, and put in at farms and monasteries to try to buy rags, paper and metal. He spoke ten words of French and not many more of English, then.

'*Might you could sell me iron, gentlemann?*' was what he said. I was often on the wagon-seat, and watched—the eldest son, though ten years old, the *b'chor* as I was called, I was supposed to go into the world with him. He was not submissive, though he appeared to be so. At least he was not submissive to men. It was to necessities that he hung down his head and not to the farmer or the Brother or housewife. He had hard matter in him. He smoked as he drove, with keen eyes. We wrapped burlap about our knees when fall weather blew. The cold little bells clinked. *'Gentlemann?'* Pa would begin, and something both anxious and bold played through him. To weigh paper, he had a scale in the wagon; his purse was in his hand to pay, a steel-billed leather purse. The term for it was also the slang word for the scrotum. The money in it was poor, seedy money, dark copper, bleak silver and a wrinkled green paper or two.

He left this business soon, never having earned more than a few dollars a week at it. In the winter it was too much for him. With Uncle Asher, Aunt Taube's husband, he went into the bag business. They rented a loft and some machines, and hired two women to operate them. It looked as if they might make good as manufacturers. Somehow Asher got an order for munitions-bags during the War. However, the contract was cancelled because the first batch was not up to specifications. When this happened, there was a big family quarrel. Everyone got into it. Aunt Taube was very haughty. Uncle Asher had great respect for Ma and was always civil to her. In fact, he was meek and good-tempered, not very clever. He boasted about his teeth and never ate candy. He was apt to repeat this too often, about candy. It was she, his sister, who said the worst things against Pa.

Ma told her, 'Don't be ungrateful, Taube.'

She meant that Taube and Asher owed their being in America to Pa. He had given them the money to marry, in his prosperous days.

'A great favour you did me,' said Taube, although her love affair with Asher was famous. The son of a mere stationmaster, he was not considered a match for her. She had seen him from a train-window while he stood idle on the platform. He was placid, and handsome because of it. My cousins, three small girls, were like him. Aunt Taube always wore a smile, but it was a shrewd smile. At the left corner of her mouth a few of the nerves were ailing and she could not govern her expressions well. She was the brainy one and wore the pants.

'It was Asher's fault,' Pa declared. 'He tried to save money on the material. That was why we lost the contract.'

'Jacob,' said my aunt, 'you must always blame someone else.'

'Well, what good does it do to fight about it now,' said Ma. 'That's what I'd like to know.'

Neither quarrelling nor peace made a difference. Pa had no trade, he would have found no work if he had had one, for there wasn't any to be found after the War. He was ready for any humiliation, even that of serving a master, and to him that was one of the deepest. He had come into the world to do business, and there was no limit to the strength and effort he would expend in this. His pride was beaten, or almost beaten, when he was ready to labour for another man.

'A beggar!' said Pa, describing himself. 'A *bettler*!'

The ragged old country *bettler*, hairy, dirty and often crazy, were to be seen then in the yellowish streets of Jewish Montreal. They carried burlap sacks in which were old rags and scraps of food. What they couldn't finish when you fed them they clutched with their beggar's fingers from the plate and stuffed into the sack: stew, bread, crumbs of sugar. Then they blessed, they mumbled insane things, and shouldered their sacks and went away. They were supposed to be like this.

Ma therefore smiled when Pa said that. 'Not yet, by any means,' was what she answered.

'Not far from it. How far do you think?'

He had gone into innumerable enterprises: jobbing, peddling, storekeeping, the produce business, the bottle business, the furniture business, the dairy business, the insurance business, matchmaking. There was no corner into which he didn't try to squeeze himself.

At one time we thought of becoming farmers. I say 'we' because my parents discussed their projects over the kitchen table. Matters of business were always brought into the open. The children had to understand. If Herskovitz the grocer or Duval the landlord came to ask for their money, the children couldn't say that Pa or Ma were at home. We grasped these necessities very quickly.

Pa had heard of a farm out beyond Huntington that was for sale or rent, and we went to see it. It was an excursion. We put on our best. Ma was very happy; she was not a city-woman by upbringing. We went down to the Grand Trunk Station on the trolley, buying some half-spoiled Bartlett pears on the way. Pa said they had their best flavour when they were like that and peeled them for us with his penknife in his neat way. Some of his habits were very trim. Tobacco made two fingers of his left hand dark brown.

There was a soft gloom in the station. The city air was heavy that day. But as we were crossing the ponderous black bridge the sun opened up on us. Beneath the funnel hole in the toilet the St Lawrence winked. Quick death should we fall in. Then the stones of the roadbed, scratched by much speed. It was bright and hot at the station when the short trip ended. We were picked up in a buggy by the farmer, an old man. Ma mounted the step with her pointed, black, button shoes, and Zelda next, with her straw hat on which cloth roses were perishing. The kids wore pongee suits with short pants, and I a pair of heavy serge knickers that made me sweat. They were picked out for me from a job lot Pa had once acquired. Blue flowers grew in the long, station-side weeds. A mill-wheel was splashing in the town.

'Ah,' said Pa. 'It's good to stand under that. It knocks your bones into place. Best thing in the world for you.'

Bentchka had a habit of dropping his head and dreaming at things with one eye. His hair was still long then. Ma would not let it be cut though he was nearly five. On her other side sat Willie with his bated-breath look; he stared at the hay, then lying over the stubble to dry. The old farmer, Archie, described the country with flaps of his whip. Ma's face softened with all the country pleasure, the warm sun and the graceful hay, and fragrance, the giant trees and hoops of birds that went about them, the perfect leaves and happy sun. She began to have smooth creases of enjoyment about her mouth and chin instead of her often sober and dark expression.

We arrived at the house. It was like silver with age, the wind had polished it so long. The old wife with her seamed skin came to the door and called in a clear voice, 'Arrrchie—the hens are in the garrrden.' Willie ran to shoo them. Pa and Ma inspected the long door, went through the house and then down toward the yard. Ma said, 'It just revives you to smell this air.' From the tone she took, Zelda and I knew that this was just a holiday in the country. And I had been imagining great things and let my mind build hopes that I could be a farmer's son and walk on those gold stubble fields from one horizon to another and not as a timid, fleshy city boy with these meek shoes, but in boots. But look! It was obvious. We couldn't live here. Glancing at me as if I would be the most prone to it, Ma said, 'We can't have the children growing up ignorant and boors.' I couldn't hide my disappointment. It filled my face.

'I don't see why they should,' said Pa.

But Ma said it was plain enough. No synagogue, no rabbis, no kosher food, no music teachers, no neighbours, no young men for Zelda. It would be good for the health of the younger children, that was true, but she wasn't going to have us grow into cowherds, no finer feelings, no learning.

'Ach, too bad,' said Pa with gloom, but he nodded. He was sizing up the beast-world of the barnyard, and I don't doubt but that he was thinking what hardship it had been for him to learn to harness a horse. And our mother had strange ideas about association with animals. If I stroked a cat she'd occasionally warn me against it. She'd say, 'You'll be cat-witted.' Or a dog, the same. 'You'll be dog-souled.'

'No, no,' she said to my pleading. Zelda was on her side; Pa was not wholeheartedly on mine.

And when we were ready to leave, we had to search for Willie. He had wandered off to the river to watch the blackbirds plunge through the bulrushes and to try to catch toads in his handkerchief. This was enough for Ma. She was in a panic. A river! Small children wandering away. There was no more discussion of farms. The farmer drove us back to the station toward night, when a star like a chopped root flared in the sky.

Pa would often say afterwards that he still wished he owned a piece of land. Losing his temper he'd exclaim against my mother, 'There could have been bread. All we needed. But you had to have your city. Well, now we've got it. We've got bricks and stones.'

The next business he tried was a dry goods store in Point St Charles, not a prosperous district. The streets ran into nothing after blocks of half-empty slum and goat-tracked snows. The store was in a wooden building. Stairs led down to it from the sidewalk. When you got down to the bottom, where the wood underfoot was shredded with age, you found a door in which there was a little pane, and when you opened it you encountered Pa and Cousin Henoch. They were setting up shop. Railroad overalls and ladies' drawers hung on exhibit, stockings, gloves, wool headwear, layettes, silk shirts and Hudson Bay blankets, and a lot of army goods. There was an odour of smoke from some of these articles; Pa had bought them at salvage sales. The business had no credit as yet and could not lay in an entirely new line. Pa got job lots wherever he could. Cousin Henoch had brought a little money into the partnership, and Pa had borrowed some from his sister Julia and her husband, who had plenty of it.

I participated in this, too. Pa, you see, thought that I was stupid and backward. He had a biased and low opinion of me and he was anxious for me to take shape, and quickly. He couldn't stand for me to remain boyish. He would say to me, 'You'll be a man soon and your head still lies in childish things. I don't know what will become of you. At twelve, thirteen, fourteen, I was already a man.' Oh, he was very impatient of childhood. One must not remain a child but be mature of understanding and carry his share of difficulty. He wouldn't have me studying magic or going to the baths with Daitch, or hiding in the free library.

Catching me there, he'd drive me into the street. When his temper was up, he thought nothing of gripping me by the ear and leading me away. Back from unseriousness. Back from heathen delusions. Back from vain and childish things. We'd march together while he gripped my ear.

'Do you know what you are?' he'd say full of rage. 'A chunk of fat with two eyes staring from it. But I'll make something of you. A man. A Jew. Not while I live will you become an idler, an outcast, an Epicurus.'

I was frightened and begged at him to let me go. I wasn't entirely a submissive son. But I didn't dare try to free my ear, though my voice went deep and hoarse when I said, 'Don't do that, Pa. Don't do that!' I yelled, 'Let me go!' while he gripped me and led me home. He made me look like a fool in the eyes of the old lady at the library. To him such things didn't matter. He kept his eye on the main business of life: to provide for us and teach us our duty.

After a family conference he often said, when it had been decided what to do, 'And you'll come with me.'

So I was with him when he went to make a loan of Aunt Julia and Uncle Jomin.

Aunt Julia was his eldest sister, a very shrewd and sharp-minded woman, and rich, and her attitude toward many things was condemnatory. She had a thin face and a pinched nose, very unfeminine to my way of thinking; her colour was flushed and it made her look threatening sometimes. Yet she was witty, also, and often kept you laughing; and when you were laughing and out of breath, then came something that took the ground from under your feet. When she said something about you, you were criticized to the heart. It was merciless, for she was a harsh judge of character. Her face, I said, was thin, but her hair was heavy and glossy. She wore it in a single stout braid down her back. Her body was also heavy, in contrast with her face, and at home she wore a few unusual and choice garments—a man's undershirt, a pair of voluminous green bloomers and over them a scarlet crêpe de Chine wrapper, wool stockings and fleece slippers. She sat heavily or, cooking, cleaning, she stood and moved with heaviness, and at all times, in that unvarying nasal tone, she uttered the most damaging and shrewd remarks conceivable: a sort of poetry of criticism, fault-finding and abuse. She was always ingenious and there were very few offences that she forgave.

Though she oppressed me, I was crazy about her. She was a great show-woman and she said whatever she pleased with utter frankness, and she and Uncle Jomin, that mild person, were extremely salty. Because, you understand, they were outstanding people; they had a right and nobody would contest it. My Uncle Jomin was a brown man and slender. His beard was tight, short and black; it surrounded the broad teeth of his smiling mouth, of which one was gold. The bridge of his nose had an intense twist, and then the cartilages broadened—it became a saddle nose. He had the brown eyes of an intelligent, feeling, and yet satirical animal. He had a grim humour about him. The odour of his breath was tart and warm. I always found it agreeable to be near him. He enjoyed playing the hand-slapping game with me, a homely game that went like this: you laid your hands on his palms and were supposed to snatch them away before he could slap them. If he missed, it was your turn to try to slap his. Despite his slight trembling—he was not well, he had an enlarged heart— he was swifter than I. With a bent head that shook slightly he would hide a deep smile and gaze at my reddened hands. His crisp beard itself made a slight sound. My hands smarted. I would laugh, like the rest of them, but be angry at heart.

My cousins, grown men and all in business, stood watching.

'Faster, you duffer,' said Cousin Abba. He was nearest to me in age and already had an enterprise of his own; in summer he operated a fruit stand. Abba subscribed to *Chums* and *Magnet*, British schoolboy magazines. He talked continually of Bob Cherry and Tom Merry and Billy Bunter and hamptuckers, and mixed 'jollies' and 'eh what's with the fantastic Yiddish they all spoke, a French-Russian-Hebrew-British Yiddish.

'Faster there, Houdini, you *golem*. Stay with it, now. Stiff upper lip does it. That's the spirit my man. Ay, what a *frask-o*. Burns, eh? Good for the circulation, I'll be bound.'

He whinnied when I cried out. He was all right, Abba. Not more open-handed than the rest of them. They didn't exactly have that reputation. But we were fond of each other and he often gave me good advice.

Jomin's business was junk. He was one of the biggest junk dealers in Montreal. In his yard there were piles, mountains of old metal shapes, the skeletons of machines and beds, plumbing fixtures. A deep, scaly red-brown beautiful rust shone like powdered chicory and dry blood to the sun. Cobwebs floated from it. I went around in the loft and tried to read funnies on the faces of paper bales or looked for locks that I could study, as Houdini had done. In the office swung chandeliers and princely metals. Long-armed and stooped in his cocoa-coloured sweater, Uncle Jomin stood in the middle of the yard and sorted scrap. He examined a piece of metal, classified it and threw it to the top of the appropriate pile. Iron here, zinc there, lead left, brass right and babbitt by the shed. Boys, Indians, old women, halfwits and greenhorns who did not know a word of English, arrived with junk in little carts and coasters. Junk men with wagons and plumed horses came. During the War Uncle Jomin did a vast business. The junk was needed at the shipyards and on the Western Front.

My aunt bought real estate, and my cousins went into business. Moneywise, they were among the first families. They lived simply, and they were known as hard dealers. In the synagogue, they rated very highly and had seats against the eastern wall, the best because the nearest to Jerusalem. The dark man and his sons, with other leading Jews, faced the rest of the congregation. Of these, most were meek immigrants, pedlars, factory workers, old grandfathers and boys. From the women's gallery Aunt Julia, thin-nosed, looked down. Her Hebrew was good and she prayed as well as any man. She wore glasses and read steadily from her book.

She'd say to me, 'What do you think of Tante Julia? Your old *Trante* is no fool.'

She could not let a word go by without giving a twist. She had a great genius with words.

One winter afternoon we came to make a touch for the store in Point St Charles. Naturally enough, Pa was a little scared of such a woman. Ma said, 'It will be hard but you have to do it. They can give you the money, and Jomin doesn't have a bad heart. Not even she can refuse her brother.'

Pa shrugged and turned his hands outward. He had been tramping the town, making his stops: he covered miles daily in his hunt for business opportunities, and did it in his outward-pointed stride, favouring the left heel, always, and his hands behind his back and his head dropped to one side. 'We'll see,' he said. He had stopped at home to get me to come with him, and so didn't take off his fox-lined overcoat—the orange fur was bald in places—and his scarf, the colour of creamed coffee, was wound thickly under his chin; it sparkled with melted frost, and so did the moustache that covered his handsome mouth. He diffused an odour of cigarettes; his fingers were dyed with the brown colour. Ma helped me into my sheepskin. She wasn't well that day, she suffered with her teeth and was heating buckwheat on the stove to apply to her cheek. Bentchka was ailing, too. He sat and looked through the bars of his bed at the sparrows as they ruffled on the wires and on the glass clusters of the telephone poles and dropped down to peck in the horse-churned, sleigh-tracked snow. You could leave him alone; he'd amuse himself for hours.

We changed cars at Place d'Armes; the snow stung like rock salt, and then we travelled another half an hour on the Notre Dame car and arrived at Aunt Julia's at sunset. Ribbons of red colour were buried in the dry snow. The sun seemed snarling, the moon pearly cold and peaceful. We went in. The stoves were hot and there was a bearskin on the sofa. The curl-tailed bitch barked. Her teeth were sharp, curved and small. My face smarted with heat and cold, and my mouth watered at the smell of gravy. Meat was roasting.

Tante Julia was thinking, as I took off my coat, how chunky I was. I knew. In her eyes this was not a bad thing, but meant I had a lot of good hard work in me.

Her floors were highly polished and gleamed with darkness, with stove lights and the final red of the roaring cold Canadian day. While she watched us take our outdoor clothes off her face judged us in a very masculine way. She knew what Pa was here for. Trust her for that.

'Come in the kitchen and have something,' she said nasally. She was not stingy when it came to food; she always fed you well. 'The lad must be hungry.'

'Give him something, yes,' said Pa.

'And you?'

'I'm not hungry.'

'Too worried to eat, ah?'

Nevertheless, Pa also ate several slices of delicious dry roast meat with carrots and grape jelly. We drank tea. Uncle Jomin was a slow eater. For every piece of bread he recited a blessing. Then he sliced away the crust and bent to the plate with a slow shake of his broad head.

'Tuck in, old top,' said Cousin Abba. 'Joshua is a *gefährlicher* trencherman.' All my cousins laughed. Everyone was present this evening. I laughed, too.

I was in an odd way a favourite with them all, although they were also sardonic with me and gave me hell. I caught it from Cousin Moses because I tracked tar one summer day into his new Ford. He had bought it to court a girl—a rich girl related to Libutsky the bottle man.

I crept into Moses's car with tar and my feet, and he lost his temper and whacked me on the head—a favourite place; perhaps everyone felt that it was a thick place and I would take no harm there. I cried and said I would get him for that, and for a while we were enemies. At Huntington, where Aunt Julia had a summer house, Cousin Moses slapped my face once and I picked up a piece of wood and tried to kill him. I would have brained him; I was in a rage. It swept me away and I no longer knew or cared what I was doing. He was sitting on the swing with his fiancée; he was swarthy and she pale. He was grinning. A vine wove fiercely around the lattices; it grew a kind of cucumber, full of prickles and inedible. Moses teased me out of the side of his mouth. I gave him an angry answer because I couldn't stand to be ridiculed before the girl, and I suddenly felt a spirit of murder in my blood and ran at him with the piece of firewood. He knocked me over and picked me up by the collar, choked me with the neckband and beat some sense into me. He slapped me till I tasted blood in my saliva and then booted me in the tail. He told Aunt Julia he wouldn't have me around. He said I was a goy, an Ishmael, and that I'd have to go back to St Dominique Street. It was a holiday, you see. They would rescue each of us a few days at a time and give us some country air at their cottage. So back I went and Willie was sent down.

I made it up afterwards with Moses. Maybe it weighed on his conscience that he had beaten me so hard; I felt ashamed, too, that I had tried to murder him. Anyway, I got along better with him than with my cousin Philip. He was a law student at McGill and behaved very slyly toward me. They were all my seniors and dealt with me more as uncles than as cousins. Cousin Thelma, two years older than I, was fat and huge and had a bold savage temper. Her hair was frizzy and her teeth were obstinate and white.

'Tell, my brother,' said Aunt Julia when everybody was present. 'I gather that things are going badly again.'

'They never went well,' said Pa. 'But I may be doing better soon, God willing.'

'Why, do you have something new in mind?'

'Yes,' said Pa.

'And why don't you stick to one thing,' his sister said. 'You jump from this to that, and here and there. You have no patience.'

'I have little children,' said Pa, in a lowered but not patient voice. 'I have to put bread on the table. I am no coward and I'm not idle, and I'm learning the language and the ways. I'm all over the city every day and digging in the cinders for a bone. I thank you for your advice. When a dog is drowning, everyone offers him a drink.'

'Yes, yes,' said my Aunt Julia. 'You don't have to tell us what it is to be poor immigrants. We know the taste of it. When Jomin came over he dug ditches. He worked with pick and shovel for the CPR and he has a hernia to this day. But I, you understand me, knew how to manage and I never thought I was a grand lady from St Petersburg with rich brothers and a carriage and summer house and servants.'

'She doesn't have them any more,' Pa said.

'You didn't know anything of such things either, before you met her,' said Aunt Julia, 'and don't pretend to *me* that you were born with a golden spoon in your mouth. I know better.'

'Yes, but what of it?'

'You cry because you've fallen so. And how humiliating it is. Common people couldn't see you, your windows were so high.'

'I never snubbed you, or anyone,' said Pa. 'My door always was open and my hand was too. I tasted prosperity once but I know something else now. Eliahu Giskin beat my bones, and *I haven't a piece of tin/To stop up a hole, or cover my skin*, as they say. I often feel as if I was buried alive.'

'My children had no pianos and violins. They knew they were poor. You have to know, and be, what you are. Be what you are. The rest is only pride. I sent them out to earn a penny. They collected bottles and bones and ran errands. They had no time to become musicians. Now, thank God, things have gone better.

28

They will hire musicians when they marry. *Then*,' she said, 'we'll dance. And I hope you'll be there to share our joy.'

The Jomins owned the house we were sitting in, and other properties around town.

'A wife has a duty to her husband not to make him a slave to the children,' said Aunt Julia. 'If you saved the dollars that you spend to make Kreislers of your boys and a princess of your daughter you wouldn't have to dig in the cinders like a dog, as you say.'

The blood had risen to her face, which never was pale, her eyes were angry and her voice high and hard. As Pa had come to confess failure and ask for aid he was obliged to listen. Also, he may not have disagreed entirely; perhaps he wanted to hear Ma blamed. He was an influenceable man and sometimes said these very things himself. Pa didn't have a constant spirit. Depending on how he felt, he changed opinion. One night he'd sit and shed tears when Zelda played Beethoven, his heart touched; another time, he'd stamp his feet and say we were ruining him: 'Food! That's my duty. Shoes!—Shoes I'm obliged as a father to put on your feet. Whatever a father should do, I will do!' he'd shout at us all. 'But I will not lay down my health and strength for luxuries and nonsense.'

Aunt Julia said, sternly, with fierce eyes turned to me, 'Children have their part to do, too.'

'Oh,' said my father, 'he's a pretty good lad.' He put his hand on my head gently. I almost burst into tears at this. A moment before I was indignant with him because he said nothing in defence of Ma. I, you see, knew what she was up against. Fear of Aunt Julia and my other hard elders kept me from speaking. It was no time to have a burst of temper and hurt Pa's chances of a loan. But now when he touched me and said I was pretty good, I wanted to take his hand and kiss it, and say how well I understood what was happening, and how much I loved him. The roof of my mouth ached, and my throat closed. I didn't dare to move or to open my mouth.

'He should be that,' said Aunt Julia. 'He's got a good father—a father who watches over his children. He's old enough to understand the difference.'

I was old enough, certainly, to understand.

'What's this new business you have gone into, Uncle?' said Cousin Moses respectfully. It came hard, because Pa was an immigrant, all but a pauper. Also, like everyone else, Pa was subject to mockery, probably, as soon as his back was turned. I had seen all the Jomins take turns at mimicking some character. I had seen them put an entire Sunday afternoon on the porch into this wicked vaudeville—how so-and-so walked, stammered, wiped his nose on his sleeve or picked bones out of fish. My sister Zelda also had a great gift for this game. She didn't spare anyone. And I am positive that Pa was often taken off in Aunt Julia's house. And perhaps he had just done something typical, and they were barely able to hold back their laughter. However, respect for elders was drummed into all of us. Pa was Moses's uncle and Moses had to speak to him with considerable civility. It was quite a thing to watch, for a man like Moses had a strong spirit of satire. He smiled at the side of his mouth. He had a powerful, swarthy face, and passed air loudly through his nose to punctuate what he said.

His engagement to the Libutsky girl, now broken off, was the result of Pa's matchmaking. My parents had tried that, too, as a sideline, and had brought Moses and the girl together. Uncle Jomin read matrimonial notices aloud to his sons from the Yiddish paper. Widows with fortunes were the chief interest, and young women with large marriage portions from the Far West who needed Jewish husbands. My Aunt Julia told her children, 'Don't hold yourselves cheap. Marry rich.' The Libutsky girl had money, but it didn't work out. Ma thought well of Moses. However, she said, the girl was too gentle for him. He would need a bolder one.

'What is this business?' Moses said.

'A little dry goods store in Point St Charles.'

'Not a bad idea,' said Moses, 'Is it a good location?'

'Yes, we can make a living there. If the Lord will send a little luck. You know I've never been a lazy man. I've had money, and I'll have it again, as surely as we're alive this day in the world . . . '

'With God's help, it happens,' said Uncle Jomin.

'It was hard for Sarah to get used to the life here, but . . . '

'You have a good wife,' said Uncle Jomin. 'I feel for her.

And it is a strange country. But you have to keep your head. That's the main thing about strangeness.'

Aunt Julia interrupted, saying, 'I don't see what's so strange. You had to make your way over there, too. Would you want to be in Russia now? A fire!' she said. 'A destruction! Millions of corpses. Ploughing with cannon. Typhus. Famine and death. Didn't you have a taste of it? Don't you thank God that you escaped from those madmen?'

She told Pa this sternly, and glared at him that he could be so weak-minded, so forgetful, so ignorant as to talk loosely about the strangeness here. She showed you how the old country was sealed up in doom and death. She spoke strongly, and as though it was a credit to her to have come here. Escape? No, it was more like a triumph.

Melba the fox terrier sat in Uncle Jomin's lap and cunningly reached for scraps on his plate. She extended her head sidewise under his arm. Melba was privileged and the reason was that one night she woke Uncle Jomin when the house was afire. She pulled the blanket from him and saved the family. Therefore she had the run of things. She escorted Jomin to the junkyard in the morning and then she came home to accompany Aunt Julia to the market. They seemed to me exceptionally lucky in their dog. We could not have one. I brought a terrier in and he gave us fleas. We had to be treated with Paris Green. Pa went out and brought it home in a paper sack, mixed a paste and smeared it on our bodies. Another time an English bulldog followed me home. I fed him peppermint hard-balls, the red and white kind. However, he ran away. I ran after him all the way to Peel Street but couldn't get him back. We had cats, instead, many of them. They belonged to Bentchka.

Then, too, Aunt Julia had pictures on the wall that seemed to me of a high degree. Of these, the best was Queen Victoria with a veil and diadem, her flesh very fair and pure. She had her elbow on the table and her chin rested on her wrist. In addition, there was a painting of a basket of fruit. A peach sliced in half with a very rich red stone was in front. Another picture was of a faithful collie who had found a lamb in the snow and wouldn't abandon it. These were powerful and influential pictures. It wasn't any old thing that turned up in the junkyard that Aunt Julia would allow to hang on her walls. At home we had only one picture, of Moses holding up the tablets.

'I have a partner for the Point St Charles business,' said Pa.

'A partner! Why a partner?' said Aunt Julia. 'Why are you afraid to do anything by yourself? And who is this partner?'

'Henoch,' he told her.

'*Gottenyu!*' Aunt Julia raised her sarcastic eyes to heaven. She clasped her hands and wrung her fingers. Her long upraised nostrils were tense with laughter and horror at Pa's idiocies.

'That one?' said Cousin Moses.

Aunt Julia cried out, 'You poor beggar. You everlasting fool.'

'Is this,' said Philip, 'the Henoch who left his wife?'

Henoch was my mother's cousin, and he had brought his wife and family over, but then there had been a divorce. No one approved of that.

'I didn't want a partner,' Pa explained. 'But I had to take in someone. I couldn't do everything myself.'

'Not if you took Joshua out of school?'

'No, not even.'

Jomin said, 'What happened to Henoch's fish store?'

'Gone,' said Pa.

'Well, that's a fine omen,' said Aunt Julia. 'He ruined his own business, and now you want to give him a second opportunity in your store.'

'They say he's living with another woman,' said Moses.

Moses had a passion for gossip. He'd come and tell his mother things. That very evening, I heard him say to her in an undertone, 'Max Feldman, you remember . . . '

'Yes.'

'Was caught.'

'With another woman?'

'His own mother-in-law.'

'No!' she said, turning her fine sharp head to him, with alarm. 'Woe-to-us-not! Those wasters! Where?'

'Where do you think,' said Moses. 'In bed, of course.'

She gave a little scream of horror and satisfaction. 'What a beast of a woman, to do this to her daughter.'

'Well,' Pa said in reply to Moses's question about Henoch. 'I don't know where he's living.' His answer was uneasy, for it wasn't truthful.

'And such a sport yet,' said Aunt Julia, 'with his little moustache, and his crooked eyes and fat lips, and his belly, and that coat he wears with a split in the back, like a Prussian.'

She was a deadly observer. Cousin Henoch's coat did bear a resemblance to the Prussian military overcoat.

'And he stinks of fish,' she added. 'And he's rotten to the bone, and lazy, and he probably has syphilis. And if you think I am going to throw away money on a business like . . . '

'I'll give you my own note,' said Pa. 'Not his, mine.'

' . . . If you think we are going to throw away hard-earned money,' she said, 'you can go out in the woods, and find a bear, and pick up the bear's apron, and kiss the bear,' she said, fiercely nasal and high, 'right under the apron.'

The mirth of the Jomin family was a curious thing—it had a devil of a twist to it. They were dark, and they were all clever and subtle, and laughed like wolves, pointing their faces.

The kitchen walls were hot. The stoves were bursting with heat. Where old pipe-holes entered the chimney there were circular asbestos plugs with flowers painted on them.

The Jomins laughed at Aunt Julia's wit, but Pa said angrily, 'You are heartless people! Hard people! One schleps himself out to earn a living for his wife and children, and another mocks him. You have it good in America. While my face is being ground.'

The hot kitchen filled with high, wrathful voices. The cries mounted.

'America is all yours, my dear brother,' cried Aunt Julia. 'Go and do as Jomin did. Work with a pick and shovel, as he did. Dig ditches and lay tracks. To this day he wears a truss.'

That was a fact. An elaborate truss with a cushion for the groin hung in the bathroom. I found it behind the bathroom door and tried it on. The pad pushed uncomfortably into the groin.

'He'll never be the same man. Don't expect me to waste his money on your wife's relatives.'

'A coarse, cruel character you have,' Pa shouted. 'Your brother's misery does you good, you devil, you.'

'You grudge me my good luck,' she cried. 'You're envious. You have the evil eye.'

'And you would murder people in the street, with your arrogant heart. And you are brazen. And you don't know what it is to pity. You're not a woman at all. I don't know what you are.'

They raged and yelled at each other. It was a quarrel of nearly forty years' duration, which now and then flared. Pa blamed her for his ruin in Canada. He called her a witch. He said she could have saved him any time she chose but preferred to see him struggle and go under.

Her face was red as Chinese paint. I am sure she knew of more sins and judgements than he could imagine if his anger lasted a month. She cried out, 'Why do you throw yourself on people? You fool! And don't you think I know better than to try to soak up the sea by flinging loaves of bread into it?'

It was Pa's outrage that she found intolerable.

'You may kiss my—!' she told him.

'You may lie in your grave before then,' he shouted, 'and not a penny will you have there.'

Melba barked at him so shrilly that Abba finally took her away, and it appeared as if her barking had incited Pa and Aunt Julia, for when her dog-shrieks ended, they both grew calmer. I too was susceptible to dogs' barking.

And Uncle Jomin on his own lent Pa 150 dollars to go into business in Point St Charles, and took Pa's note for the amount. He sternly warned him against his partner. Uncle Jomin had a pair of eyes of gloomy strength; they had great power to warn and threaten. But what good does it do to threaten a desperate man?

For one brief year we had the feeling of a family that owned a business. It was a store. People went everywhere else to buy their dry goods—if the French and Irish families in this sparse slum bought anything at all. But there was a little store, nevertheless. The partner, as predicted, was no good. He put his entire trust in Pa, and so did nothing. Every afternoon he took a nap on an old bench at the back of the store, which must have come out of the waiting-room of a station. He flirted with the Ukrainian and French women who came, and Pa said we had to keep an eye on him, he might give things away. All the men in Ma's family had this weakness for women, he told me. Henoch snoozed, during vacant summer afternoons when the air was warm and grey. Pa went out to hunt bargains, job lots, and to check on prices in other stores. I read books and practised tricks, and tried to discipline my body. I was ambitious to learn to tie knots with my toes. Houdini could both tie and untie them. I studied the books of spiritualists, too: Oliver Lodge, A. Conan Doyle, and a book called *The Law of Psychic Phenomena*, by Hudson.

The dry goods store soon went on the rocks.

HUGH COLLINS

HARD MAN

I'm five and a half years old, attending the Saint Roche primary school in Glasgow. The teacher, Miss O'Donnell, has asked us each to stand, walk to the front of the class and tell the others what our fathers do.

My da's a railway worker, says one and sits down.

My da makes ships, says another.

My da's a postman. He delivers the mail.

It is my turn and, with considerable pride, I walk to the front of the class. My da, I say, is the famous Wullie Collins. He's the Robin Hood of Scotland. He takes from the rich and gives money to the poor. My da's a bank robber.

The class erupts into screaming, shrieking laughter, and I'm taken by surprise. I can feel my face reddening. Miss O'Donnell is also surprised. And panicking. She puts an immediate halt to the exercise and marches me out of class to phone my granny.

Granny arrives. She is concerned.

He's not a bank robber, Hughie. You mustn't say that. You mustn't ever say that.

But where did I get the idea from?

Didn't I get it from Ginger McBride? Ever since Granny Collins told me to write my da at Peterhead Prison, we've had regular visits from those who have been in with him and now been released. They come to tell me and my granny stories—how Wullie has the run of the prison; how all the screws are scared of him; how he won't speak to them, even to give them the time of day; how he's still the boss. They always come with something—a little gift for Wullie Collins's only son. Tony Smith, the skinny man with a nose hooked like a claw hammer, brings me a small jewellery-box. He is younger than my da, but one of his best mates (Skinny's brother, Granny tells me one night in a solemn voice, after Skinny has just left us, will be hanged in the new year). Gypsy Winning is another. Gypsy is tall—six foot two, he says—and towers over my granny and me. He's another one of my da's best mates. When he comes, he brings me a toy gun. And then there is Ginger McBride.

I'm sure in fact that it was Ginger McBride who said that my da is the Robin Hood of Scotland, a bank robber who helps the poor. The last time he was here Ginger McBride brought me a knife. The knife is very heavy and has a tartan handle and a long, narrow blade like a dagger. It is my first knife.

My first memory is not of my da—I know him only by the pictures my granny shows me: it's of my ma on a cold, blustery night. I cannot be more than two years old and am wrapped in a blanket and held in her arms. We're walking fast, looking into deserted buildings. I remember the gaslights and the shadowy emptiness of the streets. My mother is frightened. She's been unable to find the address that she is looking for and knows that she needs to find a place for us to sleep. She is crying and her face is wet from tears. We spend the night in a room in an empty tenement. I sleep on the floorboards, my mother huddled next to me, clutching her knees.

The next morning we cross the city to Granny Collins's house, near the Royston Road. Granny Collins has such a large family—there's Alex, Jack, Shug, Charlie and Cathie—and now there will be me as well. I'm to live with Granny Collins. I don't remember my mother going. I look for her and she's gone.

I will have two mothers. My 'ma': my real mother, whom I will rarely see again. And my 'maw': my granny. At school, I start to invent parents; I seem to have so many. I take them from comic strips and make them into heroes.

I learn later that my mother's parents were against her marrying my father. Wullie Collins was a troublemaker and always in fights: he was notorious, even then. And my mother's father—a Clyde shipyard worker and lecturer for the Socialist party, a conscientious objector during the war who then spent the rest of his life fighting the label of coward—wasn't going to have Wullie Collins in the house. He was a bad sort. My mother's father refused to take her back, even for the night, even with a child in her arms. She'd just have to sleep out in the cold.

That's the night my father is sent to prison. My granny has to explain what a prison is and why my father has been sent to one. Later I will learn about the Glasgow knife fights and the razor slashings and the judge—one Lord Charmont—who was determined to make an example of my father: as a deterrent to the other slashers. Until then, no sentence for a slashing had been longer than two years. Usually no one did time at all. But knife slashings had become a Glasgow epidemic, and my father, having slashed the manager of the Locarno, a dancehall in the city centre, was given ten years. The dancehall manager got nine stitches. Ten years for nine stitches. That's thirteen months and ten days for each stitch. It doesn't seem right. Everyone tells me it isn't right; every visitor who comes with stories and gifts says it isn't right. Later still, in prison myself for a slashing, I will hunt out the newspaper clippings and trace my father's fame. I will tape them on to the wall and stare at them. His name and picture were in all the papers. There was even a 'bin the knives' campaign on television—led by Frankie Vaughan—and every bampot in the city came out to make a show of dropping off their sticks and broken bottles and used razor-blades.

It didn't seem right. It still doesn't. A judge, for his own private purposes, took Wullie Collins away from me, deprived a child of his father.

I don't know this man, the father I've never lived with, but my loyalty to him is powerful and undeniable. Where do they come from, feelings like these: so strong and yet based on so little? The man, after all, is just an idea, a thought, existing before I have any experience of being his son, and yet I want to look after and defend him. I want to protect him from injustice. And I want to be looked after by him. I want him to teach me—things, everything: how to be like him. I want to be a son he is proud of. When, later, my real mother remarries while my father is still in prison, I explode with rage at the terrible unfairness of it all. I long for my parents to be together. How can she take up with another man, when her real man, her husband, my father, is in prison, suffering from a publicity-stunt jail sentence? I will never forgive her, and years later, still inflamed by the treachery, will call her a whore (and then hate myself afterwards for saying it).

Another picture. I am eight years old, asleep, in the same cot with Alex. I think of Alex as my brother, but, even then, I know he's not. He's my granny's son, and, although only eighteen months older than me, is really my uncle. Granny is shaking Alex by the shoulders. She is fully dressed, and crying.

Wake up, Alex, she is saying. Wake up. Yer faither's just died.

For days, everyone is crying. I cry, too, although I'm not sure why. I don't think I understand what has occurred, but I'm infected by the sadness.

I remember that several days later the children—me, Alex

and Cathie—find ourselves alone in a room with Granpa. He is in a coffin. We poke his face, and the skin is cold and tough like a football. Someone finds some lipstick. What would Granpa look like with red lips? Alex is giggling as I rub great gobs of the stuff across Granpa's face. He's like Coco the Clown, I say, and everyone laughs uncontrollably.

It's when we arrive at the funeral that I see my da. He's been let out of prison to attend his father's funeral. I've seen him only once before, but it was behind a plate-glass window: he was dressed in blue and had black curly hair and a big smile. He is different now. He doesn't acknowledge me, his only son. He doesn't acknowledge anyone. He is there to witness the burying of his father. Wullie Collins is dressed in black—a long and immaculate black overcoat, a black suit, shiny black shoes, a black tie and steel handcuffs. He is surrounded by four screws and stands by the grave, silent. Everyone around him—the family, the friends—are weeping. My father is still. His face, covered with scars, doesn't reveal a thing. I study the face and will remember it for ever: it is hard, like a stone. Wullie, the hard man, people say. Yes, my da, the hard man.

(He will attend another funeral with a prison escort, my granny's, in 1968. By then, he will have completed his ten-year sentence, but will be in prison on another conviction—assault of some kind. But this time, so am I. I am only seventeen and have been sentenced to Borstal for a knifing. This time, I'm the one surrounded by screws and held in steel handcuffs: I'm the hard one, who doesn't speak and is too dangerous to be allowed near anyone else. I'm kept far from the grave. I see my father on the other side. He has been accompanied by a single copper. His hands are free. He is telling someone a joke and laughing. And then I am taken away.)

(And then, twenty years later—at the age of thirty-seven—on my first weekend's leave from a life sentence, I will return to that grave to grieve properly and pay homage to this small, heavy woman who was stronger than so many men I've known and who was more of a parent than my real parents. I found her grave some time after midnight and broke down into hysterical crying and couldn't leave. I spent the night with her, sleeping atop her, and then, in the morning, returned to prison.)

In 1977, I was given a life sentence for murdering a man by stabbing him in the heart and sent to Perth Prison in Scotland. In the first months of my imprisonment, I stabbed three prison officers, was tried for attempted murder, pleaded guilty, and was given an additional seven-year sentence. I was put in solitary confinement, where I remained for a year. In 1978, I was transferred to the Special Unit at Barlinnie Prison, in Glasgow. The transfer, I remember being told, was meant to create in me a feeling of hope: faced with an eternity in prison, a living death sentence, I would now find, people said, a reason to live.

I had no reason to live, although I knew all about the Special Unit, and was, I admit, pleased to have been sent there. The Unit had come into existence following the abolition of the death sentence; prison officers had found they were unable to cope with this new generation of lifers: what is to stop a murderer from murdering again? What does he get—another life sentence? Cages and disciplinary regimes and long bouts of solitary confinement weren't working, and the idea was advanced by the officers themselves to create a new environment—one characterized by trust and a limited sense of freedom.

In the Special Unit, the cells are not locked; there is a public telephone; visitors are welcome; there is a kitchen where prisoners prepare their own meals (with real plates *and* knives and forks), a weight-room where they can exercise, a studio where they can draw and paint, a computer where they can write. Prisoners are not automatically punished for bad behaviour, but encouraged by specially trained staff to talk through their problems. That, in any case, was the theory. It was not always the practice, but there was no denying that the Special Unit was different. Only five prisoners were accepted at any one time; there were fifteen officers to take care of them.

The Unit opened in 1974 and, in Scotland at least, has never been long out of the news. Journalists seem incapable of accepting that a murderer can be rehabilitated or placed in something other than a locked cell with a bucket for slopping out. And since 1974, there has been a steady run of stories about drugs and drink and sex. In 1978, just before I was admitted, there was a suicide, Larry Winters, who died from a barbiturate overdose. The suicide, in the eyes of many, was conclusive evidence of both the availability of drugs and, more damningly, the experiment's failure: as much as society might like to see its murderers killed off, the idea was not that the murderers should do it themselves.

The Unit's most famous member was Jimmy Boyle. While there, he was the subject of a television documentary and wrote a book, *A Sense of Freedom*, about his experiences as 'one of Scotland's most dangerous men.' Jimmy Boyle now lives in Edinburgh, drives a Rolls-Royce, and is a highly successful wine merchant, specializing in vintage champagnes. But in 1978, when I first arrived at the Unit, Jimmy was its undeniable leader.

I was, I now understand, extremely confused when I was admitted into this odd, L-shaped section of Barlinnie Prison, a space suddenly so large, especially for me, emerging from solitary confinement, that I spent days wandering along its walls, trying to understand its layout. Several times I got lost. I thought, though, that my disorientation was probably normal, because, otherwise, I didn't believe there was anything wrong with me. But there did seem to be something wrong with the people around me. They weren't behaving like prisoners. For a start, they were all friendly with the screws, joking and laughing and talking, as if they were normal people. It made me uncomfortable; more than uncomfortable, it made me sick: I was stuck in a place surrounded by sanctimonious bastards looking for parole—or maybe this was the pay-off for the treats and favours that they all got in the Unit. It was ugly, and I didn't like it. Then I noticed that even Jimmy Boyle was friendly with the screws. Boyle's reputation preceded him: he had attacked prison officers in Inverness and had been involved in the rioting there. He knew that he was never to fraternize with the enemy.

On the second day, Jimmy invited me into his cell. He knew my father—he was about halfway between my father's age and mine.

You're fucked up, he said. You don't think you are, but you're completely fucked up. So was I when I arrived here. It took me six months to recover.

And he was right: I was fucked up. A few days later, a visitor brought me some drugs, and by the afternoon I had 'snowballed'— a concoction of cocaine and heroin, a subdued high, but one intense enough to allow my feelings to erupt. I threatened to attack the prison staff unless I was transferred immediately. What was I asking for really? I know what I was expecting: punishment or solitary or a beating or even the very transfer I demanded. What I got instead was the 'hot seat', a meeting where I was questioned by all of them—officers *and* prisoners. The meeting's resolution was not to mete out punishment, but to develop ways of supporting me through my difficulties.

What the fuck was going on?

I woke the next morning and, before breakfast, drank a bottle of whisky. I don't drink whisky and had never had a whole bottle before. I was full of anger and feelings of rebellion and defiance. I walked round to Jimmy Boyle's cell and had a go at him, until the other prisoners had to restrain me. Again, I expected to be punished; perhaps I wanted to be punished, if only to reinforce my sense of self and place. Instead another meeting was convened, and I was put back into the 'hot seat'. This time, though, I wasn't going to be interrogated; I was spewing with rage—at everyone about everything: the prisoners for being such obsequious arse-lickers, the staff for being so intrusive and nosy, the endless visitors who came parading through the Unit as if we were all animals in the zoo, and these stupid meetings that we had every day, sometimes twice a day, sometimes more.

I was bundled up—I had expected this—and put in a cell: but, again, not to be punished, as I had thought I would be. No: I was put in a cell so I could sober up in peace.

I didn't understand.

The next morning, Jimmy asked to see me again.

You have to understand, he said, how really fucked up you are. You don't believe me, but you need to write out all these different emotions. There are too many of them. They're all jumbled together. Get them on paper. Try to find out who you are and what has made you this way.

But how do I do that?

W ho is Hugh Collins?
Caucasian male, born of William Collins and Betty Norrie Collins on 17 June 1951.

Height?

Five feet, ten inches.

Weight?

Eleven stone.

Build?

Muscular.

Hair?

Grey-brown.

Eyes?

Grey.

Vision?

A slight astigmatism. Corrective lens required for reading and watching television.

Tattoos or distinguishing characteristics?

A tattoo the length and width of my back, consisting of a network of concentric circles and different-coloured stars.

Other distinguishing characteristics?

Scars. From the bottom up. One in the shape of a *W* on my calf: from a gang fight with the Tongs when I was fifteen. Twelve stitches.

What else?

Two scars on my back. The first is about an inch to the left of my spine. After I was arrested for murder, and while awaiting trial, I tried to escape. My plan was to become so 'ill' I'd be removed to the Royal Infirmary, where a friend had stashed clothing and a weapon in a closet. The trick was to get there. Another friend had been arrested with me. I had a piece of a mirror, which I broke into long slivers, wrapping the end of one with a blanket to make a crude dagger. I got my friend to ram it into my back, but, in his enthusiasm, he pushed it both too far in and too close to the spine. I lost consciousness before I had a chance to make my getaway.

And the second?

On the right, higher up. Another gang fight with the Tongs. I was eighteen. I was stabbed with a bayonet.

Other scars?

One on my hand, from the day that Wee Joe, a school friend, pinned my hand to a table with a carving knife. A scar on my upper arm, the right one, from Saughton Prison, when I tried to break up a fight.

The head?

About five on my scalp, mainly from the police. One is from a steel bar—from when I was beaten up in prison by William Mooney, the man I later killed. Also, a scar behind the right ear, which Wee Joe had tried to lop off in 1971.

And the face?

Principally the seven-inch scar along the jaw line. It's my badge, my calling-card. Nobody fails to notice it: shop detectives single me out, children ask me if it still hurts, civilized people at dinner parties stare at it when they think I'm not looking. In prison, a psychiatrist suggested that I have plastic surgery—that, unless removed, the scar, like the scars on my father's face, would mean that people always responded to me as a violent man. An operation was arranged, but on the day I changed my mind: the scar is me, and to remove it would be to deny what I am.

How did it happen?

I was surprised by a butcher's cleaver. I believe the intention had been to kill me and that the jugular in my throat had been the target. They missed.

They?

My school friends.

There were four of us, all from the Royston Road. We met between the ages of five and ten at Saint Roche's: Catholic boys from a rough Catholic school. But by the time we were ten, none of us remained: we'd all been expelled. (In my case, it was after head-butting the headmaster when he tried to lash my hands because he found the length of my hair unacceptable—'Do you wear girl's clothing when you get home as well?' he asked. I broke his nose, knocked him unconscious and then ran away, never to return.)

There was the Bear, who even at five years old was large for his age. Since I can remember, the Bear was in fights, at first with the other boys at our school, usually held at the 'coop', the area behind the football parks. A day didn't pass when the Bear hadn't thumped someone (it was why I first sought his friendship: to protect me from him). Soon the Bear was thumping the boys from the next school. And then it was boys from the other side of Glasgow. The Bear had a knack for finding trouble and putting himself at the front of it—for 'steaming in'. In fact, it was the

Bear who taught me how to head-butt, my first experiment being the headmaster's unhappy nose. As the Bear got older, he got bigger. He developed curious, brooding moods and a taciturn manner and had unpredictable fits of rage. He also developed an impeccable sense of dress, with a gangster's flair for long coats: it's where he concealed his weapons.

There was Joe Mulligan. Wee Joe, we called him. While he wasn't all that short—he probably came to about five-foot-seven—he had a terribly wee frame, and a relentless capacity for violence to make up for it. Wee Joe looked like some kind of animal, a weasel or ferret, a ferocious rodent-like thing that you'd never want to feed with your hands for fear that he'd sink his teeth in and never let go. He had an animal's head—slightly snout-like, as if he could sniff things out that normal humans might miss—with slitty eyes and thin, pointy, jagged teeth. Wee Joe had a small man's dexterity with an open razor, and whenever things became a little violent, he would become hysterical and start slashing. Wee Joe and I also had our difficulties. It was Wee Joe who surprised me when I stopped at the Yellow Bird café on Buchanan Street to pick up some fish and chips by chopping the side of my head with a butcher's cleaver. I can still recall the crunching sound as it slammed into my back teeth. And then, as I spun round, he sliced across the gums above my front teeth with a razor-blade. It was his 'comeback': the two scars that run in tandem from the top of his forehead, through his eyelid and down his cheek, came from me.

I met Albert Faulds the year I was expelled. He was Irish, with jet-black hair that he kept cropped close and short to accommodate fighting: to ensure that no one had anything to grab. Albert rarely spoke—it was his way—and was always superbly fit. He had just got out of an approved school, and the two of us used to spend afternoons in the upstairs cafeteria in Woolworth's, pretending to our parents—or, in my case, to my granny—that we were in class. At one point, we got proper jobs working in a garment factory; but, having spotted some fabric that I was convinced was mohair, and having clocked the fire escapes and alarms (out of habit, if nothing else), I couldn't resist returning late on the Saturday night and making off with great rolls of our rare cloth (which we then sold on to friends and punters to make suits; but our rare cloth turned out to be synthetic—it was intended to line suits, not to make them—and as it stretched and sagged and came apart, more and more unhappy customers came looking for us).

Our employment, however, was an aberration (it turned out to be the only job I held). And after one week, Albert and I were back at the cafeteria in Woolworth's. Soon, the Bear was joining us, and then Wee Joe, and before we knew it, we had the makings of a gang. We called it the Shamrock and would eventually have about fifty members. We were fourteen years old. We'd all been in fights and had a brief history of trouble of one kind or another with the authorities. We'd all done a bit of shoplifting or some burglaries—going through the floorboards of derelict tenements, say, so as to break through the ceilings of the places below. But the point was this: we hadn't done that much. We weren't criminals. Nor were we all that violent—yet. We were just boys in search of an adventure, looking for our part in the black-and-white gangster movie that was playing inside our heads. One moment we were hanging out; the next we had a gang.

That was 1965. My father was finally out of prison. Everywhere you heard the Beatles. I'd grown my hair long. I had money in one pocket and a lump of hashish in the other. On Saturdays, I'd be at the Celtic match. And I'd become a good fighter—I knew this because people were already afraid of me. I had a wildness about me and I loved it.

And I loved being in a gang. I don't know what I was getting from it, but it had something I wanted. I lived for the gang. We all did. I was seeing girls and going to clubs, but my heart was down on the South Side, fighting with open razors, the adrenalin crack. And, from the ages of fourteen to twenty-two, from 1965 to 1973, when I was released from Perth Prison, that was my life. It's a Glasgow story that has been told and retold; its history is carved into my body; it's the *W* across my calf; the crusty lump that has formed along my back; the knot still bulging, arthritic now, that rests atop my hand. But it was, more than anything else, the period that made me.

Now, when I think back to that time, I see it in two parts. In the first, I'm fifteen years old—out of school, on the loose, on my own. That ends when I'm seventeen and sentenced, for the second time, to Borstal (where I'll be when my granny dies).

In the second, I'm in custody: always (or so it seems). I'm in Borstal or the Young Offenders' Prison at Barlinnie. Most of the offences are absurd—silly mistakes made by an arrogant guy who doesn't know better. One evening I go out to rob a bank—me, aged eighteen, on my own, standing outside the Royal Bank of Scotland with a brick in my hand, at two in the morning, until chased away by an old woman in the flat above, who suddenly throws open her window—startling the hell out of me—and tells me to bugger off before I get arrested. So what do I do? I walk down the street until I come across a display of red apples looking so delicious that, with the brick still in my hand, I feel compelled to break the window and grab one. *Three months*. In another instance, I, along with Wee Joe and Albert, have been asked to testify about a gang fight (the one where I got bayonetted in the back). The case is heard on the very day that I'm released from the Young Offenders' Prison, and I'm confused and disoriented. I should have realized what I needed to do on learning that Wee Joe has absconded to England. I have no excuse when, later, Albert appears, having purchased a bottle of lemonade which he insists I break over his head. I do, knocking him out, and when he regains consciousness, he thanks me profusely. He then goes to the Royal Infirmary, declares that he has concussion and is unable to testify. I, however, do testify: and (determined not to grass on anyone, including the guy who stabbed me in the back) I am caught out committing perjury. *Eighteen months*. In all, between 1968 and 1973, I am sent to prison five times, for sentences totalling four years. Is that where my real education took place?

I ask myself that, I have to, it's the assumption: prison is where hard men get educated. But I also ask because I now see how I am changed by my time inside, and how the person who now emerges is different from the child who was sent to Borstal. He's a man now, quick and violent, a slasher, with few scruples or regrets. This is the third part, my final chapter. It begins in 1973. I'm twenty-three and am returning to Glasgow from Perth Prison. But this is not the Glasgow I left. There are still gangs—there will always be gangs—but there is something else: drugs. And a lot of money.

Today, the drug scene is different: more sophisticated, more dangerous. Today if there's trouble, you get shot: no argument. But this was 1973. There were only about twenty people dealing in all of Glasgow, and many were still the hippy-types, middle-class, with long hair, attracted to the city centre for the glamour of its violence or its atmosphere of danger. In a few years, these dealers would have gone: if not dead, then they'd be back at a university or in a job somewhere.

The drugs had been here before, but the money hadn't. You could find acid, but you'd never pay for it. Now it was being sold—fifty pence a tab, a pound, sometimes five pounds. There was hash, as there always had been. And there was also morphine and heroin, and everyone was using needles. There were downers, diconal, mandrax: and money, everywhere.

It's easy to picture: arrogant, young Glasgow hard man arrives home to find naïve hippy-types, unused to fighting of any kind—not to mention knives, bayonets, open razors and guns— making lots of money. What does arrogant, young Glasgow hard man do?

My day began by visiting my six regular dealers in preparation for the evening. (Before I was finally put away, I had stabbed most of them. Three are now dead.) I'd then return to the flat or else meet up with a friend and have a drink. Around six o'clock, I'd start my rounds. On a normal evening, I might have had, say, fifty tabs of LSD, two or three ounces of hashish and some tablets; occasionally I had heroin. A gram fetched eight pounds.

Everything took place in the pubs in the city centre, and eventually the pubs themselves became part of my routine. Most were owned by the big breweries who were always afraid of losing their licences if too much violence occurred on their premises. Therefore, with the help of some friends, I made a point of introducing too much violence and then demanding protection money. It was a time when—with a little imagination and a great deal of fearlessness—anything was possible. The drug squads were just starting out, but they weren't working undercover yet. They'd arrive in suits, looking conspicuously like policemen, with the result that, in the drug-friendly pubs, someone usually flicked the lights off and on to warn of a possible bust. What, therefore, would the arrogant, young Glasgow hard man do? He'd put on a suit—expensive, handmade, silk—and, with one or two mates, go out for the evening pretending to be the drug squad: he'd enter a pub; its lights would be flicked off and on by the accomplice already in place; and drugs, in little pouches and sachets, would be dropped on the floor as their owners fled through the first available door; arrogant, young Glasgow hard man then had the opportunity to increase his stockholding by a brief, highly efficient sweeping operation.

What had I become? I cite an incident as an illustration. I could cite any number of others.

A publican approached me and asked if, for a hundred quid, I would slash someone who was giving him trouble. I performed my service and was duly paid. The following week I returned for another hundred quid. The publican was surprised to see me and refused to pay. I returned the following week. This time, I demanded two hundred quid—one hundred for this week, and one hundred for the week before. Again, the publican refused to pay, but I could tell that he was frightened. And with good reason.

My success in this new Glasgow rested on my reputation for being capable of limitless violence. I was both menace and protector, and I couldn't be one effectively without being the other. When the publican refused to make another payment, he knew that, eventually, he would have trouble: from me. He then made another mistake. Just as he had hired me to slash a man who had been a problem, so now he asked his bouncer to slash me—for an extra hundred quid. The news, when I learned it from a friend, filled me with an icy rage.

The bouncer did not have to look for me. That evening I presented myself at the pub. He was at the door.

'Are you looking for me?' I asked. I stepped right up to him, with my face inches from his. I had an open razor in the palm of my hand.

'Why, Collie,' he said, surprised, but very, very friendly. 'How the fuck are you?'

I then reached up behind him, grabbed him by the hair, jerked his head back and slashed him—straight along the jaw line, the blood spurting suddenly on to my face and hair and shirt, a steady stream. He buckled, knowing he had been slashed, and I pulled back harder on his hair.

'Naw, mate,' he said, 'I'm not looking for you. There's been some mistake.'

'You're right there's been a mistake,' I said. 'Tell your fuckin' gaffer that he owes me money.' And then I slashed him across the other jaw.

I had known, from the moment I heard the news that morning, what I was going to have to do that evening. The entire operation was carried out mechanically; no reflection, no regrets. It was business. (But then, later that night, I went home, smoked a joint, relaxed, and, as I was sitting on my own, listening to some music, I saw his face, the skin stretched back from the way I was holding his hair, and him looking confused and frightened. It was the eyes: suddenly so vulnerable in a man otherwise so hard. And I hated myself, grew sick and vomited.)

It is a feature of this kind of memoir—a villain's autobiography, a murderer remembering—to dress up the nasty bits. I've read books of this kind in which the murderer disappears entirely, and you're left with this nice guy telling lots of nice, colourful stories. What was all the fuss about, you want to ask? I don't want to prettify what was ugly. I don't want to persuade anyone that I was innocent, when I wasn't. From 1973 to 1977, my life was as I describe it here. I was at war—with everyone, even the members of the Shamrock. Albert, Wee Joe, the Bear: during this time, I slashed them all. And many, many others. I never went anywhere without being armed—tooled up—and would never tool myself up unless I was prepared to use my weapons. I knew what it was like to savage someone with a blade; I had felt the thrill of it, the intensity of the experience. I knew what it was to take someone's life. I was a very powerful man, and I was powerful because I was dangerous, and I was dangerous because I was prepared to be, and everyone knew I was fully capable of being so very, very violent. I had become my father.

Or perhaps I had become nothing more than what I thought my father was.

For the first time in my life, I was seeing him regularly. History and chance had conspired to keep both of us out of prison. He was living nearby, a ten-minute bus-ride away. But I didn't like what I saw.

HARD MAN

I was at some awful club—everyone in platform shoes and three-piece suits—when I was tapped on the shoulder: there was an old man at the door asking after me.

An old man? I didn't know any old men. I went to the door and discovered my father, covered in blood. He'd been done over and had come to me for help. His face had been slashed and he was without his dentures. His hair was long and unkempt, and his clothes smelt of drink and urine.

My father: the old man.

I took him home in a taxi. I cleaned him up and discovered who'd slashed him. Once he was in bed, I went out and stabbed the guy who did it. I returned home and assured my father that the guy would no longer be a problem.

Which he wasn't. But the next week, late, there was a knock on the door. It was my father: the puckered face without its dentures, the hair, the blood, the soiled clothes, the smells. And so the routine: I brought him inside, cleaned him up, asked him who did it, put him to bed, then went out and did the guy. And so it continued. And every time it happened, I duly went out into the night and chibbed the person (except one, a black guy, whose flat I broke into—perfectly prepared to stab him as well—when I came upon an old-fashioned iron; I used that instead; I learned later that, having cracked his skull, I had put him into Intensive Care).

I started to suspect that my father was allowing himself to get into trouble—or at least wasn't too bothered when he found himself in a bit of bother—knowing that his son would sort it out for him. I started to suspect that he was revelling in my reputation as Glasgow's violent hard man—as if he was living off me in some way: or, more frightening, living through me.

And then one night, I couldn't take any more. And I beat him up. He was there in the flat with his girlfriend, a prostitute he picked up every night at the end of her run—the tartan miniskirt, the white plastic boots, the battered, swollen face. He was pissed again, knocking over the furniture, spraying beer on the carpet, repeating, in his drunken slur, that I was his boy, his fuckin' boy.

And I hit him: I smacked him across the forehead with the butt of my sawn-off shotgun, then aimed it at him. Both barrels were loaded, and I went as far as pulling back the hammers. I was within a muscle's twitch of blowing my father away.

He lay there in the recess of the flat, his flies undone, his genitals hanging out, his hard, scarred face in a spasm of fear.

And for the first time, I saw him for what he was. My father was not a hard man. The hard man was a lie. Robin Hood? He was a drunk, poncing money from a burnt-out prostitute half his age. He was not someone I wanted to be. What I wanted to be had been a lie. It didn't exist.

But just look at what the lie had created.

I knew William Mooney, the man I murdered. I didn't like him, but I didn't like a lot of people. In any case, it's not the reason I murdered him. There was no reason to murder him.

Mooney was a big man, about my age, and weighed about fourteen or fifteen stone: stocky, but fit. I'd heard of him—he was from a gang called the Peg—but I didn't meet him until 1968. We were both at the Young Offenders' Prison at Barlinnie: he was on his way out just as I was settling in to serve an eighteen-month sentence. I had my father's firm principles, not to talk to, or in any way be friendly with, the screws, and so Mooney's manner was bound to irritate me. He was a screws' pet, making them tea, doing them little favours. The day before he was due to be liberated, we had an argument. I don't remember what it was about. I suspect I resented that he was about to walk free—that he'd probably got parole because he got on so well with the screws—whereas I was on my way to serving my full sentence, down to the last possible minute. I offered him a 'square go', but he wasn't having any of it: after all, he'd be having a pint with his friends by this same time the next day. I then went to the screws and asked if Mooney and I could have a square go. They almost always obliged, leaving the two of you in a room alone, intervening only if the fighting got out of hand. But the screws told me to fuck off. I drifted back into the television room and then went to bed.

At Barlinnie, the cells are opened at six-fifteen on the dot, but the next morning they were opened at six. I had been asleep and just opened my eyes to see Mooney rushing through my cell door, coming at me with a steel bar. He hammered my nose with it, then pulled a blanket over me, picked up the steel washing-basin nearby and slammed it repeatedly on my head. He went on to pound my joints, one after the other: one shoulder, then the other, the elbows, the spine, the pelvis, the knees. Then he left, closing the door behind him. I couldn't follow even if I'd been able to; I was locked in. In fact, I could hardly walk.

Mooney was freed fifteen minutes later.

I didn't see him again until the day I killed him. I had run into Wee Joe, who asked me if I could score some dope for Johnny Gemmell. Johnny Gemmell had been the husband of the woman I was living with, but Johnny and I remained good friends. Johnny was in prison, and Wee Joe would be seeing him the next day. By this time, there was no trust between me and Wee Joe, but I liked Johnny and wanted to help, so I told Wee Joe that I would meet him later at a pub called the Lunar Seven—around seven o'clock.

With Wee Joe was Mooney (Mooney, I learned later, was seeing Wee Joe's sister, and each of them—Wee Joe, the Bear and Mooney—had an informal gang of sorts). I hadn't come upon Mooney in nearly ten years, and, while I hadn't forgotten the beating, I was happy to let it pass. I was pleased to see him.

Wee Joe went off, and I joined Mooney for a drink. Mooney was already half-pissed and in a boisterous mood. Two women were with them and he was showing off a bit. He wanted to do things: shoplifting or thieving. He asked if I'd help him slash a guy—that there was money in it and that, in any case, the guy was a mug. I agreed, mainly to keep Mooney happy, although I thought that he'd been watching too many gangster movies. He kept jabbering away. He had a round, innocent face, with a turned-up nose and a permanent half-smile while he talked. As the pub closed, he suggested that all of us head off to one of the women's flats.

And so we set off, running into a nephew of mine along the way. He was with his mates, a gang called the Pickpockets, and Mooney decided to have a go at him. The Pickpockets was one of Glasgow's most organized gangs. It had about a dozen members, all young, between the ages of twelve and sixteen, and dedicated to making money. They avoided violence; they were thieves, especially adept at stealing jewellery. They travelled regularly—the previous week, they'd been in Switzerland—and always had cash. They could also be remarkably generous: if you stepped in front of a copper during a chase, they'd make a point of rewarding you later—as much as three hundred quid. But they didn't respond to bullying, and Mooney was bullying them: he wanted money.

I think I would have objected to the bullying in any case. That the one being bullied was my fourteen-year-old nephew— who couldn't fight sleep, let alone a fifteen-stone, body-building maniac in a half-drunken state—meant I was bound to get involved. And so it happened: Mooney pulled out a bread knife, threatening my nephew; I told him to leave it out, and he turned on me instead. 'I'll give it to you again,' he said.

It appeared that Mooney, too, hadn't forgotten the beating. In the circumstances, it wasn't going to take much to provoke me; this was certainly enough. And I told him so: I told Mooney to meet me at the Lunar Seven that evening; then, I, too, would be tooled up and we could go for a walk. By now, I was extremely angry, and my nephew—who, a moment before, I was protecting—now stepped between us to calm things down.

As the day wore on, I became angrier still. A friend, Felix, sought me out and told me not to go the pub that night: that it wasn't going to be a fair go after all, that everyone knew there was going to be trouble and that Mooney would be bringing a whole gang of people—the Bear among them—to do me. He was convinced that they were going to kill me. But I couldn't back out now. Besides, I had the dope for Johnny.

I don't know if Felix's suspicions were true, although it was the case that trouble had been expected. When the police arrived later to do their search and interrogation, they discovered that just about everyone was tooled up, with a blade or two secreted somewhere on his body.

I remember walking down Sauchiehall Street, very slowly, looking at everything, missing nothing. I had a blade up my sleeve, a new one, a twelve-inch Bowie knife. I kept fingering the handle, feeling its shape. I was making a picture for myself of what the pub would look like. It would be dark—the only light would be near the bar—and very crowded. Mooney wouldn't be far from Wee Joe. The Bear would be nearby. They'd be at the back, close to the exit. They would have made a point of being near the exit. At the Lunar Seven, the exit is through a swinging door, down some stairs and out on to the street.

My stomach was tightening into a ball. Sauchiehall Street was busy, with lots of people out, some already drunk.

As I walked into the pub I was aware of everything. The noise, the shadows, the smell of cigarettes and beer. It was very crowded, and I had to push my way to the bar, faces turning towards me as I did so, knowing, expectant. I spotted my friend Felix—he was standing next to Wee Joe—and the Bear. They were by the bar, at the back, near the swinging door.

'Collie,' the Bear shouted, arm outstretched to greet me. 'Over here! What're you drinking?'

Everyone was wearing a coat and drinking a glass of tomato juice: no alcohol. I stood next to Wee Joe. The scars on his face—like two railway tracks running down the length of it—still looked raw.

'Have you got the dope?' he asked.

'In a minute,' I said.

Mooney brushed my shoulder—not a word spoken between us—and I turned to follow him, watching him carefully. Then, as I turned back to the bar, a tumbler flew past my head. I twisted round, and there was Mooney, coming straight at me. Bottles were being broken and thrown, and someone was screaming. Instantly, the knife was in my hand. I slammed it into Mooney's chest just as he reached me. I could feel the fabric of his jacket on my knuckles from the force of the blow. He seemed stunned. I pulled the knife out, and my friend Felix grabbed me by the arms, trying to drag me away.

'Collie, you've done him. You've killed him.' He was whispering in my ear. 'Put the knife away and walk out quietly.' But I was staring at Mooney, who had only been stunned and was now reaching into his coat for the bread knife. He was coming back at me.

'Let me go, Felix.' He was holding on to my arms. Mooney was roaring now. 'Let me go.'

And then something snapped. It was as if my mind had liberated itself from my body, had floated up and away to the corner of the pub and, no longer able to control me, was watching what I was doing from a distance. Nothing was going to stop me.

I went for Mooney's arm and yanked it upwards, to give me a full, unobstructed view of his ribs, and then plunged the blade in between them. 'Fuck you,' I shouted. 'Fuck you, fuck you, fuck you.' I pulled out the knife and plunged it back into the ribs. 'Fuck you, fuck you, fuck you.'

But Mooney had me by the hair and threw me into the swinging door of the exit: down I fell, rolling down the stairs, pulling Mooney with me, clinging to my hair, my blade in his ribs. We hit the landing at the bottom, and he ended up astride me. Blood was pouring from his chest, but still he came at me. He had a beer tumbler in his hand, already broken, lifted it into the air and slammed it into the side of my head. I fumbled for my knife, gripped it firmly and plunged it into his throat.

He stopped and got off me, swaying. There was a gurgling sound, and he leaned back into the wall and slid down.

I got to my feet, exhilarated, covered in Mooney's blood, still warm, hot even, the knife in my hand. And then I stared at him, and realized what I was witnessing: these were his last moments; he was dying; I had killed him; he was dead.

'What the fuck have I done?'

I was dazed and staggered out into the street. I heard sirens and moved on, turned down a lane, dropping the blade in a dustbin along the way. I found myself in a fish and chip shop. What was I doing? I didn't want to eat. The people were staring at me. I was covered from head to toe with blood. I shuffled out and stopped. I had a view of the pub. The police had arrived and had cordoned off the area. I could see Mooney's legs sticking out.

I got the late bus home. It was packed with passengers. No one said a thing, but everyone stared at me.

'What the fuck are you looking at?'

Silence.

I got home, pulled off my clothes, got out my shotgun, put my chair in front of the door, and waited. When the police appeared, I would blow them away. I waited until dawn.

Hugh Collins was arrested the next day, 7 April 1977, and charged with the murder of William Mooney. He was also charged with three other attempted murders. Before he came to trial, he was impeached for two further murders. At the trial, three months later, the charges for the attempted killings and the two murders for which he had been impeached were found not proven. He was found guilty of the murder of William Mooney and sentenced to life imprisonment.

ANGELA CARTER

SUGAR DADDY

I would say my father did not prepare me well for patriarchy; himself confronted, on his marriage with my mother, with a mother-in-law who was the living embodiment of peasant matriarchy, he had no choice but to capitulate, and did so. Further, I was the child of his mid-forties, when he was just the age to be knocked sideways by the arrival of a baby daughter. He was putty in my hands throughout my childhood and still claims to be so, although now I am middle-aged myself while he, not though you'd notice, is somewhat older than the present century.

I was born in 1940, the week that Dunkirk fell. I think neither of my parents was immune to the symbolism of this, of bringing a little girl-child into the world at a time when the Nazi invasion of England seemed imminent, into the midst of death and approaching dark. Perhaps I seemed particularly vulnerable and precious and that helps to explain the over-protectiveness they felt about me, later on. Be that as it may, no child, however inauspicious the circumstances, could have been made more welcome. I did not get a birthday card from him a couple of years ago; when I querulously rang him up about it, he said: 'I'd never forget the day you came ashore.' (The card came in the second post.) His turn of phrase went straight to my heart, an organ which has inherited much of his Highland sentimentality.

He is a Highland man, the perhaps atypical product of an underdeveloped, colonialized country in the last years of Queen Victoria, of oatcakes, tatties and the Church of Scotland, of four years' active service in World War One, of the hurly-burly of Fleet Street in the twenties. His siblings, who never left the native village, were weird beyond belief. To that native village he competently removed himself ten years ago.

He has done, I realize, what every Sicilian in New York, what every Cypriot in Camden Town wants to do, to complete the immigrant's journey, to accomplish the perfect symmetry, from A to B and back again. Just his luck, when he returned, that all was as it had been before and he could, in a manner of speaking, take up his life where it left off when he moved south seventy years ago. He went south; and made a career; and married an Englishwoman; and lived in London; and fathered children, in an enormous parenthesis of which he retains only sunny memories. He has 'gone home', as immigrants do; he established, in his seventh decade, that 'home' has an existential significance for him which is not part of the story of his children's independent lives. My father lives now in his granite house filled with the souvenirs of a long and, I think, happy life. (Some of them bizarre; that framed certificate from an American tramp, naming my father a 'Knight of the Road', for example.)

He has a curious, quite unEnglish, ability to live life in, as it were, the *third person*, to see his life objectively, as a not unfortunate one, and to live up to that notion. Those granite townships on the edge of the steel-grey North Sea forge a flinty sense of self. Don't think, from all this, he isn't a volatile man. He laughs easily, cries easily, and to his example I attribute my conviction that tears, in a man, are a sign of inner strength.

He is still capable of surprising me. He recently prepared an electric bed for my boyfriend, which is the sort of thing a doting father in a Scots ballad might have done had the technology been available at the time. We knew he'd put us in separate rooms—my father is a Victorian, by birth—but not that he'd plug the metal base of Mark's bed into the electric-light fitment. Mark noticed how the bed throbbed when he put his hand on it and disconnected every plug in sight. We ate breakfast, next morning, as if nothing untoward had happened, and I should say, in the context of my father's house, it had not. He is an enthusiastic handyman, with a special fascination with electricity, whose work my mother once described as combining the theory of Heath Robinson with the practice of Mr Pooter.

All the same, the Freudian overtones are inescapable. However unconsciously, as if *that* were an excuse, he'd prepared a potentially lethal bed for his daughter's lover. But let me not dot the i's and cross the t's. His final act of low, emotional cunning (another Highland characteristic) is to have lived so long that everything is forgiven, even his habit of referring to the present incumbent by my first husband's name, enough to give anybody a temporary feeling.

He is a man of immense, nay, imposing physical presence, yet I tend to remember him in undignified circumstances.

One of my first memories is how I bust his nose. (I was, perhaps, three years old. Maybe four.) It was on a set of swings in a public park. He'd climbed up Pooterishly to adjust the chains from which the swings hung. I thought he was taking too long and set the swing on which I sat in motion. He wasn't badly hurt but there was a lot of blood. I was not punished for my part in this accident. They were a bit put out because I wanted to stay and play when they went home to wash off the blood.

They. That is my father and my mother. Impossible for me to summon one up out of the past without the other.

Shortly after this, he nearly drowned me, or so my mother claimed. He took me for a walk one autumn afternoon and stopped by the pond on Wandsworth Common and I played a game of throwing leaves into the water until I forgot to let go of one. He was in after me in a flash, in spite of the peril to his gents' natty suiting (ever the dandy, my old man) and wheeled me dripping in my pushchair home to the terrible but short-lived recriminations of my mother. Short-lived because both guilt and remorse are emotions alien to my father. Therefore the just apportioning of blame is not one of his specialities, and though my mother tried it on from time to time, he always thought he could buy us off with treats and so he could and that is why my brother and I don't sulk, much. Whereas she—

She has been dead for more than a decade, now, and I've had ample time to appreciate my father's individual flavour, which is a fine and gamy one, but, as parents, they were far more than the sum of their individual parts. I'm not sure they understood their instinctive solidarity against us, because my mother often tried to make us take sides. Us. As their child, the product of their parenting, I cannot dissociate myself from my brother, although we did not share a childhood for he is twelve years older than I and was sent off, with his gas mask, his packed lunch and his name tag, as an evacuee, a little hostage to fortune, at about the time they must have realized another one was on the way.

I can only think of my parents as a peculiarly complex unit in which neither bulks larger than the other, although they were very different kinds of people and I often used to wonder how they got on, since they seemed to have so little in common, until I realized that was *why* they got on, that not having much in common means you've always got something interesting to talk about. And their children, far from being the *raison d'être* of their marriage, of their ongoing argument, of that endless, quietly murmuring conversation I used to hear, at night, softly, dreamily, the other side of the bedroom wall, were, in some sense, a sideshow. Source of pleasure, source of grief; not the glue that held them together. And neither of us more important than the other, either.

Not that I suspected this when I was growing up. My transition from little girl to ravaged anorexic took them by surprise and I thought they wanted my blood. I didn't know what they wanted of me, nor did I know what I wanted for myself. In those years of ludicrously overprotected adolescence, I often had the feeling of being 'pawns in their game' . . . in *their* game, note . . . and perhaps I indeed served an instrumental function, at that time, rather than being loved for myself.

All this is so much water under the bridge. Yet those were the only years I can remember when my mother would try to invoke my father's wrath against me, threaten me with his fury for coming home late and so on. Though, as far as the 'and so on' was concerned, chance would have been a fine thing. My adolescent rebellion was considerably hampered by the fact that I could find nobody to rebel with. I now recall this period with intense embarrassment, because my parents' concern to protect me from predatory boys was only equalled by the enthusiasm with which the boys I did indeed occasionally meet protected themselves against me.

It was a difficult time, terminated, inevitably, by my early marriage as soon as I finally bumped into somebody who would go to Godard movies with me and on CND marches and even have sexual intercourse with me, although he insisted we should be engaged first. Neither of my parents were exactly overjoyed when I got married, although they grudgingly did all the necessary. My father was particularly pissed off because he'd marked me out for a career on Fleet Street. It took me twenty years more of living, and an involvement with the women's movement, to appreciate he was unusual in wanting this for his baby girl. Although he was a journalist himself, I don't think he was projecting his own ambitions on me, either, even if to be a child is to be, to some degree, the projective fantasy of its

65

parents. No. I suspect that, if he ever had any projective fantasies about me, I sufficiently fulfilled them by being born. All he'd wanted for me was a steady, enjoyable job that, perhaps, guaranteed me sufficient income to ensure I wouldn't too hastily marry some nitwit (a favourite word of his) who would displace him altogether from my affections. So, since from a child I'd been good with words, he apprenticed me to a suburban weekly newspaper when I was eighteen, intending me to make my traditional way up from there. From all this, given my natural perversity, it must be obvious why I was so hell-bent on getting married—not, and both my parents were utterly adamant about this, that getting married meant I'd give up my job.

In fact, it *did* mean that because soon my new husband moved away from London. 'I suppose you'll have to go with him,' said my mother doubtfully. Anxious to end my status as their child, there was no other option and so I changed direction although, as it turns out, I *am* a journalist, at least some of the time.

As far as projective fantasies go, sometimes it seems the old man is only concerned that I don't end up in the workhouse. Apart from that, anything goes. My brother and I remain, I think, his most constant source of pleasure—always, perhaps, a more positive joy to our father than to our mother, who, a more introspective person, got less pure entertainment value from us, partly, like all mothers, for reasons within her own not untroubled soul. As for my father, few souls are less troubled. He can be simply pleased with us, pleased that we exist, and, from the vantage point of his wondrously serene and hale old age, he contemplates our lives almost as if they were books he can dip into whenever he wants.

As for the books I write myself, my 'dirty books', he said the other day: 'I was a wee bitty shocked, at first, but I soon got used to it.' He introduces me in the third person: 'This young woman . . . ' In his culture, it is, of course, a matter of principle to express pride in one's children. It occurs to me that this, too, is not a particularly English sentiment.

Himself, he is a rich source of anecdote. He has partitioned off a little room in the attic of his house, constructed the walls out of cardboard boxes, and there he lies, on a camp-bed, listening to the World Service on a portable radio with his cap on. When he lived in London, he used to wear a trilby to bed but, a formal man, he exchanged it for a cap as soon as he moved. There are two perfectly good bedrooms in his house, with electric blankets and everything, as I well know, but these bedrooms always used to belong to his siblings, now deceased. He moves downstairs into one of these when the temperature in the attic drops too low for even his iron constitution, but he always shifts back up again, to his own place, when the ice melts. He has a ferocious enthusiasm for his own private space. My mother attributed this to a youth spent in the trenches, where no privacy was to be had. His war was the War to end Wars. He was too old for conscription in the one after that.

When he leaves this house for any length of time, he fixes up a whole lot of burglar traps, basins of water balanced on the tops of doors, tripwires, bags of flour suspended by strings, so that we worry in case he forgets where he's left what and ends up hoist with his own petard.

He has a special relationship with cats. He talks to them in a soft chirruping language they find irresistible. When we all lived in London and he worked on the night news desk of a press agency, he would come home on the last tube and walk, chirruping, down the street, accompanied by an ever-increasing procession of cats, to whom he would say good night at the front door. On those rare occasions, in my late teens, when I'd managed to persuade a man to walk me home, the arrival of my father and his cats always caused consternation, not least because my father was immensely tall and strong.

He is the stuff of which sitcoms are made.

His everyday discourse, which is conducted in the stately prose of a thirties *Times* leader, is enlivened with a number of stock phrases of a slightly eccentric, period quality. For example. On a wild night: 'Pity the troops on a night like this.' On a cold day:

> *Cold, bleak, gloomy and glum,*
> *Cold as the hairs on a polar bear's—*

The last word of the couplet is supposed to be drowned by the cries of outrage. My mother always turned up trumps on this one, interposing: 'Father!' on an ascending scale.

At random: 'Thank God for the Navy, who guard our shores.' On entering a room: 'Enter the fairy, singing and dancing.' Sometimes, in a particularly cheerful mood, he'll add to this formula: 'Enter the fairy, singing and dancing and waving her wooden leg.'

Infinitely endearing, infinitely irritating, irascible, comic, tough, sentimental, ribald old man, with his face of a borderline eagle and his bearing of a Scots guard, who, in my imagination as when I was a child, drips chocolates from his pockets as, a cat dancing in front of him, he strides down the road bowed down with gifts, crying: 'Here comes the Marquess of Carrabas!' The very words, 'my father', always make me smile.

But why, when he was so devilish handsome—oh, that photograph in battledress!—did he never marry until his middle thirties? Until he saw my mother, playing tennis with a girlfriend on Clapham Common, and that was it. The die was cast. He gave her his card, proof of his honourable intentions. She took him home to meet her mother. Then he must have felt as though he were going over the top, again.

In 1967 or 1968, forty years on, my mother wrote to me: 'He really loves me (I think).' At that time, she was a semi-invalid and he tended her, with more dash than efficiency, and yet remorselessly, cooking, washing up, washing her smalls, hoovering, as if that is just what he'd retired from work to do, up to his elbows in soapsuds after a lifetime of telephones and anxiety. He'd bring her dinner on a tray with always a slightly soiled tray-cloth. She thought the dirty cloth spoiled the entire gesture. And yet, and yet . . . was she, after all those years, still keeping him on the hook? For herself, she always applauded his ability to spirit taxis up as from the air at crowded railway stations and also the dexterous way he'd kick his own backside, a feat he continued to perform until well into his eighties.

Now, very little of all this has to do with the stern, fearful face of the Father in patriarchy, although the Calvinist north is virtually synonymous with that ideology. Indeed, a short-tempered man, his rages were phenomenal; but they were over in the lightning flash they resembled, and then we all had ice-cream. And there was no fear. So that, now, for me, when fear steps in the door, then love and respect fly out the window.

SUGAR DADDY

I do not think my father has ever asked awkward questions about life, or the world, or anything much, except when he was a boy reporter and asking awkward questions was part of the job. He would regard himself as a law-and-order man, a law-abiding man, a man with a due sense of respect for authority. So far, so in tune with his background and his sense of decorum. And yet somewhere behind all this lurks a strangely free, anarchic spirit. Doorknobs fall from doors the minute he puts his hand on them. Things fall apart. There is a sense that anything might happen. He is a law-and-order man helplessly tuned in to misrule.

And somewhere in all this must lie an ambivalent attitude to the authority to which he claims to defer. Now, my father is not, I repeat, an introspective man. Nor one prone to intellectual analysis; he's always got by on his wits so never felt the need of the latter. But he has his version of the famous story, about one of the Christmas truces during World War One, which was *his* war, although, when he talks about it, I do not recognize Vera Brittain's war, or Siegfried Sassoon's war, or anything but a nightmarish adventure, for, as I say, he feels no fear. The soldiers, bored with fighting, remembering happier times, put up white flags, moved slowly forward, showed photographs, exchanged gifts—a packet of cigarettes for a little brown loaf . . . and then, he says, 'Some fool of a first lieutenant fired a shot.'

When he tells his story, he doesn't know what it *means*, he doesn't know what the story shows he really felt about the bloody officers, nor why I'm proud of him for feeling that; nor why I'm proud of him for giving the German private his cigarettes and remembering so warmly the little loaf of bread, and proud of him for his still undiminished anger at the nitwit of a boy whom they were all forced to obey just when the ranks were in a mood to pack it in and go home.

Of course, the old man thinks that, if the rank and file *had* packed it in and gone home in 1915, the Tsar would still rule Russia and the Kaiser Germany, and the sun would never have set on the British Empire. He is a man of grand simplicities. He still grieves over my mother's 'leftish' views; indeed, he grieves over mine, though not enough to spoil his dinner. He seems, rather, to regard them as, in some way, genetically linked. I have inherited her nose, after all; so why not my mother's voting patterns?

She never forgave him for believing Chamberlain. She'd often bring it up, at moments of stress, as proof of his gullibility. 'And what's more, you came home from the office and said: "There ain't gonna be a war."'

See how she has crept into the narrative, again. He wrote to me last year: 'Your mammy was not only very beautiful but also very clever.' (Always in dialect, always 'mammy'.) Not that she did anything with it. Another husband might have encouraged her to work, or study, although in the 1930s, that would have been exceptional enough in this first-generation middle-class family to have projected us into another dimension of existence altogether. As it was, he, born a Victorian and a sentimentalist, was content to adore, and that, in itself, is sufficiently exceptional, dammit, although it was not good for her moral fibre. She, similarly, trapped by historic circumstances, did not even know, I think, that her own vague discontent, manifested by sick headaches and complicated later on by genuine ill-health, might have had something to do with being a 'wife', a role for which she was in some respects ill suited, as my father's tribute ought to indicate, since beauty and cleverness are usually more valued in mistresses than they are in wives. For her sixtieth birthday, he gave her a huge bottle of Chanel No. 5.

For what it's worth, I've never been in the least attracted to older men—nor they to me, for that matter. Why *is* that? Possibly something in my manner hints I will expect, nay, demand, behaviour I deem appropriate to a father figure, that is, that he kicks his own backside from time to time, and brings me tea in bed, and weeps at the inevitability of loss; and these are usually young men's talents.

Don't think, from all this, it's been all roses. We've had our ups and downs, the old man and I, for he was born a Victorian. Though it occurs to me his unstated but self-evident idea that I should earn my own living, have a career, in fact, may have originated in his experience of the first wave of feminism, that hit in his teens and twenties, with some of whose products he worked, by one of whose products we were doctored. (Our family doctor, Helen Gray, was eighty when she retired twenty years ago, and must have been one of the first women doctors.)

Nevertheless, his Victorianness, for want of a better word, means he feels duty bound to come the heavy father, from time to time, always with a histrionic overemphasis: 'You just watch out for yourself, that's all.' 'Watching out for yourself' has some obscure kind of sexual meaning, which he hesitates to spell out. If advice he gave me when I was a girl (I could paraphrase this advice as 'Kneecap them'), if this advice would be more or less what I'd arm my own daughters with now, it ill accorded with the mood of the sixties. Nor was it much help in those days when almost the entire male sex seemed in a conspiracy to deprive me of the opportunity to get within sufficient distance. The old man dowered me with too much self-esteem.

But how can a girl have *too much* self-esteem?

Nevertheless, not all roses. He is, you see, a foreigner; what is more, a Highland man, who struck further into the heartland of England than Charles Edward Stuart's army ever did, and then buggered off, leaving his children behind to carve niches in the alien soil. Oh, he'd hotly deny this version of his life; it is my own romantic interpretation of his life, obviously. He's all for the Act of Union. He sees no difference at all between the English and the Scots, except, once my mother was gone, he saw no reason to remain among the English. And his always unacknowledged foreignness, the extroversion of his manners, the stateliness of his demeanour, his fearlessness, guiltlessness, his inability to feel embarrassment, the formality of his discourse, above all, his utter ignorance of and complete estrangement from the English system of social class, make him a being I puzzle over and wonder at.

It is that last thing—for, in England, he seemed genuinely classless—that may have helped me always feel a stranger, here, myself. He is of perfectly good petty-bourgeois stock; my grandfather owned a shoe shop although, in those days, that meant being able to make the things as well as sell them, and repair them, too, so my grandfather was either a shopkeeper or a cobbler, depending on how you looked at it. The distinction between entrepreneur and skilled artisan may have appeared less fine, in those days, in that town beside the North Sea which still looks as if it could provide a good turnout for a witchburning.

There are all manner of stories about my paternal grandfather, whom I never met; he was the village atheist, who left a fiver in his will to every minister in the place, just in case. I never met my Gaelic-speaking grandmother, either. (She died, as it happens of toothache, shortly before I was born.) From all these stories I know they both possessed in full measure that peculiar Highland ability, much perplexing to early tourists, which means that the meanest, grubbing crofter can, if necessary, draw himself up to his full height and welcome a visitor into his stinking hovel as if its miserable tenant were a prince inviting a foreign potentate into a palace. This is the courtly grace of the authentic savage. The women do it with especially sly elegance. Lowering a steaming bowl on to a filthy tablecloth, my father's sister used to say: 'Now, take some delicious kale soup.' And it was the water in which the cabbage had been boiled.

It's possible to suspect they're having you on, and so they may be; yet this formality always puts the visitor, no matter what his or her status, in the role of supplicant. Your humiliation is what spares you. When a Highlander grovels, then, oh, then is the time to keep your hand on your wallet. One learns to fear an apology most.

These are the strategies of underdevelopment and they are worlds away from those which my mother's family learned to use to contend with the savage urban class struggle in Battersea, in the 1900s. Some of my mother's family learned to manipulate cynically the English class system and helped me and my brother out. All of them knew, how can I put it, that a good table with clean linen meant self-respect and to love Shakespeare was a kind of class revenge. (Perhaps that is why those soiled tray-cloths upset my mother so; she had no quarrel with his taste in literature.) For my father, the grand gesture was the thing. He entered Harrods like a Jacobite army invading Manchester. He would arrive at my school 'to sort things out' like the wrath of God.

This effortless sense of natural dignity, or his own unquestioned worth, is of his essence; there are noble savages in his heredity and I look at him, sometimes, to quote Mayakovsky, 'like an Eskimo looking at a train.'

For I know so little about him, although I know so much. Much of his life was conducted in my absence, on terms of which

I am necessarily ignorant, for he was older than I am now when I was born, although his life has shaped my life. This is the curious abyss that divides the closest kin, that the tender curiosity appropriate to lovers is inappropriate, here, where the bond is involuntary, so that the most important things stay undiscovered. If I am short-tempered, volatile as he is, there is enough of my mother's troubled soul in me to render his very transparency, his psychic good health, endlessly mysterious. He is my father and I love him as Cordelia did, 'according to my natural bond'. What the nature of that 'natural bond' might be, I do not know, and, besides, I have a theoretical objection to the notion of a 'natural bond'.

But, at the end of *King Lear*, one has a very fair notion of the strength of that bond, whatever it is, whether it is the construct of culture rather than nature, even if we might all be better off without it. And I do think my father gives me far more joy than Cordelia ever got from Lear.

IAN JACK

FINISHED WITH ENGINES

My father wrote a kind of autobiography in the years before he died. I have it now beside me in a big, brown-paper envelope, a hundred and fifty pages of lined foolscap covered with the careful handwriting—light on the up-stroke and heavy on the down—that he learned on a slate in a Scottish schoolroom eighty years ago. He called these pages 'a mixture of platitudes and nostalgia.'

My father's life spanned eight decades of the twentieth century, but he met nobody who mattered very much and lived far removed from the centre of great events. He was born in the year the Boer War ended, in a mill town in the Scottish lowlands. A Co-operative Society hearse took him to a crematorium in the same town six months before Britain fought what was probably the last of its imperial wars, in the Falklands. He was too young for the Somme and too old to be called up for El Alamein. He never saw the inside of Auschwitz and knew nobody who did. He neglects to tell us his role (if any) in the General Strike. He worked for most of his life as a steam mechanic (though he always used the word 'fitter'); a good one, so I have been told by the people who worked beside him.

He started work as a fourteen-year-old apprentice in a linen mill on five shillings a week and progressed through other textile factories in Scotland and Lancashire, into the engine-room of a cargo steamer, down a coal pit, through a lead works and a hosepipe factory. He loved applying for jobs—would study the advertisements, remove the cap from his fountain-pen, rest the lined foolscap on a chessboard he had made for himself, and write steadily in an armchair near the fire—and only fate in the shape of unwelcoming managements prevented his moving to work in jute mills on the Hoogli or among a colony of French progressive thinkers in the South Pacific.

He did not prosper. Instead he ended his working life a few miles from where he began it, and in much the same way: in overalls and over a lathe and waiting for the dispensation of the evening hooter, when he would stick his leg over his bike and cycle home. He never owned a house and he never drove a car, and today there is very little public evidence that he ever lived.

Few of his workplaces survive. The cargo steamer went to the scrapyard long ago, of course, but even the shipping line it belonged to has vanished. The coal pit is a field. Urban grasslands and car parks have buried the foundations of the mills. The house he grew up in has been demolished and replaced with a traffic island. The school where he learned his careful handwriting has made way for a supermarket. As a result, I am one of the sons of the manufacturing classes whom de-industrialization has disinherited; in many respects it is a benign disinheritance, because many of the places my father worked were hell-holes, but it is also one so sudden and complete that it bewilders me.

Still, there is this 'mixture of platitudes and personal nostalgia.' But I'm exaggerating the paucity of what he left behind. There was actually *much* more than the contents of the brown envelope. There were books, suits from Burtons, long underpants, cuff-links, shirt armbands, pipes that continued to smell of Walnut Plug, the polished black boots he always preferred to shoes, half-empty bottles of Bay Rum, tools in tool-boxes, shaving-brushes, cigarette cards, photograph albums, photographs loose in suitcases, tram tickets, picture postcards sent from seaside resorts and inland spas—Rothesay and Llandudno, Matlock and Peebles. *Here for the week. Weather mixed. Lizzie and Jim.* What a man for collecting! Even here, interleaved among the foolscap, I find a card from the Cyclists' Touring Club for the Christmas of 1927, a bill from the Spring Lodge Hotel (family and commercial) for sixteen shillings and fourpence and a menu from the mess of the cargo steamer *Nuddea* dated 12 October 1928 (that day's lunch, somewhere in the tropics, comprised pea soup, fried fish, roast sirloin of beef). And in a small envelope inside a larger one is a pamphlet on humanist funeral ceremonies, for 'when it is desired that no reference should be made to theological beliefs but, rather, to the ethical and natural aspects of human life.'

He left no explicit instructions, but the hint is clear enough. We only half-obliged. We did not stand at the lectern and read aloud, from the scraps of card that tumble from this smaller envelope:

I want no heaven for which I must give up my reason
and no immortality that demands the surrender of my
individuality.

Or:

Forgive me Lord, my little joke on thee
and,
I'll forgive your one big joke on me.

The truth is that a strident proclamation of my father's doubt would have sat strangely out of kilter with the last quarter of the twentieth century in Britain. Who, in this country of the don't-knows, now doubts doubt? It would have been like listening, that day in the crematorium, to the proposition that the earth moved round the sun.

I was born in 1945 and grew up in the Scotland of the 1950s. But in our house we lived in the 1910s and 1920s as well, concurrently. The past sustained us. It came home from work every evening with flat cap and dirty hands and drew its weekly wages from industries that even then were sleep-walking their way towards extinction.

Our village lay at the northern end of the Forth Bridge, three large cantilevers that had been built with great technical ingenuity, and at some cost to human life, to carry the railway one and a half miles over the Firth of Forth. It was opened by the Prince of Wales in 1890. The village was unimaginable without the bridge. Its size reduced everything around it to the scale of models: trains, ships, the village houses—all of them looked as though they could be picked up and thrown into a toy-cupboard. The three towers rose even higher than our flat, which stood in a council estate two hundred and fifty feet above the sea. On still summer mornings, when a fog lay banked across the water and foghorns moaned below, we could see the tops of the cantilevers poking up from the shrouds: three perfect metal alps that, when freshly painted, glistened in the sun. Postcards sold in the village post office described the bridge as the world's eighth wonder, and went on in long captions to describe how it had been built. More than five thousand men had 'laboured day and night for seven years' with materials that included 54,160 tons of steel, 740,000 cubic feet of granite, 64,300 cubic yards of concrete and 21,000 tons of cement. They had driven in six and a half million rivets. Sixty workers had been killed during those years, some blown by gales into the sea and drowned, others flattened by falling sheets of steel.

For several decades the bridge dazzled Scotland as the pinnacle of native enterprise, and then slowly declined to the status of an old ornament, like the tartan that surrounded its picture on tea towels and shortbread tins. People of my father's generation had been captivated by its splendour and novelty. Pushing his bike as we walked together up the hill, he would sometimes say ruefully: 'I became an engineer because I wanted to build Forth Bridges.'

From quite an early age I sensed that something had gone wrong with my father's life, and hence our lives, and that I had been born too late to share a golden age, when the steam engine drove us forward and a watchful God was at the helm. Scotland, land of the inventive engineer! Glasgow, the workshop of the world! I hoped the future would be like the past, for all our sakes.

My father began his apprenticeship in 1916 in one of Dunfermline's many linen mills. The town was famous for the quality of its tablecloths and sheets—'napery' used to be the generic word—and ran along a ridge with a skyline spiked by church steeples and factory chimneys. The gates of my father's first factory were only a few hundred yards from his home. He writes:

> We oiled and greased and greased and oiled . . . pirn-winding frames, bobbin-winding frames, cop-winding frames, overpick and underpick looms, dobbie machines, beetles, calenders and shafting. There was never an end to shafting! A main shaft approximately two hundred and fifty feet in length driving thirty-two wing shafts of an average length of seventy-five feet. This was all underfloor . . . and eight of these wing shafts had to be oiled every day when the engine stopped for the mill dinner hour.

Later he moved to the blacksmith's shop, where he made 'hoop iron box-corners' for the packing department and learned how to handle a hammer and chisel. 'Chap, man, chap!' said the blacksmith. 'Ye couldnae chap shite aff an auld wife's erse.' Eventually, towards the end of his apprenticeship, he was transferred to the engine house:

> Sometimes I would be allowed to attend the mill engine for a week or a fortnight . . . taking diagrams from each cylinder with an old Richards Indicator, and studying the cards. I felt just as a doctor must feel when sounding his patient's lungs with a stethoscope. If the cards were all right and the beat of eighty-five revs per minute had become automatic listening, then I could relax, and, as smoking was just tolerated in the engine house, have a Woodbine. It is said that the ratio of the unpleasant to the pleasant experiences in life is as three to one. The engine 'tenting' [tending] was one of those pleasant intermissions.

Reading this, I try to construct a picture of my father thirty years before I knew him. There he sits next to the cascading, burnished cranks of the mill engine. I know from snapshots that he has curly black hair and a grave kind of smile. Perhaps he's reading something—H. G. Wells, a pamphlet from the Scottish Labour Party, the Rubáiyát of Omar Khayyám. The engine pushes on at eighty-five revolutions per minute. Shafting revolves in its tunnels. Cogs and belts drive looms. Shuttles flash from side to side weaving tablecloths patterned with the insignia of the Peninsular and Oriental Steamship Company and the Canadian Pacific Railway. Stokers crash coal into the furnaces—more heat, more steam, more tablecloths—and black clouds tumble from the fluted stone top of the factory chimney, to fly before the southwest wind and then to rise and join the smoke-stream from a thousand other workplaces in lowland Scotland: jute, cotton and thread mills, linoleum factories, shipyards, iron-smelters, locomotive works. Human and mechanical activity is eventually expressed as a great national movement of carbon particles that float high across the North Sea and drop as blighting rain on the underdeveloped peasant nations to the east.

In 1952, after twenty-two years working in Lancashire, my father returned to Scotland, to his old factory. It was his tenth move, and a complete accident: the result of yet another letter to an anonymous box number underneath the words 'Maintenance Engineer Wanted'.

My mother, surrounded by people who called her husband Jock (his name was Harry) and talked of grand weeks in Blackpool, had fretted to be home among her 'own folk', but my father hadn't minded Lancashire. He liked to imitate the dialect of the cotton weavers and spinners; it appealed to his sense of theatre, just as the modest beer-drinking and potato-pie suppers of the Workers' Educational Association sustained his hope that the world might be improved, temperately. The terraced streets shut my mother in, but my father, making the best of it, found them full of 'character': men in clogs with biblical names—Abraham, Ezekiel—and shops that sold tripe and herbal drinks, sarsaparilla, dandelion and burdock. He bought the *Manchester Guardian* and talked of Lancashire people as more 'go-ahead' than the wry, cautious Scotsmen of his childhood. Lancastrians were sunnier people in a damper climate. They had an obvious folksiness, a completely realized industrial culture evolved in the dense streets and tall factories of large towns and cities. Lancashire meant Cottonopolis, the Hallé Orchestra playing Beethoven in the Free Trade Hall, knockers-up, comedians, thronged seaside resorts with ornamental piers. In Fife, pit waste encroached on fishing villages and mills grew up in old market towns, but industry had never completely conquered an older way of life based on the sea and the land.

Later he would talk of Bolton as though he had been to New York, as a place of opportunity, with witty citizens who called a spade a spade. A Lancashire accent, overheard on a Scottish street, would have him hurrying towards the speaker. Often he was disappointed:

'Do you mind me asking where you're from?'

'Rochdale.'

'Och, I'm sorry, I thought it might be Bolton.'

We moved back to Fife. The furniture went by van while we came north by train, behind a locomotive with a brass name-plate: *Prince Rupert*. I was seven. I held a jamjar with two goldfish, whose bowl had been trusted to the removers, as *Prince Rupert* hauled us over the summits of Shap and Beattock. The peaks and troughs of telegraph wires jerked past like sagging skipping-ropes. Red-brick terraces with advertisements for brown bread and pale ale on their windowless ends gave way to austere villas made of stone. The wistfulness of homecoming overcame my parents as we crossed the border; Lancashire and Fife then seemed a subcontinental distance apart and not a few hours' drive and a cup of coffee on the motorway. Our carriage was shunted at Carstairs Junction, and we changed stations as well as trains in Edinburgh. Here English history no longer provided locomotive names. We had moved to new railway territory, with older and quainter steam engines named after glens, lochs and characters from the novels of Sir Walter Scott. At dusk we sped across the Forth Bridge behind an Edwardian machine called Jingling Geordie, sailing past our new home and on towards the small shipbuilding town where my mother's father had settled.

When I awoke the next morning riveters were already drilling like noisy dentists in the local shipyard, and express trains drifted, whistling, along the embankment next to the sea. The smells of the damp steam and salt, sweet and sharp, blew round the corner and met the scent of morning rolls from the bakery. Urban Lancashire could not compare with this and, like my mother, I never missed it. But what was linear progress for a seven-year-old may have been the staleness of a rounded circle for a man of fifty: this little industrial utopia of my childish eye had foundations that were already rotting.

Two days later we moved a few miles down the coast and into our home beside the Forth Bridge, and my father went to work in his new old factory. It was a shock:

> The scrap merchants were at work; they had removed most of the looms and machinery from the old weaving shed, which made it a most cheerless place. The blackbirds were nesting in the old Jacquard machines. All the beam engines had gone, and the surface condenser on top of the engine house in the mill road was now standing dry and idle. The latest engine (installed in 1912) was a marine-type compound; it was also standing idle with the twelve ropes still on the flywheel. The engine packing and all the tools were still

in the cupboard, the indicator, all cleaned, lay ready to take diagrams; there was even a tin of Brasso and cloths for polishing the handrails. It seemed as if everything was lying in readiness for an unearthly visitor to open the main steam valve. But there was no steam, everything was cold and silent . . .

The views from our new house were astounding. On the day we moved in, in October 1952, I stood at the top of the outside stair and watched a procession of trains crossing the bridge and a tall-funnelled cargo steamer passing below, unladen and high out of the water, its propeller playfully flapping the river. Pressing my nose against the front-room window and squinting to the left I could see Edinburgh Castle. In Lancashire all we could see from our windows were back gardens and washing and more houses like our own, with all the doors painted in council green. My parents' phrase, 'moving up home to Scotland', took on a literal meaning. It was as though we had been catapulted from a pit bottom to daylight.

In 1956, the summer before Suez, my father took us to Aberdeen. It was my first proper holiday and the first evidence, perhaps, of a slightly increased disposable income: all previous excursions had been to the homes of aunts and grandparents. That spring we studied the brochures which declared Aberdeen 'the Silver City with the Golden Sand', and the word 'boarding-house' became part of our evening vocabulary. My father chose a name and address and corresponded with the landlady. My mother didn't like the sound of it: she noticed that the address did not carry the distinguishing asterisk that marked the approval of Aberdeen's town hall. But my father tutted and persisted: it would be fine; the landlady sounded a nice wee woman. We went by train (an express; high tea in the dining-car) and then by bus to a grey suburb in the lee of a headland where the North Sea sucked and boiled. It quickly became obvious that the house was 'off the beaten track', a phrase and a situation that always recommended themselves to my father. It lay a change of buses away from the beach but very close to a fish-meal factory. The smell of rotting fish hung over the street and crept into the house, to slide off the polished Rexine of the sofa and chairs but impregnate permanently the dead collie dog that the landlady had converted into a rug. The whiff of more marine life, cooking in pots, came from the kitchen. We ate boiled and fried haddock for a week and were reminded constantly that Aberdeen was then the premier fishing-port of Europe. This was twenty years before the oil came in.

At night I shared a room with a young man who had an institutional haircut and dug for a living in a market garden. Other young men, equally shorn, emerged for the breakfast kippers. Mrs MacPhail, the widowed landlady, had claimed them after they had reached the age limit of the 'special schools' that contained them during adolescence. On the first morning we walked to the lighthouse and stared forlornly across the harbour mouth towards the inaccessible beach. My father said we would just have to make the best of it; the other lodgers were 'decent enough laddies . . . a wee bit simple but hardly proper dafties . . . there's no harm in them.' And there wasn't. On wet evenings the hardly-dafties took me to the cinema, and on the night before we left they gave us a concert in the room with the dog rug. My room-mate, Johnny, sang 'If I Were a Blackbird I'd Whistle and Sing'. Another hummed 'A Gordon for Me' through a comb and paper. A third placed a favourite new record on the radiogram and again and again we heard: 'Zambezi! Zambezi! Zambezi! Zam!' The next morning my father—who had a terrible fear of missing trains—rose at an extraordinarily early hour to pay the bill and surprised the landlady, naked and trying to cover herself with the remains of the pet collie.

More than twenty years later, he would mention the experience whenever the word Aberdeen looked likely to occur in a conversation, even if the rest of us had been talking about the oil rigs now moored in the firth outside the house, or what would happen to the country when the oil ran out.

My father went on cycling back from his lathe until well into the 1960s. The new decade was good to us both. I left home at eighteen and gladly entered pubs, football grounds and dancehalls. Films and television plays began to represent British life as we thought we knew it. When *Saturday Night and Sunday Morning*, the film of Alan Sillitoe's novel, came to the local

Regal, I was thrilled to see scenes of conscientious men working at milling machines and lathes. 'Poor bastards,' says Albert Finney in the role of the new British hero, the young worker who sticks up two fingers at respectability and grabs what he can get.

The film kindled a suspicion within me that this was the definitive verdict on my father, apparently a dupe who had worked for buttons for nearly fifty years. It was an ignorant adolescent judgement: my father was not a 'poor bastard', and surprising things began to happen to him. I came home late one Saturday night and found him roaring with laughter at a satire show on television. He joined the Campaign for Nuclear Disarmament and worked for it long after I, an earlier but more faint-hearted member, had left. He won a couple of thousand pounds on the football pools (a total ignorance of football led to the correct forecast; virtue, for once, had its reward) and took my mother on sea voyages to Egypt and the Soviet Union, two countries that had fascinated him since Howard Carter found Tutankhamun's tomb and the Bolsheviks stormed the Winter Palace. He grew jollier and, rather than offering bitter homilies against masonic foremen and the unfairness of piece-work, settled into a new role as a teller of quaint stories.

In 1967 he retired with a present of twenty pounds in an envelope and a determination to enjoy himself. He read books on Egyptology, went to evening classes in Russian, cultivated his garden and watched quiz shows and documentaries on television. This is the passage of my father's life I know least about. Somehow we missed our connection. I neglected him, no longer went out with him on our bikes, barely listened to the stories I thought he would always be there to tell.

As the old died, the village filled up with new people: wives who wore jeans and loaded small cars at the nearest supermarket, husbands who drove what twenty years before would have seemed an impossible distance to work. Couples gutted old cottages and painted knock-through rooms white, hung garlic from their kitchen shelves. In these houses 'lunch' and 'supper' supplanted 'dinner' and 'tea', but their owners, searching for a past to embellish their modern lives, went burrowing into history to uncover village traditions that had been invisible for forty years. The only village celebration of my childhood had been the one to mark the Coronation, when New Testaments and children's belts in red, white and blue had been distributed. Now an annual gala day was revived, with a bagpiper at the head of the procession, and a 'heritage trail' signposted in clean European sans-serif as though it were an exit on an *Autobahn*. Meanwhile most of the village shops closed, and vans stopped calling with the groceries. Steam locomotives no longer thundered up the gradient. My father gave up reading newspaper stories which told of 'fights to save jobs'. Once he threw down the local weekly in disgust: 'There's nothing in here but sponsored walks and supermarket bargains.' He cycled still, taking circuitous routes to avoid the new motorways and coming home to despair at the abundance of cars. Usually on these trips he would revisit his past. The Highlands, fifty miles away, were now beyond him, but even in his seventies he could still manage to reach the Fife hills and the desolate stretch of country that had once been the Fife coalfield. He brought back news to my mother. 'Do you mind the Lindsay Colliery? It's all away, there's nothing there but fields.' Factories had gone, churches were demolished, railway cuttings filled up with plastic bottles and rusty prams.

Once around this time we visited an exhibition of old photographs in Dunfermline, his birthplace. One picture showed a street littered with horse dung and small boys standing in a cobbled gutter: the High Street, *circa* 1909. My father went up close. 'That's me on the left there. I remember the day the photographer came.' We looked at a boy with bare feet and a fringe cropped straight across the forehead. The photograph and the man beside it were difficult to reconcile. Quite suddenly I realized how old my father was. Afterwards he talked about writing his 'life story', and we encouraged him; for months of evenings and afternoons he sat in the easy chair with the chessboard and foolscap on his knee, writing with his fountain-pen and smiling.

He became, I suppose, like the people he had always cherished: a character. Like the photograph, he was now of historic interest, and sometimes when I came up from London I expected to find him surrounded by tape recorders and students from the nearest university department of oral history. That did not happen. One day he collapsed into the potato patch he'd been digging. Cancer was diagnosed, eventually, but he never asked for the diagnosis and was never told. For many weeks my mother nursed him as he slipped in and out of pain and consciousness. The pills did not seem to work; he whimpered and cried aloud like an abandoned baby, an awful sound. The doctor decided to change the medication to an old-fashioned liquid cocktail of alcohol, morphine and cocaine. After the first dose he rose bright-eyed from the pillows and saw me, up from London.

'What's yon big lazy bugger doing here?'

Those were his last words to me, and my mother worried that I'd been hurt. 'He's never spoken about you like that before. I don't know what came over him.'

We decided that it was bravado induced by alcohol, but I wondered. I remembered all the times I'd failed to help him in the garden; my uselessness with a chisel and saw; and my job, where I never got my hands dirty, or at least not literally. Or perhaps he was simply bored and had decided to liven people up.

The crematorium was a new building, concrete and glass, which had been built (as my father would have been the first to tell his mourners) near the site of one of the first railways in the world. The moorland to the east held mysterious water-filled hollows and old earthworks, traces of an eighteenth-century wagonway that had carried coal from Fife's first primitive collieries down to sailing barques moored at harbours in the firth. Here my father had played in the summers before 1914, uncovering large square stones with bolt-holes that had once secured the wagonway's wooden rails. Here also we had gone for walks on Sundays in the 1950s, smashing down thistleheads and imagining the scene as it must have been when horses were pulling wooden tubs filled with coal. The world's first industrial revolution sprang from places such as this; it had converted our ancestors from ploughmen into iron moulders, pitmen, bleachers, factory girls, steam mechanics, colonial soldiers and Christian missionaries. Now North Britain's bold participation in the shaping of the world was over. My father had penetrated the revolution's secrets when he went to night school and learned the principles of thermodynamics, but as the revolution's power had failed so had he. His life was bound up with its decline; they almost shared last gasps.

BLAKE MORRISON

AND WHEN DID YOU LAST SEE YOUR FATHER?

1

A hot September Saturday in Cheshire, 1959. We haven't moved
for ten minutes. Ahead of us, a queue of cars stretches out of sight
around the corner. Everyone has turned his engine off, and now
my father does so too. In the sudden silence we can hear the
distant whinge of what must be the first race of the afternoon, a
ten-lap event for saloon cars. It is five minutes past one. In an
hour the drivers will be warming up for the main event, the Gold
Cup—Graham Hill, Jack Brabham, Roy Salvadori, Stirling Moss
and Joakim Bonnier. My father has always loved fast cars, and
motor racing has a strong British following just now, which is why
we are stuck here in this country lane with hundreds of other cars.

My father does not like waiting in queues. He is used to
patients waiting in queues to see him, but he is not used to waiting
in queues himself. A queue to him means a man being denied the
right to be where he wants to be at a time of his own choosing,
which is at the front, now. Ten minutes have passed and my father
is running out of patience. What is happening up ahead? What fat-
head has caused this snarl-up? Why are no cars coming the other
way? Has there been an accident? Why are there no police to sort
it out? Every two minutes or so he gets out of the car, crosses to
the opposite verge and tries to see if there is movement up ahead.
There isn't. He gets back in. The roof of our Alvis is down, the
sun beating on to the leather upholstery, the chrome, the picnic
basket. The hood is folded and pleated into the mysterious crevice
between the boot and the narrow back seat where my sister and I
are scrunched together as usual. The roof is nearly always down,
whatever the weather: my father loves fresh air, and every car he
has ever owned has been a convertible, so that he can have fresh
air. But the air today is not fresh. There is a pall of high-rev
exhaust, dust, petrol, boiling-over engines.

In the cars ahead and behind, people are laughing, eating
sandwiches, drinking from beer bottles, enjoying the weather,
settling into the familiar indignity of waiting-to-get-to-the-front.
But my father is not like them. There are only two things on his
mind: the invisible head of the queue and, not unrelated, the
other half of the country lane, tantalizingly empty.

'Just relax, Arthur,' my mother says. 'You're in and out of the car like a blue-tailed fly.'

But being told to relax only incenses him. 'What can it be?' he demands. 'Maybe there's been an accident. Maybe they're waiting for an ambulance.' We all know where this last speculation is leading, even before he says it. 'Maybe they need a doctor.'

'No, Arthur,' says my mother, as he opens the door for a final time and stands on the wheel arch to crane ahead.

'It must be an accident,' he announces. 'I think I should drive ahead and see.'

'No, Arthur. It's just the numbers waiting to get in. And surely there must be doctors on the circuit.'

It is one-thirty and silent now. The saloon race has finished. It is still an hour until the Gold Cup itself, but there's another race first, and the cars in the paddock to see, and besides . . .

'Well, I'm not going to bloody well wait here any longer,' he says. 'We'll never get in. We might as well turn round and give up.' He sits for another twenty seconds, then leans forward, opens the glove compartment and pulls out a stethoscope, which he hooks over the windscreen mirror. It hangs there like a skeleton, the membrane at the top, the metal and rubber leads dangling bow-legged, the two ivory earpieces clopping bonily against each other. He starts the engine, releases the handbrake, reverses two feet, then pulls out into the opposite side of the road.

'No,' says my mother again, half-heartedly. It could be that he is about to do a three-point turn and go back. No it couldn't . . .

My father does not drive particularly quickly past the marooned cars. No more than twenty miles an hour. Even so, it *feels* fast and arrogant, and all the occupants turn and stare as they see us coming. Some appear to be angry. Some are shouting. 'Point to the stethoscope, pet,' he tells my mother, but she has slid down sideways in her passenger seat, out of sight, her bottom resting on the floor, from where she berates him.

'God Almighty, Arthur, why do you have to do this? Why can't you wait like everyone else? What if we meet something coming the other way?' Now my sister and I do the same, hide ourselves below the seat. Our father is on his own. He is not with us, this bullying, shaming, undemocratic cheat, or rather, we are not with him.

My face pressed to the sweet-smelling upholstery, I imagine what is happening ahead. I can't tell how far we have gone, how many blind corners we have taken. If we meet something on this narrow country lane, we will have to reverse past all the cars we have just overtaken. I wait for the squeal of brakes.

After an eternity of—what?—two minutes, my mother sticks her head up and says, 'Now you've had it,' and my father replies, 'No, there's another gate beyond,' and my sister and I raise ourselves to look. We are level with the cars at the head of the queue, which are waiting to turn left into the brown ticket holders' entrance, the plebs' entrance. A steward steps out of the gateway towards us, but my father, pretending not to see him, drives past and on to a clear piece of road, where, two hundred yards ahead, the half a dozen cars that have come from the opposite direction are waiting to turn into another gateway. Unlike those we have left behind, these cars appear to be moving. Magnanimous, my father waits until the last one has turned in, then drives through the stone gateposts and over the bumpy grass to where an armbanded steward in a tweed jacket is waiting by the roped entrance.

'Good afternoon, sir. Red ticket holder?' The question does not come as a shock: we have all seen the signs, numerous and clamorous, saying RED TICKET HOLDERS' ENTRANCE. But my father is undeterred.

'These, you mean,' he says and hands over his brown tickets.

'No, sir, I'm afraid these are brown tickets.'

'But there must be some mistake. I applied for red tickets. To be honest, I didn't even look.'

'I'm sorry sir, but these are brown tickets, and brown's the next entrance, two hundred yards along. If you just swing round here, and . . . '

'I'm happy to pay the difference.'

'No, you see the rules say . . . '

'I know where the brown entrance is, I've just spent the last hour queueing for it by mistake. I drove up here because I thought I was red. I can't go back there now. The queue stretches for miles. And these children you know, who'd been looking forward . . . '

By now half a dozen cars have gathered behind us. One of them parps. The steward is wavering.

'You say you applied for red.'

'Not only applied for, paid for. I'm a doctor, you see . . . '—
he points at the stethoscope—'and I like being near the
grandstand.'

This double *non sequitur* seems to clinch it.

'All right, sir, but next time please check the tickets. Ahead
and to your right.'

This is the way it was with my dad. Minor duplicities. Little
fiddles. Money-saving, time-saving, privilege-attaining
fragments of opportunism. The queue-jump, the backhander, the
deal under the table. Parking where you shouldn't, drinking after
hours, accepting the poached pheasant and the goods off the
back of a lorry. 'They' were killjoys, after all—'they' meaning the
Establishment to which, despite being a middle-class professional,
a GP, he never felt he belonged; our job, as ordinary folk, trying
to get the most out of life, was to outwit them. Serious law-
breaking would have scared him, though he envied and often
praised those who had pulled off ingenious, non-violent crimes,
like the Great Train Robbers or, before them, the men who
intercepted a lorry carrying a large number of old banknotes to
the incinerator. ('Still in currency, you see, but not new, so there
was no record of the numbers and they couldn't be traced.
Brilliant, quite brilliant.') He was not himself up to being
criminal in a big way, but he'd have been lost if he couldn't cheat
in a small way: so much of his pleasure derived from it. I grew
up thinking it absolutely normal, that most Englishmen were like
this. I still suspect that's the case.

My childhood seems to be a web of little scams and
triumphs. The time we stayed at a hotel near a famous golf
course—Troon, was it?—and discovered that if we started at the
fifth hole and finished at the fourth we could avoid the clubhouse
and green fees. The private tennis clubs and yacht clubs and
drinking clubs we got into (especially on Sundays in dry counties
of Wales) by giving someone else's name: by the time the man on
the door had failed to find it, my father would have read the
names on the list upsidedown: 'There, see, Wilson. No, Wilson, I
said, not Watson.' If all else failed, you could try slipping the
chap a pound note. With his odd mixture of innocence,

confidence and hail-fellow cheeriness, my father could usually talk his way into anything and, when caught, out of anything.

Oulton Park, half an hour later. We have met up with our cousins in the brown car park—they of course arrived on time—and have come back with them to the entrance to the paddock. My father has assumed that, with the red tickets he's wangled, we are entitled to enter the paddock for nothing—along with our guests. He is wrong about this. Tickets to the paddock cost a guinea. There are ten of us. We're talking serious money.

'We'll buy one, anyway,' my father says to the man in the ticket booth and comes back with a small, brown-paper card, like a library ticket, with a piece of string attached to a hole at the top so you can thread it through your lapel. 'Let me just investigate,' he says, and disappears through the gate, the steward seeing the lapel ticket and nodding him through: no stamp on the hand or name-check. In ten minutes or so my father is back, in a state of excitement. He whispers to my Uncle Ron, hands him the ticket and leads the rest of us to a wooden slatted fence in a quiet corner of the car park. Soon Uncle Ron appears on the other side of the fence, in an equally quiet corner of the paddock, and passes the ticket to us between the slats. Cousin Richard takes the ticket this time and repeats the procedure. One by one we all troop round: Kela, Auntie Mary, Edward, Jane, Gillian, my mother, myself. In five minutes, all ten of us are inside.

'Marvellous,' Father says. 'Four pounds, twelve shillings and we've got four red tickets and ten of us in the paddock. That'd be costing anyone else twenty guineas. Not bad.'

We stand round Jack Brabham's Cooper, its bonnet opened like a body on an operating table, a mass of tubes and wires and gleamy bits of white and silver.

Later, Brabham is overtaken on lap six by Moss, who stays there for the next sixty-nine laps. A car comes off the circuit between Lodge Corner and Deer Leap, crashing through the wooden slatted fence along from where we're standing. My father disappears 'to see if I can help'. He comes back strangely quiet and whispers to my mother: 'Nothing I could do.'

2

She will sleep with him tonight. She worries that it is macabre, but I encourage her: she must do what she feels right. This is, she says, the last night she'll ever have him here, and she wants them to spend it together.

Round midnight, we are sitting on the bed, and she is stroking his hair and kneading his face and then tweaks his nose and says: 'Icy. But you never did complain of the cold, did you?' We have kept the window open, which is just as well because we've not been able to turn the radiator off, and from time to time I catch a whiff of something I don't much want to think about. His face, the chin propped up on its hod or golf tee or sock darner, is still perfect. He has always been a great sleeper ('I was really hard on,' he'd say when he woke from his afternoon nap or evening pre-pub *zzz*), and all this sleeping he is doing now seems his apotheosis—the hardest sleep of all. 'No, the easiest,' says my mother when I try this conceit on her: 'No dreams, no worries about oversleeping, nothing.'

She leaves the room, and I lift back the sheet. There is a deep blackberry bruise spreading across either side of the stomach scar—the skin looks papery-thin and in danger of oozing or bursting. Little red lines have appeared on parts of his bleached hands. The back of his neck, from what I can make out, has gone purple and discoloured, all the blood gathering there.

When I come in at seven next morning, she's asleep beside him. I return later and find she's been crying.

'I've just been talking to my little man.'

'What about?'

'Oh, I've been telling him he shouldn't have gone and left me alone like this—not so soon.'

'I'm sure he didn't want to.'

'No, I know, but the fact remains: he's upped and gone.'

She berates him some more, and I am reminded of Shakespeare's Cleopatra, berating Antony:

Hast thou no care of me, shall I abide
In this dull world, which in thy absence is
No better than a sty.

This is the way the world goes, the men running out on the women, running out *before* the women. A shorter life expectancy: there's one inequality men can brandish on their placards, can grumble about to women, who endure most of the others. But perhaps even in this women—as the ones left painfully behind while their husbands move beyond pain—end up suffering the most.

3

A skiing trip to Lech, Austria, 1971. Long after the time when most parents would have written off their children as surly adolescents scarcely to be endured even for a weekend, and long after the time when most children would be holidaying only with their peers, here we all are for a fortnight together, father, mother, daughter, son. Friends at university have spoken enviously of the wonderful *après-ski* life awaiting me—parties, cocktails, drugs, girls—but I can't see how I'm going to come by all this with my parents inhibitingly omnipresent and my sister, supposing I did get away from them, lumberingly in tow. On the slopes I'm tormented by glimpses of beautiful faces and long hair streaming from bobble hats. In the long waits for the lift or cable-car, I dream about the evening ahead and how I will come upon her at the bar, the special one I have been waiting for. But the accommodation is a 'small family hotel'; my sister and I seem to be the only humans aged between nine and forty-nine; the disco action is somewhere else in town, not here. At least there's nothing to distract me from my work: while everyone else is sitting in the bland pine-and-whitewash meliorism of the hotel lounge, I sneak back to my bed to read a bit more Marlowe or Tourneur or Webster, blackness and murder, infinite torture in a little room.

'*There* you are,' my father says, from the doorway of the twin-bedded room I'm sharing with him, chaps-chaps/girls-girls being the way my parents—or, rather, *he*—has chosen to divide this up, instead of husband-wife/daughter-(third room or dividing curtain)-son, as other married couples might. 'Bit antisocial, wasn't it, to skip off like that? We didn't know where you'd gone.'

'I said, Dad. I've got this work to do.'

'Well, if you said, I never heard, you mumble so much. Look at you: unshaven, scruffy hair, in need of fresh air and exercise.'

'I wouldn't be getting that in the bar, would I?'

'Don't get smart with me. We're all family together. Come on, it's time to eat.'

At the next table sit a pair of middle-aged Scottish women, who when greeted by my father—'Nice day on the slopes? Snow to your liking?'—seem even bonier, pricklier and more dour than they were last evening.

'Rather puir conditions. And the queues to the chair-lift wair tairrible. We took a little lunch: would you believe it, two sandwiches and two lemon teas came to over five pounds?'

These ladies are on the same package as ourselves, and I wonder whether their relentless itemizing of the holiday's shortcomings have contributed to yesterday's sudden departure of the tour rep—a muddly fuzz-blonde from Manchester—to 'a meeting at head office'. The Scottish ladies turn disapprovingly back to their meal. I reach for another glass of Liebfraumilch.

'Dr Morrison, I presume?'

A young woman is standing beside the table. She is tall, dark, with big sensual lips, heavy make-up, a long nose and hair down to her shoulders. She looks as if she has just stepped out of one of those plays I've been reading, or dreams I've been dreaming.

'I'm Rachel Stein, your new rep. This must be your family. I hope you're all having a good holiday.'

'Smashing, love,' says my father, pulling over an extra chair beside him and ordering her a drink before she has time to refuse. He takes it upon himself to fill her in on the hotel, the town, the best ski-lifts to use, the restaurants to avoid, the deficiencies of the laundry system. He also fills her in on where we live, what he does, what we're all called, our ages, our stages in life. When he talks proudly of me at school and now university, I wait for recognition to flare in her eyes, for her to acknowledge the feeling which I'm feeling and she surely must also feel. But she looks back to my father. A second drink arrives. The Scottish ladies, her other charges, to whom she has nodded a brief hello, look on frostily as she begins to talk. She is due to read English at Bristol University next autumn, she says, but is having a year off first—the travel company who took her on have a super scheme for reps, a month here, six weeks there, always on the move. She had Agadir in Morocco last, and it will be Greece next. She's used to moving around: her father worked abroad a lot, being uprooted by his firm every two years.

Her eyes swim suddenly: 'He died last year. My mother thought it would do me good to get away, though I miss her.'

She is on her third beer. We are on sweet and coffee. I am in love, and she has barely looked at me yet. How artful of her to seem to be so interested in my boring old dad, not me. Suddenly she's up and gone in pursuit of the Scottish ladies—'Must catch a word with them: they're sisters, you know, the Misses Laidlaw from Kirkcaldy.' We watch her flounce into the distance.

'Always a good idea to get on with the rep,' my father says. 'Nice girl—she'll look after us.'

She certainly looks after him. Over the next evenings it becomes a ritual for her to join us at the table and for my father to relate the events of the day, every little skiing feat and mishap. Even with half a bottle of wine inside me, I'm out of my mind with embarrassment at his banal chat (how does she hide how bored she must be feeling?) and veer between looking away in shame and trying to catch her eye. She speaks often of her poor little rich girl's childhood, and I want to take her away and comfort her in her pain and loss. I wait vainly for my mother to help me out by signalling some disapproval of my father's monopolizing of her. I wait vainly for my father to say: 'Why don't you young people take off for the evening?' But he's too obsessed with Rachel, even by his own obsessive standards, to let her go. Despairingly, I join my mother and sister in the television room while my Dad and Rachel sit on high stools at the bar.

Back in our room, my father's snores reverberating round the pine and whitewash, I think of how the bit of him that wants the best for me, makes things easy for me, takes pride in me, is up against a different, more competitive bit I haven't admitted to seeing before. Last June, when he came to collect me at the end of my first year at Nottingham, he insisted we play squash, which I had recently—at his encouragement, seeing my face pasted by two terms of parties and drugs and seances—taken up: 'Perfect game for busy people: short, sweet and very active. I got quite good at it myself when I was a medical student.' I anticipated a gentle, non-competitive knock-up as the best thing for both of us: I'd not slept the night before, and he hadn't (he claimed) played for twenty-five years. But after a few minutes' limbering up, he said, 'What about a game then?' He was stiff and erratic, and I let him have the first game, knowing that I'd be able to crank myself up for the next one.

What I hadn't reckoned on was his getting more confident. And as he cracked his shots low and irretrievably into the court's four corners, or sent me scrambling in nausea after one of his feinted drop-shots, and the whoops and ironies echoed from the dozen or so of my friends whom he had invited into the gallery, I realized that he was simply better at this than me, that I was not going to beat him, that I was going to be trounced. He eased off a bit towards the end to make a game of it, but that only made me angrier and more wayward than ever.

Now, as his snores vibrate through me, I see this is what it's been like for at least five years now. I learned to water-ski; so did he. I invited friends down to our North Wales caravan; somehow, on those weekends, he always happened to be there. I talked them into going for midnight swims; he was the first out into the night-cold in trunks and towel. Lately I mentioned a vague plan to go to Canada to read for an MA after I graduated. 'Great,' he said: 'Gill and Mum and I will sail out and join you. We'll buy a Dormobile and get it kitted out and we can tour North America. I'll have four months off and hire a locum. Why not?' Why not, except that this was a man who, when we were small, never had time for a holiday; why not, except that the whole point of Canada is to get away from him. When is the old bugger going to admit he's old? Next thing he will tell me he's given up medicine and applied to read English at Nottingham.

Not quite: the next thing he does is to announce, when he wakes up, that he has strained his back in some way, that he thinks it unwise to ski today and in any case fancies a day off sitting on his balcony in the sun. My mother jokes, as the three of us troop off to the slopes, that he'll 'No doubt be seeing his girlfriend.' It is the kind of thing she's said before, about other women he's latched on to, as if calling them 'girl-friends' is her way of convincing herself that they aren't. I leave my mother and sister on the nursery slopes and join my own class higher up.

We're practising parallel turns, and with my father absent I seem to get the hang of it at last. After lunch, I become fascinated by the figure in front of me in the chair-lift. I can see the backs of her shoulders as she reclines languidly and unfazed, long blonde hair pouring from beneath her hat. I prepare myself as I come in behind her at the landing-stage. I'll quote Eliot, I decide, 'Here in the mountains you feel free,' and then, if she seems uncomprehending, the German bits: '*Frisch weht der Wind/Der Heimat zu*' (terribly genteel and polyglot). She's almost into the station and I swing my bar up in readiness to leap out. Twenty yards ahead of me she alights and turns, and I see that she has a large belly and bad acne. I also see that she is a twenty-five-year-old man.

Back in the room, at dusk, my father and Rachel are sitting on the balcony: they have drinks in their hands and are smoking, and, with the mountains and ice-blue skies beyond, look like a Martini advertisement. I pour myself a whisky. My mother begins to witter about our time on the slopes, and they listen politely, like a married couple smiling condescendingly at a nanny or grandma's account of her day out with the little ones. I look at the bed—unrumpled—but they'd have had time to straighten it, so who can tell? I feel a sudden disgust, not just with him, for stealing Rachel before I could even get hold of her, but with her, for her sophistication and cosmopolitanism and orphan's wide-eyed fascination with an older man. As soon as I decently can, I flounce off to read some more of *The White Devil*.

> *To dig the strumpet's eyes out; let her lie*
> *Some twenty months a-dying; to cut off*
> *Her nose and lips, pull out her rotten teeth;*
> *Preserve her flesh like mummia, for trophies*
> *Of my just anger! Hell, to my affliction,*
> *Is mere snow-water . . .*

When I wake next morning, my father's not there. I find him with my mother, in her room. My parents are giggling. There's an odd pranky collusiveness between them.

'Shall we do it now?' my father asks.

'Yes, ring her,' my mother says.

'What's this about?' I ask.

'You'll see—just keep a straight face.'

My father dials three numbers. 'Could you come to the room?' he mutters bleakly into the receiver. 'Something terrible has happened.'

Rachel is up two minutes later. She looks pale, worried, no make-up, her face the colour of a Russian winter, her lovely black hair without its sheen.

'What happened?' she asks.

'There was this man on the balcony,' my mother says, sitting on the bed, her head bowed, wringing her hands.

'When was this?'

'Last night, when I came back to my room—Gillian was already asleep, thank God.'

'What did he do?'

'He just stood there.'

'He didn't come in?'

'No.'

'But you were frightened. You thought he was going to come in?'

'More than that.' My mother looks down at her hands. 'He . . . you know.'

'You mean he exposed himself?'

'Yes, he got out his, you know, and just stood there.'

'What did you do? Did you ring reception? You should have rung reception, or screamed, or something.' Rachel is sitting on the bed beside my mother, stroking her hands.

'I was going to, but next thing he disappeared.'

'But this is terrible. You must have been horribly frightened. You didn't sleep?'

'No.'

'Right,' says Rachel, getting up from the bed. 'I'm going straight down to reception to report it and to get on to the police.'

'There's one other thing you should tell them,' my father says.

'What's that?'

'That it's April the first.'

'Sorry, I'm not with you.'

'It's April Fool's day.'

'I still don't . . . '

'You've been April-Fooled,' my father says. 'We made it up, it didn't happen, it's a story, we were having you on, love.'

Rachel sits down on the bed again and bursts into tears.

They give her coffee, calm her down, say, 'There there, you've had a nasty shock, love,' themselves shocked that the joke has worked too well. She still doesn't really see it, and nor can I see why my father wanted to play it on her. For my mother to invent a tale of sexual violation makes sense: it's probably what she's been feeling for several days. But what was in it for him? Is it because he has slept with her and wanted to punish himself for it—the joke as atonement? Or that he hasn't slept with her and he wants to punish her for it—the joke as revenge?

4

Twenty minutes after his death, I'm wading in boxes and boxes of photographs. It's something I do every Christmas, but Christmas has come a little early this year. Even now I can see it's some futile struggle to resuscitate and preserve him. His face swims up from the bendy sheens of black and white, the cardboard transparencies, the tiny sepia squares—in RAF uniform in the Azores; in his wedding suit in 1946; with a litter of twelve labrador pups; with babies, with toddlers, with his leg in plaster; being carried downstairs half-drunk ('fresh') by a collection of male friends at his retirement party. There is something boyish and little in these that won't do, won't measure up to how I want to remember him. Then I find something better: a photograph of him outside our Georgian rectory, leaning dandyishly against the side of his black Mercedes and drawing on a cigarette, his beautiful wife, fortyish then, posed beside him—an image not just of wealth and health and substance to set against the poverty and sickness and insubstantiality of the body we've lived with for the past month, but also of the aspirations and even affectations death has snuffed out.

My mother comes in to say that she has rung the vicar. It is not yet eight, so he can say a prayer at matins and word will get round the village without our having to phone: the church still has

its uses after all. She asks was that me who's just been in her
bedroom—somebody had seemed to be walking about. This is the
one haunted moment. Otherwise the house feels unspooky; my
father (I know) is too much of a materialist to become a ghost,
and the room in which we've watched him die is unwaveringly
bright and rationalist. It isn't him but we who move about like
ghosts, pale and hovery and traumatized. There he lies, solid on
his bed. I touch his skin. An hour after his death, his forehead has
cooled to marble already, but when I slip my hand under the
covers and across his huge ribs the chest is hot.

And it is still warm when Dr Miller, the GP, comes at nine:
'Poor Arthur, you didn't deserve this,' he says. And it is not much
cooler—I know, I check—when Malcolm, the undertaker, arrives
four hours later. He is fortyish, remembers me from primary
school, is gangly in a grey suit with a Rotary Club badge on his
left lapel: 'Oh dear, oh dear, Arthur,' he says, and doesn't know
where to put himself.

He asks for a bowl of water, and while my mother is out of
the room uses a long tweezery implement to shove a piece of
cotton wool into my father's open mouth, where it rests (visibly)
at the back of the tongue—'To stop any gases coming up,' he
explains. My mother returns with the warm water. Malcolm takes
a razor and for the next hour or so works away at my father's
week-old stubble, 'just tidying him up.' I look at my mother and
see that she is thinking what I am thinking—why bother with
these cosmetics? Who will see him in the coffin? And even if he
were to lie open for public viewing in a Chapel of Rest, who
would mind the stubble? He might, I suppose: he was always a
great one for checking whether I'd shaved. But he didn't like this
sort of shaving himself—used only an electric razor—and would
have resented the waste of manpower: better to have got
Malcolm out doing something useful in the garden. If he'd been
here, *really* been here, that's what he'd have been arranging.

But my mother and I are new to all this and yield to
Malcolm's sense of etiquette. And at least it gives him something
to do while he chats.

'I've done forty-eight of these this year—about one a week it
works out, usually. It's a sideline, really, the undertaking. My main
business is joinery. But I don't get much call for that these days,

and you've got to make ends meet. There's nothing special you want, is there? No? Fine. Of course some people want the works, you know, the whole waxworks. It's amazing what you can do these days—some undertakers, they inject the client with formalin by sticking this tube into the neck artery, or you can drain the blood and urine off with an electric pump, and put these caps under the eyelids to make the eyes more rounded, sleep and peace, like. I don't hold with that: making a corpse like a plum instead of a prune, it's not right. Simple and clean, that's my philosophy.'

I wait for the moment when he will nick my father's chin—do the dead bleed less or more profusely than the living?—but he does it all spotlessly. I help him roll my father on to his side, so he can remove the pads from under him, wash his bottom and put a fresh nappy between his legs: it's dirty work. 'There may be more fluids,' he says. My father's body is a little stiffer now, but his back, as I hold him, is still warm, the skin red and corrugated where the sheet has wrinkled under him. 'This is why we come in fairly sharpish,' says Malcolm, 'before the rigor mortis. After twelve hours they can be very stiff and hard to move. After four or five days they go floppy again.'

My father always said that he'd never wear a shroud in his coffin, and he would not have wanted to waste a good suit. So now I help dress him in a pair of fawn cotton pyjamas. Malcolm hasn't batted an eyelid yet, any more than my father has, but as I hold the torso upright for him, he slips the right arm in the left sleeve and realizes his mistake only after finding the pyjama buttons are underneath my father's back. We lift the body and get the pyjamas off, then on again the right way. They won't button up over the swollen stomach and zip scar, so we leave them open. There's one final cosmetic act: the chin support, a small white plastic hod or T to keep the jaw from dropping too far open. Malcolm has some trouble adjusting the length of this: it's either too short, leaving my father dopily open-mouthed, or too long, clamming him up, unnaturally tight-lipped. Finally he jams the stick end into the collar-bone, an awkward riving process, and I have to remind myself that this won't be hurting. My father, at any rate, looks better for it: peaceful, no teeth showing.

'I should have said earlier,' Malcolm remarks as we draw the sheets back up to the chin, hiding the hod support. 'That's a pacemaker there, isn't it? I'll have to get the doctor to remove it or come back with a scalpel myself. We have to take it out, you see, if he's being cremated: it says so on the form, no HPMs. There've been cases where they exploded.'

'I'd like to have it in that case—if it's not going to be used by anyone else.'

'I'll check with the doctor. I'm sure that will be fine.'

Once Malcolm has gone I sit with my father again and touch the little pacemaker box in his chest and slide it about under the skin. Still warm, that chest, though it is six hours now since he died and for two hours he has been exposed to cold air. But the forehead is damp and Siberian. My mother sits across from me, holding his hand. She has not cried properly yet: with each phone call—and as the morning wears on there are more and more of these—her eyes water and her lips tremble, but she does not howl. Now, finally, she throws herself across him and sobs into his cold neck and chest.

5

When did you last see your father? Was it when they burnt the coffin? Put the lid on it? When he exhaled his last breath? When he last sat up and said something? When he last recognized me? When he last smiled? When he last did something for himself unaided? When he last felt healthy? When he last thought he might be healthy, before they brought the news?

The weeks before he left us, or life left him, were a series of depletions; each day we thought, 'He can't get less like himself than this,' and each day he did. I keep trying to find the last moment when he was still unmistakably there, in the fullness of his being, *him*.

When did you last see your father? I sit at my desk in the big cold basement of a new house, the one he helped me buy, his pacemaker in an alcove above my word processor, and the shelves of books have no more meaning than to remind me: these are the first shelves I ever put up without him. I try to write, but there is only one subject, him. I've lost sight not only of his life, what it meant and added up to, but of mine. When my three children come back from school, their cries echo emptily round the house, and I feel I'm giving them no more than a stranger could give them: drinks, attention, bedtime stories. Never to have loved seems best: love means two people getting too close; it means people wanting to be with each other all the time and then one of them dying. I feel as if an iron plate has come down through the middle of me, as if I were locked inside the blackness of myself, cold and futureless. I thought that to see my father dying might remove my fear of death, and so it did. I hadn't reckoned on it making death seem preferable to life.

When did you last see your father? The question hangs about, waiting to be answered. I try to remember where I first heard it asked, or saw it written. I invent contexts for it: in some sixties film, late at night, two drop-out bikers have begun to confide in each other about their pasts, and one asks the other, their Harley-Davidsons nearby, 'When did you last see your father?' A television documentary this time, and in the horrid brightness of a police interview room a kindly woman constable is coaxing what information she can from a fourteen-year-old Geordie boy found bruised and shivering in a shop doorway near King's Cross: 'When did you last see your father?' Or maybe it was my own father who had used the phrase. I remember him telling me, at some point in my late teens or twenties when I was drifting away from him, seeing less of him, how badly he'd taken the death of his father, and how he didn't want this to happen to me. Maybe it was then he said it: 'I used to see Grandpa every weekend. But for some reason I'd not been over to Manchester for about six weeks, and he hadn't come to Thornton, and then he had his heart attack and was dead. There were rows we'd had we hadn't really settled, and that made me very guilty after. I remember someone at the wake asking "When did you last see your father?" and me feeling terrible.'

I want to ask the question of others and warn them: don't underestimate filial grief, don't think because you no longer live with your parents, have had a difficult relationship with them, are grown-up, a parent yourself—don't think that will make it any easier. I've become a death bore. I embarrass people at dinner parties. I used to think the world divided between those who have children and those who don't; now I think it divides between those who've lost a parent and those whose parents are still alive. Once I used to get people to tell me their labour stories. Now I want to hear their death stories—the heart attacks, the car crashes, the cancers, the morgues.

Letters come. They begin: 'I know no words can help at such a time.' Words like these do seem to help, a bit. No one can live inside another's body, feel another's pain; grief, like joy, must be experienced in isolation. But the letters suggest something different, a commonality, that is both a solace and a chastening. Others have known worse: how much worse for a spouse than for a son; how much worse to die at thirty-one (as a beautiful, intelligent woman I sit next to at a dinner does, of cancer, two weeks later) than to die at seventy-five, like my father.

Beside me on the desk is a new anthology, *A Book of Consolations*. There are plenty of brisk, snap-out-of-it sorts in there, like Walter Raleigh ('sorrows are dangerous companions . . . the treasures of weak hearts'), or Dr Johnson, who thought sorrow 'a kind of rust of the soul' and recommended, much as my father would have, the healing powers of fresh air and exercise. There is plenty of speciousness about death, too: nothing to worry about, says Plato; a 'dreamless sleep', a migration of the soul; the ruins of time becoming the mansions of eternity. I hate all this lying cheeriness and evasion. I think of Larkin in 'Aubade' seeing off religion,

> *That vast moth-eaten musical brocade*
> *Created to pretend we never die,*
> *And specious stuff that says* no rational being
> Can fear a thing it will not feel, *not seeing*
> *That is what we fear—no sight, no sound,*
> *No touch or taste or smell, nothing to think with,*
> *Nothing to love or link with,*
> *The anaesthetic from which none come round.*

The cursor pulses on the screen in front of me. What can I say about my father that others haven't said, more memorably, of theirs? Some of my friends and contemporaries have written moving elegies for their fathers. Even when my father was in the best of health, I used to sit mooning and tearful over their words

107

as if they were for me, as if I'd written them myself. I wanted my father to hurry up and die so that I could join the club. I wrote an elegy for a friend of his, as preparation. I ran elegiac lines for him through my head. Now he's given me my opening, and the poems won't come.

I tell the therapist this. Yes, Dad, a therapist. I know that you don't approve, that you're down on analysts, male or female (and this one's female), and that, yes, *of course*, I should have shopped around, found a cheaper one, or at least asked: 'How much for cash?' (I supinely write the cheque.) But I have to talk to someone.

There is no couch in her room, though there are beanbags, and a baseball bat to hit them with. Myself, I don't use the baseball bat, nor scream, nor weep. I sit in a white canvas chair, the sort film directors have, and play back bits of my life. She asks me how I'm feeling, where I've got to now, what my body's telling me, and I find that sure enough my stomach's taut and hurting. She tells me I don't listen enough to my feelings, that I'm all head, no body or heart. She catches me smiling at critical points of my psycho-story, and this, she says, or gets me to say, is because I'm trying to distance myself ironically from my emotions. She tells me I'm a poor communicator, that I give out ambivalent signals. All of this is true, and helpful—so helpful that soon, I think, I shall stop seeing her.

In July I go up to Yorkshire—back at the house for the first time in seven months—the wind blowing through the delphiniums and the roses not yet deadheaded. The rustic fencing you put up is starting to rot. The raspberries have mildew—they're grey and squelchy like a dead mouse and dissolve ashily in the wind.

The ashes themselves, your ashes, have been kept in a big sheeny-brown plastic jar at the bottom of the wardrobe. Today is when we've chosen to scatter them. I take the jar down the garden, unscrew the lid, dip my hand in and taste a few grey specks: a smoky nothingness on my tongue. You, or your coffin, or a crematorium pick 'n' mix, how can I tell? My mother and sister come, having waited months for this moment, and we start to pour helpings of you among your favourite bits of the garden. We take it in turns, filling the lid of the jar with fine shale (like those upturned lids we used to fill with mouse poison and leave behind the fridge), then tossing the shale to the wind. The wind blows powder back in our faces; a speck catches in my sister's eye, her good eye; my trouser bottoms are sifted in volcanic dust. You cover the flower-bed like fine spray, every leaf variegated. We keep on scattering till the jar is tipped up for the last time—empty. My mother hugs my sister. I walk off with the jar, which is like a giant pillbox, and hear your voice in the wind: 'Useful container that—I should hang on to it.' I stow it in the garage between the jump-leads and a shrunken plastic bottle of antifreeze.

Back in London, the therapist asks: 'How long did you say it had been now?'

'How long has what been?'

'Since the death. When did you last see your father?'

When did you last see your father? I remember the answer then. I tell her.

6

He isn't drinking, isn't eating. He wears his trousers open at the waist, held up not by a belt but by pain and swelling. He looks like death, but he is not dead and won't be for another four weeks. He has driven down from Yorkshire to London. He has made it against the odds. He is still my father. He is still here.

'I've brought some plants for you.'

'Come and sit down first, Dad, you've been driving for hours.'

'No, best get them unloaded.'

It's like Birnam Wood coming to Dunsinane, black plastic bags and wooden boxes blooming in the back seat, the rear window, the boot: herbs, hypericum, escallonia, cotoneaster, ivies, potentillas. He directs me where to leave the different plants—which will need shade, which sun, which shelter. Like all my father's presents, they come with a pay-off. He will not leave until he has seen every one of them planted: 'I know you. And I don't want them drying up.'

We walk round the house, the expanse of rooms, so different from the old flat. 'It's wonderful to see you settled at last,' he says, and I resist telling him that I'm not settled, have never felt less settled in my life. I see his eyes taking in the little things to be done, the leaky taps, the cracked paint, the rotting window-frames.

'You'll need a new switch unit for the mirror light—the contact has gone, see.'

'Yes.'

'And a couple of two-inch Phillips screws will solve this.'

'I've got some. Let's have a drink now, eh?'

'What's the schedule for tomorrow?' he asks, as always, and I'm irritated, as always, at his need to parcel out the weekend into a series of tasks, as if without a plan of action, it wouldn't be worth his coming, not even to see his son or grandchildren. 'I don't think I'll be much help to you,' he says, 'but I'll try.' By nine-thirty he is in bed and asleep.

I wake him next day at nine, unthinkably late, with a pint-mug of tea, unthinkably refused. After his breakfast of strawberry Complan he comes round the house with me, stooped and crouching over his swollen stomach. For once it's me who is going to have to do the hammering and screwing. We go down to the hardware shop in Greenwich, where he charms the socks off the black assistant, who gives me a shrug and a pat at the end, as if to say, 'Where'd you get a dad like this from?' Back home again, he decides that the job for him is to get the curtains moving freely on their rails. 'You know the best thing for it?' he says. 'Furniture polish. Get me a can of it and I'll sort it out for you.' He teeters on a wooden kitchen stool at each of the windows in the house, his trousers gaping open, and sprays polish on the rails and wipes it over with a dirty rag. His balance looks precarious, and I try to talk him down, but he is stubborn.

'No, it needs doing. And every time you pull the curtains from now on, you can think of me.'

I ask him about the operation: is he apprehensive?

'No point in being. They have to have a look. I expect it's an infarct, and they'll be able to cure that, but if not . . . well, I've had a good life and I've left everything in order for you.'

'I'd rather you than order.'

'Too true.'

I make sure there are only two light but time-consuming jobs for us. The first is to fix a curtain pole across the garden end of the kitchen, over the glazed door, and we spend the best part of two hours bickering about the best way to do this: there's a problem on the left-hand side because the kitchen cupboards finish close to the end wall, six inches or so, and you can't get an electric drill in easily to make the holes for the fixing bracket. The drill keeps sheering off, partly because I'm unnerved by him standing below, drawing something on the back of an envelope. I get down and he shows me his plan: a specially mounted shelf in the side wall to support the pole rather than a fixing bracket for it on the end. Sighing and cursing, I climb back up and follow his instructions in every detail—not just the size of screws and Rawlplugs needed, but how to clasp the hammer.

'Hold it at the end, you daft sod, not up near the top.'

'Christ, Dad, I'm forty-one years old.'

'And you still don't know how to hold a hammer properly— or a screwdriver.' Infuriatingly, his plan works—the shelf mounting, the pole, the curtain, all fine. I try not to give him the satisfaction of admitting it.

We bicker our way into the next room and the other job: to hang the chandelier he once gave me, inherited from Uncle Bert. At some point in the move, many of the glass pieces have become separated, and now, in the dim November light behind the tall sash-window, we spend the afternoon working out where they belong, reattaching them with bits of wire, and then strengthening the candelabra from which they dangle. 'This really needs soldering,' he says, meaning that he will find an alternative to soldering, since to solder would mean going out and spending money on a soldering iron when he has a perfectly good one at home. I watch him bowed over the glass diamonds, with pliers and fractured screw-threads and nuts and bits of wire: the improviser, the amateur inventor. I think of all the jobs he's done for me down the years, and how sooner or later I'll have to learn to do them for myself. The metal clasps joining glass ball to glass ball are like the clasps on his King Edward cigar boxes, and like those on his old student skeleton, Janet, whom we'd joined together once, bone to bone.

'I think that's it,' he says, attaching a last bauble. 'Three pieces missing, but no one will notice.' He stands at the foot of the stepladder, holding the heavy chandelier while I connect the two electrical wires to the ceiling rose, tighten the rose-cover and slip the ring-attachment over the dangling hook. He lets go tentatively—'Gently does it'—unable to believe, since he has not done the fixing himself, that the chandelier will hold. It holds. We turn the light on, and the six candle-bulbs shimmer through the cage of glass, the prison of prisms. 'Let there be light,' my dad says, the only time I can ever remember him quoting anything. We stand there gawping upward for a moment, as if we had witnessed a miracle, or as if this were a grand ballroom, not a suburban dining-room, and the next dance, if we had the courage to take part in it, might be the beginning of a new life. Then he turns the switch off and it's dark again and he says: 'Excellent. What's the next job, then?'

Leonard Michaels

My Father's Life

Leonard Michaels

Six days a week he rose early, dressed, ate breakfast alone, put on his hat, and walked to his barber-shop at 207 Henry Street on the Lower East Side of Manhattan, about half a mile from our apartment. He returned after dark. The family ate dinner together on Sundays and Jewish holidays. Mainly he ate alone. I don't remember him staying home from work because of illness or bad weather. He took few vacations, but once we spent a week in Miami and he tried to enjoy himself, wading into the ocean, being brave, stepping, inch by inch, into the warm, blue, unpredictable immensity. Then he slipped. In water no higher than his *pupik*, he came up thrashing, struggling back to the beach on skinny white legs. 'I nearly drowned,' he said, very exhilarated. He never went into the water again. I think he preferred his barber-shop to the natural work. He retired after thirty-five years, when his hands trembled too much for scissors and razors and angina made it impossible for him to stand up for long periods. Then he took walks in the neighbourhood and carried a vial of whiskey in his shirt pocket. When pain stopped him in the street, he'd stand very still and sip his whiskey. A few times I stood beside him, as still as he, waiting for the pain to end, both of us speechless and frightened.

He was vice-president of his synagogue society, keeping records attending to the maintenance of the synagogue's building. He spoke Yiddish, Polish, maybe some Russian, and had the Hebrew necessary for prayers. He spoke to me in Yiddish until I began, at about the age of six, speaking to him mainly in English. Sometimes, when he switched from one language to the other, I'd not even notice. He could play the violin and mandolin. As a youth in Poland, he'd been in a band. When old friends visited our apartment, he'd drink a schnapps with them. He smoked cigars and pipes. He read the Yiddish newspaper, the *Forward*, and the *Daily News*. He voted Democrat but had no faith in politicians, political systems or 'the people'. Aside from family, work and synagogue, his passion was friends. My mother reminded me, when I behaved badly, of his friends. She'd say, 'Nobody will like you.' Everybody liked Leon Michaels.

He was slightly more than five feet tall. My mother is barely five feet. Because I'm five-ten, she thinks I'm a giant. She came from Brest-Litovsk. He came from Drohiczyn, a town on the river Bug near the Russian border. When I visited Poland in 1979, I asked my hosts about Drohiczyn. They said, 'You'll see new buildings and Russian troops. No reason to go there.' So I didn't go there. It would have been a sentimental experience, essentially empty. My father never talked about the town, rarely said anything about his past. We also never had any long, deep talks of the father-and-son kind, but when I was fifteen, I fell in love, and he said a memorable thing to me.

The girl had many qualities—tall, a blonde, a talented musician—but mainly she wasn't Jewish. My father learned about her when we were seen together watching a bastetball game at Madison Square Garden, among eighteen thousand people. I'd been foolish to suppose I could go to the Garden with a blonde and not be spotted. My father had many friends. You saw them in his barber-shop, 'the boys', the snazzy dressers jingling coins in their pockets or poor Jews from the neighbourhood who came just to sit, to rest in their passage between miseries. Always a crowd in the barber-shop—cab-drivers, bookies, waiters, salesmen. One of them spotted me and phoned my father. When I returned that night, he was waiting up for me with the fact. He said we would discuss it in the morning.

I lay awake in anguish. No way to deny that the girl I loved killed Jews because she wasn't one. I'd been seeing her for months. Her parents knew about the secrecy. I was so ashamed of it that when I called for her, I'd ring the bell and then wait for her in the street. She pleaded with me to come upstairs, meet her parents. After a while, I did so. Maybe they understood. Her previous boyfriend was the son of a rabbi.

In the morning my father said, 'Let's take a walk.' We walked around the block, then around the block again, in silence. It took a long time to walk twice around the block, but the silence was so dense, it felt like one infinitely heavy, immobilized minute. Then, as if he'd rehearsed a speech and dismissed it, he sighed. 'I'll dance at your wedding,' he said.

Thus we spent a minute together, just he and I, father and son, and he said a memorable thing. The sentence speaks for itself. It is concise, its burden huge. If witty, it is so in the manner of Hieronymus Bosch, making a picture of demonic gaiety. My wedding takes place in the middle of the night. My father is a small figure among dancing Jews, frenzied, hysterical with joy.

For a fifteen-year-old insanely in love, this sentence was a sentence—judgement, punishment—and, at the same time, a release from brutal sanctions. He didn't order me not to see her. I could do as I pleased. As it happened, she met someone else. I was very shocked and hurt. I was also relieved. The light of her hair returned to me in dreams.

My father did dance at my wedding, twelve years later, when I married a black-haired, dark-skinned German Jew. Because her parents were dead, the traditional ceremony was held in our apartment. Her aunts and uncles sat along one wall, mine along another. The living-room was small. Conversation, forced by closeness, was lively and nervous. The rabbi, delayed by traffic, arrived late, and then the ceremony was hurried. Everyone seemed to shout instructions. Did she circle me or I her? My father was satisfied, maybe delighted. The marriage lasted five years, and when we fought, which was every day, she threatened to tell my father the truth about me. 'It will kill him,' she said. After we separated, she had a series of love affairs, then killed herself. At her funeral, the only person I noticed crying was my father. What he felt exactly I don't know, but somebody in her family or mine had to cry. He cried alone. Before the wedding, he didn't say, 'Let's take a walk,' then tell me this marriage would lead to horror. I had tried to talk to him about her psychotic violence, but he was unable to assimilate the details; he couldn't hear what I was saying. He said, 'She's an orphan. You cannot abandon her.'

If he ever hit me, I don't remember it, but I remember being malicious. A bad boy. My brother, three years younger than I, was practising scales on my father's violin one afternoon. When he finished, he started to carry the violin across the room. I put out my foot. He tripped, fell. We heard the violin hit the floor and crack. Instantly—quicker than instantly—I wanted to undo the act, not trip my brother. But it was done. I was stuck with myself. I think I smiled. My father looked at the violin and said, 'I had it over twenty years.'

Maybe I tripped my brother because I'm tone-deaf and

could never learn to play any musical instrument. Nothing forgives me. I wish my father had become enraged, knocked off my head, so I could forget the incident. I never, never, never felt insufficiently loved, and yet I think, *When Abraham raised the knife to Isaac, the kid had it good.*

In all photos of my father, however badly lit or ill-focused, he looks like himself, whereas I almost never look like myself, despite the competence of the photographer. I see perversions of musculature about the eyes and mouth, lids weirdly, sickishly drooping, lips stiffening through a sneer toward a smile that will never be natural. This isn't me, I think. Like a baby, my father appears, inevitably, like himself. Perhaps in our similarities it is guaranteed I'll always be other than myself, whatever that is. When someone admires me, I think there's been a mistake; when someone disapproves of me, I want revenge. Like my father, I have a lot of friends, but when I wake up alone in a strange motel and I can't remember what city I'm in and there's nobody to phone, I feel unbearably happy.

My father never owned a car or flew in an airplane. He could imagine no alternatives to being himself. He had only his neighborhood, the hectic variety in human traffic, the barbershop. Looking out my window, I can see San Francisco Bay and how the world bends towards China.

I was in London, returning from three months in Paris, when he died. My flight to New York had been cancelled. I was stranded, waiting for another flight. Nobody in New York knew where I was. I couldn't be phoned. At last, the day after the funeral, I arrived. My brother met me at the door of the apartment, where my mother still lives, and told me the news. I went alone to see my parents' bedroom and sat on the bed. I didn't want to be seen crying.

Day after day, people visited the apartment to offer condolences and to reminisce. Then a rabbi came, a tiny, fragile man dressed all in black, with a white beard twice the length of his face. He asked my mother to give him some of my father's clothes, particularly things he'd worn next to his skin. As the rabbi started to leave, a bundle of clothes in his arms, he noticed me sitting at the kitchen table. He said in Yiddish, 'Sit lower.' I didn't know what he was getting at. Did he want me to crouch?

I was doing nothing, sitting there alone, but I was somehow susceptible to criticism. My mother interceded. 'He feels,' she said. 'He feels plenty.'

The rabbi said, 'I didn't ask how he feels. Tell him to sit lower.'

I got up and left the kitchen, looking for a lower place to sit. I was very angry but not enough to start yelling at a fanatical midget. Besides, he was correct.

One Friday night, I was walking to the subway on Madison Street. My winter coat was open, flying with my stride. I wore a white shirt and a sharp red tie. I'd combed my hair in the style of the day, a gorgeous pompadour fixed and sealed with Vaseline. I was nineteen-years-old terrific. The night was cold, but I was hot. The wind was strong. My hair was stronger, imperturbable in its rigid gleam. As I entered the darkness below the Manhattan Bridge, where it strikes across Madison Street and makes a high, gloomy, mysterious vault, I met my father. He was returning from the barber-shop, following his usual route. His coat was buttoned to the neck, his hat pulled down to protect his eyes. He stopped. As I approached, I saw him study me, his creation. We stood for a moment beneath the bridge, facing each other in the darkness and wind. An American giant, five feet ten inches tall. A short Polish Jew. He said, 'Button your coat. Everyone doesn't have to see your tie.'

I buttoned my coat.

'Why don't you wear a hat?'

I shrugged. 'I'm all right.'

'You need a haircut. You look like a bum.'

'I'll come to the barber-shop tomorrow.'

He nodded, as if to say 'Good night' and 'What's the use?' He was on his way home to dinner, to sleep. He'd worked all day. I was on my way to sexual adventure. Then he asked, 'Do you need money?'

'No.'

'Here,' he said, pulling change from his coat pocket. 'For the subway. Take.'

He gave.

I took.

SUSAN J. MILLER

NEVER LET ME DOWN

O ne night, at an hour that was normally my bedtime, I got all dressed up, and my mother and father and I drove into New York, down to the Half Note, the jazz club on Hudson Street. I was thirteen, maybe fourteen, just beginning teenagehood, and had never gone anywhere that was 'nightlife'. I had heard jazz all my life, on records or the radio, my father beating out time on the kitchen table, the steering-wheel, letting out a breathy 'Yeah' when the music soared and flew. When they were cooking, when they really swung, it transported him; he was gone, inside the music. I couldn't go on this trip with him, but I thought I could understand it. It seemed to me that anyone could, hearing that music. Bird, Diz, Pres, Sweets, Lester, Al, Zoot. It was my father's music, though he himself never played a note.

I knew the players, for about the only friends my parents had were musicians and their wives. When I was a little kid, I'd lie in bed listening to them talk their hip talk in the next room. I knew I was the only kid in Washington Heights to be overhearing words like 'man' and 'cat' and 'groove', and jokes that were this irreverent and black. I knew they were cool and I loved it.

At the Half Note that night, the three of us walked through the door, and the owner appeared, all excited to see my father, and, in the middle of this smoky nightlife room, he kissed my hand. This was real life, the centre of something. We sat down. In front of us, on a little stage, were Jimmy Rushing, a powerful singer, and two sax players, Al Cohn and Zoot Sims, whom I'd known all my life. And there was a whole *roomful* of people slapping the tables, beating out time, breathing 'Yeah' at the great moments, shaking their heads, sometimes snapping their fingers, now and then bursting out with, 'Play it, man,' or, 'Sing it.' When the break came, Zoot sat down with us and ate a plate of lasagne or something and didn't say much except for these dry asides that were so funny I couldn't bear it. Too funny to laugh at. And there was my dad: these men were his friends, his buddies. They liked the things about my father that I could like—how funny he was, uncorny, how unsentimental, unafraid to be different from anyone else in the world: how he was unafraid to be on the edge.

A s a child, I didn't know that my father and many of the musicians who sat with their wives in our living-room, eating nuts and raisins out of cut-glass candy dishes, were junkies. It wasn't until I was twenty-one, a college senior, that my father told me that he had been a heroin addict, casually slipping it into some otherwise unremarkable conversation. The next day, my mother filled in the story. My father had begun shooting up in 1946, when my mother was pregnant with my brother, who is nineteen months older than me. He stopped when I was around thirteen and my brother was fifteen—the same age as my father's addiction.

I never suspected a thing. Nor did my brother. We never saw any drug paraphernalia. There was a mysterious purplish spot in the crook of my father's elbow, which he said had something to do with the army. His vague explanation was unsatisfactory, but even in my wildest imaginings I never came near the truth. In the fifties, in the white, middle- and working-class communities where we lived, no one discussed drugs, which were synonymous with the utmost degradation and depravity. My parents succeeded in hiding my father's addiction from us, but, as a result, we could never make sense of the strained atmosphere, our lack of money, our many moves. The addiction was the thread that tied everything together. We didn't know that such a thread existed, and so decisions seemed insanely arbitrary, my mother's emotions frighteningly hysterical. My father was often away, staying out late or not coming home at all. My brother and I fought often and violently. My mother was terribly depressed, sometimes desperate. I regularly found her sitting, eyes unfocused, collapsed amid the disorder of a household she was too overwhelmed to manage. She would beg my father not to go out at night. As I got older, I tried to figure out what was going on. An affair? This was a logical explanation, but it didn't fit.

My father was a man of socially unacceptable habits. He was fat, he picked his teeth, he burped, he farted, he blew his nose into the sink in the morning, he bit his nails until he had no nails and then he chewed his fingers, eating himself up. He was a high-octane monologuer, a self-taught high-school drop-out who constantly read, thought and talked politics and culture, gobbling up ideas, stuffing himself as fast as he could—with everything.

He was from Brighton Beach, Brooklyn, and earned his living dressing windows in what were called 'ladies' specialty shops'—independently-owned women's clothing stores in and around New York City. He went from store to store in his display-laden station-wagon, visiting them every month or so when they changed their windows. Being a window-dresser was a touch creative, but most importantly it meant he didn't have to fit in; all he had to do was get the job done.

How did a bright Jewish boy from Brighton Beach become a junkie in the late forties? It was partly the crowd he hung out with: white musicians deeply under the influence of Charlie Parker—and Parker's drug, heroin. Stan Getz, Al Cohn, George Handy—all were junkies and all were my father's friends.

My father began with marijuana—at age fifteen. Although drafted during the Second World War, he never made it overseas; he was, I was told, 'honourably discharged' from boot camp in Georgia for health reasons: he was deemed too weak to fight, having lost weight because of the heat. I've always found the story rather odd, if only because, in the army pictures I've seen, he looks so happy and active, even if a little thin, clowning in front of the camera with his friends. Perhaps the story is true, but it seems unlikely. By his late twenties, he was a heroin addict. Ten years later, he was taking amphetamines as well. He occasionally gave me some when I was in college to help me stay up all night writing papers; they were very strong. When he was about fifty, he was taking LSD, mescaline, peyote, whatever he could get.

At college, I received long letters from him, written when he was coming down from an acid or mescaline trip. Often he tripped alone in the living-room of my parents' New Jersey apartment, awake all night, listening to records, writing and thinking while my mother slept. I read pages of his blocky, slanted printing, about how the world is a boat and we are all sinking. So many pages with so many words. Usually I threw them away without finishing them, scanning his stoned raps in front of the big, green, metal trash-can in the college mail-room, picturing him in the living-room with the sun rising, wired up, hunched over the paper, filling up the page, wanting me to know all the exciting things he had discovered. Part of me wanted to hear them and love him—and indeed did love him for taking the acid, for taking the chance. But another part shut down, unable to care. I would look out of the mail-room window on to the college's perfect green lawn, scenic mountains in the distance, little white houses with green shutters, the place of my willed exile, my escape.

One day when I was home from college on vacation, my father and I went into New York together. He was going to retrieve his car from .a garage in the West Forties, take me to a friend's downtown and then pick up my mother at her midtown office and drive her home. We took the bus across the bridge, then got on the subway at 178th Street. After the doors shut, my father edged close to me, putting his mouth up to my ear to make himself heard over the screech of the train. I took acid before we left the house this morning and I'm just starting to get off, he said. He was smiling; a naughty kid out in the big grown-up world. My heart sank. My father had swallowed a psychic explosive that might detonate him and then me, if his trip turned bad. The train rocked furiously back and forth, its lights flickering, racing at sixty miles an hour through its pitch-black tunnel on the longest non-stop run in the city, from 125th to 59th Street. At any moment, the subway car might turn into a sealed tomb on an endless nightmare ride. Acid makes you vulnerable, a sponge. It would take only seconds, a quick switch in his head, and he would be gripping my arm and saying, Susan, I've got to get out of here. Now, right now.

We reached our stop, and I stayed close, following him through the smelly, mobbed, low-ceilinged station where at every turn I saw something I feared might set him off: glistening hot dogs revolving under infra-red lights; a legless man on a wheeled board, selling pencils. But at the garage my father understood the Puerto Rican mechanic's broken English better than I did. He checked the bill and counted out cash and coins the right way the first time. Last time I took acid, I found myself in a little family grocery in Santa Fe, staring dumbfounded at the meaningless discs of silver in my hand, unable to buy an orange popsicle without help, thunderstruck by the very concept of money, its simultaneous brilliance and folly. My dad was having no such problems. He was energized; he was having fun. He got behind the wheel and headed out into the river of cars, the honking, swerving cabs, the sticky stop-and-go jams. He dropped me off, waved goodbye, headed back uptown to pick up my mother.

Watching him trip was like discovering that your father was an accomplished deep-sea diver or high-wire artiste. Yet I knew that even the best tightrope walker slips. I limped up to my friend's, exhausted.

Never marry a musician, my mother admonished me when I was growing up, in the same way, I suppose, that other mothers warned their daughters off criminals or *schvartzehs* or Jews. I suspected she had a point; life married to a man always on the road would be no picnic. I had heard about the hotel rooms and buses and daytime sleeping. I also knew she meant something more complex; that these men were not to be trusted. She could say, don't marry one, because she had seen so many. What she didn't say, and what I didn't know, was that so many were junkies. Because I didn't know what lay behind her warnings, they seemed mysteriously exaggerated.

The musicians who came to our house fascinated me: their pants with black satin stripes down the sides, their hip talk, their battered horn cases. My father could hear anyone on the radio and know who was playing. He'd say, That's Pres, or, Listen to Diz swing. I loved the fame of these men, the fact that the world knew their names, their sounds, that there were pictures of them in *Down Beat*. I knew some, like Al and Zoot, but most of them I never met. They were part of the life my father lived apart from us children. To me, these were names, or sounds on records, or sometimes faces in our photo album; they belonged to men leaning against lampposts in the Village, or sitting with their arms around attractive women on rocks in Central Park. Allen Eager, Tiny Kahn, George Handy, Stan Getz, Johnny Mandel, Georgie Auld, these names resonate in my heart like the Yiddish that I heard so often then.

I don't know what went on between my father and these men. All I know is that for my father, his junkie years were the greatest of his life. He wanted to tell me about them, so I would understand why he wasn't sorry about what he did. He wanted me to know about the great and wild people he had met, the music he had heard, the crazy underworld places he had been to. He needed to explain that, while being a junkie sounded bad to other people, it had been really wonderful for him. But I couldn't listen. For me, those years of his heroin addiction had been a time of fearful poverty, violence at the hands of my brother and terror that my mother would cease to function. No, I said, I don't want to hear. Each of us was furious: my worst times were his best.

As a child, I was convinced that if my father saw me walking down the street in an unexpected place, away from the clues that linked me to him, such as our apartment or my mother or my school, he would not recognize me. He didn't know what I looked like. But I knew nothing about the drugs; lacking knowledge, I could not say, he is stoned, he is high.

He would not have been a good father even if he hadn't been an addict. By his own admission, he came to parenthood ignorant of love and acquainted only with hate.

My mother told me about my grandmother Esther, the wicked witch of Brighton Beach. According to my mother, my grandmother despised men. She lavished attention on her daughter, my father's only sibling. She dealt in machinations, lies and deceptions, feeding the fires of hate between father and son, sister and brother, so that for weeks this one wouldn't speak to that one, that one wouldn't speak to this one, everyone crushed together in the one basement room where they lived. When my father did well in school, his mother scorned him. She tore up a citation he'd won—and then spat on it. She never kissed him, except on the day he went off to boot camp. His mother and my mother, then his young wife, were standing on the platform, saying goodbye. Seeing the other mothers tearfully embracing their sons, his mother was shamed into touching hers: she pecked his cheek.

We sometimes took her to Ratner's for dinner. Ratner's was a kosher dairy restaurant on lower Second Avenue, where, twenty-four hours a day, an aged waiter with a heavy Yiddish accent brought you baked fish or *kasha varniskes* or blintzes or icy *schav*. Later, when the neighbourhood became the East Village, I would occasionally return to Ratner's for a plate of blintzes, after seeing the Grateful Dead at the Filmore East next door. But at the time, I was ten, eleven, twelve and trying to learn the rules of public behaviour. My grandmother, the urban peasant, did not give a shit about public behaviour. The peasant: belching, slurping, sucking the fishbones. Picking her teeth with the corner of a matchbook. Unbuttoning her blouse to adjust her straps. It was amazing to watch her, truly not giving a damn about anyone or anything except the food in front of her. Across her broad face, she wore a thick layer of dead-white powder and a bright red circle of rouge on each cheek. Her hair was so thin you could see her waxen scalp and the dark roots of each strand. It was dyed a shade that was probably meant to be auburn but was actually a bright, rusty orange.

When Esther belched, my mother said nothing. The daughter of immigrants herself, she was shy and scared inside, afraid to make a mistake. But I was ashamed, sitting there in silence, eating my baked fish and looking up at the huge ugly oil portrait of old Mr Ratner that hung over the cash register.

I really wanted to learn what to do, how to eat, talk, act, seeking self-confidence the only way I could, from the outside in. But I was tethered with doubt and embarrassment. I suffered bourgeois afflictions that must have come from my mother, *and* the desire not to be downtrodden by convention, which came from my father. My mother was a slave to rules she wasn't sure of; my father knew there were rules and he loved to break them; my grandmother didn't even know rules existed.

Occasionally Esther spoke to me, addressing me brusquely in rapid-fire Yiddish (she never learned English, even though she had come here at sixteen: a fuck-you to the New World). Was she really trying to communicate with me, forgetting I didn't know Yiddish? Or did she care so little that she had no memory of what I knew or didn't know? At my look of incomprehension, her expression would turn to disgust: what use is this child, if she can't even speak? *Feh*— she would dismiss me with a wave of her hand. I felt as though I was nothing more to my grandmother than a body sitting on the aqua, padded chair, a body with no one inside, much as I felt with my father. And again, if I had appeared before her without my parents, without those usual clues to my identity, she would have been unable to place me.

I didn't trust grown-ups. They didn't protect me; they didn't see me. To Esther, I was a speck, a smudge.

My father only once told me a story about himself and his mother. I was a college student at the time. The two of us were driving on the highway on a beautiful, clear, cold winter day. My father was behind the wheel. Fourteen years earlier, in 1956, when he was thirty-eight, his father, who had been very sick, died in the hospital while my father and Esther were visiting him. My father took Esther home to Brooklyn, where she asked him for a favour. There were some terms in her will she wanted to review. Would he read it out loud to her? (Even in Yiddish my grandmother was illiterate.) My father was tired and upset and somewhat puzzled that his mother wished to go over her will on the night of her husband's death, but he agreed. (As my father talked, I pictured Esther unlocking the black metal strongbox with the key she wore around her neck and handing him the will. They would have been in her tiny living-room, sitting on her overstuffed flowered chairs, knees almost touching, her heavy-featured face impassive, his eyes wary but hoping to please.) The will turned out to be simple: Esther's house and savings were to go to Sarah, her daughter. Then he heard himself, the fly in the web, reading: And to my son Sidney, I leave nothing, because he is no good.

My father stared at the road ahead.

Why, I cried, would she have you read that to her? What did you do?

My father's voice was tired and bitter. She wanted to see what I would do, he said; she wanted to watch my reaction. Ma, I said, I gotta go home now. I'm tired and it's late. I didn't want to show her how bad I felt, I didn't want to give her the satisfaction. It wasn't the money. I didn't care about that. Let my fucking sister have the money. But why did she have to write that sentence? Why did she have me read it?

My father started to cry. He had never cried in front of me. His hands loosened their grip on the wheel. The car began to drift into the opposite lane, across the white unbroken line.

Look out, I yelled. He grabbed the wheel and turned us towards safety. Look out, I had yelled, and he did. Look out, I had yelled, for what else could I have said?

In 1973, two years after my father told me about his addiction, he stopped in to visit me at my apartment on Charlton Street. He was distraught, not an unusual state for him. Damaged merchandise, he said, are the words that I see in front of me when things get bad, and when I see those words I know it's all over. Do you understand that? He fixed me with his wild, wide-open, hazel eyes. Do you understand what I am trying to say?

Yes, I said, over and over. Yes, I understand what you are trying to say, but I knew he could scarcely see or hear me through the haze and buzz of electric cloud around his head.

Damaged merchandise. He was a window-dresser; he spent hours making signs on thick, white rectangular cards with a creamy, smooth surface, writing them out in front of the television the night before the job. SALE, they said, HANES HOSIERY, $1.99 A PAIR, or whatever. Next day he propped them up in front of the displays, a bra folded carefully, skilfully, and laid out on the floor, cups pointing up and out. Stockings draped over the Lucite stand, the card tipped in front. At Christmas, he piled mounds of fake snow, hung tinsel, attached big red bows, positioned empty packages wrapped in foil paper, red and green and silver. In the summer there were palm trees and beach balls. He was the window-dresser, his station-wagon filled with displays and rolls of no-seam paper, sprays of stiff flowers, thick cotton sockettes over his shoes to protect the floor, eyes bugged out, seeing in his mind's eye *himself*, on sale, marked down, damaged merchandise, an item nobody, not even the most inveterate bargain-hunter, would want.

And he told me this, he spelled it out for me, and I listened even though I didn't want to. I hadn't yet learned how to tell him no; I still thought it was my job to listen to what anyone in my family wanted to say to me: as I had when my brother told me the details of his sex life; or my mother told me how horrible she felt about herself and us. My father paced around my living-room, his voice ranting, careening, echoing in the big empty room that was his sad and lonely and frightened heart. It scared me to listen because I knew that I had been damaged, too: by his not seeing me, as he was not seeing me right then. The room was turning into a funnel, and I felt myself being sucked down into it. I acted very polite, trying to remain a whole person. I asked him some questions. I tried to change the subject. And then I don't remember what I did. Maybe I yelled at him, or maybe I just asked him to leave, telling him I had to go somewhere. Or maybe I said, Oh Daddy, it's awful you feel that way. I was trying to hold on to myself, and no response I could choose would have been any better than any other. Nothing woke him up to me.

NEVER LET ME DOWN

In August 1988, my father was diagnosed with liver cancer, the result of chronic hepatitis, a disease associated with heroin addiction. The doctors correctly predicted he would live for five months. He tried chemotherapy, ate a macrobiotic diet, enrolled in an experimental holistic treatment programme. When I visited him in November, it was clear that things would not turn around.

Al Cohn had died of liver cancer as well—that same year. Zoot Sims had been done in by alcohol in 1985. In the weeks before my father died, he played their records, and only theirs, as if they were calling to him and he could hear them.

My mother, who had stuck by him through everything, was still by his side. He was eager to share his latest revelation. A social worker in the treatment programme had asked him what he would miss most when he died. It was an interesting question, and I was interested to hear his answer. He said: I told her that, yeah, sure, I'll miss my wife and my kids, but what I'll miss most is the music. The music is the only thing that's never let me down.

That the revelation would hurt us—my mother especially—never occurred to him. He never kept his thoughts to himself, even if it was cruel to express them. Neither my mother nor I said a word. The statement was the truth of him—not only what he said, but also the fact that he would say it to us, and say it without guilt, without apology, without regret.

MICHAEL IGNATIEFF

AUGUST IN MY FATHER'S HOUSE

Michael Ignatieff

It is after midnight. They are all in bed except me. I have been waiting for the rain to come. A shutter bangs against the kitchen wall and a rivulet of sand trickles from the adobe wall in the long room where I sit. The lamp above my head twirls in the draught. Through the poplars, the forks of light plunge into the flanks of the mountains and for an instant the ribbed gullies stand out like skeletons under a sheet.

Upstairs I can hear my mother and father turn heavily in their sleep. Downstairs our baby calls from the bottom of a dream. What can his dreams be about? I smooth his blanket. His lips pucker, his eyes quiver beneath their lashes.

I have been married seven years. She is asleep next door, the little roof of a book perched on her chest. The light by the bed is still on. Her shoulders against the sheet are dark apricot. She does not stir as I pass.

At the window, the air is charged and liquid. The giant poplars creak and moan in the darkness. It is the mid-August storm, the one which contains the first intimation of autumn, the one whose promise of deliverance from the heat is almost always withheld. The roof tiles are splashed for an instant, and there is a patter among the trumpet vines. I wait, but it passes. The storm disappears up the valley and the first night sounds return, the cicadas, the owl in the poplars, the rustle of the mulberry leaves, the scrabble of mice in the eaves. I lean back against the wall. The old house holds the heat of the day in its stones like perfume in a discarded shawl. I have come here most summers since I was fifteen.

When I was fifteen, I wanted to be a man of few words, to be small and muscular with fine bones, to play slide guitar like Elmore James. I wanted to be fearless. I am thirty-seven. The page is white and cool to the touch. My hands smell of lemons. I still cling to impossible wishes. There is still time.

The house was once a village wash-house. At one end of the pillared gallery, there is a stone pool—now drained—where women used to wash clothes in the winter. At the bottom of the garden under the lyre-shaped cherry tree, there is the summer pool where the sheets were drubbed and slopped between their knuckles and the slanted stones. That was when the village raised silkworms for the Lyons trade a hundred years ago. When that trade died, the village died and the washing pool was covered over with brambles.

The house became a shepherd's shelter. He was a retarded boy, crazed by his father's beatings, by the miserable winter pastures, by the cracked opacity of his world. One night in the smoke-blackened kitchen, he and his father were silently drinking. When the father got up to lock away the animals, the son rose behind him and smashed his skull into the door-jamb. After they took the boy away and buried the father, the house fell into ruin, marked in village memory by the stain of parricide.

When we came to look at the place that evening twenty-two years ago, my father sent me up the back wall to check the state of the roof tiles. The grass and brambles were waist-high in the doorway. A tractor was rusting in the gallery and a dusty rabbit skin hung from a roof beam. One push, we thought, and the old adobe walls would collapse into dust. But the beam took my weight and there were only a few places where the moonlight was slicing through to the dirt floor below. The tiles were covered with lichen and I could feel their warmth through the soles of my feet. When I jumped down, I could see they had both made up their mind to buy it.

It is my mother's favourite hour. Dinner has been cleared away from the table under the mulberry tree, and she is sitting at the table with a wineglass in her hand watching the light dwindling away behind the purple leaves of the Japanese maple. I sit down beside her. She is easy to be with, less easy to talk to. The light is falling quickly, the heat it bears is ebbing away. After a time she says, 'I never expected anything like this . . . the stone wall that Roger built for us, the lavender hedges, the bees, the house. It's all turned out so well.'

Her voice is mournful, far away.

A Toronto schoolmaster's daughter, squint-eyed and agile, next-to-youngest of four, she rode her bicycle up and down the front steps of her father's school, the tomboy in a family of intellectuals. I have a photograph of her at the age of ten, in boy's skates with her stick planted on the ice of the rink at her father's school. She is staring fiercely into the camera in the

133

manner of the hockey idols of the twenties, men with slick side-partings and names like Butch Bouchard.

It is nearly dark and the lights have come on across the valley. She twirls her wineglass between her fingers and I sit beside her to keep her company, to help the next words come. Then she says, out of nowhere, 'When I was seven, my father said "Who remembers the opening of the *Aeneid*?" as he stood at the end of the table carving the Sunday joint. "Anyone?" They were all better scholars than me, but I *knew*. "*Arma virumque cano* . . . " Everyone cheered—Leo, the cook, Margaret, Charity, George, even Mother. My father slowly put down the knife and fork and just stared at me. I wasn't supposed to be the clever one.'

There is some hurt this story is trying to name, a tomboy's grief at never being taken seriously, never being listened to, which has lasted to this moment next to me in the darkness. But her emotions are a secret river. She has her pride, her gaiety and her elusiveness. She will not put a name to the grievance, and silence falls between us. It is dark and we both feel the chill of evening. She gets up, drains her glass and then says, 'Mother always said, "Never make a fuss." That was the family rule. Good night.' I brush her cheek with a kiss. We will not make a fuss.

She was a painter once, and her paintings have become my memory for many of the scenes of my childhood; playing with a crab in a bucket on a rock in Antigonish, Nova Scotia, and watching her painting at the easel a few paces away, her back, her knees and her upraised arm making a triangle of concentration, her brush poised, still and expectant before the canvas, her face rapt with the pleasure of the next stroke.

When I was six she painted my portrait. It was an embarrassment at the time: my friends came to point and laugh because I looked so solemn. But I see now the gift she was handing me across the gulf which divides us from the vision of others: a glimpse of the child I was in my mother's eye, the child I have kept within me. She doesn't paint any more. For a time, marriage and children allowed her a room of her own. But then it was swallowed up or renounced, I don't know which. She says only, 'Either I do it well, or I do not do it at all.'

S he whispers, 'Have you seen my glasses?'

'Your glasses don't matter. You can do the shopping without them.'

'I know they don't matter. But if he finds out . . . '

'Tell him to . . . ' But now I'm the one who is whispering.

When I find her glasses by the night-table where she put them down before going to sleep, the lenses are fogged and smudged with fingerprints. A schoolgirl's glasses.

She says, 'I know. I know. It runs in the family.'

'What? Forgetting?'

'No.' She gives me a hard stare. 'Dirty glasses. My father's pupils used to say that he washed his in mashed potatoes.'

She owns only one pair. She could hide a second pair in a jar by the stove so she wouldn't be caught out. But she won't defend herself.

I take her into town and buy her a chain so that she can wear them around her neck and not lose them. She submits gaily but in the car on the way back home, she shakes her fist at the windscreen: 'I swore I'd never wear one of these goddamned things.'

When we lived in the suburbs of Ottawa in the fifties, she used to come out and play baseball with the kids in the street on summer evenings. She could hit. In my mind's eye, I see the other boys' mouths opening wide as they follow the flight of the ball from her bat and I see them returning to her face and to her wincing with pleasure as the ball pounds on to the aluminium roof of the Admiral's garage. She puts the bat down with a smile and returns to make supper, leaving us playing in the street under her amused gaze from the kitchen window.

When the Yankees played the Dodgers in the World Series, she wrote to the teacher to say I was sick and the two of us sat on her bed and watched Don Larsen pitch his perfect game and Yogi Berra race to the mound throwing his mask and mitt into the air. We saw Sandy Amaros racing across centre field chasing a high fly ball which he took with a leap at the warning track. In life, the ball hits the turf. In memory, its arc returns unendingly to the perfection of the glove.

Michael Ignatieff

The *notaire* arrives as dusk falls. We sit down for business under the mulberry tree. When my mother and father bought the house and fields twenty-two years ago, the *notaire* was a rotund Balzacian figure who observed with amused contempt while the peasants from whom we were purchasing the property passed a single pair of wire-rim glasses round the table so that each in turn could pore over the documents of sale. The new *notaire* is a sparrow of a woman, my age, a widow with two young sons and a motorcycle helmet on the back seat of her car.

We pore over deeds of sale and cadastral surveys of the fields: one planted in clover once and now overgrown with mint and high grass. The goat is staked there under the walnut tree and eats a perfect circle for his breakfast. Framed between the poplars in front of the house is the lavender field. Once a year in the first week of August, the farmer comes with a machine which straddles the purple rows and advances with a scrabbling, grinding sound, tossing aside bound and fragrant bunches. We watch from the terrace as the field is stripped of its purple and is left a bare, spiky green. The butterflies and bees retreat ahead of the mechanical jaws and, at the end of the day, are found in a desperate, glittering swarm on the last uncut row, fighting for the sweetness of the last plants like refugees crowded into an encircled city.

Then there is the orchard behind the house. It was once full of plums, but the trees were old and wormy and, one by one, they were dropping their branches, tired old men letting go of their burdens. Father called in the bulldozer, but when it came, we all went indoors and clapped our hands over our ears so that we wouldn't have to listen to the grinding of steel on the bark and the snapping of the tap roots. In a quarter of an hour, the planting of generations had been laid waste. But it had to be done. The field is bare now, but olive saplings are beginning to rise among the weeds.

The deeds of sale are all in order. My mother runs a finger over the old papers and stops at her name: *'née à Buckleberry Bradford, Angleterre, le 2 février 1916, épouse sans profession,'* and at his *'né à Saint Petersbourg, Russie, le 16 décembre, 1913, profession diplomate.'*

'"*Épouse sans profession*" sounds sad, doesn't it?' she says.

They are transferring the title of the property to me and my brother. 'Just once more,' she asks, 'tell me why we have to.'

'Because,' I reply, 'it is cheaper than doing it afterwards.'

Sometimes on the airless August nights, I lie in bed and imagine what it would be like to sell the house, turn it over to strangers and never come back. I find myself thinking of hotel rooms somewhere else: the echo of the empty *armoire*, the neon blinking through the shutters, the crisp anonymity of the towels and sheets. I remember the Hôtel Alesia in Paris, eating brie and cherries together on a hot June afternoon; the Hotel San Cassiano in Venice and its vast *letto matrimoniale*. I remember the next morning lying in bed watching her comb her hair at the dressing-table by the open window. A curl of smoke is rising from the ashtray and the swoop of her brush flickers in the facets of the mirrors. Through the window comes the sound of lapping water and the chug of a barge. We have the whole day ahead of us. I think of all the writing I might do in hotel rooms. Words come easily in hotels: the coils spring free from the weight of home.

In my father's house every object is a hook which catches my thoughts as they pass: the barometers which he taps daily and which only he seems to understand; the dark *armoire* they bought from the crooked *antiquaire* in Île sur Sogue; the Iroquois mask made of straw; the Russian bear on a string; the thermometer marked *gel de raisin, Moscou 1812* at the cold end and *Senegal* at the hot end. My thoughts, cornered by these objects, circle at bay and spiral backwards to the moods of adolescence.

'Old age is not for cowards.' My father looks at me angrily, as if I cannot possibly understand. 'I have no illusions. It is not going to get any better. I know what she goes through. Don't think I don't. You wake up some mornings and you don't know where the hell you are. Just like a child. Everything is in the fog. Some days it lifts. Some days it doesn't.'

He paces slowly at the other end of the long room, at the distance where truth is possible between us. It is late. Everyone else has gone to bed. We are drinking *tisane*, a nightly ritual usually passed in silence. There are thirty-four years between us: two wars and a revolution. There is also his success: what he gave me makes it difficult for us to understand each other. He gave me safety. My earliest memory is rain pounding on the roof of the Buick on the New Jersey Turnpike. I am three, sitting between them on the front seat, with the chrome dashboard in front of me at eye level and the black knobs of the radio winking at me. The wipers above my head are scraping across the bubbling sheet of water pouring down the windscreen. We are all together side by side, sharing the pleasure of being trapped by the storm, forced to pull off the road. I am quite safe. They made the world safe for me from the beginning.

He was never safe. His memory begins at a window in St Petersburg on a February morning in 1917. A sea of flags, ragged uniforms and hats surges below him, bayonets glinting like slivers of glass in the early morning sunlight. The tide is surging past their house; soon it will break through the doors, forcing them to run and hide. He remembers the flight south in the summer of 1917, corpses in a hospital train at a siding, a man's body bumping along a dusty road in Kislovodsk, tied by one leg behind a horse. I see it all as newsreel. He was there, with the large eyes of a six-year-old.

As he gets older, his memory scours the past looking for something to hold on to, for something to cling to in the slide of time. Tonight, pacing at the end of the room while I sit drinking the tea he has made for both of us, it is Manya who is in his mind, his nursemaid, the presence at the very beginning of his life, a starched white uniform, warm hands, the soft liquid syllables of a story at bedtime heard at the edge of sleep. She followed them south into exile. She was the centre of his world, and one morning she was no longer there.

'I woke up and she was gone. Sent away in the night. Perhaps they couldn't afford her. Perhaps they thought we were too close. I don't know.'

Across seventy years, his voice still carries the hurt of that separation, a child's helpless despair. He was her life. She was his childhood.

I try to think about him historically, to find the son within the father, the boy within the man. His moods—the dark self-absorption—have always had the legitimacy of his dispossession. Exile is a set of emotional permissions we are all bound to respect.

He is still pacing at the other end of the room. He says suddenly, 'I don't expect to live long.'

I say: 'It's not up to you, is it?'

He stokes the prospect of his death like a fire in the grate. Ahead of me the prospect beckons and glows, sucking the oxygen from the room. He says he is not afraid of dying, and, in so far as I can, I believe him. But that is not the point. In his voice, there is a child's anger at not being understood, an old man's fear of being abandoned. He does not want a son's pity or his sorrow, yet his voice carries a plea for both. A silence falls between us. I hear myself saying that he is in good health, which is true and entirely beside the point. He says good night, stoops briefly as he passes through the archway, and disappears into his room.

On some beach of my early childhood—Montauk Point? Milocer?—he is walking ahead of me, in those white plastic bathing shoes of his, following the lines of the water's edge, head down, bending now and again and turning to show me what he has found. We decide together which finds go into the pocket of his bathing-suit. We keep a green stone with a white marble vein in it. He takes it to a jeweller to have it set as a ring for her. In some jewellery box back home, it is probably still there.

I don't believe in the natural force of blood ties. There is nothing more common, more natural than for fathers and sons to be strangers to each other. It was only on those silent beach walks together, our voices lost in the surf, our footprints erased by the tide, our treasure accumulated mile by mile, that we found an attachment which we cannot untie.

There was a period in my twenties when that attachment foundered on my embrace of victimhood. It is a natural temptation for sons of powerful fathers. I was elated with destructiveness, righteous for truth. They had sent me away to school when I was eleven, and I wanted to know why. We had ceased to be a family in the flesh, and became one by air mail and transatlantic telephone. Once a year, for a month, in this house, we tried to become a real family again. Such is the story which the victim writes. I wanted to know why. I see his hands covering his face.

Why did I cling to the grievance? The truth is I loved going away from home, sitting alone in a Super Constellation shuddering and shaking high above Greenland on the way back to school, watching the polar flames from the engines against the empty cobalt sky. I won a first-team tie in football. I listened to Foster Hewitt's play by play of Hockey Night in Canada on the radio under my mattress after lights out in the dorm. I was caned for a pillow-fight, a wild and joyful midnight explosion of feathers, the only true uprising that I have ever taken part in. After such an uprising, the punishment— twelve stripes with a bamboo cane— was an honour.

I read *King Lear* in Gallimore's English class. He frog-marched us through every scene, battering us with his nasal southern Ontario intonations: until I fell in love, for the first time, with the power of words.

I went to my first dances and breathed in that intoxicating scent of hairspray, sweat, powder and the gardenia of girls' corsages, that promise of lush revelations in the dark. I became an adult in a tiny tent on a camping ground north of Toronto. The gravel was excruciating on my knees and elbows. The girl was very determined. She guided my hands in the dark. Afterwards she slapped my face, like a caress.

I did what I wanted. Because I was at school, I didn't have to bring her home; I could keep sex a secret. But I clung to the grievance of banishment.

I clung to another grievance too, but this one as much my making as his. I said to him, You have crushed her. She used to paint. Not any more. She has wishes for you and for me, but none for herself. Not any more.

He never forgave me for that, for the absolution I had given myself in blaming him. I see his hands covering his face.

'Truth is good, but not all truth is good to say.'

My son is sitting on his grandfather's knee, working over his grandfather's hands with his gums. I notice that my father's signet ring, a carving in amber of Socrates set in a gold oval— one of the survivors of exile and the pawnshop—is missing from the little finger of his left hand. In its place there is a small university ring which seems to pinch. He notices me looking at it.

'I gave it to your brother. You'll get the watch.'

The tops of his hands are strong and sunburned, but the

palms are gullied and clenched with arthritis. He no longer wields the axe.

He is tender and wary with his grandson, this messenger of life and his mortality. He strokes the child's chest absently, as if relearning a long-forgotten gesture. My son turns in his lap, and with infantile deliberation removes his grandfather's spectacles. They exchange a blue glance across seventy years. 'In the year 2000,' my father says, 'he will be sixteen.'

When I come through the beaded curtain with my breakfast, my mother is whirling the baby around slowly beneath the mulberry tree, cheek to cheek, holding his arm out against hers in the old style and crooning, 'Come to me, my melancholy baby.' My son has a wild look of pleasure on his face.

'You dance well,' I say.

She whirls slowly to a stop and hands him to me: 'No, I lead too much.'

She whispers in the baby's ear, 'Crazy old granny, crazy old granny.' She is not crazy. She is afraid. Her memory is her pride, her refuge. The captions of *New Yorker* cartoons not seen for forty years; lyrics of Noël Coward and Gerty Lawrence songs from the London of the thirties; the name of the little girl with Shirley Temple curls at the desk next to hers at Bishop Strachan School for Girls; the code-names of all the French agents she helped to parachute into France during the war: her memory is a crammed shoebox of treasures from a full life. It is what happened five minutes ago that is slipping away—the pot on the stove, the sprinkler in the garden, what she just said.

The memory which frightens her, which portends the losses still to come, is of the last time she saw her mother. They spent a week together, and as they were leaving, her mother turned to my father and said, 'You're Russian, aren't you? And who is this charming girl?'

Your daughter.

When I was eight, I spent a weekend with my grandmother in the large, dark house on Prince Arthur Avenue in Toronto. We ate breakfast together: tea on a silver service, Ryvita biscuits imported from England, with the London *Times* in a feathery edition two weeks late. I sat on the end of her bed and we had a conversation, tentative and serious across the gulf of time. I had never seen her hair down before, masses of it—grey, austere and luxuriant against the pillows. There is a kind of majesty in some old women, the deep red glow of a banked fire. I talked on and on, and she followed me with her eyes and a whisper of amusement on her lips.

Then there came a Sunday, not many months later, when I was ushered into the dark mahogany dining-room and knew at once from the slope of her shoulders, the terrible diminution of her presence, the slowness with which she turned to meet my eye, that she had no idea who I was. She stared out through the window at the blank wall of the new hotel rising to block her view. She said nothing. Her eyes were still and grey and vacant. I was speechless through lunch with her, and, when I left, I knew I would never see her again. She died several years later in a nursing home north of the city. Her will, that last relinquishing gesture of generosity in a generous life, enabled my father and mother to buy this house.

My mother is cool and lucid about her own prospects. I do not believe these things run in the family, and I tell her so. She nods and then says, 'I'm sure I would make a cheerful old nut. Don't you think so? In any case,' and here she picks up her drink and walks into the kitchen to look to her cooking, 'it's much worse for those you leave behind.'

In the next village, a theatre troupe is staging *Oedipus* on a tiny stage built into the sandstone cliffs at the foot of the village. There is a little boy in front of us in the stands, sitting between his mother and his father. He is about five. Oedipus and Jocasta circle each other slowly against the towering folds of sandstone: the eternal story unfolds in the night air. Oedipus turns his bleeding eyes upon us: 'Remember me, and you will never lose your happiness.'

The little boy rocks backwards and forwards on his seat. He says to himself in a small voice, 'Now I understand everything.'

Then he falls asleep on his mother's lap.

We stay behind afterwards while they dismantle the set. From the top row of the stands, the valley stretches out below us in the amber afterglow of nightfall. The vines and cane wind-breaks are drained of colour. The first lights in the village appear. It was this landscape which made me into a European: man's hand is upon it, the millennia of labour, the patient arts of settlement. The stillness is human: the rim of light at the edge of a shutter, the snake of a headlight, the swish of the irrigation sprinklers drenching the earth in the dark. In Canada the silence among the great trees was menacing. No light for miles. The cold. I had no quarrel with the place. I just wanted to get out.

She is standing beside me looking out into the dark valley. She leans her weight against my shoulder. I met her in a street dance in London eight years ago. Within two weeks I had brought her here, knowing that this was the place which would reveal us to each other.

My favourite photograph of her was taken in the first week we spent in this country. She is on the terrace walking towards me, wearing a white dress and a red Cretan sash. Her right hand is pushing the hair back off her forehead. She is smiling, her gaze directly into mine, shy and fearless. It is the last photograph in which she is still a stranger, approaching but still out of reach, still on the other side of the divide, before we fell in love.

The valley below us is black now. A breeze lifts up from the earth and the olive groves. She points to the sparkling village perched ten miles away on a promontory of ochre: 'It's like an ocean liner.'

I am thinking of the *Andrea Doria*. She went down off Nantucket when I was nine. They sent divers down, and they took photographs. She was lying in shallow water, and the lights of her bridge, by some impossible chance, were still on. Like the livid eyes of some great beast staring at the hunter who has brought her down, the ship's lights streamed through the ocean darkness. As a child I used to dream about those pictures of the great ship glowing on the bottom of the sea. It seems to me now that those dreams were an image of what it would be like to die, sinking in the folds of the ocean, your own eyes blazing in the salty dark.

On the way down the hill from the village, through the vaulted tunnel of the plane trees, white and phosphorescent in the headlights, she sings to me. Verdi as always. Flat as always, her head leaning back, her eyes staring up at the trees rushing by through the sun-roof.

'I am *not* flat.'

I am laughing.

She ignores me and sings on in a husky voice, '*Libera me . . . de morte aeterna.*'

From the village road, the house looks low and small, its back hunched against the mistral. By Christmas, when the *notaire* has filed the deed, it will belong to my brother and me. But whatever the deeds say, it will always be my father's house. I cannot sell it any more than I can disavow the man I became within its walls, any more than I can break the silences at the heart of family life.

The lights are out. My parents are both asleep, and our son is in his cot.

She says, 'Let's not go in yet.'

We climb up into the field behind the house where the bee-keeper has his hives, and where you can see the whole of the Luberon mountains stretched out against the night sky. The shale is cool and the dew is coming down. We watch for satellites and for the night flights to Djibouti, Casablanca and Rome. There are many bright, cold stars. A dog barks. In the house, our child floats in his fathomless sleep.

'Cassiopeia, Ursa Major, Orion's Belt . . . I must learn the names, I want to teach him the names.'

Out of the dark, as if from far away, she says, 'What do you need to name them for?'

MONA SIMPSON

RAMADAN

'Welcome in Egypt,' a large man said.

Egypt, that first brass afternoon in spring, may have been the most stylish place I ever saw on the earth. Nobody had ever told me about the cars. The cars were old German and American models from the fifties and sixties, black and rounded. They honked and shined everywhere, and I found a driver to Alexandria with my guidebook propped between two pronged fingers like a piece of music. Alexandria was a long way—two guys turned me down before this one. He was handsome and young, with many teeth, and he had a dry grassy smell the closer I stood to him. We bargained a price in dollars. I still had to get pounds. He knew almost no English. He had a book. I sat in the back of the old Mercedes on deep leather seats made soft with time and watched out of the rolled-down windows as we left Cairo in a circle like a maze and drove north into the horizon of cypresses, eucalyptus and olive trees. It was good.

There was so much sky. The ground and trees, people and even buildings rose about an inch and the rest was sky. It was 24 February. I wanted to remember the day. I lay my head back on the seat and the smell of earth rolled over me. This wasn't desert as I'd expected. It was dirt, not light sand; the vegetation was scarce and sombre. Ragged trees moved slightly in the soft wind, and they seemed to whine and creak. Date palm and sycamore. Closer in, there were acacia, juniper, jacaranda and grass.

I felt looser in my clothes when I couldn't see Cairo behind us any more. We were on an old road. The structures you saw in the distance looked small, made of concrete and mud. A rich weedy taste came through the air. I thought of my father and how, even though he was a boy who grew up here in this old slow country, he'd moved in suits and silk ties all over the world. I'd travelled too. I'd driven cross-country, had my college summer in Europe; even my grandmother, in Wisconsin, had been around the world. But do we, any of us, love more?

If this was Egypt, maybe that explained Wisconsin. His existence there. On the road ahead of us I saw a small lake and then a mountain, which disappeared when we came close. I'd been told about mirages in school, when I learned the word, but I'd never seen one. Maybe it took a desert to produce them. Once in a while the driver turned to me and we'd try to talk but it was too hard, so he'd fall back to driving, which he did with an evenness and a happy hum that seemed as odd and discordant as sitar music. He had a vague smile which seemed to move through a sort of plot sequence. I rested back on the seat, thinking how I'd like to sleep with this boy just once, tonight, in my hotel room and wondering if I could, how this worked and whether I should give him money. This was so foreign no one would know. No one ever. For the rest of my life no one would know.

I stared at the back of his neck. His hair was cut short but it still curled. Below the line of hair were two lines of sweat, tiny drops balanced on the dark taut skin. At that moment I thought how hard it was to be a man. The distance between imagining and placing a hand in the world on to someone's skin—I didn't know how that happened. That seemed enormous. Even when there were two cultures and no language and you had the money. But no. That wasn't good. Being bought with money could harm anyone.

I tapped his shoulder—his skin through the cotton was warm—and pointed for him to stop at a market, a bazaar of some kind by the side of the road. It looked like a farm food stand anywhere in America, except the trees were high date palms. I was hungry. He pulled over the Mercedes, its bulk calming smoothly on the dirt gravel pass. We got out. The canvas- and tin-roofed tents shaded jars of oil, dates still on the branch, almonds, pine nuts, diamond-cut pastries in tin pans that ran with honey, hazed by close thick black flies, pomegranates, olives, figs open and red, dusty purple on the outside. A thin man, dark-skinned with almost no hair on his legs and arms and head, sat cross-legged on a striped rug on the uneven ground. His eyes were nearly closed. A clear glass jar, like one you would buy jam in, sat full by his knee. I tried to get close. I browsed by a table with nothing recognizable on it, some kind of cheese in water, I thought. I saw then in his jar: a coiled snake; I couldn't tell dead or alive.

I wanted figs, dates and almonds and started to gather them in a brown-paper bag, but my driver came up and with elaborate arm motions pointed to his chest, establishing, I'll do this, without words. The thin man's flat sunken mouth smiled a big smile. He tried to take her and was caught. She's an American, it's all game.

147

Walking back to the car with my bag of fruit, I heard a familiar monotonous sound. I walked across the sand and looked behind the tent. A rickety ping-pong table was set up on the ground and two dark boys were playing. Then we were driving again, and he conducted a long speech to me in Arabic, probably about how much money he'd saved me, and I murmured something to make it seem I understood. 'Is no good for you, is better for you,' was all I made out from his speech. His arm sometimes lifted off the wheel, articulate and graceful, but I wished I could settle it back to driving and I ate the fresh dates, the skins crumbling like sugar and the fruit inside melting like honey. I could eat like this for a hundred years. In the back seat there was a long soft breeze and sun on the left side, so I took off my shoes and my long shirt and just lay down in my tank top and skirt, legs bare, feet on the leather, feeling it almost like another skin. I was sort of asleep but not really. The breeze played on my belly, my upper arms, the bones of my neck. It was good. The smell of the fruit on the foot-space swelled up in shells of air.

Before I left, I'd wanted to find some Arabs to write things down for me. I stopped at the place across from the school that sold hummus and tabouli and shish kebab in pita. But the guys there turned out to be Israelis. Nice guys. They gave me a felafel and suggested that I check the university. It would have to have some kind of Arab Studies department.

I asked directions and went upstairs. On a third floor corner, I found Near Eastern Studies. A woman in black jeans and a black turtle-neck stood near a floor-to-ceiling wire cage which held a parrot. Inside the cage, which looked home-made, was a large, driftwood branch where the parrot perched. The woman held a finger to the bird. From the glint of jewel, I saw she was married. She was dark-skinned, wide-eyed, with an extremely full, flower-shaped mouth. She sounded younger than she looked.

'I'm Mayan Atassi.' That was the first time I'd said it since Ted Stevenson broke our names and then returned to randomness. 'I'm looking for someone Egyptian.'

The parrot flapped its long wings and squawked. She laughed. 'Egyptian. Let's see. Professor Kamal is,' she said, 'but he's on leave in Paris this year.'

'You're not Egyptian?' I said.

'No, I'm from the Lebanon,' she said. My whole life I'd heard of Beirut and how it was the Switzerland of the Middle East. I knew that I had been conceived there.

'Do you know Arabic?'

'Yes, mmhmm.'

I began to explain. My mother never wanted me to be alone with my dad. 'He could have you on a plane to Egypt in ten minutes,' she'd snap her fingers, 'and they'd have you married off and swelled up pregnant at fourteen. That's what they do to girls over there. Girls are nothing.'

'What about going to college?' I'd said.

'College, in Egypt?' she said. She burst out with a bitter-rinded laugh. 'Forget it.'

I was grown up now and being pregnant didn't seem only shame. It appeared even beautiful, a common thing. It was strange having outlived the life with my mother: I was forever rediscovering little things that I had believed and assumed and were not true. Anyway, I might never be able to get pregnant and that was because of me. I'd dieted too much when I was in high school.

On three sheets of paper, the woman with the parrot wrote in Arabic the Station Street address, my address in America, and a little paragraph that I dictated saying who I was and that I was looking for my father whom I hadn't seen in years, and his name. I looked at her ring while she wrote. It was dark gold, the diamond capped on either side by bright blue-green gems cut in squares.

I opened my wallet and slipped the three papers in the deepest part. They became treasures. She asked me if I would come back when I returned and tell her what happened.

I was halfway down the hall, a clean echoing hall of black tiles, and then I ran back. 'Do you know what the weather is like there?'

She stepped out from behind the desk. She was a plump-cheeked woman, big-breasted, wonderful-looking. 'Nice. Perfect. Like your San Francisco.'

Some time later he made a punctuating noise in the front and I sat up. I saw Alexandria in the distance, like a series of half-staircases on a hill. This was the place my father grew up. It was early evening, seven o'clock and not much light. The roads (some

149

of them) looked older than the Ottoman empire but were still used, not kept for antique. There were geraniums in the windows, like Paris. The stone and plaster were crumbling and dirty. A lot of the houses had clay pots on the roofs. I wondered why. Some of the buildings had a white sheen, with mosaic. The streets were quieter than Cairo, the neighbourhoods lower, the old sun like a bucket full of water spilled on the bricks. This was a smaller city, I guessed, and was supposed to be holy. I knew that. Not only for me.

'*Mumkin ahgiz ohda ghur-fa min hi-na?*'

I read to him from the guidebook but he didn't understand. Then I gave up and moved behind his shoulder and showed him where it was printed in Arabic calligraphy, pointing with my fingernail while the car moved unevenly over the bricks. I wanted a hotel. He put his hand to his forehead, and then exploded in head-nodding. He was so young. His shirt was striped, yellow and green. Just then I noticed a band aid on his right arm, near the elbow, a band aid printed with circus animals, the kind we always wanted as children. Is that what became of circus band aids? The surplus shipped to the Third World?

We turned a corner and beyond us was the Mediterranean, blue and green and moving with unrest, a sea of barking dogs. He drove me to an ugly hotel, modern and run-down. I said no, crossed my arms, and found the word for old in the guidebook. This made him think a moment and then he got it, and the next place was right: white and Persian-looking, with small cracks snaking down the towers. He parked the Mercedes, pulled the keys out and came inside with me, carrying the pack. It seemed too hard to argue. He wanted to deal with the desk for me, so I stood next to him, holding out my credit card. The man behind the desk took it, produced a key and that was the end of it. An old cage elevator, with script I could not read, lyrical cursives strewn in fancy metal painted white, stopped at the ninth floor where the smell of old geraniums came profuse and dusty and breath-stopping almost: I followed and he opened the door of my room and it was good.

French doors opened to a small terrace and the sunset fired outside. I looked in the bathroom: it was completely tiled, even the ceiling. You could wash it out with a hose. The bed was plain and white; a small prayer rug waited in one corner. The carpet was a very faded red, and dirty.

My driver put my backpack down and stood there.

I pulled my wallet out of the pack and paid him the amount we agreed, plus ten dollars.

He counted slowly, with complication, twice, then his face cleared and he handed me back ten one-dollar bills.

I shook my head no, pointed—for you—then I grabbed the phrase book and tried to find the words that meant 'for the children.' In the guidebook, it said you were supposed to say 'for the children.' He looked pretty young to have children and I couldn't find the damn phrase anyway, so I pushed the money back into his hand and he shook his head no, and I put my hands behind my back meaning I won't take it and then he pushed my shoulders, gentle but a real push, the money held up in his hand between us, and for a minute we didn't know what was happening and then we were falling back, first me on the bed and then him.

His skin stretched and spread taut wings from his neck to his top chest bones. I remembered that he was young, probably younger than twenty. I wanted to hear his name. I didn't want it to be Atassi. He could have been. My father might have come back. Then I remembered my father telling me around the old kitchen table, 'If I went back, I'd be running the country. I was the John F. Kennedy of Egypt.' Well, he wasn't running the country. I read the newspapers. I knew those people's names. He said so little to us that I saved every sentence. I could lift one up like a bracelet or strand of pearls from a box. As if any young man could be held responsible for grandiose dreams whispered to an infant daughter, when he was new in a country and still thought everything was possible.

But he could have come back. It was more than twenty years ago he'd said that. He was a very young man then.

I rolled over on my belly, reached down for the guidebook. My shoes fell off the side of the bed. He pulled me back by my ankle. I felt his fingers like a bracelet. I riffled through the pages. There it was; 'My name is Ismee Mayan Atassi,' I said.

He pointed to his chest. 'Ramazan el-Said. I was born during the Ramadan, so my mother called me that.'

OK. Fine. I lay back on the bed; the book dropped. This was good. We couldn't say a word and I'd stopped trying, but maybe because of that something else worked. I always talked too much in bed anyway. I lay back and wished he would touch my neck for some reason, I don't know why, and I don't know if I'd ever wanted that or thought that before, my neck, but he did, first with his fingers, hard so I felt my pulse flutter. I didn't know if it would be different or the same so far away with someone not in my language, a complete stranger, but I watched the fan in the ceiling slowly mark the room with carousel shadows and in a minute I was lifting my hips to shrug my skirt off and then we were both naked, he was dark and thin and not different really. I touched him and looked in his face, his cheeks seemed to spread wider apart and questions stood like cool statues in his eyes and I wanted him and started it and then it began. It went on a long time, well into first dark, it never really stopped. I'd turn over on my side and clutch some sheet around me and look out of the windows at the clear stars and he'd be on my back with his hands and mouth and then something would feel like a shot, absolute and four-pointed but blooming pleasure and we'd begin again and it went on so long sometimes I'd forget. I'd feel I was the man, entering him and he seemed that way too, opened, split, eyes shallowing up like hungry fish on the surface, as if in the night we traded who owned the outside and the inside, who could penetrate and who could enclose. The stranger was in me and I wanted that. I finally fell asleep. He woke me and I heard water rushing. It was still dark. I dragged the sheet behind me to the window, where there was one star that almost hurt to look at, a too proud diamond, somebody else's, and I wondered why he'd woken me so late or so early, and then he pushed me to the bathroom where he'd run a deep tub with a flower floating on the top. The whole thing smelled almond and he put me in it. I saw blood. It wavered in the water like a frilly ribbon. I stepped out and saw him kneeling by the bed. The sheet was soaked red. I was bleeding. He started kissing the inside of my thighs, which were bloodstained like some all-directional flower. I couldn't tell him how happy I was with the guidebook; there was no way to explain. Before I lost my period, like a stitch in knitting, I'd minded blood in a prissy way, hated the bother of it, worried

about spotting. Now I could have tasted it. I felt like shouting.
That was over, the long punishment for what I'd done to myself.
I had my choices again. He was looking up at me now with
different eyes, submissive. He knelt by the bed and capped my
knees with his hands. He said words I didn't know.

Then he rampaged through the room. I found him squatting
over the guidebook. He said in English, I love you. He kept
looking up at me in this slave way. Then I understood. The
blood. He thought that meant virgin, that I'd given that to him.
'No,' I tried to tell him. 'No.' He picked me up, an arm under
the crook of my knees and one under my back. He took me to
the tub again. He was carrying me like a fragile child. I had to
clear this up. But there was no way. His brown eyes fixed. I
slipped down into the water, and heard him in the other room
pulling up his pants, the clink of keys and change. He stole out
of the door. I figured I'd never see him again and that was fine,
like a sealed perfect envelope. A tangerine peeled, every section
intact. I got up out of the water to latch the door behind him.
Then I went back to sleep, thrilling even in dream every time I
felt the trickle of blood.

The next morning, I felt proud because with the guidebook I
ordered room service coffee and it came with a wet rose on
the tableclothed tray. The petals fell off easily when I pulled
because the flower was full and seedy. Outside, the hills were raw
brown with a haze of purple on the surface. The ocean was a
plain grey colour. I took a bath and remembered the night. I sat
with the coffee on the tiled rim of the tub. A line of blood ran
jagged like the thinnest twig. The blood was going to be a
problem. I went to the guidebook but there was nothing under
Tampax. I called the desk and sat with the guidebook and finally
sputtered 'Tampax' in English. The man said, 'Oh, Tampax,' and
a few minutes later the elevator creaked and a boy appeared with
a blue unopened box on a cloth-covered tray with a new rose. I
put on a white shirt, brushed on mascara and left.

His car was parked across the street. The sight hit me like a
sling. I tiptoed up: he was asleep on the back seat. He looked
pathetic. He was too big for the car, and he slept with one leg
folded under him and his head bent against the window. I left him

153

be and walked downhill to ask directions at a fruit stand. I waited my turn. The high citrus smell tickled my face and behind the server two towers of orange and lemon hulls hovered. I showed him my scrap of paper with the Station Street address that the woman with the parrot had written, and he pointed. I wanted to buy lemonade but I remembered I hadn't changed my money. I started walking.

I passed a movie theatre with calligraphy on the marquee. The photographs by the ticket booth showed a huge Omar Sharif, older now, with salt-and-pepper hair. I had seen all his movies. I had wondered whether he was even still alive. He was never in anything any more. But his career hadn't fallen to ruins. He was here.

I heard birds as I climbed the winding streets and I smelled myrtle and sage. There was also the distant hammer sound of construction. I hadn't expected the whirring of bicycles everywhere. They were black and old, like the cars. After a few minutes outside I was used to camels. I'd stopped and touched the black lips of one, wet and soft, gumming my hand. Then I felt something nudge my hip. It was the Mercedes. At first I was mad. I twisted my skirt to see if it had made a mark. He sat at the wheel, grinning, motioning me to get in. I didn't see what else I could do, so I got in the front seat, giving up my adventure but glad anyway. I showed him the Station Street address.

He put a hand, softly, on my lower belly. I wriggled away. But it was good he found me. He studied a map and it took us fifteen minutes of turns and curves, in opposite directions. Then we were at the house.

It still stood. A tall straggly eucalyptus waited in front. It was a wooden and concrete house, three floors with two balconies, brownish coloured with old rusty metal and stucco. The roof was red tile, Spanish-looking. I saw a metal drain-pipe like the one at home. The eucalyptus moved in the wind above me. I wanted to get rid of the driver. I didn't know how long I would be. I didn't want anyone waiting for me.

I returned to the car, knocked on the window and motioned to him wildly, to say it could be a long time. He pointed to his chest, then to the floor of the car. I guess he meant that he'd be there. I shrugged, tapping my watch. I spread out my hand wide. Eternity. He folded his arms and closed his eyes.

The sky was clear blue with no clouds and I heard the drift of a slight wind in the eucalyptus leaves, a tired and very old sound. Patience, they seemed to whisper, patience. Summer is long. My heart beat like something flung against a wall. There was no bell, and I knocked. A wind chime of crude glass and metal pipes hung from the eaves. Nobody answered. The porch was cool, clay-tiled. I knocked again.

I checked my slip of paper against the number on the door. Yes, twenty-two was the number. Outside the door was an old orange plastic chair and on the ground, the dish for a plant, filled with what looked like rainwater. I heard a window shoved open in the house next door to the right, and a woman's hot fast voice spilled through and I said, 'Isam Atassi. American.' There was a noise inside her building of feet on a staircase. A door whipped open and the woman stood there looking me over.

She crossed her arms firmly over her substantial chest and spoke to me, her head shaking. The only words I recognized were 'no America, no America.' For a moment I thought she was trying to chase me away but then she was showing me into her house with her arms, almost bowing, big loops of arm hanging down like stretching dough from shoulder to elbow, from elbow to hand. She stood with her ample back to me, hands on hips, calling up the stairs; a little girl ran down, a round-limbed blue-eyed blonde. The woman said something to the child, and the child gathered her skirts in both fists and started running. 'No America,' the woman said again, this time bending in a near curtsy. I finally got it; she didn't speak English. She motioned me to sit and I did. She sat across from me and folded her hands on her lap and her feet one behind the other. I couldn't help noticing her legs. Her calves were enormous, over the dainty gesture of her feet, and patterns of black hair were trapped under her nylon stockings. Then she sprang up, graceful and light, and slowly lifted the lid off a green cut-glass bowl of candy. To be polite I took one. It was a date wrapped around nuts, and rolled in sugar and ground pistachio. It was good. She slowly pantomimed drinking from a glass, then lifted her eyebrows to ask if I wanted anything. I shook my head no, not wanting to get into a beverage charade.

We sat politely in the still living-room on fancy maroon velvet couches with gold tassels, our hands folded, looking in

155

different directions. She smiled at me every few moments. After a long while the girl skidded in with a boy who might have been her brother but didn't look like it. They were calling back and forth in avid musical conversation. The boy stood before the woman, probably his grandmother, hands at his sides and chin down, awaiting an order. More fast Arabic. I rested with the ease of understanding absolutely nothing.

Then the boy turned to face me and said, 'I know English.'

'Oh, good,' I said, loudly, 'Are you learning in school?'

'Yes,' he said. 'School.'

'What is your name?' I said.

'My name is Nauras Awafti.'

I reached out my hand. 'My name is Mayan Atassi.'

'Yes. There are many here,' the boy said.

The grandmother became impatient and pulled the boy to her by the back of his shirt. He turned and translated for her. She fired questions at him hard and fast. Then he swivelled back to me. She smiled, and showed her teeth, some of them not white, and lifted her old plump hand in a wave.

'I am American,' I said. 'My mother is American, my father is from here. Egyptian. He grew up next door. My father is Mohammed Atassi and I came here to find him.'

'Mohammed ah-yah,' the old woman said, her head going up and down. The boy translated what I had said.

'He left my mother years ago. I haven't seen my father— Mohammed—since I was twelve years old.' I marked the height with my hand. 'Around your age. I wonder if you, or your grandmother, knows where he is.'

He grinned and said, 'She's not my grandmother,' as if this were a hilarious mistake. I hoped to hell she was not his mother. 'She's my grandmother's sister. My grandmother's upstairs.' He pointed to the ceiling.

The old woman grabbed his collar again sternly to get him back to business.

'Does she know where my father is?' I repeated.

She shook her head and I knew my answer even before he translated.

'You come all the way from America to find him?' the boy said.

'Yes,' I said. The woman closed her eyes and continued rocking her head.

She spoke and the boy translated. 'He hasn't been there for a long time. Not thirty years. She says he's somewhere in America. When his father die, next door, he wasn't at funeral. You have bad luck because they live there next door, Farhan's wife and daughter. But they went for two months already to America.'

America. I was astonished. 'Where in America?' I said.

She shrugged.

'She says she doesn't know. But she thinks California.'

I looked at the little blonde girl. She was sitting in a big chair, her arms clutched to the armrests, her round legs ending in blunted sneakers. She stared up at me, the American.

The boy said that my father's mother was very old but still in the house next door. He asked if I would like to meet her.

I thought I'd heard the translation wrong. 'Yes!' I said. 'Yes!' My other grandmother.

The old woman spoke and the boy said that she had invited me to eat a meal with them first. She stood up, with her huge knees facing out, bent them in a *plié* and lifted and spread her arms to encompass the room. The woman's repertoire of gestures belonged to a clown. A fat clown. I liked her very much, I appreciated her exaggerated courtesies, but I wanted to go. I tapped my watch and pointed at the house next door. I was sick of people—even Egyptians, even neighbours—who saw my father once thirty years ago. I didn't want strangers. I had a grandmother locked in the house next door.

The old woman rose, negotiated her weight around the furniture and motioned me with a plump fluid wrist to follow. The kids stood on either side of me, looking at me as if I were the strangest being they'd ever seen. We went through a mint-green kitchen, like an old-fashioned one at home, and out of the back door. The backyard went far. Three goats faced us. There was a chicken coop too, with loud dirty-white chickens. From a eucalyptus tree, an old tyre hung and the lawn was worn smooth and grassless. Past the yard and a shed was a field, just weeds, down the hill to a stand of olive trees. I knew my father must have run there.

I could have stayed. But the woman and the boy and girl were entering the next house's back door and I followed. We walked into a cellar full of vegetables and fruit in clear jars, cans with faded labels, jars of honey and vats of olive oil and sacks of grain. I picked up a jar of olives that were still attached to their branch. The woman tapped at a jar that contained something like yellow peanut butter. Her lips opened on her teeth in a large expression that strained for meaning. 'Mohammed,' she said, and moved a hand on her ample belly.

The boy translated. 'He liked that for his meal every day.' I didn't know what it was.

We entered a kitchen that looked as if it had been remodelled twenty years before, in matching black-and-white checks. The cupboards seemed safe and ample, the corners rounded, the surfaces used and worn. It was clean and plain. We passed into a large living-room with plush emerald-green carpeting and fancy satin and velvet couches and chairs. Gold ropes marked off parts of the room. An old inlaid chess table and some brass trays looked Middle Eastern; the mahogany console stand holding an RCA colour television could have been anywhere. I stopped at some chrome-framed pictures on a shelf. The photographs showed a wedding. The bride was a full, young, curly-haired girl who looked nothing like me. There were eight pictures of her sitting in her flower-decked throne and in each one she was wearing a different dress. My father was not there. The old woman shook her head sadly, with raised eyebrows. 'Mohammed, no,' she said.

We climbed upstairs, the children ahead. The woman ascended slowly, holding the gold velvet rope that served as a banister. On the first landing, there was a family room, with another sofa and chairs, a bookshelf, a standing globe, and corridors leading to more bedrooms. We started up the second stairs. Near the top, the woman called the children back. She explained something to the boy and he ran ahead, two steps at a time, arms scissoring with purpose.

We entered the top room. A young woman with her hair held back pressed by us out of the door. She stood on the landing, holding one elbow. She was wearing a nurse's uniform with a long zipper. It was a wide, low-ceilinged room, pink and white in the eaves. Outside, eucalyptus leaves fingered the window-panes. The room was full of roses, their petals falling from the night table on to tabletops, the floor, the lush satin bedspread. There she was, rising from a chair with great effort, collapsing down again, an old woman with a deeply lined dark face, a mouth large as a harmonica, with many teeth and a puff of white hair. Her eyes were clear blue. She was large and short.

'Momo,' she said, her whole face crumbling over the words. She hugged me and she smelled a way I hadn't ever known an old woman to smell, warmly sweet like caramel. We sat in white, satin-cushioned chairs and the boy translated between us. She had a clear sad look when she shook her head after the boy asked if she knew where her youngest son was. She had not heard from him for ten years, she said. Her eyebrows lifted and her large mouth formed a beautiful shape. She told the boy she had not seen him for almost twenty. She lifted her hands and I went close and knelt down so she could hold my face.

She told us that when my father was a boy he liked the animals. He was always out in the air with animals. I asked if he had been smart. She shrugged, frowning, then slowly nodded her head to say that she supposed so.

I moved to the small attic window. I could see the field and the goats. My father had run there, a boy like any boy. There was a muddy pen. A sandbox. The woman from next door tilted her head and made a gesture that we should let the old woman rest.

I knelt and kissed her goodbye. We walked out and she called us back in words I didn't recognize. She'd lifted herself up and got to a bureau. From the top drawer, open now, I saw a thousand things—threads, thimbles, scissors, papers, cards, scarves, veils, stockings, lipsticks, jewellery. She extracted a tiny photograph of my father, about an inch square, black and white with a white ruffled edge.

She gave it to me and I closed my hand around it. I couldn't look at it until later. In the cellar again, the woman from next door gave me the jar of what my father had liked. She pointed to the ceiling.

'She wanted you to have,' the boy said.

Before I left I gave them the scrap of paper where the woman with the parrot had written my address. 'You can visit me in America someday,' I said.

'*Inshallah*,' the boy said. He copied the address down and returned the paper to me.

I asked him what the word meant. I'd heard it all around me.

'God willing,' the boy said, 'in Egypt nothing for sure. Everything is *inshallah*.'

I asked him what my name meant.

'It's just a name like other names. A common name here.'

'I thought it meant light,' I said. That's what my parents had told me.

'No. Nora means light.'

'What about Amneh?' That was my middle name. I thought it meant to wish.

'No. Believer.'

I hoped that Ramazan was still outside and we could drive back to Cairo. He would rub my back and I would fly home into the dawn. I wanted to leave. I felt like a person who had thrown a diamond ring down off a bridge and watched it disappear into the dark water. It was over, I'd lost the gamble, he'd eluded me this time for ever and now I wanted to go home. But I felt calm. I didn't care any more. I'd had my Arab experience. As I looked around me, up at the tall slow trees, I knew I'd be back another time, for different reasons.

The car was there and they walked slowly with me to it. I opened the front passenger door and the old woman rapped her knuckles on the window of the back seat and pointed.

I shrugged. 'It's OK.'

Ramazan, who had just woken up, slumped over the steering-wheel. He looked up from his dropped head like a yoked animal. The old woman kept rapping; she seemed upset. Ramazan pointed to the back seat. I got out and went in the back. I didn't understand, but I wanted to go. I rolled down the back window and looked for a moment at the house and the yard beyond, the three goats, their black heads, the shimmering yellow-green weeds of the plain field. It was as shabby as my grandmother's house in Wisconsin, the land as old. I was sad over how many different lives there were and we only got once.

Ramazan explained with the guidebook. 'Rich,' he said and he looked at me, nodding his head. He said the word again, repeating to memorize. I shook my head. He persisted. The wind tore through the open windows. My mother had always told me we were royalty over here. I laughed out loud. Twenty-two Station Street was a good house, but it wasn't royal anywhere in the world. The car stopped: I didn't know why. There was a small stand of dusty olive trees by the side of the road. Ramazan got out and I heard him pee on the dry leaves. Below him was an old stone amphitheatre. I came up behind him, toppled him, and we lay there on the cool stone, toying. I hurt my back once on a eucalyptus button.

'Greco-Roman,' he said, pointing to the stage below. It was a small, perfectly tiered circle. There was life there once.

'Arabs have everything, huh?'

'No, Egyptians.' He tapped his chest. 'We have got pyramids. Antiquities. History.' He made a sound by letting air out of his mouth.

When I put my underwear on again, the good pair, drops of blood trickled to the cotton, staining like a water-colour. I found the last scrap of paper from my wallet, on which the woman with the parrot had written that I was looking for my father who might be in Alexandria and that I hadn't seen him for seventeen years. I gave it to Ramazan. He spent a long time reading it.

In the car his face took on a new cast and he lost the plot of his smile. His hands stayed on the wheel, not playful any more. I showed him the word in the book that means airport. I made wing motions with my arms, pointed at myself—'Me, America.' We drove a long time keeping the silence and arrived in Cairo. On the way to the airport, he drove through a district of mansions on the Nile. They had domed towers, minarets, columns and mosaics, like mosques. They looked a thousand years old, or older. This was the royalty of Egypt.

'Heliopolis,' he said. He stopped before one mansion and pointed. 'Omar Sharif.'

At the airport, he came into the terminal with me. I studied the English television screen. There was a flight in the evening at eight o'clock. It was only three. He took my hand and I followed him to a phone booth. He was carrying my pack again and it felt easy to let him. It was a modern phone booth. He lifted a book, paged through, found a spot and showed me. I remembered from his hand that Arabic scans from right to left.

His hand brailled over the whole page. 'Atassi,' he said. 'Atassi. Atassi. Atassi.'

I smiled and shook my head. It was too late for that. I wanted to go home. I sat on his lap. I didn't want to close the book over a page of Atassis. He ripped the page out, folded it up, put it in my backpack, zipped the zipper. We had time to eat. He drove me to a neighbourhood of low two-storey tenement buildings. Children played in the bare street. The restaurant was small and underground, and we sat cross-legged on the floor. A short-stemmed pink rose leaned in a tin can on our table. Two of the petals, cleft in the centre, had fallen to the cloth. Light slanted into the room from back and front. Ramazan ordered in Arabic and I sat low against a pillow. We looked at each other and sometimes smiled, sometimes didn't; we had stopped trying to use words. The food began to come and set our clock. Olives and new cheese, then kibbe, then my father's layered pancake with a different butter and burnt sugar. He'd always talked about the Bedouin food, about sleeping outside with them as a boy, the open fires in the morning. The pancake tasted of honey and deep caramel and rose-water. I handed Ramazan a pencil and paper for the name. He drew and whispered: 'Fatir.'

Then we used the guidebook. He pointed to his chest and showed me the word 'poor'. I smiled a little, embarrassed for him. He didn't have to ask me. I'd already decided to give him all the money I had and save only twenty dollars for the bus home from the airport. He pointed to himself again, made wing motions and said, in an accent I'd never heard, 'America.' He pointed to me and I smiled. I gave him my address, and he put it in the little bag he had around his neck where he kept money, and clasped it shut. He took my left hand and banded a cleft rose-petal over my third finger. I knew before looking in the book. 'Marrying,' he said. I got up to leave. He's so young, I was thinking.

It was still light when we walked outside. I wanted to buy a souvenir. We had more than an hour. With the guidebook I showed him the word for bazaar and I shrugged. We walked into a district of close streets and corners, brown buildings and smells of burning meat. We came to a square filled with market stands and around the sides were the neon-lit fronts of casinos. He pulled me over to the edge of the square, where there was a tiled drinking-fountain and a man standing with a camera draped in black cloth and a camel tied to a palm. He spoke and seemed to be asking if I wanted to have my picture taken with the camel.

We surveyed the stands of the bazaar. From a dusty market table, we picked out an everyday Turkish coffee pot, a little one. I wanted to open the jar of what my father had liked. When the woman had given it to me, I thought I'd save it for my father and give it to him as a present the first time I saw him, if I ever found him and we met again. But I didn't want to wait. I'd waited and saved enough for him. The lid stuck. I gave it to Ramazan. He held it against his belly, straining, and again I thought, he's young, and then it was open. It was a rich distilled paste that tasted of almonds and honey. We ate it with our fingers as we walked past fabric bolts and animals that licked our hands. We finished the whole jar. I turned my back for a moment and he bought me a dress. I had been staring at a painted wooden cut-out of a bride and groom propped outside a casino called The Monte Carlo. The heads were open circles for people to stand in and have their picture taken. BE THE BRIDE, it said.

In the airport I bought a snowball paperweight that showed a scene with camels and tents in the desert. Ramazan paid for it. He'd paid for the coffee pot, for dinner, for the dress, and he'd tried to pay for the wedding photographs. We passed a bar called the Ramadan Room, where an orchestrated version of 'Home of the Brave' was playing. At the departure gate I tried to give him my money. I had two hundred and ten dollars in cash. I wanted to give him all of it. He wouldn't take it. I pushed the crinkled bills into his pockets. His mouth got hard; his chin made a clean line; he took it all, balled it, jammed it down in my pack.

At the metal security bar we drank a long goodbye kiss. His articulate hands moved around my face as if fashioning an imaginary veil there.

'Goodbye,' I said. I knew absolutely that I would never see him again.

He said words I didn't understand but I made out Allah. Everything in his language had to do with God.

DORIS LESSING

IMPERTINENT DAUGHTERS

Aphotograph of my mother shows her as a large, round-faced schoolgirl, full of the confidence I have to associate with her being Victorian. Her hair is tied back with a black bow. She is wearing her school uniform, a full white blouse and a long, dark skirt. In a photograph taken forty-five years later, she appears as a lean, severe old thing, bravely looking out from a world of disappointment and frustration. She stands by my father, her hand on the back of his chair. He has to sit: as always, he is ill. It is clear that he is only just holding himself together, but he is in a proper suit, certainly because she has told him he must make the effort. She wears a rather smart tailored dress, made up out of a remnant bought in the sales.

The difference between these photographs is what this memoir has to be about. It seems that it has taken me a lifetime to understand my parents, with astonishments all the way. There is a mysterious process, frightening because there is nothing whatsoever you can do about it, that takes you from fierce adolescence—as if parents and you stood at either side of a battlefield, hands full of weapons—to a place where you can stand where they did, in imagination, any time you want.

Only when I sat down to write this did it occur to me that I could write about my father and hardly mention that dread word 'class', but with my mother it is a different matter. She never freed her judgements from thoughts of class, but then she did not see why she should. Class was then a straitjacket, an imperative, a crippler. Only that time, that place, could have produced her: London, Britain, the British Empire. But the Empire was in its last days: a thought she would have dismissed as treacherous, wrong-headed, soft.

On a mud wall of the old house on the farm in Africa where I was brought up was a large, ornately-framed portrait of my grandfather McVeagh. He is standing beside his second wife. He was fat-faced and overfed, with hair slicked down on either side of a parting. He wore a tight, smug suit and a golden chain across his chest. I loathed him, this self-righteous prig, with a violence that stopped me from listening to my mother, whose reminiscences seemed only another attempt to bind me to her. Had she, had my father, not escaped from England? Why, then, was she winding me back into that shroud? I closed my ears, and I am sorry now I did. For instance, who was that elegant, fastidious lady he married? She was Jewish, with a fine curved nose and exquisite hands. Her dress was a miracle of embroidery and little tucks and lace. She came from a different world, by nature if not by class. I think she was a governess. Yet she had chosen to marry him: a thought that didn't enter my head for years; he made two romantic marriages, this philistine bank manager.

Once I had a fit of wanting to know who my forebears were, and before I found what a fussy and tedious business it is and gave it up, I came across birth certificates of McVeaghs from Exeter and Maidstone. They were all called John and Edward and James, and were sergeants in cavalry regiments. In short, my grandfather McVeagh, or his father, had made the jump up into the middle classes, and he was as snobbish as one would expect. Yet his first marriage had been to Emily Flower, the daughter of a contractor for lightering. A marriage for love. There is no picture of Emily Flower. This is because she was such a misfortune. All my childhood I heard of this grandmother thus: 'She was very pretty, but all she cared about was dancing and horses.' It was said with the little cold sniff that probably derived from the servants who brought the children up after wicked Emily died, which was—my mother's tone said it served her right—in childbirth with her third child. That was in 1888, and she was thirty-two. But how was it that the wife of a suburban bank manager was able to dance all the time and be mad about horses? In Blackheath? Blackheath was where my mother said the tall, grim, cold house was; but on Emily's death certificate it says Canning Town.

My mother, Emily Maude, was the first child. Then came Uncle John. Then Muriel, who disgraced herself and the family by marrying back into the working class. Hardly a surprise, judged my mother, for Muriel was always happiest with the servants. In other words she was not happy in the competitive, striving atmosphere of getting on and doing well.

It was a cold home. Her father, so romantic in love, ruled his children as Victorian papas are reputed to have done, with the rod, and without love. There was no affection from the elegant stepmother, who was dutiful and correct and did not understand children. I never once heard my mother speak of her father with warmth. Respect, yes; prescribed admiration, certainly. Never love. As for her stepmother, she might have been a visitor or a distant relation.

Emily was clever at school, much cleverer than her brother, John, who was destined for the Navy, and who found the exams difficult. He had to be coached and pushed and prodded. She loved examinations, came first in class, adored mathematics and was expected for a time to become a professional pianist.

The children, as was proper in this Forsytian world, were taken to all public occasions of rejoicing or grief; and my mother spoke of Mafeking night, Queen Victoria's funeral, the coronation of Edward VII, exhibitions, the visits of the Kaiser and of foreign heads of government, as if these milestones were the only possible way to mark the passing of a childhood.

If there was little family life, there was an energetic social life full of friends she kept in touch with for years, even from the farm in Africa. She played tennis and lacrosse and hockey and went on bicycle trips. There were musical evenings. They drew portraits of each other and pictures of appropriate landscapes; wrote humorous and sentimental verses to mark anniversaries. They pressed flowers and collected shells, birds' eggs and stones. They visited the theatre with suppers afterwards at the Trocadero. All this went on in London; she was essentially urban, this woman who would find herself on a farm in the veld.

Modern-minded John William McVeagh, proud of his clever daughter, was thinking of university for her, but was confronted with a rebellious girl who said she wanted to be a nurse. He was horrified, utterly overthrown. Middle-class girls did not become nurses, and he didn't want to hear anything about Florence Nightingale. Any skivvy could be a nurse, and if you become one, do not darken my door! Very well, said Emily Maude, and went off to the old Royal Free Hospital to begin her training. It was hard: conditions were bad, the pay was low, but she did well, and when she brilliantly passed her finals, her father was prepared to forgive her. She had done it all on her own, without him.

Whom, then, did she love, this poor girl brought up without affection? She was fond of her brother, John, but this was a far from simple emotion, and of course he was at boarding-school most of the time. Her sister, Muriel, was not her sort. Her many and varied friends? They were good sports, pals . . . Why did she fight so hard to become a nurse, if not that she needed to care for and to nurture people and to be loved for it? I have only just had this thought: I could have had it before.

Her training completed, she resumed, as far as possible, her social life. She had given up dreams of being a pianist, but continued to play the organ for churches, for instance, in Langham Place. She was part, in a small way, of the musical life of London. 'I could have been a real concert pianist,' she would say, until the end of her days. 'I had my LRAM. The Examiners told me I should go on.' I wonder at her energy. Nurses worked harder then than now. Yet there were musical evenings, and concerts and excursions. Also, holidays—always sea trips, for she loved the sea. She read, too, as did my father. Both knew enough of Wells and Shaw to be affected, and both judged society from a perspective of critical independence. There was a generation of young people, before World War One, for whom Wells and Shaw played the same tutoring role as Orwell did later.

Then began the war. 1914. She was a sister at the Royal Free Hospital, nursing the wounded soldiers who arrived in train-loads from the trenches. She had an album with verses written by the men she nursed back to life, and she appears as the traditional martinet with a heart of gold.

My father, at that time, was fighting in the trenches. He had two periods there. The first was ended by a timely appendix, otherwise he would have been killed with all his company in the Battle of the Somme. The second, timely again, was when he was wounded—shrapnel in the leg—preventing him from being killed with every other man in the company, at Passchendaele. I do not know exactly how long he was in the trenches, but altogether it was months. He said he was lucky not to have been killed a dozen times over. But the war did him in nevertheless: he lost a leg, and was psychologically damaged. He went into the fighting active and optimistic, and came out with what they then called shell-shock. He was in bed for months. My mother nursed him.

He was very ill, she said, and what was so worrying was his state of mind. I have a photograph of him in bed in the Royal Free Hospital, a handsome man, but minus a leg and inwardly in torment. Beside him Sister McVeagh sits wearing her full white veil, sewing, her eyes on her handiwork. 'Before she was thought of,' says the caption, meaning me, their first child. The date is September 1917.

She was thirty-three, a year older than her mother had been when she died giving birth to her third child. Sister McVeagh was facing a hard, a very hard, choice. She had been asked if she would accept the matronship of St George's Hospital—an honour, at her age. Usually much older women became matrons and ran great hospitals. But she liked nursing: did she want to become an administrator? Besides, matrons were such martinets! She had suffered under these formidable women, did she want to become one? And here was Captain Tayler, of whom she had become very fond, wanting to marry her. There were no men left, they were all killed. Would she be asked again? She had always thought of herself as—had always been told she was—very plain. Did she want to marry him? Did she want to marry at all, since her real love, the man she ought to have married, was dead?

He had been a young doctor in the hospital with whom, my father confirmed, she had had an understanding. His little picture, torn out of a newspaper that recorded his death by drowning in a ship sunk by the Germans, stood for ever on her dressing-table. He had a soft, boyish face. The understanding between them, the death, my mother's unhappiness were observed by my father who always spoke of him with pain. 'Your poor mother,' he would say, 'he was a good chap, that young doctor.'

It took her a long time to decide, and she became ill with the strain of it all. As a nurse she should have known what she had to face in a man so damaged. Later she would say, often: 'If we knew when we were young what was going to happen to us, then . . . '

She really had no idea, then or ever, of the mental world my father lived in. I am not only talking of his depression after the war. Quite simply, he had a dimension that she lacked. For a long time I thought it was the awfulness of the war that had given him his sensitiveness to other people, his broadness of outlook. Their experiences, after all, had not been so different.

His upbringing had been as bad as hers—savage, I was going to say, and yes, the word can stand: her impatient ruthlessness, I once thought, was the legacy of her childhood. But he had been much beaten at school and at home, over-disciplined, and harshly misunderstood. He, like her, had escaped as soon as he could. Years later I met people who had known him as a young man— and what the war had done was to confirm his essential nature: he had always been contemplative and philosophical. 'Your father had his own way of seeing things,' cried a former girlfriend, 'and I would often rather not have known what he was thinking.' And another said, not without ambiguity, that she had never been so well understood. He was kind; he was generous; she had not met anyone like him; but there was something detached in him which was hard to take. And this detachment was a part of his deepest characteristic—an understanding of impermanence, change.

I believe that his nature, so different from hers, was why my mother married him. She knew she had limitations—how could she not, brought up constantly against this magnanimity in everything? 'Don't you see, old girl, that's how things *are*?' he would say, amazed at her pettiness, her inability to see: he had been watching Life at it again, working out one of its little games. He was unsurprised, interested: she, always, rebellious.

To put her dilemma squarely: what she respected most in him, what gave her access to a largeness she would never have known without him, was precisely what did both her and him in: these fine ways of thinking, his scope, were always overthrowing her best self, which was a magnificent common sense. She had married a weak man, then? But his weakness was obviously stronger than her strength, always pulling her further away from what would best suit her. A weak man? Yet he was not weak by nature; it was the war that had distorted him. *Weak!* How else could you describe him? Always refusing to make judgements, take stands; always insisting on what he called the long view— you'd think there was nothing he respected . . . And yet. Life was not a simple business; she suspected he was nearer to understanding it than she would ever be.

I have an image of them, confronting Life in such different ways. He looks it straight in the face, with a dark, grim, ironical

171

recognition. But she, always being disappointed in ways he could never be, has a defiant, angry little air: she has caught Life out in injustice *again*. 'How can you!' she seems to be saying, exasperated, to Life. 'It's not right to behave like that!' And she gives a brisk, brave little sniff.

They were married. They did not feel up to a proper wedding. For one thing they were Wells and Shaw people, and white weddings were ridiculous (obviously soon to become obsolete!), and for another, his mother disapproved of Sister McVeagh: she was going to rule him with a rod of iron, said this ruler with the rod. My father was elegant, as always, when he still cared about clothes. My mother wore a dress she clearly had given a lot of thought to: only recently, when I was writing the Jane Somers books, did I realize that my mother (who could, I think, be something like Jane Somers if she lived now) very much enjoyed clothes, even though for most of her life she did not have the money to buy them, or the opportunity to wear them.

It was on the wedding night, they joked, that my mother must have got pregnant, though they were armed with the works of Marie Stopes, and had decided not to have a baby yet, if at all. He was still so low in spirits: he simply did not seem able to pull himself out of his ugly state of mind. And she was ill, she did not know why, but it was probably overwork from the war. And there was all that flu about, so many people dying everywhere: everything was so depressing about the war. It was 1919.

They left for Persia. He had to leave England—he couldn't stand it—so why not Persia? My mother, being a woman of her time, was ready to go off and live in the Middle East, even though she knew nothing about it. A close friend was a missionary in Japan; her brother, John, never at home in the Navy, was about to become a rubber planter in Malaya.

Persia was then divided into spheres of influence, mainly French and British. Britain had finance, and my father was going to manage a bank in Kermanshah. Before the war he had been a clerk in a bank, and to have to go back to it was awful for him; but at least he was getting out of England, where he knew he could never live again. Coming back from the trenches he felt as all the soldiers of that war did: betrayed by the politicians who had lied to them and did not keep promises; betrayed by the civilians who talked patriotic nonsense and had no idea of what the trenches were like; betrayed by the jingoistic newspapers; betrayed by the Armistice which would make another war inevitable. It was stupid to treat the Germans like this, one should take the long view. None of the Tommies felt vindictive. Any Tommy could tell the politicians they were being stupid. A funny thing, wasn't it? he would demand all his life (my mother half agreeing with him, feeling that she should, while her nature rebelled): any ordinary person could see it, the politicians couldn't. Why is it that ordinary people have so much more sense than politicians when it is the politician's job to be sensible?

This was the first time in her life when my mother would need a lot of clothes, and she took trunks full of them. She also took the necessities for a middle-class nursery as prescribed by one Dr Truby King and other mentors. The layette for a baby then consisted of dozens of everything. Napkins thick and thin, and napkin liners. Vests long and short, inner and outer. Petticoats of various lengths, of flannel and of lawn, embroidered and tucked and edged with lace. Long and short dresses of pin-tucked and embroidered lawn. Caps. Shawls. Not to mention binders made of thick material which supported the baby's stomach as if it were a wound from which entrails might spill. This layette itself must have been enough to dismay any woman, make her feel helpless, feel at least that an ordeal lay ahead. It all assumed servants of course. Those exquisite dresses alone took hours to iron, not to mention the dressing and undressing of the helpless infant, who was also supposed to be fed every two or three hours, day and night, and, if bottle-fed—a recommended practice—the preparations were like those for a surgical operation.

I used to read those lists on the farm in Rhodesia, dazzled by incredulity: I was surrounded by black babies living contented and naked inside a fold of cloth on their mothers' backs.

It was 'Maude' and 'Michael' Tayler who arrived in Persia. My mother had always disliked Emily, I suppose because it was the name of her mother, but she liked Maude, because of Tennyson's Maud. She had been trying to shed Emily for years. She would not have Alfred for my father: a common name. And what did he think about it? I can hear him: 'Oh Lord, old thing, who cares? What does it matter? If it makes you happy, then . . . ' He was made Michael because of *Peter Pan*.

The Westminster Bank allotted Maude and Michael an enormous house, made of stone that was carved and fretted, with great arches along the verandas and arched windows, and surrounded by wonderful gardens. Servants—gardeners, cooks, people who cleaned the house, shopped—did everything. My mother hardly mentioned the servants, except to say that households were regulated by protocol, and that the mistress of the house knew her place and did what she was told. She thought this amusing: not a hint here of what in Africa became a neurotic preoccupation: the shortcomings of the black servants.

For my father Kermanshah was what he had dreamed of: an ancient town on a high, empty, brown landscape, the high, blue sky, the mountains all around with the snow on them. When I went to Granada for the first time I knew it was like Kermanshah: gardens, the sounds of water running everywhere, the smell of the dust . . . My father was managing the bank; he was not at anybody's beck and call. He rode everywhere, for he would not allow his wooden leg to make him less active. He liked the spacious house, and the release, at least to an extent, from English respectability.

My mother was having a difficult pregnancy, morning sickness being only one of the complications. She was expecting a son, Peter John. Why did she not even consider the possibility of a daughter? Her passionate identification with a son was, I think, because of her brother, John, who was not clever, did not care very much what he did, and yet went as if by right into the Navy. I think she most bitterly envied him, but to feel like this was not being a good sort. She was the one born to be an officer in His Majesty's Navy! She was the clever one, who adored everything about the sea, about ships, was never seasick. She was resourceful and quick-witted. She was decent and good-humoured and able to get on with people. An authoritarian person, happy in a structured life, she was able to take and to give orders. Of course, the negative aspects of this particular personality were also hers: the inability to put herself into the shoes of people who were different; a contempt for weakness; a lack of understanding of what she described as 'morbid': the ambiguous, the witty, the equivocal—these areas would always be suspect, and she was threatened by them.

I can only guess, hurt for her, at how much she must have felt frustrated as a girl, seeing her slow brother get what ought to have been hers too. And yet she never said anything, except in jolly little jokes, brave jokes. What she felt had to come out indirectly.

The birth was difficult. I was delivered with forceps that left a scarlet birthmark over one side of my face. Above all, I was a girl. When the doctor wanted to know my name, and heard that none had been prepared, he looked down at the cradle and said softly, 'Doris?' This scene: the doctor's weariness after the long night, his soft, tactful, but reproachful query, was vividly enacted by my mother, like many other scenes.

Of course I resented it all bitterly, particularly that she did not even see that it was likely to make me angry. How could she stand there, with her customary determined little smile, her brisk social manner, telling me that I was not wanted in the first place; that to have a girl was a disappointment that nearly did her in altogether after that long labour; that she had no milk for me and I had to be bottle-fed from the start and I was half-starved for the first year and never stopped screaming because she did not realize that cows' milk in Persia was not as rich as real English milk; that I was an impossibly difficult baby, and then a tiresome child, quite unlike my little brother, Harry, who was always so good. And so she let the nurse cope with me, and looked after Harry herself.

Better say, and be done with it: my memories of her are all of antagonism, and fighting, and feeling shut out; of pain because the baby born two-and-a-half years after me was so much loved when I was not. She would recognize none of this, nor accept it. The way she saw it was that her childhood had been cold and loveless, and she would make sure that her children were governed by love. Love was always being invoked; and I became an expert in emotional blackmail by the time I was five. She didn't like me—that was the point. It was not her fault: I cannot think of a person less likely than myself to please her. But it would have been impossible for her to admit it: a mother loves her child, a child its mother. And that's that!

My father hated it when he was transferred to Tehran, to a branch of the bank where he was not manager and had to work under someone else, and where he had to live in a house he thought English and stuffy. But my mother loved it. At last, suitable nurseries, instead of those great stone rooms that curtains and rugs could not soften. I remember the tall, square day-nursery, the heavy red velvet curtains and the lace ones behind them, the brass fender with the tall dangerous fire, the suffocating plenty of things, things, things. And, of course, my brother, the 'baby' (he was called Baby until he was seven and fought for self-determination) who was the centre of everything. And the scolding, fussy nurse.

In Tehran my mother also loved the social life, which was like the pleasures of her girlhood over again. About 'the Legation set' she would talk wistfully in Africa, while my father, half sighing, regarded her with his familiar expression: incredulity, curiosity, held in check by irony. How could she enjoy those boring jolly evenings with boring jolly people? He loathed musical evenings with people singing the 'Indian Love Lyrics' and 'The Road to Mandalay' to each other, while my mother played. (She played alone, for her own pleasure, music these people found highbrow.) He hated the dinner parties, receptions, garden parties and picnics; she could not have enough of them. He would tell the story of a certain Englishman in Persia who, urged by his family to let them have a picnic, put his children on donkeys, blindfolded them, and had them led around and around the garden for an hour, when they were unblindfolded, and saw the feast prepared for them in a corner of their own garden. Meanwhile he retired to the library. A fellow spirit! My mother only laughed. 'Don't you dare try it,' she said.

Persia, particularly Tehran, was the best time in my mother's life.

When they had been in Persia for five years, leave was due, after which they intended to come back. He did not much want to: would he really have to work in a bank for the rest of his life? He had had a country childhood, and always wanted to be a farmer.

It was summer, the Red Sea a furnace, and dangerous for

children. They decided—which means, my mother decided—to travel back across Russia. Ours was the first family to use that route after the Revolution, through the Caspian to Moscow. 1924, and everything was in chaos. On an oil-tanker in the Caspian, my mother sat up all night to keep the lights on us, for there were swarms of lice. A shadow fell on an arm: mine, which became red and swollen with bites. Typhus abounded. The trains were ancient, also lice-ridden, no food on them. On every station were crowds of starved children, orphans; and the peasant women selling a hard-boiled egg or some bread had to defend themselves against these *bezprizorniks*, when my mother got off to buy something, anything at all, to eat. She was still on the platform once when our train left without her. I remember the terror of it: she had vanished. It took her a day and a half to catch up. She had to fight her way on to a goods train, had to 'tell them what to do—*they* didn't know—I had to make them telegraph our train to wait for me.' All in English, of course. At the frontier, informed that we did not have the right visas, she had told the man at Immigration not to be so silly. For years my father collapsed into laughter, remembering the poor, ragged, half-starved Bolshevik with a rifle 'that wouldn't bring down a pigeon,' confronted by a British matron. 'Oh Lord,' wept my father, 'I can see it now. Don't be silly, she said, and he was raring to shoot the lot of us.' 'Did I get us in or did I not?' demanded my mother, not really understanding why he laughed so much, but knowing she was in the right. 'Oh, you got us in all right!'

In Moscow, in the hotel, the chambermaids begged to bath and dress us, because they had not seen normal, well-fed children. My mother spoke of this with calm, proprietary pride: that the Russians were in this terrible disorganized condition was of course only another proof of the virtues of the British and our Empire.

Six months' leave, in England. My memories of it are many, all of cold, damp, dreariness, ugliness, a series of snapshots illustrating my loathing for the place. My parents took us to visit relations, such as my mother's stepmother, now a distinguished old lady living on a minute pension. They did not enjoy it. My father wanted only to leave England, even more stuffy than he remembered, and my mother yearned to return to Tehran. They visited the 1924 Empire Exhibition at Wembley, and the Southern

Rhodesia stand had maize cobs eighteen inches long, and the posters, yards high, claimed that anyone could make his fortune in maize-farming within five years.

My father had about a thousand pounds' capital and a pension because he had lost his leg in the war. This was his chance.

What did they imagine they were going to? Certainly they expected a social life not unlike that in Tehran, for my mother had trunks full of clothes from Harrods. Also curtains and hangings from Liberty, and visiting-cards. Also a governess, Biddy O'Halloran, aged twenty-one. Perhaps they had heard of the lively goings-on in Nairobi? Not that my mother would have approved of those fast ways. She could not approve of Biddy, who had shingled hair and wore lipstick. These modern girls . . . all her life my mother would use phrases like this, without inverted commas.

It must have been painful, giving up Tehran, to go off to be a farmer's wife in yet another new country. She would not really have minded staying in England—that is to say, London. She was still, every fibre of her, a Londoner. Remembering England, she thought of the streets, buses, trams, theatres, parks, of London. She did not mind the conventional in the way my father did. If he had been prepared to go back into the Westminster Bank somewhere in London, she would have given up the pleasures of Tehran with equanimity. And then she would have lived out her life in conformity with her nature, a useful and energetic middle-class woman in, let's say, Wimbledon.

Instead, she set off for the middle of Africa with her crippled husband, who was steadily getting more prickly and solitary, with practically no money, and her two children, one of whom was born to be a trouble and a sorrow to her. Did she know anything about Africa, or about farming? Not a thing! But it didn't seem to matter.

I think she saw Africa as some little interlude, a station on her way, soon to be passed. Nothing had ever happened to my mother to prepare her for what she would find.

It was a slow German boat. My mother loved the gales that sent the other passengers below, leaving her on the bridge with the captain. This, and the deck games and the fancy-dress parties, made up for her husband, who wanted only to sit and watch the sea, and for her daughter, who was being consistently impertinent, and who cut up her evening dresses with scissors when she was forced to go to bed early so as not to interfere with the evening's good times. The boat loafed around the Cape to Beira where they caught the train to Salisbury. Outside Salisbury was a place called Lilfordia that boarded settlers while they were buying farms. (Lilfordia was the farm of 'Boss' Lilford, later Ian Smith's guide and mentor.) My mother left her children with the governess and went with her husband by Scotch cart to look at farms. The settlers were being offered land at about ten pounds an acre (at today's values), the money advanced by the Land Bank. The land had been cleared of the black people who had been living on it: they were dispatched to the Reserves, or told to move to land that hadn't yet been allocated to whites. This was 'opening up the country for white civilization,' a description my mother never could see any reason to criticize.

The farm they bought was in Lomagundi, seventy miles from Salisbury, a modest fifteen hundred acres, but we were free to run our cattle and to cut grass and wood on the miles of government land which was at the frontier of 'white civilization' with nothing between us and Portuguese East Africa a couple of hundred miles away.

The land was sparsely settled, the farms huge. The nearest farmhouses to ours were three, four, five miles away. It was virgin bush: a few trees had been cut for mine furnaces. Every kind of animal lived there: sable, eland, kudu, bushbuck, duiker, anteaters, wild cats, wild pigs, snakes. There were flocks of guinea-fowl, partridges, hawks, eagles, pigeons, doves—birds, birds, birds. Dawns were explosions of song: the nights noisy with owls and nightjars and birds whose names we never knew; all day birds shrilled and cooed and hammered and chattered. But paradise had already been given notice to quit. The leopards and baboons had gone to the hills, the lions had wandered off, the elephants had retreated to the Zambezi Valley, the land was emptying.

But it was still a wilderness that my parents were taking on. The farm itself was approached by a disused mine track, a dirt road. The railway was seven miles away. Not one acre had been cleared for planting. The labourers were people who had been savagely defeated in a war thirty-five years before, and who left their villages and came out to work only because they had to pay the poll tax imposed on them precisely to make them work.

Having found their farm, my parents came back to collect the children. Their daughter as usual had been very naughty indeed, much worse than ever before: she had lied, stolen, run away, sulked and screamed. My mother knew it was all the fault of this travelling about: children need an ordered existence. She got us into a covered wagon drawn by twenty or so oxen, while her husband rode alongside it on his horse. The journey took five days. Inside the wagon was everything they possessed.

While the trees were being cleared off the hill where the house was to be built, we lodged at the gold-mine just over the ridge.

Settlers always built themselves mud-and-thatch huts, joined by verandas and expected to last only a year or so, to be replaced after the first good season by brick and tin. Our house was a single elongated hut, divided into four rooms. Its walls were of mud smeared over poles and whitewashed, the roof thatch cut from the grass in the vleis, the floor of stamped mud and dung.

All the floors were covered with black linoleum, and furniture was made from petrol and paraffin boxes stained black and curtained with flour sacks that were dyed and embroidered by my mother. In the front room, which had windows all around it, 'like the prow of a ship,' as my mother insisted, were Persian rugs, Liberty curtains, a piano and the heavy display silver of the period.

While my mother supervised the gang of black men building the house, my father watched the teams who cleared the bush for planting.

Then there was the business of Biddy O'Halloran, who turned out so badly. She had definitely expected something like Nairobi, and found herself stuck in this lonely and savage place with suitors of the wrong class. Every unattached male for fifty miles came visiting to propose to her, and she did not have as much time for the children as my mother thought was due. There were quarrels, and she departed back home. Then, about a year after the arrival in Africa, my mother became ill and took to her bed and stayed there. It was her heart! It is clear now that she was in an acute anxiety state, was having a breakdown. Neither her doctor in Salisbury, nor she (a nurse) could see it. The worst for her, of course, was the isolation. What my father revelled in—for he had at last found the life that suited him—was destroying her. Having always been surrounded by people, she now had only the blacks, towards whom she had had from the start all the attitudes typical of the settler: they were primitive, dirty, stupid. She was never able to see that there was anything interesting in them. Her neighbours were lower-middle-class and working-class, mostly Scottish, who had come out before the War and had got rich on maize. She did not want to seem snobbish, but what did she have in common with them? She had no intention of spending her life talking about gardening and recipes and dress patterns. But that was what her life now was, just like theirs.

She got out of bed, complained of a thousand aches and pains, went back again. She complained continually, and it was unlike her, for it simply wasn't done to make a fuss! She lay in a bed specially made by a neighbour who ran a timber mill, with attachments for books and magazines, and summoned her children to her throughout the day to comfort her. 'Poor sick Mummy,' she insisted, and we responded with fervent but (in my case at least) increasingly resentful embraces.

But this was certainly not all that went on at her bedside. Early childhood is when children learn best, and nothing was going to get in the way of our instruction, according to Montessori. In and out of bed, she read to us, told us stories; she was a marvellous teacher of small children. We were taught geography by means of piles of mud and sand left over from the housebuilding—making continents and countries and mountains that hardened in the sun and that, for oceans and rivers, could be filled with water. She taught us arithmetic with seeds and hens' eggs and baby chicks. She made us understand the solar system through games in which we were planets, the moon, the sun. We were made to notice stars, birds, animals. For a while we were taught by a correspondence course, but its lessons were not nearly as good as hers, and she ordered us books from England and two periodicals whose impossibly high standards of writing would find no equal today. The *Children's Newspaper* offered news about discoveries, inventions, archaeological finds, beasts and birds, and the *Merry-Go-Round* printed stories and poems by

writers like Walter de la Mare and Eleanor Farjeon. It was my
mother who introduced me to the world of literature into which I
was about to escape from her.

And then my mother got herself out of bed, and went on
living. She had been ill for a year. I wonder if she ever understood
that her illness had been a way of denying what she knew she had
to face. What courage that must have taken! I know it and I
admire it, but I can't put myself in her place. It was the farm, the
veld, that she hated, that trapped her. She was planning, scheming,
dreaming of escaping from it, from the moment she arrived. But
the farm, the veld, Africa is to me, quite simply, the luckiest thing
that ever happened.

Writing about my mother is difficult. I keep coming up
against barriers, and they are not much different now from
what they were then. She paralysed me as a child by the anger
and pity I felt. Now only pity is left, but it still makes it hard to
write about her. What an awful life she had, my poor mother!
But it was certainly no worse than my father's, and that is the
point: he was equipped by nature for hard times, and she was
not. He may have been a damaged, an increasingly sick man; she
was strong and full of vitality. But I am not as sorry for him as I
am for her. She never understood what was happening to her.

Candia McWilliam

The Many Colours of Blood

Candia McWilliam

We lived much of our life in the houses of others, and in our own house there lived with us most of the time people other than ourselves. My father worked for the National Trust for Scotland and had to travel all over the country. We stayed sometimes in green castles, sometimes in fish houses, sometimes bothies, while my father worked on the recording and saving of these buildings with their poetic names: Crathes, Culross, Tantallon, Pittenweem, Kirriemuir, Culzean, Craigievar.

My parents' house had been full of dry rot when they bought it in 1954, a modest grey sliver in a terraced Edinburgh crescent with steps up to the front and what is known as an 'area' beneath for storing coal, which came, as did milk, and beer for the pub at the end of the street, by dray. We gave the horses oats for their nosebags, and lump sugar; my mother collected their rotund droppings for the garden. Boys on their way to dig the allotments behind the crescent sometimes threw bangers under the hooves of a dray horse. The gunpowder in the firecrackers smelt more intoxicating than the heavy pall of fermenting hops from the Ushers Vaux brewery that set upon our part of town when there was no wind from the sea. All the time one smelt coal. The first brush Edinburgh children had with sex was a joke; in Edinburgh, sex is what you carry coal in.

In our basement was a large kitchen with an old range that must once have served the whole house. The range had to be fed by my parents with coal twice a day, and riddled more often to stir it into action, when it would produce a swelling, short and sulky heat that caused the laundry, hung above it on a pulley with curly wrought-iron brackets, to steam like a winded man in the cold. If the weather was fresh without the wetness of haar to it we hung the washing in the garden on the line between spindly six-foot-long wooden props. We did the washing in two stone sinks, using a washboard whose surface was covered with a metal at once hard and soft that may have been zinc. Round her waist my mother wore a bag of pegs; a peg bag was an acceptable womanly gift at that time, and to be able to sew a peg bag was part of my education, so important that I was three times taught how to do it at my emphatically, Scottishly, academic school. The third time we sewed a peg bag we did it against time, as though the task were a competitive event in the race to domesticity.

The pegs themselves had a ruthless look like tribal jewellery. Around my middle I too had a peg bag, whose toy pegs were bright and fragile. These were stocked by Mr McDonald the newsagent, who kept a basket of crunchy Cellophane sachets of toys priced around threepence and made in Hong Kong. Those seemed exotic words; I see them printed on cheap card, acid green lettering misaligned or incorporated in the moulding of a doll's pink neck, MADE IN HONG KONG, a declaration suggesting to me a glamour all the more vivid for its certainty of short life. The colours of these frail toys were harsh and tropical in Edinburgh, whose granite and sea mist and inhabitants' clothing hardly ever pushed beyond the seemlier shades. My mother and I took a bus to look at an avocado once, as Londoners at one time had visited the camelopard, or giraffe. No one bought the green leather pear, and I am not sure if anyone knew how it might be opened.

My mother pined for colour in her short life. Sometimes she forced it into being, for which I as a native Scot found it hard to forgive her then. Towards the end of her life she began collecting me from school in wigs that were not intended to imitate reality. Her own fair hair was long; over it she might helm herself with her silver wig, or a strawberry blonde *coup sauvage* that gave her the look of an actress who has at short notice had to fill in for the man playing opposite her. She did not seem even to hope to convince. What she sought was, paradoxically, an inconspicuousness impossible for a woman of her appearance. She was held to be 'too friendly with tradesmen' and I was once told at school that the greengrocer 'had tried to kiss the Englishwoman among the greens'; it was Christmas time and the ceiling was all mistletoe in the bunch, so she was very likely kissing him in seasonal innocence. Her accent made her 'the Englishwoman'; she didn't have a gout of English blood, but a radio-drama quality of overemphasis that was dated even then seems in my memory to mark her speech, as it does mine. It comes from my grandmother, who, as an actress and singer on stage from the age of five, spoke to carry, from the pit of her breath. My mother spoke Italian in Valvona & Crolla, the Italian grocer that was like an unofficial club for many war-exhausted people homesick for a Mediterranean they had not, or had only briefly, seen. Edinburgh is still full of Italians. Sweet teeth and a passion for starch married happily. The best fish and chips (Brattisani's) and the best ice-cream (Lucca's of Musselburgh) and generations of handsome, double-accented children are the issue.

It wasn't as though my mother had been transplanted from somewhere strange and fiery up to the north. The laurel and brick of her English childhood were actually less exotic than Edinburgh's silver and pearl and black and the river roaring along behind our garden, prone to flood, and all but classically named the Water of Leith. But the forms of eccentricity encouraged by Edinburgh's bracing traditions did not yet include her particular flavour, in which staginess combined as it often does with absence of vanity. Her energies were curiosity, inventiveness and an affectionate nature that did not understand how to tally, invest or calculate. In a city of thrift where things were made to last, the ephemeral was glorified by attendant disapproval. Neighbours watched for waste. A bit of income might have allowed her to be euphemized as bohemian; she had a way with rubbish, of turning what she had totted from street sales into something rare until the time of dusting and falling to dust. It might not tolerate much light and there were holes in everything and too many cats, but she deployed her flotsam like precious cargo.

Costume and making do seemed to be part of her, as they were of her mother. For her beauty my grandmother was married by my builder grandfather who was as Scots as harling. They had my mother only, with whom they were not invariably pleased. Her talents and dramatic appearance seemed to them wilful defiance of what they had worked for.

My mother's clothes came from a dress agency with a sad name such as the Scottish Ladies' Benevolent Frock Exchange. This discreet ossuary of fashions was known as 'The Dead Women's', with a long 'o' as in 'womb'—'The Dead Woo-men's'. My mother went through racks of coats that had represented thrift and respectability and regular attendance at the kirk with her eagle eye for something a bit off-key, the off-centre thing she hunted.

Occasionally we would go into a shop that sold things first hand. (Apart from food, I hardly recall her having anything first hand. It was a necessity that became a preference.) I had to be restrained in what might be called fresh shops from smelling the merchandise. Inserting myself in between crisp scented frocks on their big cartwheel rail, I would tread the circle like a drunken donkey, round and round in the stirring stuff with its nylon waft of blossom and insecticidal net. I was used to the smells of mothballs and cats from our hours among reeking mattresses, bargaining underground with old women who wore hats indoors. I did not dislike the junk shops but had a childish intolerance of kind overtures from the very old and the peculiar. I wanted the smoothness and flawless good humour of a life I saw on hoardings: *'You'll wonder where the yellow went/When you brush your teeth with Pepsodent.'*

Both my parents, all their lives, fell easily into conversation with strangers. Neither of them liked to miss a story, and they were curious and not easy to embarrass—kinder to these strangers than to themselves or each other. A need for talk that began in her childhood was perhaps another reason for my mother's listening; she had no idea of when to stop, of how to preserve herself. My father's similar habits were to do with his anarchist's openness to life and a patience that could drive you mad. They could not resist drunks, tramps or beggars. Approached by such a person, whichever parent it was would listen to the story, even if it contradicted the one told two days before.

The Grassmarket was where the drunks with blue faces lived. They drank Blue Billy, a mix of meths and Brasso. They did not often wear shoes and had no understanding of cars, which occasionally blethered down the black sweep of setts, as the deep, orderly Edinburgh cobbles are called, granite dovetailed with the precision of igloo blocks. The drinkers would freeze when a car came as though at Medusa's passing. Most of the men had been at sea, in the war or on the fishing boats. Tears came to them, after so long being awash with the drink, with a tidal ease. My mother responded as though to romance, aware that politeness was too dim a mode for the drunk man's intense register. So surprising for those times was her appearance that perhaps they considered her one of them, in spite of the solid child at her side.

Such encounters could be alarming to a child. The worst was

just after we got our first car, when my father was driving me and himself to England overnight on some business for the Trust, not then the plump institution it is now. We had an old, black Humber Snipe, with red leather seats, which was just as well.

Rain, the zippy repetitions of windscreen wipers and the for some hours certain presence of my elusive father composed a selfish bliss for me. I was six. We passed through the cooked-meat coloured town of Biggar. In the headlights was a man with a big head, waving astride the centre of the red metalled road. He had on a belted mackintosh. His shoulders and bent head seemed dark with the rain. He had the raw build of someone in the services, but new to it, not fully hardened to the life. We stopped and my father rolled down the window on my side, smiling his kind dog's smile, leaning over me.

The hitchhiker lowered his head and looked down at us, a child and a friendly man. Before he spoke he put his hands in at the window. They were wet and red and in one of them was the top half of a bottle, which he did not brandish so much as flourish, loosely, as though offering tired flowers. His head and shoulders were bloody too. He was asking to be taken to a sea port, any one at all. He seemed indifferent to the pain that must accompany the blood, which seemed to be coming up out of the top of his head and spilling slowly down to be thinned by the rain. At the top of the head among the hair the blood was slow. It lay along his shorn red curls.

My father told him to hop in. The rest of the night was spent in stopping off to wash, feed and at last, when dawn came up over the chemists of the Borders, bandage this man, out of whose head came further bits of his, or someone's, bottle, that my father picked out. The reason for the fight was forgotten, and its subject, also its other participant or participants.

When the Biggar man had gone off to sleep, my father stopped the car and got out in order to rearrange him in the back so that he might be more comfortable. 'If he wakes up and sees a child, at least he won't be alarmed,' he said. 'You jump in next to him.'

Blood red is a newly terrible colour every time, worse when it is in the dark and temporarily black, the odd lasso of advancing and withdrawing headlights pulling tight to remind you of its unshaded redness. The man snored, with his head right back on the red leather, his broken pink lips and red eyelashes coming to colour slowly in the Lowland dawn.

When he woke up, he pleaded to be back in Biggar. Back we went. Can this be so? The order of events is sketchy to me now, but I remember the many colours of his blood. Perhaps he is always there at the roadside, each night, to tempt those who feel they can help things at all, a drunken sailor for all weathers.

With my mother, the victims were mainly women. Just as she would not allow mangled birds or shrews to perish in their absent tiny way without bringing them in for warmth and hopeless last rites, she picked up wrecks. One walk we took regularly was along the river down to a row of working men's houses called the Colonies. These were serried rows of terraced cottages, each with its small washing green. There was a stone staircase set sideways up the front of each, leading to a top-storey front door, where the old might sit in the weather to grumble. Now favoured by middle-class couples with no children, these houses swarmed with families who gathered by the railings that dropped down to the river to gossip and play and chuck leftovers to the swans that begged there, braking in the water with their rubber feet. The water was clear and bright coppery brown and through it could be seen shards and remnants, bedsprings, broken tiles, bottle glass. I collected these treasures, using my minnow net, and watched them dry out, until like fish they lost their shine.

The walk was a short cut behind the big houses of Inverleith and the expanses of the Botanical Gardens (known as the Tanics to children thereabouts). It was called the Rocheid Path and it was dark and green and stank bitterly. A trembling bridge on chains led from the Rocheid Path over the river into the Colonies. So long fallen that the moss clipped it, a tree all but barred the mouth of the bridge, its branches gone for firewood. We would sit sometimes and make a picnic, spreading my mother's handkerchief and laying out a Pan Drop each. Squirrels came and once or twice she told my father that she had seen a red one, though I cannot remember ever doing so. Once in the country she said she saw a golden pheasant, one of those trailing glories with cadmium yellow earflaps, a neck thick with minute bevelled ruffles and a lorgnette-lifting gait.

Perhaps she did just want to see more colour than there was. But on a seemingly featureless field she would spy a hare standing among stalks in its own dry colour, and she saw spring flowers in the hours before they solidified into being open, so perhaps she was preternaturally sharp-eyed.

We were on the bridge over the Water of Leith, looking back down the Rocheid Path, when there was suddenly a woman and the abrupt running departure of a man in blue. His hair was black and all in one shining piece as if he had just risen from a deep dive. I saw clearly because he moved at such speed that he compressed the attention. The woman had hair the sheepish gold of the chiropodist's wool my mother wound around her two broken toes so that she could wear winklepickers.

Not young, but busty, in an apron and a coat thrown over the shoulders, the woman turned her face to us, patting at her neck with her finger ends as though feeling in surprise for sudden rain.

The blood was coming down fresh from her face, from cuts you could not see but for the rising red, that seemed thin, like water or spirits. It stung to see the thin razor cuts.

My mother took off her own headscarf as though it was too formal and took the shorter, older woman in her arms.

I suppose the woman had done her washing, pinned it up and crossed the bridge over from her family life in the Colonies for that assignation in the dark leafy short cut, so certain of warmth that she had not even put her arms into the sleeves of her coat. I feel certain that the man was her lover, because she kept on saying, 'He done it for he was so young.' My mother was calm. For all I knew, this might have been what happened as a rule when men and women met. We took the woman home. Her hands were freezing with shock and we each chafed one, I imitating my mother, who kept up a steady, encouraging flow of endearments that I recognized many years later as the words of exhortation used by midwives and other chance yet crucial helpmeets.

THE MANY COLOURS OF BLOOD

Living in the basement of our house there were always lodgers who would invite me down the inside stone stairs to visit them. A curtain hung at the bottom of the stairs; through it I passed from one set of habits to another. I became fond of disappearing and of trying on different lives. The lodgers were often students, and 'thesis' became a word by whose constipated mystery I was early oppressed. I associated the disordered reams of notes with a kind of outlaw freedom that seemed to have fled by the time the thing appeared, caught and bound. The poet with his staring hair who lived at one point below us seemed to have a happier relation to paper, using it like birdlime, waiting for words to fly and settle in their order.

For my parents, the lodgers were sometimes a means of escape from each other. My father came down to draw in the basement whenever he and my mother fought. Taking his delicious alcohol-scented FloMaster pen, he would hesitate, cigarette in mouth, breathing with his inadequate lungs, then stab at the whitewashed wall, sweeping, whirling and cross-hatching with the black pen, not stopping until he had completed a man-sized pastiche of a nineteenth-century zoological drawing. A chameleon with a Vitruvian scroll of tongue looked down with its turreted eyes to where the egg of a monstrous lyre-bird was hatching, the egg just burst to display a quivering tuning-fork.

My mother increasingly complained about my father's absences, so it was also for company that she passed through the curtain on the stone stair. Of all the lodgers it was Mr Sapietis the Latvian who was the most comforting for her, not because he intended to be but because nothing could surpass what he had seen. He had no fingernails or toenails. They had been pulled from him. He was a handsome man with a thin profile and a blue jersey dingleberried with clay, a potter. When I played in our garden he would come and talk to me and sometimes he would cry as he watched me play with my invented companions. Perhaps he was amazed at my assumption that invisible presences might be benevolent. He touched things quite slowly, as though he felt them more sharply than nailed men. He would hold my fat face and look into its want of knowledge as though trying to get something through my blank trust.

But the lodgers I loved most were Bengali. The wife stood

me on the table and wound me up in a green sari with a black mackerel zigzag; she brushed and oiled and braided my dull brown hair and finished off its diminishing point with tassels threaded with silver. The rice she cooked rose high on the dish instead of sinking into a milk pudding. The husband was training to be a doctor; his wife was at home all day. They had left at least one child back at home with the wife's parents, so I suppose that it was in some ways pleasant to have me around. There must have been days when she wanted me to be gone, because I hung around staring at everything she did, rinsing and rinsing and rinsing the rice, the hair, the washing, and spreading her hair out down from her overturned head as she dried it in front of the pale cream range with its hardly glowing mica windows.

My mother and I were continually cold. The Bengali woman must have been cold to the bone. We gathered round one of two paraffin heaters that leaked a sick-making but reassuring smell. When it was bitter we used a squat heater that plugged in and made a noise like an old dog. Dust came off it like midges in the beams of its heat.

The Bengali husband I recall less pictorially although he was among the first men whose elegance I noticed, one evening as he worked by very little light and I saw a poised white shirt sitting up in a chair, folded and turned back over each hardly visible forearm. As the light withdrew the shirt's wearer was included in the gloom, leaving only the white mauve shape deepening at the table.

While these welcome strangers came and went, my father was away attending to the residences, abodes, castles, byres, doocots, follies, palaces, huntingtowers, keeps, but and bens and ruins of Scotland. The country then was full of houses lying open to its consuming rain, their roofs dynamited off by owners no longer wanting to pay rates.

The damp air and the salt of the sea ate into lath and plaster even where there was a roof. Mouldings got fat with moisture like fruit and, like fruit, fell. An Englishman of predominantly Irish blood who assumed a satirical manner when speaking of Scotland's smugger, frowstier, more snobbish self-delusions, my father developed a feeling for the country's rational yet eccentric architecture that came to rule his life, and my own and my mother's lives with his.

I grew up jealous of buildings. Buildings were inexhaustible, work and recreation. The matter of saving houses is associated now with styles of life and with an upholstered luxury that is as destructive as the death-watch beetle. My father was suspicious of comfort; he preferred cigarettes to food. Tentative and ironic in speech, he mocked the gap between gloss and truth. He never went grey, but did not display a threatening boyishness because there was clearly no strength in his slimness; he was thin and never well, with a bad heart and dodgy lungs and a cough that pained its hearer. He trespassed everywhere (in Scotland there is no law of trespass, he said, and scaled a fence blaring with prohibitions) hunting the forgotten, the untraced, the deserted brides among houses. When involved with a house, he was dangerous. I do not remember often suspending a tension and concern for either of my parents. He climbed up ruins and along cracking beams, with more relish the higher and fainter the structure. Then he would forget his camera up there, so that he had to go back, past the willow-herb and toads and lifting roof-lead, or on his stomach along the splintering joists.

When I was lucky I went with him. It could be horrible, standing holding his T-square in rain while he sketched a neglected contemporary masterwork in Glenrothes, or when he rang the doorbell of a house whose entrance was grown over with giant hoary thistles and the reluctant interior footsteps began.

Once, we broached a house whose façade was a big classical dishface, curving in to a pediment yellow and crumbling as demerara sugar. A deer-faced woman in many old garments answered. Prepared by my self-consciousness and by experience for someone deranged or very old, I wasn't expecting this alert character. My father asked about the house and whether he might come in, somehow making it clear he was not selling anything nor wanting to do more than share his enthusiasm for William Adam.

The lawn was full of groundsel and plantain. It was moving by entanglement over the gravel to the house.

'Go away, we fly to America tomorrow,' lied the I realized beautiful woman with spirit.

Fly to *America*! A place so other that it might be brandished in that way, to hold off the little man. The woman used the exotic name as a spell to keep the sleep on her house that was swooning into ochre dust.

My father, understanding but frustrated, got back into the car, and we spun and jarred our way back down the drive under the settling rookeries, pursued by a blue dog the height of the brambles, heavy mayoral fat on its walrus back.

Suddenly the dog fell back, recoiling on to its crupper as though pulled. We caught on a high stone between the wet ruts of the drive. Fists pummelled the back window and then, holding on to the car for a footing, the beautiful liar came round to my father's side window and put her hand flat up to it till the palm was pale. He wound down the window with a can-opening movement, and the woman's voice said, 'Come in for a drink. We think we like you.' Like another deer, her husband had been watching us from the wet roses beside the house.

In the drawing-room that was cold as a disused quarry the dog was the source of heat. Batons of Brussels sprout tops like green maces stuck out of a jug in the fireplace. Perhaps the deer couple cracked off some sprouts when it was time to dine, in a dining-room whose ceiling rested for the most part on its long, oxblood-red, plaster-dimmed table.

One of the best outings my father and I took, away from my mother's neglected and in consequence tarnishing dazzle, was by steamboat to the Cathedral of the Isles on Great Cumbrae, a green island in the mouth of the River Clyde. My mother had told me that God did not exist. The car deck was aseethe with sheep whose malicious eyes rolled at the forcible enclosure, noses upon each other's backs as though to browse sweeter air, restive hooves tittupping on the iron deck, perilous as the small shoes of fat women.

The minister of the cathedral met us and took my father and me to his house through a sunken field of hard cold green daffodils. There in his bare kitchen we had bottled coffee, tinned milk and cake like masonry, with a brown sugar crystal on a string that he dangled briskly in each cup before pulling it out like a mouse by the tail. No slices were separable from the cake, which remained a rich idea, solid with potential but unresolved by practicalities.

The creation of a single building in which might worship people living on islands separated by hundreds of miles of bad-tempered water was a notion as potentially rich and impractical as the indivisible cake.

Unlike all the many other churches I had been into, almost always visiting for secular reasons, this large grey building held no sense of small accumulated human gestures. There were no notices, no blush of heating, no flowers, no kneeling woman to one side or abandoned mitten by the stoop. It might as well have been full of seagulls.

Aged nine, I took this as impersonal truth and perpetual magnificent indifference made manifest. I was comforted by what I thought was a revelation that all pain was temporary, everything solved by distance. It was as though I were being swung through the lenses on a telescope until the planet I lived on became a grain in the pollen pocket at the knee of a bumble-bee in some vast afternoon. It is a technique of painkilling that is unreliable but involuntary in the pessimistic adult mind, and I have been grateful more often than not that it came to me young.

The nervousness around my mother centred upon the absence of my father, and her thwarted glamour. It was probably I who thwarted it. Her impulse was to work and paint and draw. She was full of plans and had just begun to find a world under the chill, hard to lift, stone of Edinburgh. The Traverse Theatre used her, I think, as a cook. She and my father made and sold toys. Her art-school training was not used. Her desire to conform to an idea of wifehood led her into impersonations best not undertaken by an intelligent blonde of six foot two; she did not convince at coffee-mornings. She was desperate to earn but over-educated for the jobs she could get, full of ideas and talk but stuck with me, to whom she talked as though I were her age. I knew too much.

My mother and I spent what turned out to be her last day on a farm where long-eared Nubian goats were reared. Their colours were those of driftwood and breakfast cereal and they would eat cigarettes as soon as apples. Their lips moved like surreptitious gossips' mouths on the flat of the hand, mouthing meanly, 'I wouldn't like to say, but . . . ' It was easy to imagine these goats snaffling a living in a dusty market under the Egyptian sun.

We had come to see some pups, pointers, liver and white, with breaks in the tail as definite and slight as breaks in a fount of type. The weight of a pup, picked up, fell to its lowest point; it was like holding living dough.

The long mother lay on her side in an army bed on a frame that twanged under the twelve lives lived on it. One pup, a bitch, was marked with sharp spatters like a carnation. My mother pulled it out repeatedly to set it on her hand and let it run inside her green knitted jacket from the Dead Women's. She held it on her lap while we spent far too much time on this farm with strangers up a lane. She talked to the dog as if to herself, with the least admissable emotion, self-pity, smuggling itself out of her.

Lying to herself and to me, she said, as we left the unforthcoming woman she had eventually charmed and made her friend, and the several matter-of-fact children who had suffered my uninvited urban presence all day, 'We'll come back tomorrow for the puppy.'

The very idea summed up normality and life above ground, a life I imagined most other children led. Seldom had I gone to sleep happier, sleeping out the last hours of my mother's life in dreams of a dog.

PETER CAREY

A LETTER TO OUR SON

Before I have finished writing this, the story of how you were born, I will be forty-four years old, and the events and feelings which make up the story will be at least eight months old. You are lying in the next room in a cotton jump-suit. You have five teeth. You cannot walk. You do not seem interested in crawling. You are sound asleep.

I have put off writing this so long that, now the time is here, I do not want to write it. I cannot think. Laziness. Wooden shutters over the memory. Nothing comes, no pictures, no feelings, but the architecture of the hospital at Camperdown.

You were born in the King George V Hospital in Missenden Road, Camperdown, a building that won an award for its architecture. It was opened during the Second World War, but its post-Bauhaus modern style has its roots in that time before the First World War, with an optimism about the technological future that we may never have again.

I liked this building. I liked its smooth, rounded, shiny corners. I liked its wide stairs, I liked the huge sash-windows, even the big blue-and-white checked tiles: when I remember this building there is sunshine splashed across those tiles, but there were times when it seemed that other memories might triumph and it would be remembered for the harshness of its neon lights and emptiness of the corridors.

A week before you were born, I sat with your mother in a four-bed ward on the eleventh floor of this building. In this ward she received blood transfusions from plum-red plastic bags suspended on rickety stainless-steel stands. The blood did not always flow smoothly. The bags had to be fiddled with, the stand had to be raised, lowered, have its drip-rate increased, decreased, inspected by the sister who had been a political prisoner in Chile, by the sister from the Solomon Islands, by others I don't remember. The blood entered your mother through a needle in her forearm. When the vein collapsed, a new one had to be found. This was caused by a kind of bruising called 'tissuing'. We soon knew all about tissuing. It made her arm hurt like hell.

She was bright-eyed and animated as always, but her lips had a slight blue tinge and her skin had a tight, translucent quality.

She was in this room on the west because her blood appeared to be dying. Some thought the blood was killing itself.

A LETTER TO OUR SON

This is what we all feared, none more than me, for when I heard her blood-count was so low, the first thing I thought (stop that thought, cut it off, bury it) was cancer.

This did not necessarily have a lot to do with Alison, but with me, and how I had grown up, with a mother who was preoccupied with cancer and who, going into surgery for suspected breast cancer, begged the doctor to 'cut them both off.' When my mother's friend Enid Tanner boasted of her hard stomach muscles, my mother envisaged a growth. When my father complained of a sore elbow, my mother threatened the old man: 'All right, we'll take you up to Doctor Campbell and she'll cut it off.' When I was ten, my mother's brother got cancer, and they cut his leg off right up near the hip and took photographs of him, naked, one-legged, to show other doctors the success of the operation.

When I heard your mother's blood-count was low, I was my mother's son. I thought: cancer.

I remembered what Alison had told me of that great tragedy of her grandparents' life, how their son (her uncle) had leukaemia, how her grandfather then bought him the car (a Ford Prefect? a Morris Minor?) he had hitherto refused him, how the dying boy had driven for miles and miles, hours and hours while his cells attacked each other.

I tried to stop this thought, to cut it off. It grew again, like a thistle whose root has not been removed and must grow again, every time, stronger and stronger.

The best haematological unit in Australia was on hand to deal with the problem. They worked in the hospital across the road, the Royal Prince Alfred. They were friendly and efficient. They were not at all like I had imagined big hospital specialists to be. They took blood samples, but the blood did not tell them enough. They returned to take marrow from your mother's bones. They brought a big needle with them that would give you the horrors if you could see the size of it.

The doctor's speciality was leukaemia, but he said to us: 'We don't think it's anything really nasty.' Thus 'nasty' became a code for cancer.

They diagnosed megnoblastic anaemia which, although we did not realize it, is the condition of the blood and not the disease itself.

Peter Carey

Walking back though the streets in Shimbashi in Tokyo, your mother once told me that a fortune-teller had told her she would die young. It was for this reason—or so I remembered—that she took such care of her health. At the time she told me this, we had not known each other very long. It was July. We had fallen in love in May. We were still stumbling over each other's feelings in the dark. I took this secret of your mother's lightly, not thinking about the weight it must carry, what it might mean to talk about it. I hurt her; we fought, in the street by the Shimbashi railway station, in a street with shop windows advertising cosmetic surgery, in the Dai-Ichi Hotel in the Ginza district of Tokyo, Japan.

When they took the bone marrow from your mother's spine, I held her hand. The needle had a cruel diameter, was less a needle than an instrument for removing a plug. She was very brave. Her wrists seemed too thin, her skin too white and shiny, her eyes too big and bright. She held my hand because of pain. I held hers because I loved her, because I could not think of living if I did not have her. I thought of what she had told me in Tokyo. I wished there was a god I could pray to.

I flew to Canberra on 7 May 1984. It was my forty-first birthday. I had injured my back and should have been lying flat on a board. I had come from a life with a woman which had reached, for both of us, a state of chronic unhappiness. I will tell you the truth: I was on that airplane to Canberra because I hoped I might fall in love. This made me a dangerous person.

There was a playwrights' conference in Canberra. I hoped there would be a woman there who would love me as I would love her. This was a fantasy I had had before, getting on airplanes to foreign cities, riding in taxis towards hotels in Melbourne, in Adelaide, in Brisbane. I do not mean that I was thinking about sex, or an affair, but that I was looking for someone to spend my life with. Also—and I swear I have not invented this after the fact—I had a vision of your mother's neck.

I hardly knew her. I met her once at a dinner when I hardly noticed her. I met her a second time when I saw, in a meeting room, the back of her neck. We spoke that time, but I was argumentative and I did not think of her in what I can only call 'that way'.

And yet as the airplane came down to land in Canberra, I saw your mother's neck and thought: maybe Alison Summers will be there. She was the dramaturge at the Nimrod Theatre. It was a playwrights' conference. She should be there.

And she was. And we fell in love. And we stayed up till four in the morning every morning talking. And there were other men, everywhere, in love with her. I didn't know about the other men. I knew only that I was in love as I had not been since I was eighteen years old. I wanted to marry Alison Summers, and at the end of the first night we had been out together when I walked her to the door of her room, and we had, for the first time, ever so lightly, kissed on the lips—and also, I must tell you, for it was delectable and wonderful, I kissed your mother on her long, beautiful neck—and when we had kissed and patted the air between us and said 'all right' a number of times, and I had walked back to my room where I had, because of my back injury, a thin mattress lying flat on the floor, and when I was in this bed, I said, aloud, to the empty room: 'I am going to live with Alison.'

And I went to sleep so happy I must have been smiling.

She did not know what I told the room. And it was three or four days before I could see her again, three or four days before we could go out together, spend time alone, and I could tell her what I thought.

I had come to Canberra wanting to fall in love. Now I was in love. Who was I in love with? I hardly knew, and yet I knew exactly. I did not even realize how beautiful she was. I found that out later. At the beginning I recognized something more potent than beauty: it was a force, a life, an energy. She had such life in her face, in her eyes—those eyes which you inherited—most of all. It was this I loved, this which I recognized so that I could say—having kissed her so lightly— I will live with Alison. And know that I was right.

It was a conference. We were behaving like men and women do at conferences, having affairs. We would not be so sleazy. After four nights staying up talking till four a.m. we had still not made love. I would creep back to my room, to my mattress on the floor. We talked about everything. Your mother liked me, but

I cannot tell you how long it took her to fall in love with me. But I know we were discussing marriages and babies when we had not even been to bed together. That came early one morning when I returned to her room after three hours' sleep. We had not planned to make love there at the conference but there we were, lying on the bed, kissing, and then we were making love, and you were not conceived then, of course, and yet from that time we never ceased thinking of you and when, later in Sydney, we had to learn to adjust to each other's needs, and when we argued, which we did often then, it was you more than anything that kept us together. We wanted you so badly. We loved you before we saw you. We loved you as we made you, in bed in another room, at Lovett Bay.

When your mother came to the eleventh floor of the King George V Hospital, you were almost ready to be born. Every day the sisters came and smeared jelly on your mother's tight, bulging stomach and then stuck a flat little octopus-type sucker to it and listened to the noises you made.

You sounded like soldiers marching on a bridge.

You sounded like short-wave radio.

You sounded like the inside of the sea.

We did not know if you were a boy or a girl, but we called you Sam anyway. When you kicked or turned, we said, 'Sam's doing his exercises.' We said silly things.

When we heard how low Alison's blood-count was, I phoned the obstetrician to see if you were OK. She said there was no need to worry. She said you had your own blood-supply. She said that as long as the mother's count was above six there was no need to worry.

Your mother's count was 6.2. This was very close. I kept worrying that you had been hurt in some way. I could not share this worry for to share it would only be to make it worse. Also I recognize that I have made a whole career out of making my anxieties get up and walk around, not only in my own mind, but in the minds of readers. I went to see a naturopath once. We talked about negative emotions—fear and anger. I said to him, 'But I *use* my anger and my fear.' I talked about these emotions as if they were chisels and hammers.

This alarmed him considerably.

Your mother is not like this. When the haematologists saw how she looked, they said: 'Our feeling is that you don't have anything nasty.' They topped her up with blood until her count was twelve and although they had not located the source of her anaemia, they sent her home.

A few days later her count was down to just over six.

It seemed as if there was a silent civil war inside her veins and arteries. The number of casualties was appalling.

I think we both got frightened then. I remember coming home to Louisa Road. I remember worrying that I would cry. I remember embracing your mother—and you too, for you were a great bulge between us. I must not cry. I must support her.

I made a meal. It was salade niçoise. The electric lights, in memory, were all ten watts, sapped by misery. I could barely eat. I think we may have watched a funny film on video. We repacked the bag that had been unpacked so short a time before. It now seemed likely that your birth was to be induced. If your mother was sick she could not be looked after properly with you inside her. She would be given one more blood transfusion, and then the induction would begin. And that is how your birthday would be on 13 September.

Two nights before your birthday I sat with Alison in the four-bed ward, the one facing east, towards Missenden Road. The curtains were drawn around us. I sat on the bed and held her hand. The blood continued its slow viscous drip from the plum-red bag along the clear plastic tube and into her arm. The obstetrician was with us. She stood at the head of the bed, a kind, intelligent woman in her early thirties. We talked about Alison's blood. We asked her what she thought this mystery could be. Really what we wanted was to be told that everything was OK. There was a look on Alison's face when she asked. I cannot describe it, but it was not a face seeking medical 'facts'.

The obstetrician went through all the things that were not wrong with your mother's blood. She did not have a vitamin-B deficiency. She did not have a folic-acid deficiency. There was no iron deficiency. She did not have any of the common (and easily fixable) anaemias of pregnancy. So what could it be? we asked, really only wishing to be assured it was nothing 'nasty'.

'Well,' said the obstetrician, 'at this stage you cannot rule out cancer.'

I watched your mother's face. Nothing in her expression showed what she must feel. There was a slight colouring of her cheeks. She nodded. She asked a question or two. She held my hand, but there was no tight squeezing.

The obstetrician asked Alison if she was going to be 'all right'. Alison said she would be 'all right'. But when the obstetrician left she left the curtains drawn.

The obstetrician's statement was not of course categorical, and not everyone who has cancer dies, but Alison was, at that instant, confronting the thing we fear most. When the doctor said those words, it was like a dream or a nightmare. I heard them said. And yet they were not said. They could not be said. And when we hugged each other—when the doctor had gone—we pressed our bodies together as we always had before, and if there were tears on our cheeks, there had been tears on our cheeks before. I kissed your mother's eyes. Her hair was wet with her tears. I smoothed her hair on her forehead. My own eyes were swimming. She said: 'All right, how are we going to get through all this?'

Now you know her, you know how much like her that is. She is not going to be a victim of anything.

'We'll decide it's going to be OK,' she said, 'that's all.'

And we dried our eyes.

But that night, when she was alone in her bed, waiting for the sleeping pill to work, she thought: If I die, I'll at least have made this little baby.

When I left your mother I appeared dry-eyed and positive, but my disguise was a frail shell of a thing and it cracked on the stairs and my grief and rage came spilling out in gulps. The halls of the hospital gleamed with polish and vinyl and fluorescent light. The flower-seller on the ground floor had locked up his shop. The foyer was empty. The whisker-shadowed man in admissions was watching television. In Missenden Road two boys in jeans and sand-shoes conducted separate conversations in separate phone booths. Death was not touching them. They turned their backs to each other. One of them—a redhead with a tattoo on his forearm—laughed.

In Missenden Road there were taxis NOT FOR HIRE speeding towards other destinations.

In Missenden Road the bright white lights above the zebra crossings became a luminous sea inside my eyes. Car lights turned into necklaces and ribbons. I was crying, thinking it is not for me to cry: crying is a poison, a negative force; everything will be all right; but I was weeping as if huge balloons of air had to be released from inside my guts. I walked normally. My grief was invisible. A man rushed past me, carrying roses wrapped in Cellophane. I got into my car. The floor was littered with car-park tickets from all the previous days of blood transfusions, tests, test results, admissions etc. I drove out of the car park. I talked aloud.

I told the night I loved Alison Summers. I love you, I love you, you will not die. There were red lights in Parramatta Road. I sat there, howling, unroadworthy. I love you.

The day after tomorrow there will be a baby. Will the baby have a mother? What would we do if we knew Alison was dying? What would we do so Sam would know his mother? Would we make a video? Would we hire a camera? Would we set it up and act for you? Would we talk to you with smiling faces, showing you how we were together, how we loved each other? How could we? How could we think of these things?

I was a prisoner in a nightmare driving down Ross Street in Glebe. I passed the Afrikan restaurant where your mother and I ate after first coming to live in Balmain.

All my life I have waited for this woman. This cannot happen.

I thought: Why would it *not* happen? Every day people are tortured, killed, bombed. Every day babies starve. Every day there is pain and grief, enough to make you howl to the moon for ever. Why should we be exempt, I thought, from the pain of life?

What would I do with a baby? How would I look after it? Day after day, minute after minute, by myself. I would be a sad man, for ever, marked by the loss of this woman. I would love the baby. I would care for it. I would see, in its features, every day, the face of the woman I had loved more than any other.

When I think of this time, it seems as if it's two in the morning, but it was not. It was ten o'clock at night. I drove home through a landscape of grotesque imaginings.

The house was empty and echoing.

In the nursery everything was waiting for you, all the things we had got for 'the baby'. We had read so many books about babies, been to classes where we learned about how babies are born, but we still did not understand the purpose of all the little clothes we had folded in the drawers. We did not know which was a swaddle and which was a sheet. We could not have selected the clothes to dress you in.

I drank coffee. I drank wine. I set out to telephone Kathy Lette, Alison's best friend, so she would have this 'news' before she spoke to your mother the next day. I say 'set out' because each time I began to dial, I thought: I am not going to do this properly. I hung up. I did deep breathing. I calmed myself. I telephoned. Kim Williams, Kathy's husband, answered and said Kathy was not home yet. I thought: She must know. I told Kim, and as I told him the weeping came with it. I could hear myself. I could imagine Kim listening to me. I would sound frightening, grotesque, and less in control than I was. When I had finished frightening him, I went to bed and slept.

I do not remember the next day, only that we were bright and determined. Kathy hugged Alison and wept. I hugged Kathy and wept. There were isolated incidents. We were 'handling it'. And besides, you were coming on the next day. You were life, getting stronger and stronger.

I had practical things to worry about. For instance: the bag. The bag was to hold all the things for the labour ward. There was a list for the contents of the bag and these contents were all purchased and ready, but still I must bring them to the hospital early in the morning. I checked the bag. I placed things where I would not forget them. You wouldn't believe the things we had. We had a cassette-player and a tape with soothing music. We had rosemary and lavender oil so I could massage your mother and relax her between contractions. I had a Thermos to fill with blocks of frozen orange juice. There were special cold packs to relieve the pain of a backache labour. There were paper pants—your arrival, after all, was not to happen without a great deal of mess. There were socks, because your mother's feet would almost certainly get very cold. I packed all these things, and there was something in the process of this packing which helped overcome my fears and made me concentrate on you, our little baby, already so loved although we did not know your face, had seen no more of you than the ghostly blue image thrown up by the ultrasound in the midst of whose shifting perspectives we had seen your little hand move. ('He waved to us.')

On the morning of the day of your birth I woke early. It was only just light. I had notes stuck on the fridge and laid out on the table. I made coffee and poured it into a Thermos. I made the bagel sandwiches your mother and I had planned months before—my lunch. I filled the bagels with a fiery Polish sausage and cheese and gherkins. For your mother, I filled a spray-bottle with Evian water.

It was a Saturday morning and bright and sunny and I knew you would be born but I did not know what it would be like. I drove along Ross Street in Glebe ignorant of the important things I would know that night. I wore grey stretchy trousers and a black shirt which would later be marked by the white juices of your birth. I was excited, but less than you might imagine. I parked at the hospital as I had parked on all those other occasions. I carried the bags up to the eleventh floor. They were heavy.

Alison was in her bed. She looked calm and beautiful. When we kissed, her lips were soft and tender. She said: 'This time tomorrow we'll have a little baby.'

In our conversation, we used the diminutive a lot. You were always spoken of as 'little', as indeed you must really have been, but we would say 'little' hand, 'little' feet, 'little' baby, and thus evoked all our powerful feelings about you.

The term ('little') is so loaded that writers are wary of using it. It is cute, sentimental, 'easy'. All of sentient life seems programmed to respond to 'little'. If you watch grown dogs with a pup, a pup they have never seen, they are immediately patient and gentle, even solicitous, with it. If you had watched your mother and father holding up a tiny terry-towelling jump-suit in a department store, you would have seen their faces change as they celebrated your 'littleness' while, at the same time, making fun of their own responses—they were aware of acting in a way they would have previously thought of as saccharine.

And yet we were not aware of the torrents of emotion your 'littleness' would unleash in us, and by the end of 13 September we would think it was nothing other than the meaning of life itself.

When I arrived at the hospital with the heavy bags of cassette-players and rosemary oil, I saw a dark-bearded, neat man in a suit sitting out by the landing. This was the hypnotherapist who had arrived to help you come into the world. He was serious, impatient, eager to start. He wanted to start in the pathology ward, but in the end he helped carry the cassette-player, Thermoses, sandwiches, massage oil, sponges, paper pants, apple juice, frozen orange blocks, rolling-pin, cold packs and Evian water down to the labour ward where—on a stainless-steel stand eight feet high—the nurses were already hanging the bag of Oxytocin which would ensure this day was your birthday.

It was a pretty room, by the taste of the time. As I write it is still that time, and I still think it pretty. All the surfaces were hospital surfaces—easy to clean—laminexes, vinyls, materials with a hard shininess, but with colours that were soft pinks and blues and an effect that was unexpectedly pleasant, even sophisticated.

The bed was one of those complicated stainless-steel machines which seems so cold and impersonal until you realize all the clever things it can do. In the wall there were sockets with labels like OXYGEN. The cupboards were filled with paper-wrapped sterile 'objects'. There was, in short, a seriousness about the room, and when we plugged in the cassette-player we took care to make sure we were not using a socket that might be required for something more important.

The hypnotherapist left me to handle the unpacking of the bags. He explained his business to the obstetrician. She told him that eight hours would be a good, fast labour. The hypnotherapist said he and Alison were aiming for three. I don't know what the doctor thought, but I thought there was not a hope in hell.

When the Oxytocin drip had been put into my darling's arm, when the water-clear hormone was entering her veins, one drip every ten seconds (you could hear the machine click when a drip was released), when these pure chemical messages were being delivered to her body, the hypnotherapist attempted to send other messages of a less easily assayable quality.

I tell you the truth: I did not care for this hypnotherapist, this pushy, over-eager fellow taking up all this room in the labour ward. He sat on the right-hand side of the bed. I sat on the left. He made me feel useless. He said: 'You are going to have a good labour, a fast labour, a fast labour like the one you have already visualized.' Your mother's eyes were closed. She had such large, soft lids, such tender and vulnerable coverings of skin. Inside the pink light of the womb, your eyelids were the same. Did you hear the messages your mother was sending to her body and to you? The hypnotherapist said: 'After just three hours you are going to deliver a baby, a good, strong, healthy baby. It will be an easy birth, an effortless birth. It will last three hours and you will not tear.' On the door the sisters had tacked a sign reading: QUIET PLEASE, HYPNOTHERAPY IN PROGRESS. 'You are going to be so relaxed, and in a moment you are going to be even more relaxed, more relaxed than you have ever been before. You are feeling yourself going deeper and deeper and when you come to you will be in a state of waking hypnosis and you will respond to the trigger-words Peter will give you during your labour, words which will make you, once again, so relaxed.'

My trigger-words were to be 'Breathe' and 'Relax'.

The hypnotherapist gave me his phone number and asked me to call when you were born. But for the moment you had not felt the effects of Oxytocin on your world and you could not yet have suspected the adventures the day would have in store for you.

You still sounded like the ocean, like soldiers marching across a bridge, like short-wave radio.

On Tuesday nights through the previous winter we had gone to classes in a building where the lifts were always sticking. We had walked up the stairs to a room where pregnant women and their partners had rehearsed birth with dolls, had watched hours of videos of exhausted women in labour. We had practised all the different sorts of breathing. We had learned of the different positions for giving birth: the squat, the supported squat, the squat supported by a seated partner. We knew the positions for first and second stage, for a backache labour, and so on, and so on. We learned birth was a complicated, exhausting and difficult process. We worried we would forget how to breathe. And yet now the time was here we both felt confident, even though nothing would be like it had been in the birth classes. Your mother was connected to the Oxytocin drip which meant she could not get up and walk around. It meant it was difficult for her to 'belly dance' or do most of the things we had spent so many evenings learning about.

In the classes they tell you that the contractions will start far apart, that you should go to hospital only when they are ten minutes apart: short bursts of pain, but long rests in between. During this period your mother could expect to walk around, to listen to music, to enjoy a massage. However, your birth was not to be like this. This was not because of you. It was because of the Oxytocin. It had a fast, intense effect, like a double Scotch when you're expecting a beer. There were not to be any ten-minute rests, and from the time the labour started it was, almost immediately, fast and furious, with a one-minute contraction followed by no more than two minutes of rest.

If there had been time to be frightened, I think I would have been frightened. Your mother was in the grip of pains she could not escape from. She squatted on a beanbag. It was as if her insides were all tangled, and tugged in a battle to the death. Blood ran from her. Fluid like egg-white. I did not know what anything was. I was a man who had wandered on to a battlefield. The blood was bright with oxygen. I wiped your mother's brow. She panted. *Huh-huh-huh-huh.* I ministered to her with sponge and water. I could not take her pain for her. I could do nothing but measure the duration of the pain. I had a little red stopwatch you will one day find abandoned in a dusty drawer. (Later your mother asked me what I had felt during labour. I thought only: I must count the seconds of the contraction; I must help Alison breathe, now, now, now; I must get that sponge—there is time to make the water in the sponge cool—now I can remove that bowl and cover it. Perhaps I can reach the bottle of Evian water. God, I'm so *thirsty*. What did I think during the labour? I thought: When this contraction is over I will get to that Evian bottle.)

Somewhere in the middle of this, in these three hours in this room whose only view was a blank screen of frosted glass, I helped your mother climb on to the bed. She was on all fours. In this position she could reach the gas mask. It was nitrous oxide, laughing-gas. It did not stop the pain, but it made it less important. For the gas to work, your mother had to anticipate the contraction, breathing in gas before it arrived. The sister came and showed me how I could feel the contraction coming with my hand. But I couldn't. We used the stopwatch, but the contractions were not regularly spaced, and sometimes we anticipated them and sometimes not. When we did not get it right, your mother took the full brunt of the pain. She had her face close to the mattress. I sat on the chair beside. My face was close to hers. I held the watch where she could see it. I held her wrist. I can still see the red of her face, the wideness of her eyes as they bulged at the enormous *size* of the pains that racked her.

Sisters came and went. They had to see how wide the cervix was. At first it was only two centimetres, not nearly enough room for you to come out. An hour later they announced it was four centimetres. It had to get to nine centimetres before we could even think of you being born. There had to be room for your head (which we had been told was big—well, we were told wrong, weren't we?) and your shoulders to slip through. It felt to your mother that this labour would go on for eight or twelve or twenty hours. That she should endure this intensity of pain for this time was unthinkable. It was like running a hundred-metre race which was stretching to ten miles. She wanted an epidural—a pain blocker.

But when the sister heard this she said: 'Oh do try to hang on. You're doing *so* well.'

I went to the sister, like a shop steward.

I said: 'My wife wants an epidural, so can you please arrange it?'

The sister agreed to fetch an anaesthetist, but there was between us—I admit it now—a silent conspiracy: for although I had pressed the point and she had agreed it was your mother's right, we both believed (I, for my part, on her advice) that if your mother could endure a little longer she could have the birth she wanted—without an epidural.

The anaesthetist came and went. The pain was at its worst. A midwife came and inspected your mother. She said: 'Ten centimetres.'

She said: 'Your baby is about to be born.'

We kissed, your mother and I. We kissed with soft, passionate lips as we did the day we lay on a bed at Lovett Bay and conceived you. That day the grass outside the window was a brilliant green beneath the vibrant petals of fallen jacaranda.

Outside the penumbra of our consciousness trolleys were wheeled. Sterile bags were cut open. The contractions did not stop, of course.

The obstetrician had not arrived. She was in a car, driving fast towards the hospital.

I heard a midwife say: 'Who can deliver in this position?' (It was still unusual, as I learned at that instant, for women to deliver their babies on all fours.)

Someone left the room. Someone entered. Your mother was pressing the gas mask so hard against her face it was making deep indentations on her skin. Her eyes bulged huge.

Someone said: 'Well get her, otherwise I'll have to deliver it myself.'

The door opened. Bushfire came in.

Bushfire was aboriginal. She was about fifty years old. She was compact and taciturn like a farmer. She had a face that folded in on itself and let out its feelings slowly, selectively. It was a face to trust, and trust especially at this moment when I looked up to see Bushfire coming through the door in a green gown. She came in a rush, her hands out to have gloves put on.

There was another contraction. I heard the latex snap around Bushfire's wrists. She said: 'There it is. I can see your baby's head.' It was you. The tip of you, the top of you. You were a new country, a planet, a star seen for the first time. I was not looking at Bushfire. I was looking at your mother. She was all alight with love and pain.

'Push,' said Bushfire.

Your mother pushed. It was you she was pushing, you that put that look of luminous love on her face, you that made the veins on her forehead bulge and her skin go red.

Then—it seems such a short time later—Bushfire said: 'Your baby's head is born.'

And then, so quickly in retrospect, but one can no more recall it accurately than one can recall exactly how one made love on a bed when the jacaranda petals were lying like jewels on the grass outside. Soon. Soon we heard you. Soon you slipped out of your mother. Soon you came slithering out not having hurt her, not even having grazed her. You slipped out, as slippery as a little fish, and we heard you cry. Your cry was so much lighter and thinner than I might have expected. I do not mean that it was weak or frail, but that your first cry had a timbre unlike anything I had expected. The joy we felt. Your mother and I kissed again, at that moment.

'My little baby,' she said. We were crying with happiness. 'My little baby.'

I turned to look. I saw you. Skin. Blue-white, shiny-wet.

I said: 'It's a boy.'

'Look at me,' your mother said, meaning: stay with me, be with me, the pain is not over yet, do not leave me now. I turned to her. I kissed her. I was crying, just crying with happiness that you were there.

The room you were born in was quiet, not full of noise and clattering. This is how we wanted it for you. So you could come into the world gently and that you should—as you were now—be put on to your mother's stomach. They wrapped you up. I said: 'Couldn't he feel his mother's skin?' They unwrapped you so you could have your skin against hers.

And there you were. It was you. You had a face, the face we had never known. You were so calm. You did not cry or fret. You had big eyes like your mother's. And yet when I looked at you first I saw not your mother and me, but your two grandfathers, your mother's father, my father; and, as my father, whom I loved a great deal, had died the year before, I was moved to see that here, in you, he was alive.

Look at the photographs in the album that we took at this time. Look at your mother and how alive she is, how clear her eyes are, how all the red pain has just slipped off her face and left the unmistakable visage of a young woman in love.

We bathed you in warm water and you accepted this gravely, swimming instinctively.

I held you (I think this must be before), and you were warm and slippery. You had not been bathed when I held you. The obstetrician gave you to me so she could examine your mother. She said: 'Here.'

I held you against me. I knew then that your mother would not die. I thought: 'It's fine, it's all right.' I held you against my breast. You smelt of love-making.

WILLIAM WHARTON

FIELD-BURNING

Will and I push our bikes along the narrow alley between the house and the fence of the house next door. We're dripping wet from a three-mile run we've just made in Asbury Park. The run is every Thursday evening at seven on the boardwalk and conducted by the local YMCA. We've ridden the mile or so from there back home. The air is soft and soothing.

Rosemary, my wife, is already home. She'd driven back. We've invited good friends who run with us to eat at our house. She's come home to set the table and put things out. Albie and Linda, with whom we run on Monday and Thursday evenings, are stopping to get the pizza. Bobbie, another friend who is joining us, is with them. Will, our younger son, and I have enjoyed riding slowly through the darkening evening and look forward to showers and good pizza with friends.

As I push my bike past the dining-room window, I just catch the movement of Rosemary coming back through the kitchen. I park my bike near the trash cans. Will parks his along the fence leaning over the marigolds we've planted. He rushes in past Rosemary to get his shower started so I can have mine after him. I figure I'll help with anything Rosemary needs.

She pauses on the little covered back porch, on the platform outside the kitchen door. I'm just stepping over the little sill into the porch when she comes quickly down the steps to me. It's enough out of the ordinary that I take notice. I see she's crying.

She comes into my arms. I hold her tight. She's sobbing so hard I can feel it through her whole body and mine. I think, what in heaven's name can be wrong, Rosemary is not an easy crier. I'm just beginning to think about all our loved ones, mostly the few older aunts and uncles who are left. Then she looks up, takes my head in both her hands, stares into my eyes. I can scarcely make her out in the dark.

'Bert, darling, a terrible thing has happened.'

She stops to take a deep stuttering breath.

'They're all dead. Bill, Kate, Mia, Dayiel. They're all dead. I just finished talking to Betty Rodewald. They were killed in a huge crash and fire on the highway in Oregon. They're dead.'

She leans her head into my sweaty shoulder and cries hard some more. I hold on to her, as much to keep myself up as anything. I'm surprised at my reaction. I don't believe it.

216

Somebody's made a mistake. I can't accept it. All the usual reactions people have to things they don't want to believe. But I'm not crying. I've just started shaking my head against Rosemary's.

'When did it happen? How? Are you sure?'

She talks into my shoulder. 'It happened yesterday at about four o'clock Oregon time. There was a fire that blew across the road. Seven people were killed. About thirty cars piled up. Betty was crying so hard it was hard to understand. I still don't understand.' Betty Rodewald is my daughter's mother-in-law.

'It happened yesterday? Are you sure? What took so long? What kind of people won't even tell you right away when something like this happens?'

'I wish it weren't true. They're dead.'

I hold her tighter. I'm beginning to shiver. I feel cold all the way inside myself. How could this happen? These are the kinds of things that happen to other people. We've always been so lucky. Bill, Kate's husband, is such a careful driver; Kate, even more so. She won't go around the block in a car with the babies unless they're strapped into baby seats, like astronauts, with wide straps crossed over them.

I turn Rosemary and lead her back up the steps into the kitchen. She's slumped against me. I'm still not crying. It hasn't registered yet. I hear the Jeep pulling in, parking out front. I lead Rosemary into the living-room, ease her into the reclining chair where she likes to read in the evenings.

Our friends are standing on our front porch. I open the door. They're wearing jackets against the chill after the run. Albie is holding the grease-stained paper box with the pizza out with two hands. He's smiling, the women are behind him. They know right away something has happened; something is wrong.

'We've just had some terrible news.'

For the first time I feel I might break down, crying. Telling it to someone else will make it more real, irrevocable.

'Kate, Bill, Mia and Dayiel have been killed in some kind of monstrous automobile accident in Oregon. Rosemary just phoned and talked to Bill's mom. It happened yesterday afternoon.'

Albie puts the pizza down on the table by the window.

'And they're only telling you now?'

It's the same reaction I had. Rosemary begins talking behind me. I know her. She doesn't want anyone thought badly of when they haven't done anything wrong.

'They didn't know themselves until just about an hour ago. It's only afternoon there. The accident was so horrible they couldn't identify the bodies for a long time. The Rodewalds were expecting them home for dinner last night. They didn't come. They thought the car had broken down or they'd decided to stay over with friends. The accident was on all the news, television, everything, all over the country, but they didn't think this kind of thing could happen to the family.'

She stops, leans forward with her face in her hands. Linda goes over, gets down on her knees, holds on to Rosemary. I'd better get off my feet or I'm going to fall down. I slump on to the floor with my head against the side of the couch, the way I watch baseball on television. Bobbie pulls some pillows off the couch and tucks them under my head. Both Linda and Bobbie are crying now. Each have children of their own.

Albie pulls my legs out straight, goes into the dining-room and brings out a chair. He lifts my legs up on to the chair; Bobbie puts another pillow under my legs. I guess from their reactions I must be going into shock. I know I feel terrible. I can't stop shaking my head back and forth, like a pendulum. It's totally involuntary.

Linda takes the pizza into the kitchen. She comes back with wet towels for both Rosemary and me. I'm beginning to feel as if things are passing me by. I want to comfort Rosemary but I'm numb. Albie is on his knees beside me now.

'Do you want me to get the first-aid people? I can call them and they'll be here in five minutes.'

I shake my head no. It interrupts my regular rhythm of head-shaking.

'No. I think we should just be alone for a while. I still have to tell Will. He doesn't know yet. We'll be all right. You people go home to your families.'

Rosemary sits up in her chair, ready to play hostess.

'Yes, please go home. We'll have many things to do. Nobody can do anything for us right now. If we do need help, we'll call.'

Bobbie leans towards Rosemary.

'I know I won't sleep tonight, so call any time, and I'll be right over. Dave can help, too. You know life-guards are trained in first aid. You don't need to take this all alone.'

Linda and Albie are standing. It's uncomfortable knowing they want to help, but all of us know there's nothing they can do. We just have to work it out ourselves.

They leave. I try to get them to take the pizza. No one feels like eating. I see them off the porch and into the Jeep. I look around at the quiet street in the night. Ocean Grove is famous for its peace. I wonder if it will ever be the same for me. I turn back into the house. I go over and kneel before Rosemary, take her hands in mine. Her crying has subsided.

I hear Will coming down the stairs. The stairs enter on to the dining-room. This house is three rooms in a row on the ground floor, living-room off front porch, then dining-room and kitchen in back. I stop Will at the bottom of the stairs.

'Will, I have something to tell you.'

Will is usually diffident. But he catches something in my voice, my face. Still he's carrying through what was for him the normal sequence.

'I left enough water for you to shower and there's still a dry towel.'

'Will, I have some bad news, something terrible has happened.'

He stands there, hanging his hands loosely at his sides. I wish I didn't have to say it. We could have let him have one more night's peaceful sleep. But it has to be done.

'Kate, Bill, Mia and Dayiel were killed in an automobile crash in Oregon. Mom just talked to Mrs Rodewald. That's how we found out.'

His face blanches. He stands there blank for a few seconds. He peers into the living-room.

'How's Mom taking it?'

'It's hard but she's OK.'

'Is there anything I can do?'

'Not now. Do you want some of the pizza? It's right there on the table.'

'No, I couldn't eat. I'll take a walk on the boardwalk. I

don't think I can handle this.'

'Just be back before ten. I don't know when we'll be leaving for Oregon and the funeral. Probably tomorrow.'

'I'll be right back.'

I can tell he's on the edge of breaking down. I don't think I've heard him cry since he was under ten. I'm not interested in hearing it now. Walking along the boardwalk in the dark, crying, is more his style. He goes out the back door. I go into the living-room again. The running costume is looking more and more ridiculous. Then I remember that on Sunday we're supposed to be part of a big family reunion outside Philadelphia at my Aunt Alice's. I'll need to call. I also have to call my sister in California.

I slip off my warm-up jacket. It's beginning to dry on me. I slip off my soaking wet running-shirt. I do these things automatically. I keep looking up at Rosemary. She's staring out of the window. I need to go upstairs to shower and put on some dry clothes but I don't want to leave her alone. I don't want to be alone either.

'Bert, you go on up and shower; I'm fine.'

She smiles. I smile back. We're being silly. Neither one of us expresses emotions easily.

I let the shower run over me for ten minutes. Here, I can cry. I wonder if Rosemary can cry downstairs. I dress in a pair of light slacks and a T-shirt, not exactly a mourning costume, but mourning costumes aren't our style either. I go down the steps slowly, preparing myself. Rosemary has moved from the chair by the window to the chair at the desk. She has the Yellow Pages in her lap and is talking on the phone. She hangs up.

'Well, we have a flight out of Newark for Portland, leaving at ten oh five tomorrow morning. We get to Portland at about noon. I'll call Betty Rodewald now and tell her what time we arrive. I think she told me the funeral is Tuesday. I'm not sure. I wasn't paying much atten—.' She breaks down. I go over and take her head to my chest. She puts her arms around my waist.

'Those beautiful young people. We're going to their funeral. It's all wrong.'

I hold her tighter and try to hold tight on to myself. I wonder how she got herself together enough to call the airlines. She amazes me. This is all a horror and a shock for me, but for her it must be impossible. Her life has been the kids. I have my painting and writing, other kinds of children in a way. But she's just lost her much loved first-born Kathleen, along with Bill and those two beautiful babies.

She gently pushes me away. She calls Betty Rodewald and tells her what time we hope to arrive. Bill's brother Steve will pick us up at the airport in Portland and drive us down.

'I guess we should call Camille,' she says.

I know the number by heart. It rings about ten times, then I hear Camille, sleepy-voiced, our only daughter now. I almost can't speak because the sobs are building up. It's three in the morning for her in France.

'Camille, this is Dad.'

I stop, take two deep breaths with my hand over the phone.

'Something terrible has happened.'

'What is it? Could you speak louder?'

I might as well get right into it. I don't have any choice. I'm sobbing as I say it.

'Kate, Bill, Dayiel and Mia were killed in an awful automobile crash in Oregon.'

'What?! Who told you that?'

I can't go on. Rosemary takes the phone. She's crying but not sobbing.

'I called to find out about Kate's gynaecologist appointment. I reached her little Wills, but Betty took the phone from him and she told me. It must be true. We can't believe it.'

I take the phone from Rosemary. Camille is crying, practically screaming. She's trying to tell Sam, her husband, what's happened. I say her name to get her attention.

'Camille.'

There's a long silence, then she says between sobs, 'I'm here.'

'Don't bother coming to the funeral. It's too far and Mom and I are sure we can handle it.'

'Whatever you say.'

That's not like Camille. She's generally against what *anybody* has to say. It's her way.

Rosemary moves into the kitchen and is unsetting the table she'd set for the pizza dinner. I go in and give her a hand.

Twice, in passing, we stop, hug and hold on to each other. Neither of us can say anything.

Will comes in as we're finishing and goes straight upstairs and into his bedroom. Rosemary sits in the reclining rocker. Her face is swollen and red, her eyes swollen, too.

'We should probably pack tonight. There won't be much time in the morning.'

'Right, I'll tell Will.'

'Give him a little more time, first, dear. I know he'll be up late, he usually is. Just before we go to bed you can tell him about packing. Be sure to tell him to pack his suit, a shirt and a tie, extra socks and underwear.'

Going up the stairs behind Rosemary I'm reminded of Sisyphus, constantly climbing and falling back. We pull out a bag each and start. It all seems so unnecessary. I pack a charcoal-grey suit, the only real suit I own. I also have a summer suit but it needs cleaning. I throw in socks, underwear, a few changes of shirts, an extra pair of shoes, more dressy than the ones I'll wear on the plane. I peek over at Rosemary packing. She goes about it in her usual methodical way, folding carefully each dress, skirt, blouse, putting rubber bands around her stockings, underwear.

I go into the bathroom. I look dreadful. I splash water on to my face. I take four Valium out of the medicine cabinet, two for me and two for Rosemary. They're the yellow kind, five milligrams. I've never taken two before. I take one once in a while when I can't sleep. I hope two will be enough. I hope Rosemary will take hers. She doesn't like taking medicine of any kind, also has a terrible time swallowing pills.

We undress slowly, turn out the light and climb into bed. The French doors on to the porch are open, letting in a fresh ocean breeze. Then I remember I haven't taken my medication. I slide out of bed and go back into the bathroom. I take my pills for blood pressure and blood sugar, plus some others. I also remember I haven't told Will to pack.

On the way back to our bedroom, I knock at his door and open it. He's stretched out on his bed fully dressed. His eyes are red.

'Will, we're leaving so early in the morning you should pack before you go to sleep. Mom says be sure to pack your suit, a good white shirt and tie. Take along your best shoes, too. A funeral is an awfully formal kind of thing.'

'OK. But I don't think I'll sleep.'

'We're not sure we will either, but we're going to try. Tomorrow will be a long day, as will the next few days. So, get in your PJs and try to relax. If you want something to put you to sleep I have some pills.'

'Oh no, that won't be necessary.'

I back out of the room, shut the door. Will is the same as Rosemary when it comes to pills. I run downstairs and pull out the phone cord.

Our bed is basically two twin beds pushed together. We don't like to sleep apart but there's really no double bed in this house we rent every summer. I usually start out in Rosemary's bed and then as she falls asleep, roll over into the other bed, the bed by the French windows.

I close the bedroom door. Rosemary is stretched out on her back in her nightgown, but not under the covers. In summer, I sleep without pyjamas. I crawl across my bed to hers, snuggle in beside her and put my arm across her breast. She has her arms up over her head against the bedstead and one leg cocked up. She often begins sleep this way. Her eyes are open, tears are rolling slowly down her cheeks but there are no spasms of crying or sobbing. She's crying quietly to herself. I put my face against hers; her tears are cold. I can't think of anything to say. I don't really want to say anything but feel I should. Her voice seems so calm, so far away, so dry and emotionless, not like her at all.

'I never knew one's teeth could hurt so much from crying.'

'For me it's the ears, from trying not to cry. It's like the earaches I used to have when I was a kid. It hurts to swallow. Probably your teeth hurt from the same thing, trying to hold in; you're biting down too hard.'

There's a long silence. We stay close. We spend an hour not moving, each pretending to sleep for the other. Finally, it's too much. I roll over to where I've put the pills and a glass of water. I turn back to Rosemary.

'I have some Valium. We really ought to sleep. Tomorrow's going to be tough.'

I hold out the pills. She doesn't move.

'I don't want to sleep. But you take something. Listen, Bert, do you really think we should go all the way to Oregon? They're dead, there's nothing we can do. Why don't we stay here where we were with them last and remember all the good times we had together. I know Kate wasn't sure I'd like Oregon. Most of the people there are roughnecks. Why don't we just keep it the way it is.'

I'm shocked. It seems so bizarre not going to the funeral of your own child, her husband and two of your only three grandchildren. I begin to wonder if Rosemary is all right. She's one for form, doing the proper thing. I keep quiet.

'Bert, if there are any bodies to see, I don't want to see them. They're probably terribly crushed and burned. I don't need that, neither do you. Why are we doing this?'

I went to my grandmother Wharton's funeral when I was nine, then to my grandfather's, my father's father, when I was fifteen. I was a pallbearer that time. Then there were the funerals for my mother and father, that's about it. That's a pretty good record for a man over sixty years old. I've been avoiding weddings and funerals all my life. In fact, I don't see much difference between the two. Rosemary knows this, I've said it often enough.

'All right, you're right, Rosemary. You know how I hate funerals. I'm sure if Kate and Bill can know what's going on, they'd agree with us. We haven't paid for any tickets so I'm sure we can cancel them. I can go in now and tell Will we're not going. I don't think that'll break his heart. I'll call our kids and tell them we're taking our own advice, staying home. If they want to go that's their business. What else? Boy, I feel better already.'

I roll out of bed to go in and tell Will.

'You're so sweet, darling. Don't. We *have* to go, there's just no way out of it, but as long as we both know that this entire farce is for others, that we don't need it, I feel better about things. I'm sorry I got your hopes up.'

I roll back on to my bed, take the glass of water and pop three Valium. Maybe we'll have a mass grave.

At first the pills don't work and I can tell Rosemary is still awake. My watch sounds midnight. I begin to think there shouldn't be anybody calling us between now and the time we

224

leave unless it's our kids trying to get in touch. I roll quietly out of bed and go downstairs. I plug the phone back in.

The pills must have worked, finally, because when I come back up, I go out like a light. I wake to the ringing of the phone downstairs. I stagger across the foot of the bed. Rosemary is rolling out of her side.

'You go back to sleep, dear, I'll get it. It's probably one of the kids.'

I dash past her and start down the steps. Rosemary is just behind me. I'm counting rings. It's the fifth ring I've heard when I pick up the phone. I sit down at a chair beside the table near to the desk. Rosemary hovers over me.

I hear the little 'dink' of a long-distance call but then nothing, except somebody breathing heavily into the phone.

'Hello, who is this?'

I hear a thick rumbling clearing of a throat, the sound of a sob. Even from this, I recognize Jo Lancaster, my best friend.

'Jo, is that you?'

'I love you.'

Then more hard sobbing. I can't respond. I'm sobbing myself. I hand the phone to Rosemary.

'Jo, is that you?'

There's a long pause, then Rosemary walks over slowly to the table and puts the phone in its cradle.

'He just said he was sorry and hung up.'

We look at each other and break down again. I hold her in my arms. She buries her head into my chin. I can feel her silken skin under her light, white nightgown. Even now, I have my same old trouble. Her hair is tickling my nose. I rub it off in her hair, knowing she'll know, and not caring. After almost forty years, she knows these things about me.

Finally, we push each other away.

'Rosemary, it's starting to get light out. I think you ought to take a shower. Who knows when we'll have a shower again.'

Without a word she starts up the steps, then turns back.

'Would you wake up Will? You know how hard it is for him to get moving in the morning. Make sure he's out of bed. I know he slept because I could hear him snoring last night.'

She goes up the rest of the steps. I turn on the light in the living-room so when the limo comes he'll know we're here and awake. Then I realize I'm stark naked and if any fool is up at this time, by Ocean Grove standards, I'm 'exposing'. I hurry up the stairs.

I wake Will and wait until I'm sure he's up and out of bed. I know better than to carry on a conversation with him. He's a slow starter but his heart's in the right place.

'I know, Dad. I'm up, honest I'm up.'

I go into the bedroom and dress myself in the clothes I laid out last night.

We're ready and on the porch when the limo arrives. We haven't packed much, so Will and I can get everything into the back. It's a real limo with a dark blue plush interior. Will sits in front with the driver because he has such long legs, Rosemary and I sit in back. The driver is good and we feel confident. I'm reminded of a funeral. I've rarely driven in a limo except in those few family funerals I've attended.

The flight is long and boring. I'm torn between mourning and fatigue. Rosemary falls asleep until we reach Chicago and need to change planes. Will drops off to sleep immediately. I try not watching the film.

Chicago to Portland is even longer. Will drops right off again but Rosemary is just staring at the ceiling of the plane with tears running down her face. I don't feel I can interrupt her thinking. I know she's with Kate. I only intrude when the food arrives. I eat, I can always eat. Usually Rosemary can, too, but this time she just plays with the food, pushing most of it aside. But she drinks a cup of tea.

At Portland, Steve, Bill's younger brother, and Wills are waiting for us at luggage retrieval. We give big hugs to Wills and try not crying too much. Our Will holds his ground, he never hugs anybody, hasn't since he was ten years old.

Steve is tall and thin, even more so than Will. His eyes are red and we hug and shake hands. We're all trying hard to hold it in. He goes to his car and brings it right to the kerb. We throw the baggage in the back and climb in. Will is in front with Steve, and Wills is in back with us. Rosemary is hunting for a third seat-belt but there isn't any, so she straps Wills and herself under one.

Steve works himself out of the airport confusion and up on to the highway. He tells us it's the same highway, I-5, on which Kate, Bill, Dayiel and Mia were killed, only they were going the other way, north.

The traffic is horrendous. Steve drives carefully and stays to the right but it seems that every vehicle is towing something, a boat, a trailer, a house trailer or it's a big RV or a huge pick-up with gigantic tyres. I've never been on a highway like this, not even in Los Angeles, and they drive like kids playing bumper cars, constantly cutting in and out, ducking between the gigantic trucks and semi-trailers, steaming along at over seventy miles an hour.

I thought after what had happened to us in the past twenty-four hours I'd never be scared to die again, but I am. I look over at Rosemary. She's white and white-knuckled. We turn our attention to Wills, who's been rattling away about some horses they have at the Rodewalds' and how this is 'neat' or that is 'neat'. I begin to wonder if anyone's told him what's happened, or is he just so childish he can't comprehend. Then he puts his head on Rosemary's chest and in a choked voice says: 'It was their nap time, Dayiel and Mia. They were probably asleep, weren't they? They just didn't wake up.'

Rosemary looks over at me and we're both breathing deeply. She leans her head down so her face is in his hair.

'That's right, Wills. They just went to sleep and never knew what happened. It's terrible that they're gone but I don't think they felt a thing.'

Steve turns off the I-5 and we're on small roads. The unkempt sides of the roads, the house trailers instead of houses, the houses that aren't kept up, make me think of the pine barrens of New Jersey. But it's green. Wills is asleep against Rosemary. He's got to be beat. He's been inside this thing since the beginning.

I begin to dread arriving at a house where I've never been, meeting on such intimate terms people I hardly know. It's *worse* than a wedding.

We twist around a few dirt roads and then pull up in front of a rambling house newly painted, a sort of dark earth pink. There's the most godawful-looking tree in the front yard. It looks like something drawn by a talented yet autistic child, too regular and not like a tree at all. It looks like something on which you'd hang your hat.

Betty Rodewald comes down from the front door and off a front porch to meet us. Rosemary unhooks the seat-belt and Wills runs to meet her.

She pulls him to her as he's babbling away.

'See, they came. I told you they would. These are Mom's Mom and Dad. They'd be sure to come.'

During the next few hours, as people keep coming with more food, country style, we learn more about what happened. They show us the newspapers. The past two days it's been the headline event in the two Oregon newspapers. The faded, poor-quality colour pictures are gruesome. I can't put it together with our family. It's unreal.

The big question, after the sensationalism of the accident itself, is field-burning and why it continues. A farmer named Paul Stutzman started the fire with what he thought was the approval of the DEQ, that is the Department of Environmental Quality, who were keeping surveillance on the valley in helicopters and light planes. Mr Stutzman won't speak to anyone and his son tells the reporters to go away. It all seems so hopeless. I don't really see what can be done. These people obviously don't have the same regard for the environment and human life that we do.

The identification of Bill was made from his dental X-rays. Kate's followed soon after. There was no other way to identify the bodies, they were so badly burned. We really should have stayed in Ocean Grove, spent the day at the beach in an isolated spot and just talked to each other. We shouldn't know this.

It turns out they've arranged with the mortician in the next town, named Dallas, to have the bodies cremated. Betty is Catholic but somewhere along the line, without my noticing, the Catholic church has let up on the temple of the Holy Ghost thing. For other reasons I'd rather they not be cremated but it turns out to be a bit late to stop this. My only insistence is that they not be cremated separately, as planned, but together. After a phone call to Dallas, this is confirmed.

There is pressure on me, as a writer, to come up with

something appropriate to have put on the flyer (or whatever it is) that will be distributed at the funeral ceremony. But I have no trouble. They hand me a pencil and paper. I haven't thought about it at all. It flows out of the end of my pencil. It isn't even the kind of thing I'd usually write. I'm more of a mystical poet. I write:

> They came together
> Lived together
> Became together
> Left together.

Everybody seems satisfied with this. Then they want me to design a monument. Again I know in my mind, as if I'm being told, exactly what it should be. It's like magic writing.

I take pieces of paper and design a slant-topped sundial with one of their names at each cardinal point. Around the sides I write the above poem. At least I have something to do. I want to carve a model of it in wax for the monument maker. We gather all the sealing-wax they use for preserves, I put it in a Number 10 can and melt it. When it's hard, I pound it on the bottom and knock it out. I figure I'll work some more on it in the morning.

We start getting telegrams and telephone calls from our friends all over the world. Several friends of ours and Kate's in Paris and in Munich are actually flying in for the funeral. Camille, Sam and Matt phone from Boston or somewhere to say they're on their way. So much for the fourth commandment.

Betty's in a dither. As I suspected, there's no hotel within twenty miles. There's no space at Steve's apartment with his girlfriend there. Jim, Bill's younger brother, has space for horses but not for people. We start pulling out quilts, blankets, sheets, sleeping-bags, blow-up mats, everything we can find. It's going to be a camping funeral. Some people will have to sleep on the lawn. It turns out that we, as sort of the guests of honour, are going to sleep in Bill's room. It's the room he had all the time he lived at home and where he and Kate spent their last night. The cribs are still up in the room. Betty volunteers to take them down but we say it'll be OK. We're so frazzled, not tired, just frazzled, nerves on edge, we can sleep anywhere, that is if we can sleep at all.

We go to bed early. Each of us, I know, is trying not to think about or mention the fact that the sheets we're sleeping on, the blankets we're under, were last slept on and under by Bill and Kate. But we can't help ourselves.

We grab hold of each other and can't stop crying. It's the whole compilation of things, the actual knowing of how they died, how horrible it was, the discussion of the cremation, the formalities. And we're absolutely dead tired. Rosemary's little snooze on the plane and mine in our bed in Ocean Grove last night weren't enough to support us.

It must be hours that we just cry, very little talk, there isn't much to talk about. How can one have a discussion? Finally, sometime after midnight, Rosemary drops off; I can hear by her regular breathing, sometimes interrupted by a pitiful mewing sound or a sob. But she's asleep. I very carefully untangle myself and stretch out on the bed beside her, on top of the covers.

I must have gone to sleep rather quickly because I have no memory of a long waiting for sleep. This one would be real sleep without chemical assistance. I'm gone.

Sometime before morning I wake. I don't need to go to the bathroom, I just wake naturally. I'm surprised by my inner calm. I know what has happened but it's somehow all inside me, integrated, accepted, in some astonishing way. I lie awake in the dark, in this strange, yet not quite strange bed, the slight fragrance of Kate's perfume, Magie Noire, in the bed sheet. I feel enormously comforted and comfortable. I begin to think I might be having some kind of psychotic experience. It isn't natural to feel so absolutely absolved, or separate, in such a circumstance. I fall back to sleep.

I wake in the morning still in a state of unbelievable calm. I even entertain the idea I might have died in the night and this might be what death is, a totally involving peace.

I turn my head slowly, just enough to see that Rosemary is still asleep. I have no desire whatsoever to move. I stay like that, in some form of suspended animation, for an undefined length of time, watching the sun pass across the low window beside the bed.

Then, the concerns of what must be done this day invade my inner quiet. I carefully slide to the side of the bed, rise to a sitting position. I stay there for several minutes looking out of the window.

Then I stand up. Immediately it is as if I am struck hard from behind. I fall to my knees. Strangely enough, my hands are in fists on the worn shag rug. It's as if I've been knocked down in a football game, clipped, and I can't get my breath for several seconds. Then I can, and begin to sob with such violence I almost throw up. I fight for breath between sobs, but that is only the outside.

Inside I am knowing things I have no way of knowing. My head is spinning. I am on the verge of fainting. I feel Rosemary behind me, hovering over me, her hands on my shaking shoulders. I feel her rolling tears on my bare back.

'What is it, dear? Are you all right? Should I get someone?'

I have just enough contact, strength, to shake my head no. I stay like that on my knees, not able to stand. Rosemary eases herself on to the rug beside me, her arm over my shoulder, her hand on my quivering wrist. It's as if we're in the starting position of the second period in a college wrestling match. The image, the memory passes through my head, but it is smothered by other images seemingly engraved in my mind, the way nothing I've ever experienced in my life has ever been imprinted.

I try taking deep breaths. Slowly, the shaking comes under control. Rosemary is asking if I think I'm having a stroke or a heart attack, should she call a doctor. I have to tell her something. My first impulse is to try passing off the entire experience, blame it on my hysterical state, keep it to myself. But, almost immediately, I know I can't do this. What I know, or think I know, must be shared, especially with Rosemary. In a certain peculiar way, I'm a messenger.

'Dearest, I've had something happen to me and I don't know how to tell you and still maintain your respect. But I know I must tell you. It is meant that I tell you, even if you can't accept it.'

I settle back to a sitting position on the floor, squatting, between my legs. I'm suddenly aware of my nakedness. I'm in the sunlight coming through the window and I'm naked.

'Rosemary, would you lock the bedroom door? I didn't lock it last night in case we might be needed.'

She pushes herself up, crosses the room, turns the old-fashioned key in the lock. She comes back, folds her legs under her and sits facing me in a modified yoga position. She looks in my eyes, waiting.

'It started, or happened in the middle of the night. We'd both, happily, finally gone to sleep. I woke with this unreal sense of calm, or clarity. It was something like the feeling you have after you've had a long fever and suddenly it's gone. The world seems new and you're an intrinsic part of it. It was something like that. I remember being frightened for my sanity. How could I feel like this when we'd just lost Kate, Bill, Dayiel and Mia. It didn't make sense. Also, it didn't really seem to matter to me that I'd arrived at this strange psychic distance. I don't think it was five minutes before I fell into a deep restorative sleep.

'Rosemary, I woke this morning, refreshed. I didn't want to move, do anything but stay in this nirvana of peace. I still didn't have any idea of why I was so content, soothed; but I knew there were a hundred different things we had to do today and they must be waiting for us downstairs. I eased myself out of bed and stood up. This is where it gets hard to believe, don't interrupt, just listen, please. I want to get it all straight and right.'

I'm trying to sound calm but inside I'm shaking as I come to this part.

'When I stood, it was as if I were knocked down by some powerful force from behind. I found myself hardly breathing, as you found me, when you woke up. But, more than that, I knew all in a flash what had happened to me in the night, what had calmed me, made me feel deeply comforted, despite everything. It all made some kind of sense.'

I take another deep breath, trying to convert something in my mind that wasn't words, into something Rosemary could understand as words, even though I knew she could never know or believe this. Still, I had to tell her. It was part of the entire experience, telling her.

'I was sitting in one of our low beach-chairs on the beach in Ocean Grove with my back to the land, the sun setting over the town behind me. You know how much I like that, the long shadows, the shadows from the ridges in the sand, the changing colour of the water, of the sky, matching the colours almost as complements to the sunset. Then there are the sounds of water at its calmest, rising and falling back on pebbles rolling at the edge of land and sea. It is the most relaxing thing I know of, a natural meditation without effort. It has always been magic.

'Then I see the long shadows of people coming up behind me. I'm disappointed. This is for me a quiet time, not a social event. But it's Kate and Dayiel going past me to the edge of the water. Kate doesn't look over at me. I'm surprised, because she's supposed to be helping you get dinner ready, but I'm even more surprised to see her on the beach. At first, I think it's because she's mad at Bill, and it turns out this is part of it. Then I remember, you know how she is about sand. She never could stand having sand between her toes. So, what's she doing at the beach, walking barefoot?

'Next, Bill comes up on my left side. Kate and Dayiel have passed on my right. He's wearing bathing-trunks and one of his loud Hawaiian shirts. He's carrying Mia, the way he does, as if she's a football, in the crook of his huge arm, and hanging over his forearm. He settles in the sand beside me, putting one leg out, his football knee, and he drapes Mia over it. She's wearing a diaper, also some kind of lightweight white shirt and a sun-bonnet with ruffles around her face. She's watching my eyes in a way she never has, not as if she's curious about my eyes, but about me. Bill has started making marks in the sand in front of her, the sand collapsing completely, totally, without trace each time. He looks up at me. He has a quizzical smile on his face. He, too, stares into my eyes a long time, in a way he never has. I'm beginning to have a terrible feeling in the pit of my stomach that something horrible has happened. It has, but I have no idea, then. Bill starts that slow shaking of his head which is a sign for me he can't comprehend or believe something.

'"You know, Bert, you're not here and I'm not either. You're in my bed in Falls City, in my bedroom, and I'm still not sure where we are. It seems right now we can be almost anywhere we want. We're hoping to find out more about all this soon. It's really weird."

'He stops. I don't know what he's talking about. It's so far from what I'm seeing, or think I'm seeing, feeling, or think I'm feeling, know, or think I'm knowing, that it's total nonsense to me, like some kind of crazy party game. I just stare at him.

'"Bert, being dead is a hell of a lot different than you might think it is. I'm still not sure what's going on, and I know I'm not supposed to be talking to you, but I wanted you to know. You deserve it. Kate's mad at me for telling you like this, sort of in your dream, but everything was perfect, the place, the time, how it happened to us so fast before we could even think. It all came together and I couldn't resist. There's not much of what we always called time, so I'll hurry.

'"You see, we didn't leave you, *you* left us. It's as if we were all on a giant train or something like that and then we stepped off while you and everybody else just kept on going. That isn't quite right either, but it's close as I can get. I've always been better at numbers than words.

'"But I want you to know we're fine, that we're still together. There's no way to know what's next but we're not worried about it. That's the important thing. So don't you worry either."

'He looks over, takes his eyes from mine. Kate's coming up the beach with Dayiel dancing around her. She's not coming towards us, she's going to pass right by us again without looking.

'"Kate says I don't know how to let go. But would you do me this one favour. Would you get hold of those bodies that used to be us and take good pictures of them. It's important. It might help stop this damned field-burning. It's the field-burning more than anything else, that killed us. You'll learn more about it in the next few days. Talk to Steve, tell him about this, he'll help you, I know."

'He pushes himself up. Mia is still watching my eyes. He passes on behind me with her and joins Kate. I can watch their shadows, long and violet-coloured in the sand. I don't turn around. Just as the last shadow is gone I hear Kate's voice.

'"Goodbye Dad, we're sorry."

'Then I turn around and they're gone. The beach is empty. I turn and watch the sea some more.

'Then I must have wakened that first time, when I was so calm. I know now. I really know and I still know.'

I stop. Rosemary is crying, tears just running down her cheeks. She looks me deeply in the eyes.

'That's the most beautiful dream I've ever heard, Bert. Even I, who didn't dream it, feel much more calmly acceptant. I know

I can live with it now. I won't say I believe this really happened because I'm not that way. But I believe you believe it happened and that's what's important. I think that's why Bill could come to you, because you could believe. Kate and I never believed this kind of thing. What are you going to do now?'

'I think that's why I've been crying so hard just now. A dream like that should never make anyone cry. But I dread taking those photographs. I can't bear the idea of seeing them like that, burned. I want to remember them the way they were with us that week, or the way they all were in the 'dream'. I don't think I can hire anyone to take those pictures, even if I could find somebody who would. It might even be illegal. I'll have to find someone to give me a hand. Bill suggested Steve. I'll try him first.'

I help Rosemary up off the floor and we make the bed together. I feel so close to her. I wonder what people are going to think when I go downstairs and seem so happy, so full of life instead of death.

After Rosemary washes up, I go in and shower. When I go downstairs, there's all kinds of breakfast fixings and it's serve yourself. I have my blood-sugar automatic test-kit with me and I need to test before I eat. I go out on to the front porch. Steve comes out behind me. He has his kit, too. It's a remarkable coincidence. We're pricking, making the blood blob, counting, wiping, waiting, while we talk.

'Steve, I don't know how to bring this up, but last night I had an amazing experience.'

Then I tell it all as I told it to Rosemary. Steve looks at me in the strong morning light.

'That's Bill, all right. He fought field-burning tooth and nail. He could never let go, even if he was dead. You should have seen him play football or basketball. Never-say-die Rodewald we called him.'

'The main thing is, can you help me, Steve? Bill sort of said you would. I need to see those bodies and take pictures of them. I dread the whole thing, but I feel it's some kind of a mandate from Bill.'

'I can call John, the mortician in Dallas, and take you there.

I have a camera, too. But let's eat first.'

'I'd like to try keeping this to ourselves, Steve. It sounds so crazy, I don't want to try explaining to anybody else.'

'I'll call from the upstairs phone.'

We have a great breakfast. There are pans after pans of good scrambled eggs. Each of us washes out his or her dishes in a huge kitchen sink. I've just finished mine when I catch Steve at the front door signalling me. I go over.

'John says the bodies are at the coroner's but he'll get them to the mortuary if we want. He says they're pretty awful and he doesn't recommend our looking at them.'

'What'd you tell him?'

'I didn't tell him anything, but I made arrangements for us to be there at one o'clock. Is that OK?'

'Thanks, Steve. I'll work on the model for the monument while we're waiting.'

'Dad had all the tools you'll ever need. They're out in the back shed. But you don't have to do this right now. It can wait.'

'I want to. I'll be better off out there working with your dad's tools than inside with everybody. I need time to be alone; this will be my excuse.'

Steve takes me out to a really great workshop, all in wood, with nails driven into the walls for hanging tools and each tool marked in outline against the wall, so anybody can know where each tool goes and his dad could know if a tool were missing. With three boys, I'm sure he had to keep track of his tools.

Steve brings out the Number 10 can with the wax mould in it and some knives. He clears the work table, putting tools back in place.

'This should be just the kind of place for you. I can't tell you how much we all appreciate your doing this, especially now, considering all that's happened.'

He goes right out. I wonder if he thinks I would be making this model for a monument if practically our whole family hadn't been killed. I'm sure he's as upset as I am.

I spend the entire morning carving away until the monument in my mind begins to appear. Around the sides I carve in the words of the poem. I find an old fourpenny nail and use it for the gnomon. I set it at an angle equal to the angle of the sundial face. For the cardinal points, I carve in Bill at north or twelve o'clock, Kate at south or six o'clock, and Mia on one side, at nine o'clock, that is, west, and Dayiel at three o'clock, or east. I find some gold paint in the paint closet, and with a small brush fill in the indentations of the carving.

It doesn't look funereal at all and it certainly makes me feel much better, as if I've done *something*, at least. Throughout the whole job, I can feel Bill hovering near but I hear or see nothing. It is only my imagination.

Sometimes one person or another will drift in but I don't look up. It doesn't happen too often, so I imagine Steve has given the word. Rosemary comes briefly to sit by and watch quietly. I look up at her, and we smile but don't say anything. I think it's as hard for her to speak as it is for me. She puts her hand on my shoulder as she leaves. I continue working, turning the model in different directions to see how it reacts to the lighting until it feels right. Steve comes in. He's enthusiastic about the monument-sundial model.

'First we should eat, then take off for Dallas. John phoned and said he managed to get the bodies from the coroner's office but they aren't happy about it.'

'Well, I assure you, Steve, it's something that has to be done. It won't be much of a pleasure, but sometimes things just have to be done. I have my camera with me, but I don't have much film. Is there a place in Dallas where we can buy film?'

'Sure, and I'll bring my camera too. We can buy any film we'll need. The same place does really good work on developing, and they're pretty fast if we make it a rush order.'

'Good, I'll clean this up and come in soon. What's the chance we can go to some place where they cut marble and granite?'

'In Salem, there's a place called Capitol Monuments. They cut the little plaque for Dad's grave. We can stop in there after we go to John's. In fact, we can do that while we're waiting for the film to be developed. Everything will be closed tomorrow, Sunday.'

'That's what we'll do then. I'll be inside in a minute or two.'

Inside there's a mob scene. Everyone is so nervous and so glad to see each other it's more like a wedding than a funeral. I say hello to everybody, trying not to act too much the hypocrite, but not wanting to offend their sensibilities. I'm just not totally broken up the way I was before. Rosemary's in good form, too. These people must think we're the most cold-hearted parents and grandparents in the world. Camille is making up for us. She and Sam also arrived this morning. She's crying up a storm. Those babies were practically like her own; she often took care of them. She and Kate were beginning to be really close, too, even though they had entirely different personalities. Her entire face is swollen and wet all over as if she's been running.

It's a quarter past twelve and I eat hurriedly. I'm not really hungry but I don't want to feel sick or weak, especially now. Steve gives me the eye and goes out of the front door. I wait about two minutes, then follow him. He has his car parked outside the gate and the motor's running. I dash into the workshop and pick up the model; I've stashed my camera in the workshop because I've been taking photos of the model as it's come along. I mount the model on a small piece of plywood. I climb into the front seat beside Steve.

The trip to Dallas is quick and we don't talk much. We stop first at the photo shop and buy three rolls of film, thirty-five millimetre, colour, print, twenty-four exposures. We figure that should do. Then we drive to the mortuary. It isn't as ugly as I thought it would be. In fact it's quite handsome, natural woods and tinted glass. It's also bigger than I'd expected.

But when we go in, it's a mortuary all right. There are the smells and also the quiet. A sandy-haired, slightly balding man comes out from a small office to greet us. Steve shakes hands with him and introduces us. John, the mortician, looks at me quizzically.

'Are you sure you want to do this? I don't recommend it.'

I nod. I don't want to talk too much. I'm on the edge of what I can handle. Being in the mortuary where my family is being stored is getting to me.

'Have you ever seen badly burned human bodies before?'

I nod again, not trusting myself to speak. I must look pretty white or green. He suggests we sit down in some comfortable chairs grouped in a semicircle in a small ante-room. We sit. I feel

I should say something but I don't want to tell him about Bill's visit to me. I'm sure morticians hear more crazy stories than they really want to. I try answering his question.

'I was in World War Two and helped pull bodies out of tanks after they'd burned, both American and German. I have a good idea of what it's like. Mostly I remember the smell.'

'Well, this will be different. This is your family, not complete strangers. I've sprinkled formaldehyde over the bodies to keep down the smell and to slow down the natural decomposition that would occur. Because we've had to hold the bodies for so long, we've also had to keep them in a cold locker. That's one of the reasons they were at the coroner's; I don't have enough cold storage space for them.'

'I understand.'

I understand, but I'm beginning to want to back out of the whole thing. I can see by Steve's colour he's having some of the same feelings. I check my camera and stand up. Steve stands, too. John gets up with us. He leads the way down a narrow corridor to the back of the building. There's a door at the end of the corridor. I guess that's the entrance through which they bring the bodies to cause a minimum of disturbance for the neighbours.

We walk in the last door on the right. There's the smell all right but it's covered partly by a chemical smell. It reminds me of biology class at UCLA. There are four tables, a small one just where we came in, then another small one, then two larger tables deeper in the room. There are high windows over the tables. Each table is covered with a waterproof cover, black on one side and yellow on the other. John steps ahead of us. He takes hold of the cover on the first small table and turns to us.

'This is going to be difficult for you. If you feel it is too much, give me a signal. I'll cover the body and we'll get out of here.'

He pauses, watching us.

'This one is the one who burned the least, the little baby, Mia.'

Steve and I back off a little and he slowly, gently, removes the cover. My first reaction is that she looks exactly like the bodies which were dug up at Pompeii and Herculaneum. She's all white and her features are obliterated but it is definitely the form of a little girl. Her left foot has been broken off just above the ankle but is still hanging by a piece of what was once flesh. In places, we can see the charred sections of her body which were not covered by the formaldehyde powder.

Steve and I look at each other. We're both sighing and taking deep breaths. John is watching us carefully.

'Do you want me to cover her again?'

I figure I can make it. I look at Steve. He nods. I think he nods that we should go on, but I'm not sure. My hands are shaking. I manage to make the settings for my camera, then focus on the baby. I know I'm crying. This is far from every memory I have of Mia. It's hard to keep it together. I take shots from the side, then from on top, leaning over, smelling the cloying yet sharp odour, the combination of the chemical and decomposition. Steve is doing the same thing. John covers Mia and leads us out into the corridor.

'Look, I don't know why you two are doing this but I don't want to have any more dead bodies around here. I think you're pushing yourselves beyond what you can handle. I'm a professional, but I don't think I could take pictures like that of my family if something terrible like this happened.'

Steve and I are leaning back against the wall of the corridor, breathing deeply, trying to recover. I could easily up-chuck if I let myself.

'We're OK. It's just hard. We really want to have these pictures, the last part of some of the most lovely people in the world. OK, Steve? Shall we go back?'

He nods his head. John opens the door again. The smell this time isn't so bad. It's in our clothes now, so the shock isn't as great. John goes to the other small table. He pulls off the cloth. This time it's much harder. Somehow, in the accident, Dayiel lost the top of her skull. The striations of her brain are visible. She's also lost her arms, from the tops above the elbows down, and her legs from above the knees. If she were alive, she'd be a 'basket-case baby', like those thalidomide cases in Germany. I can't believe this is the beautiful Dayiel, a child who never stopped, with deep blue eyes, a lively expression and golden hair. There is a clump of darkened hair at her neck that I think could be her hair.

I start photographing and feel the room beginning to spin around. I grab hold of the edge of the table Dayiel's on. John moves towards me, but I'm better. I lean over to take a photo from above. I hear Steve. He's leaned against the wall behind us and is slowly sliding down. John grabs him by the arm and takes him out. I stay on and take a few more photos of Dayiel, knowing it isn't really her, impressed by how we are all so fooled by the physical, into thinking that this is what we *are*. What must it be for her having to change everything, be in another world when she is so young. But then the whole idea of age is only one part of our limitations. It only deals with how long we've been in a particular body, or some such thing.

Thinking these thoughts comforts me. So I regain my equilibrium. I go out to the corridor. Steve and John have gone up to the antechamber again and are sitting down. I join them. John turns towards me.

'Steve says he's ready to go back. He wants to see his brother for the last time. I'm not so sure it's a good idea.'

I look at John and then at Steve.

'Don't come back, Steve, if it's too much. I know your family is Catholic. I don't know how much of it you believe; but if you accept the idea of the spirit, then you know that what we're looking at in there is only the empty body they left behind. I know it's horrible from a human point of view but it just isn't them any more.'

Steve has leaned over and is looking at his hands, fooling with his camera. His colour is coming back. He looks up at me.

'OK, you're right. I'm ready. I have a feeling this is what Bill meant and this is a kind of test or something. Let's go.'

We walk down the corridor again, John leading the way. I check to see how much film I have left on the roll; enough for two pictures, then I'll need to change rolls. I have a roll in my pocket.

We go into the room. I try not to breathe deeply. John lifts the cover off one of the larger tables. It takes my breath away. It's Bill! He has his head arched back so I can see under his neck. This time it's like that wonderful statue in Rotterdam by Zadkine. The stumps of both his arms are thrown up over his head as if he's reaching for the sky. His mouth is open as in a scream. It's a dreadful sight as a reality. Steve just stares. I look into his face. He's smiling a mirthless smile.

'It's exactly the way he'd go, screaming, reaching for a way out. I'm glad I've seen this. It helps me accept things. Bill was my big brother. He never gave up. Part of this whole horror for me has been that he didn't do anything. I can see now he was trying the best he could. He was Never-say-die Rodewald, right up to the end.'

We start photographing. Even burned down to the bones as he is, it's obvious he was a big and powerful man. His legs are shattered in pieces, not more than three inches each. His arms are above his head but his shoulders have been driven right out of the sockets. In his open, screaming mouth all his teeth are visible like a skull, the skin of the face burned away.

I note all this as I take the first two photos, then change film. Mine is an old-fashioned camera with no automatic rewind and load. I rewind by hand, then engage the spool with shaking hands, close the cover, cock it a few times and start taking pictures. Steve is finished with his and stands looking at his brother. He's crying.

I ask if we can take a little break before I look at Kate. I know this is going to be the hardest for me. All the games we played together, the thousands of books I've read to her, the nights up with her when she was sick, the fun pushing her on a swing or around on a playground carousel, or sometimes on a real carousel, trying to grab rings and never getting any, and she'd laugh. There's so much binding people together it's hard to let go.

We go back in. John pulls the cover down towards her feet. The yellow-and-black plastic reminds me of so many auto accidents I've seen or helped with in my more than fifty years on the road. I never thought I'd see our first-born wrapped up in one.

She's the least recognizable. The lower part of her trunk is a mass of unburned but seared intestines, other organs. Here, she seems the least burned. But her legs, her wonderful long legs are broken into pieces like a jigsaw puzzle or the bones found in the ground and pieced together to make a dinosaur. When I look at her face, calm, the mouth closed, her beautiful green eyes, now only holes in blackened bone, I almost can't make it. I keep trying to keep my eye to the viewfinder of my camera. It's more as if I'm seeing it on television or something else artificial, not real.

I can't take any more. I go out of the door into the hall. Steve follows me. John covers Kate, then comes out too. Steve and I are soaking wet from sweat. My knees feel weak. The sweat on my forehead is cold. John leads us down to the couches and comes back in a few minutes with a shot of whiskey for each of us. I sip mine, Steve downs his like a true Oregonian. John stands in front of us.

'Well, I didn't think you'd make it. That was bad. I want you both to know how sorry I am this had to happen. There's no excuse for a civilized state like Oregon to have field-burning still going on. These four young people aren't the first field-burning victims I've buried from around here. It's a disgrace.'

We take the film out of our cameras. John goes back into his office. By the time I finish rolling the film out of my camera I feel somewhat better. At least I'm not sweating. I head for the restroom. It is such a hot, sweaty day I want to freshen up. I find the restroom in the corridor leading away from the one where we saw the bodies.

I take off my shirt and undershirt. They are soaking wet. I'm a big sweater. I fill the little basin with water and dunk both shirt and undershirt into it. I push down and slosh them around to get the nervous smell out. I can't be any wetter. Then I wring them out as best I can and slide them back on. It is refreshing. Steve comes into the restroom. I tell him what I've done. He's only wearing a T-shirt. He pulls it over his head and does the same thing. He is thin, with strong arms and more hairy than I thought he'd be but not as hairy as Bill.

'What a great idea. I smell like a horse with scurvy.' He uses his wet T-shirt to wipe under his arms and down his stomach, then rinses it again before he wrings it out and slides it back on. We leave the restroom refreshed and ready for the Oregon heat.

The film place is nearby. We ask to have only the negatives made. We'll choose which ones to have printed. It seems they can do it all in one day.

We head for Salem, the capital of the state of Oregon. I'm wondering if the monument place is CAPITOL MONUMENTS or CAPITAL MONUMENTS. Most Americans don't know or pronounce the difference. The *capitol* building has to be here in Salem, but Salem is the *capital* city of Oregon.

It turns out to be CAPITOL MONUMENTS. They're open. I take the model out of the car. Steve begins talking to a round-faced man. They're surrounded by all kinds of monuments and slabs of marble. It's like an indoor cemetery. Steve is saying he's the brother of Bill Rodewald who was killed in the I-5 crash. He introduces me and the man is very sympathetic. I guess tombstone builders have to learn sympathy as much as morticians.

I show him the model and explain what I want. He has trouble catching on to the idea that I'm not as concerned about its being a functioning sundial as I am that it be a symbol of everlasting life, the constant revolving of the sun.

We talk about the kind of stone. There must be fifty different kinds to choose from. I want one which is a rich, warm grey but he tells me it won't weather the way another granite called Sierra would. There's not much difference so I agree to the Sierra. He doesn't have any in stock but he can order it. That's OK with me. There's no way I can stay to see it finished. I'm hoping I'll never come back to Oregon again in my life. I'll most likely never see it.

The CAPITOL man, whose name I forget, begins making drawings to approximate my model. He must have flunked industrial drawing in high school. I keep correcting his perspective and isometric projections. Steve and I decide to have the two family names carved on the front of the monument. Under it, the brief poem. The cardinal points, as on my model, would be carved as well. We tell him we want the colour in the engraving to be black, not gold as in my model. He tells us he'll mail a full-sized styrofoam mock-up to me in New Jersey. I give him my address. He says the monument in the cemetery will come to about five thousand dollars. I tell him I'll pay after I've seen the mock-up and made corrections.

Steve looks at his watch. We get out of the graveyard of polished stones and into the heat again. We drive back to the film place. Steve has air-conditioning, but even so, it's hot. We get to the film store just as it's reopening. I realize we haven't had anything to eat.

We're shocked when we look at the negatives. Practically none of them are usable. We were so nervous and shaken we seem to have made every mistake possible. It's three o'clock. The next day is Sunday and then there's the funeral. We ask how soon they'd need new negatives in order to have them ready by Monday. They close at six. Steve uses their phone and phones the mortuary. John says he hasn't sent the bodies back but can't hold them past four because the coroner's office closes at five on Saturdays.

We buy more film. We drive like madmen to the mortuary. We're out and in the back room in five minutes. John shows us some Polaroid shots his son has taken. They'll probably be good enough if we don't do it right this time.

We're much more calm and collected this time. I check every move, every setting on my camera to get it right. It's astounding how the human mind can adjust to almost anything. We get the photos shot in half an hour. We're both crying as we go along but we're functioning. We thank John profusely. Nobody could be nicer under such conditions.

We get the film out of the camera and delivered to the photo shop in plenty of time. Steve takes his camera from me. I was unloading as he was driving. They tell us we can see the negatives and maybe positive direct prints before they close, if we want to wait. I think they've looked at the work we did before and know what we're doing. They're very considerate. Two young women run the place. We say we'll be back at ten minutes to six. We walk out into the heat again. Nobody should have to die in weather like this. Steve turns away from his car.

'I need a beer. I know a good, dark, air-conditioned place about half a block from here.'

'Sounds good to me, Steve. I'm starving and I'll go any place that's cool.'

We go into the back of a wood-panelled place with the bar up front. Steve orders two draught beers on the way in. I can feel myself fading. I lean back in my chair. Steve quaffs off his beer with only one stop. It's so cold it hurts my eyes.

'Steve, you know what I'd like to do while we're waiting for those photos?'

It's obviously a rhetorical question, but I think Steve's expecting anything from me.

'How far is it from here to where the accident happened? Do you think we could get from here to there and back before the photo shop closes?'

Steve stares at the ceiling, then sucks out the foamy dregs of his beer.

'We could do it, but it'll be close. I don't think we'll find anything anyway. The road is black and the grass is burned there, but they cleared everything away with big equipment. I watched some of it on television.'

'I'd really just like to see the last things they saw. It would bring me closer to them.'

Steve stands up, pushes back his chair.

'OK, let's go then. We have about two hours, that should do it.'

He's out of the door. I take a last slug of beer. I catch up with him. The heat hits us again. The car's still where we left it at the mortuary.

Steve drives faster than before but still not so fast that I'm uncomfortable. We don't talk too much. Steve keeps looking at his watch.

'We'll make it and have about ten minutes to look around if we want. I haven't been here myself, just didn't have the nerve. We'll need to go down about twelve miles past to find an on-ramp to the I-5. There's some kind of construction going on in the southbound lane there. But I think we'll make it.'

We drive on to the I-5 going north and I'm looking out of the windows, wondering just what Kate or Bill or any of the kids might have seen. I'm hoping for some contact from them. I'm so close to where they last were in this world, although four days have passed. The newspapers said the accident seemed to have happened around four o'clock. It's around four, a little after.

But all I experience in the landscape is a weird frozen quality, as if nobody has ever been here. There's a lovely little hill in the generally flat country to my right. Kate must have noticed that. As a geologist, this strange formation would mean something to her.

Both north- and southbound traffic is on the north side with us. The trucks are enormous and are going too fast for the density of traffic. There's no passing. These guys have got to make up time. We open up again, the south traffic back in its own lane, and we see where the accident was. Steve pulls over. We get out in the slanting sun and look. The roadbed is cracked from the intense heat of the crash. I only looked briefly at the newspapers everybody kept pushing into my face last night because I wasn't ready. But I remember the fire burned for hours. It seems diesel fuel leaked out of a truck and combined with a truck filled with wood chips, making quite a fire. I find a piece of metal on the road. I shine it up and it's the nameplate of a Corvair. We have to be careful because the cars are tearing by, nobody going under seventy.

'Bert, we'd better get going. I don't know if I can take this any longer and that photo shop might close on us. It's hard to predict traffic at this time of night.'

We hop back in the car and head north, continuing the trip that Kate, Bill, Dayiel and Mia never finished.

We arrive at the photo shop before a quarter to six. The girls pull out both the film and prints. They have a back light wall and magnifying glasses for us to look at the negatives and prints. It's almost worse than the reality. This time we did it right. Steve wants me to choose. I'm not sure what Bill wanted except somehow these photos were supposed to help fight the field-burning. I try selecting photos which best show the terrible damage done to their bodies. I know that after this, only the photos can ever show that. Two days from now, the rest of the cremation will be done and as far as we mere mortals are concerned, they won't exist any more.

I select twenty of the photos for full-scale enlargement. The rest of the negatives and proofs I put in a separate packet. I'm glad I have a significant amount of cash with me because I forgot my cheque-book. I don't want to use plastic. One of the girls, the smaller, not so pretty one, gets up her nerve.

'Are these photos of the victims of the I-5 crash Wednesday?'

'That's right.'

Steve looks at me to see if it's all right to tell them.

'Are you from the police? How did you get these pictures? I couldn't help looking at them. They're terrible!'

We're quiet. She has a right to know.

'No. I'm the father of the woman and grandfather to the two babies. My friend here is the brother to the man. We took these pictures so we'd have something to remember them by.'

She looks to see if I'm kidding, sees I'm not, puts her hand to her mouth.

'But what a terrible way to remember them. I don't know how you could have taken these pictures. Didn't I just say that to you, Diana?'

'Well, we did. In a way, we had to. How much will I owe you for all this work? It's very well done. Would you please write out the bill for the enlargements, and for the development and proofs? I'll pay now. My friend will pick them up when they're ready.'

She takes a form and checks off the negatives to be enlarged, peering at the numbers in the margin. She notes the cost of the development and proofs separately. It comes to just under two hundred dollars. I take two hundred-dollar bills out of my pocket. She peers at them, to check if they're real, I think. She gives me the change.

'We're terribly sorry about what happened. Isn't that field-burning awful?'

'I don't know, except it killed my family. We don't allow things like this where I live.'

We turn and leave. It's hot in the car. Even at six o'clock in the evening it's hot. But it is August. Steve turns up the air-conditioner. I lay my head back on the headrest. My eyes feel bare. But we did get it done: everything, the monument, the pictures. Maybe I can sleep tonight. I should, I'm dead tired. I dread the funeral. I own one suit, one white shirt, one tie, one decent pair of shoes. Getting dressed up for things is not my style.

GEOFFREY WOLFF

WATERWAY

Geoffrey Wolff

One May afternoon, at the end of Nicholas Wolff's junior year at college, aboard our boat, *Blackwing*, drinking beer so cold we needed mittens to hold the cans, reaching rail-down into the sun and towards the beach at Mackerel Cove on the New England island where we live, Nicholas and I struck a deal: on graduating from Bowdoin, Nicholas would take this boat to the Bahamas with one or two chums.

There was nothing to it: other than taking full responsibility for our boat which *I* pay for, and teaching his friends to sail, navigate, cook on a galley stove without blowing up the galley, other than maintaining the sails and gear and engine and electronics, and troubling that the dinghy wasn't stolen, and earning enough money before he sailed from home to keep himself afloat without work for six months, and making certain the anchor didn't drag when autumn and winter gales blasted him, and learning first aid, and keeping his friends out of the ocean and clear of the boom . . . Why, there was nothing to the venture but a nod, a wink, another beer and a far-away look on Nicholas's face that I took to be gratitude for my trust, but was in truth cogitation.

During the following year, when friends would remark what a generous fellow I was and how trusting (how could I bank on a mere boy with so much boat? wasn't he grateful?), that circumspect countenance would steal on Nicholas's face, and he'd catch my eye, and I'd shrug. In fact, I had every reason to trust him: he was handy; he didn't get seasick; he knew (as I didn't and don't) celestial navigation; he'd been trained to strip down and repair a diesel engine; he'd sailed offshore weeks at a time on a tall ship; he'd been aloft in great seas and screaming winds; his instincts on the water seemed flawless. We'd been together on the water since he was ten, and in trouble he had never failed to come through.

Besides, *Blackwing* would either winter over in my back yard (while I paid the bank and watched her cradled in blocks, swathed in tarps and crusted with snow a few yards from a blue spruce) or in the Bahamas. Which would she prefer?

He got her there. He and two college buddies provisioned her and prepared her for sea in September, while hurricane Hugo made its way up the east coast from the Caribbean. When it passed, Nicholas gave them a crash course in the rudiments of sailing, and slipped our Jamestown, Rhode Island, mooring the first day of October: Block Island, Fishers Island, the Thimbles, Long Island, City Island, the East River, Sandy Hook, Manasquan, Atlantic City, Cape May, Chesapeake City, Sassafras River, Annapolis, Smith Island, Norfolk, the Dismal Swamp, Elizabeth City, the Alligator River, Ocrakoke, Oriental, Beaufort, Wrightsville Beach, Waccamaw River, Charleston, another Beaufort, New Teakettle Creek, St Simon's Island, St Augustine, Daytona, Cocoa Beach, Vero Beach, Fort Pierce, Palm Beach, Fort Lauderdale, Key Biscayne, the Gulf Stream, Gun Cay, the Bahama Banks, Chub Cay, Nassau, Allan's Cay, Hawksbill Cay, Sampson Cay, Pipe Creek, Staniel Cay, Georgetown, Eleuthera, Governor's Harbour, the End Of The Road.

That road was six months unwinding, bristling with pitfalls and Sirens and drug dealers and drug agents and anxiety and shoals and snags and reefs and the worst gear-busting winter winds ever recorded in the southern Bahamas.

Priscilla and I had agreed to meet our son and our boat at Governor's Harbour on the hundred-mile-long island of Eleuthera on 20 March. Such rendezvous are laughably quixotic. On our end we had flu to avoid, blizzards to pray against, semi-tropical airlines with semi-tropical attitudes toward confirmed reservations and clockwork schedules. On Nicholas's end was a complex of nautical machinery, his body's machinery, weather systems, kismet.

On 20 March, we landed at Eleuthera's little airport and took a taxi to the harbour. In the harbour, swinging from a mooring thousands of miles from home, were our boat and our son. The boat was impeccable, the sun shining, the son tan and grinning.

With what mixed feelings Nicholas surrendered command of *Blackwing* might be imagined. With what mixed feelings I took responsibility for safely returning Priscilla, the boat and me to Rhode Island might be imagined. The idea was to take it easy, to laze three hundred miles through the islands of the northern Bahamas and back across the Gulf Stream; then to push about a thousand miles up the Waterway to Norfolk; then to bring her the final six hundred miles home, reading the seabag-full of paperbacks we'd brought, catching some good rays, watching the handsome world float by at five miles per hour—less, if we wanted to hang out. I had finished and revised a book; Priscilla was on leave from teaching. We felt we deserved this, and we knew we needed a jolt to our routine. Back home we were owned by a house and trees and gardens and processes of maintenance that had become habitual. We were past due for a sea change.

During the transition week we stayed in Eleuthera at a friend's beach house. Most mornings that week Nicholas instructed me an inch at a time in the foibles of the boat I had taught him to sail. The boat looked different. It looked better. It had always looked good, I think, but Nicholas had made it look better. He had finished *Blackwing*'s cherry interior bright, laying up coat after coat of varnish. (And where did three six-footers sleep while the varnish was drying?) Above decks he had taken all the brightworked teak down to bare wood, and brushed on eight coats. Below, the bilge was dry, smelled sweet. The sails had been cleaned and spot-mended. You would not guess looking into my son's bedroom at home that *Blackwing*'s icebox would have been scrubbed, but it had been scrubbed.

He had made our boat sound and clean, and made us happy. There was nothing more that he could do, except sail with us twenty miles north up the west coast of Eleuthera to Hatchet Bay, and say goodbye.

The day we sailed, as all Eleutheran days so far, was clear; the wind was fair; *Blackwing* moved fast through twenty-five feet of water. We could see the bottom; we disciplined ourselves not to look down. We instead stared ahead, trying to make out distinguishing features along what seemed to be an undifferentiated coast. There are no navigational aids in the 'Bahamas'—a corruption of the Spanish *baja mar*, low sea.

In less time than it takes to tell, we were sailing through a hole in the wall, and making our way to a mooring of the Hatchet Bay Yacht Club. A few feet from the mooring pickup Nicholas said the water looked to him 'thin', and I was on the point of requiring him to define his terms when I ran us aground in soft mud.

I don't run aground. Ask anyone. Maybe I *used to* run

aground, in Chesapeake Bay, but *I do not run aground.*

'Dad, we're high and dry. Tide'll ease you off in a couple hours. Mix a Mount Gay and juice. Be mellow in the islands, mon. Gotta blaze, Ma. I've got a plane to catch.'

There was water enough to float the dinghy, and I rowed my son ashore, and asked him how often this had happened to him.

'Well, that's a weird thing. Never, actually.'

(Well, actually: would *you* believe him?)

2

After Nicholas said goodbye, Priscilla and I had a long, hard look at our hole cards. Neither told the other, then, but both wondered, what did we think we were doing? After Priscilla reminded me of our agreement, that (after we crossed the Gulf Stream) she could jump ship whenever she was fed up with *Blackwing* or its crew, we decided to feel laid-back. We put a Zoot Sims tape on the deck, were pleased to have verifiable corroboration that a rising tide floats all ships, ate a fine meal. The harbour was snug and pretty, bordered by the little settlement of Alice Town.

This Saturday night a volleyball game was being played under arc lights against a neighbour from the archipelago now called the Family Islands. It was a sweet occasion: we could hear bellows of enthusiasm, and Priscilla and I smiled a private smile, happy to share (at a little distance) the Bahamians' childlike pleasures, to hear their boisterous huzzahs.

The next morning, in transit to Royal Island, trying with what would become comic inefficiency to get a weather forecast, we heard a news report. Dozens of people injured last night during a fracas at half-time of a volleyball match in Alice Town. A mêlée. Bottles had been thrown, police and ambulances sent for. How the world seems is not how the world is.

At Royal Island we anchored in a palm-fringed lagoon that resembled a movie set of Eden: water as clear as crystal, abandoned plantation, coconut palms backlit by a Tintoretto sunset, soft evening. Sixteen boats were anchored in the large, nearly land-locked harbour; the moon rose, showing its sharp-edged silver face like a cheerful, goofy neighbour peering over a fence, *hey guys, what's cooking?* The nautical almanac had said the moon would rise and it was so, the spheres in their regulated cycles, time and tide right with the world. As the night lavished softness, the moon spilling such unpolluted light that we could see by its beams our anchor dug into the chalky white sand below our keel, and as the breeze piped up we heard the voices of wine and beer and rum drinkers float across the water, singing the songs sung in the back of school buses ('Roll Me Over'), and around camp-fires ('Row Row Row Your Boat'), and by God we joined in. Was this OK or what?

We were gathered into the anything-goes euphoria of strangers sharing a discovery. Then it got rowdy, as though the whole harbour were drunk on liberty. Someone shot off a parachute flare and we heard chivvying gasps: Bad Form. This Is Not Done. Flares were reserved for Mayday emergencies, to signal grave distress. To set off a flare back where we thought of as *back home* would bring the Coast Guard down on a mariner. Back home, playing with flares was much deplored; horsing around with flares, a rum job, a hanging offence back home. But we weren't back home. For sure. So another boat lofted a parachute flare, and another, and soon the lagoon was bathed in moonlight, starlight, phosphorus. Phosphorus in the velvet water, phosphorus aloft. The harbour was lit and so were we.

I went below, and spread out the charts. Again. I'd been studying the ungiving things since the night we met Nicholas in Governor's Harbour and, to my disenchantment, they weren't more inviting tonight than a week ago. The problem was simple: to get to Little Harbour in the Abacos, the northernmost Bahamas chain, we had to navigate more than fifty miles (fifty-three, to be precise, which is what I had to be) of Northeast Providence Channel. To sail the reef-strewn Bahamas at night was unthinkable, so we had ten hours from dawn (seven a.m.) till sundown. *Blackwing* could do five and a half knots under power in calm seas and neutral current. We had to hit Little Harbour Bar on the button. I spent the next several hours calculating courses and tidal sets.

If the wind (or tidal current) was on *Blackwing*'s nose, we wouldn't make it. On the other hand, if the wind was behind us, or abeam of us, we probably would, unless something went wrong. Moreover, if we *almost* made it, there was no escape hatch, no harbour of refuge. We'd cross a line of no return five hours out from Royal Island, and if we went for Little Harbour, and the wind clocked around on us, coming to blow against us, we were out of luck.

The rum was beginning to wear off. I had shut down Jimmy Buffet for the night, and was playing a tape of Pablo Casals doing Bach solos. He was working his way through a threnodic patch, and I explained to Priscilla that I was 'apprehensive'.

She cocked her head at me.

I said I was 'anxious'.

She asked me what I was talking about.

I said it was going to be a 'tricky' passage. Maybe 'chancy'. Not 'tranquil'. In fact, I was looking at alternate routes back to the coast of Florida. An easy passage would take us home by way of Nassau and Freeport, shit-holes.

Priscilla said she'd hang her head in shame. When it came down to it, Priscilla seemed always to be the one of us who put the thing in gear, and stepped on the gas. She likes to know the pros and cons, but I'm not sure why; it takes a lot of cons to turn her off course.

So next morning we got our hangovers out of our berth an hour before dawn. While Priscilla made peanut butter sandwiches with Ritz crackers, and packed them in Ziploc bags, I tried to tune in Charley's Locker on the transistor radio. In the Bahamas, on weekdays, at six forty-five a.m., maybe, if reception was good, it was possible to tune in Charley's Locker from Coral Gables, Florida, to get a rough prophecy of weather in the Caribbean. This followed a round-up of sports news from Trinidad and Jamaica, and was preceded by a maddening hornpipe shanty, 'Barnacle Bill the Sailor' or the like. The velocity of Charley's weather report was remarkable; someone was paying by the second. It was possible, if the boat was pointed in just the right direction, and if the seas were quiet, and wind wasn't shrieking in the rigging, and Priscilla remembered not to talk while I listened, and I kept alert despite a numbing chatter of cricket scores, to hear every third or fourth word in the only experience in the Bahamas (other than trouble) that befell us fast. I tuned in Charley, and he sort of seemed to bring passably OK news. Windsouthwest-somethingknots-somethingelse-by afternoon.

'Let's go,' I said.

It was a hairy passage.

We jumped off at the first hint of light, got up in oilskins and wool caps and gloves. The wind was up and at 'em, twenty knots at first, gusting to twenty-five. The day was grey and ominous, with low clouds scudding in from the west-south-west. The rusted wreck of a fertilizer freighter was the last vessel we saw that day. We were headed due north into great cresting rollers; but as the wind increased, spindrift blew off the tops of the surge, spraying us with warm water. When a gust hit, it came from the west. The wind was beginning to clock around, and I was tense, racing the sun to cross Little Harbour Bar before dark, and safely.

Priscilla noted loran fixes—read from an electronic position calculator—and nautical miles accumulated on the log, and kept me equipped with hot tea and peanut-buttered crackers. I hadn't eaten peanut-buttered crackers since I was a kid, and neither had Priscilla; she reinvented them for this voyage and this is why she's so smart: she knew that a quantity of those crackers, dry in zip-locked bags, would give our windswept, water-soaked cockpit a milk-and-crackers-at-recess comfyness. This passage was a trial for her. All these years she'd fought seasickness, and now we were trying a timed-release drug taken by way of a patch worn behind her ear, and either it was working, or she was too busy hanging on and helping out to be sick. That was the good news. The bad news: I was working hard to keep *Blackwing* on course in those wilful seas, with the wind building and coming more and more off her beam. Plus: beginning just after noon, past the line of no return, we could see lightning on the horizon, and hear thunder. Plus: the steering felt sloppy, and I heard the rudder creak when I adjusted it to counter the violent push of a roller on our port stern quarter.

There is no worse destiny in heavy seas than to lose a rudder (other than being stove in, or catching fire). Nicholas had had a steering cable break a few weeks ago, while cruising in the Exumas, navigating a tricky reef. He'd been sailing with a flotilla of friends, and they'd provided him with a spare cable after he'd managed by skill (and maybe luck) to get out of trouble. But now the cables would be impossible to replace or adjust. I had an emergency tiller, but it would take all my strength to keep *Blackwing* on course with it, and I was cold and tired. I felt short-handed; I *was* short-handed, and I elected to keep my anxieties about our steering system to myself.

A simple truth we couldn't ignore: Priscilla—smart, brave and calm—is not strong. She has an unerring sense of place, so that she could thread us through a reef. She would cheerfully go below and make food in wild seas. She kept a running record of our time and probably location by the process known as dead reckoning. But to ask her to douse and furl a sail in huge seas, or to trim a sheet, or to wrestle the wheel out here where all was too big for our britches—this was to ask too much. Unspoken between us was a contract: I sail, she thinks. Her will wasn't in question, or her nerve; she was overpowered, and I wasn't, quite. But there was only one of me (alas, alas!), and that one was now wearing out.

The thunder and lightning hit us with full force at four in the afternoon, just after we'd caught sight of a landfall on Great Abaco. When the rain hit us in wind-driven horizontal sheets, we could see nothing but grey wet and evil electric bolts, and the concussive thunder scared us silly. I wondered to myself what it would be like, if I couldn't find Little Harbour Bar, to ride this out at sea, through the night, waiting for dawn, hoping to find my way across. Wondering this, I heard Priscilla say, 'that's it'. The 'it' to which she referred was a reef, forbiddingly named The Boilers, a mile or so south of the bar. If 'it' wasn't 'it', all bets were off, and we'd rolled snake eyes. Time was short now. But 'it' *was* 'it', and now all that remained was to follow the *Yachtsman's Guide to the Bahamas*, which Priscilla read to me above the scream of the wind and the thunder and the smash of the sea.

> Little Harbour Bar should be negotiated with care, according to the following directions. Approaching Little Harbour Bar from the south, stand off the coast

not less than one mile until Little Harbour Point and Tom Curry's Point are in transit. (See sketch chart of Little Harbour.) They will then be bearing roughly 305°. Alter course to port to keep them on this bearing until in mid-channel between the point and the line of breakers on the reef that extends south from Lynyard Cay. Then alter course to north, running parallel to the land for about 400 yards, in order to clear the reef that extends for about 300 yards north from Little Harbour Point. You will then be in 18-24 feet. As you alter course, rounding the reef to the port, a cove behind the lighthouse will open up. This will be easily recognized by the white sand beach and a group of coconut palms in the eastern corner. This is not a good anchorage.

See what I mean? Clear as mud? If you don't see what I mean, if you see instead what the *Yachtsman's Guide* shows, if you see it with utmost clarity so that you could put a hand on *Blackwing*'s wheel, and guide her over the reef, then you're of Priscilla's tribe. 'Look,' she said. 'Look there!'

I looked, terrified what I might see. It was a pretty beach, our anchorage, which was a very good anchorage. A pink sand beach. And over it, arched from way out at sea, near the ungodly depths called The Tongue of the Ocean, to the spot off Lynyard Cay where we dropped anchor, a rainbow.

I thought of it as her rainbow, and do. When I met Priscilla in 1963 she was temperamentally unlike anyone I'd known; I fell in love with her for the inexpressible reasons people fall in love but also for a character I can try to articulate, her unimpeded clarity of vision and expression. Of course Priscilla had understood the *Yachtsman's Guide*, and of course she had translated its dense instructions into a rational course of action. If I couldn't have counted on Priscilla to continue to see and say unambiguously, we wouldn't have come to this place in this way. Imagine someone who sees things and systems whole, and who says precisely what she thinks. Not that she says whatever she thinks: she says only what she thinks. Such a person can neither be fooled nor fool, and to live with her is to live with the recurring surprise of hearing a sane consciousness expressed with insanely serene candour. It is frightening to be wholly understood; it is bracing; it is fun; it keeps me off reefs. Because Priscilla's relentless good sense has no interest in prudence, because her comprehension is a renewable resource driven by curiosity, because to see the world through her eyes is to see a misbegotten human comedy rather than a blighted human tragedy, because she said something crossing Little Harbour Bar that made me laugh, because I associate her with light—warmth and buoyancy and illumination—that was her rainbow, and is.

It is worth feeling wet and cold to feel dry and warm. It is worth being scared to be secure. It is worth leaving sight of land to make a landfall. More than a few times, *Blackwing* had been an instrument of instruction in these truisms, but to be safe aboard her, with Priscilla, in the lee of those very reefs that caused such dread, was to feel the kind of gratitude that it is irrational to feel for inanimate objects. Perhaps this was why Priscilla—bringing a tray of rum drinks and cheese to the cockpit—found me below in the engine compartment, tightening the steering cable. It had been well secured and abundantly greased by Nicholas, but it had stretched, as new cable will, under the strain put on it today.

'Come on out of there,' Priscilla said. 'The sun's setting.'

'I know,' I said. 'I need the last of the light to adjust her steering.'

I saw Priscilla make that ancient sign of schoolyard and marriage, eyes rolled upward while forefinger circles ear clockwise.

'What's the matter with you?' she said. 'What's wrong with tomorrow?'

The question was sensible, as far as it went. It failed merely to accommodate how I'd feel tonight leaving undone what ought to be done to thank our boat for bringing us safely to this place, the rainbowed and sundowned glow of which I was missing to thank our boat for bringing us to this place. Well, it confused me, too.

3

Last night we'd seen through our open hatch the stars clear and sharp in the flawless atmosphere—Arcturus, Spico, Regulus, the Southern Cross—and the next morning came in clean and bracing. Studying the charts, planning our complicated passage from Lynyard Cay to Marsh Harbour (the metropolis of the Abacos) to Hope Town, I noticed over the tops of my sunglasses an inflatable dinghy, pushed by an outboard, grinding towards us. The irritating noise (irritating when someone else was making it but not when I was making it, when it was *necessary* and *up-and-about* noise) reminded me how quiet was the world here in these Out Islands. We were anchored off a pretty beach—down here we were always, when we were anchored, anchored off a pretty beach—not a boat or person in sight, except this one, nearing from Little Harbour. It was churlish to resent company; call me churlish. Here he came: 'Ahoy, *Blackwing*! Where's the Cap?'

'I'm the captain. And owner.'

'Oh.' The fellow bobbing alongside, a little more or less my age, was disappointed. 'Where's Nick?'

This question would be repeated all the way home: *where's Nick?* To meet returning north the people he had met migrating south was an odd sensation. He'd made many friends, and these were not the friends I predicted he'd meet. The water south to the Bahamas is so well-ploughed by yachts that the Inland Waterway is sometimes called the Blue Flag Expressway, for the blue flags flown from boats whose owners are not aboard. I had predicted that Nicholas and his friends would meet the paid hands of boats much bigger than *Blackwing*, crews of young men and women not much older than Nicholas. In fact, the boys of *Blackwing* preferred the company of people like us, oldsters looking for an adventure, middle-class couples (with an occasional remittance man or woman thrown in to raise the tone of the venture) who had cashed in their chips, sold the pencil factory or software patent or house in Shaker Heights, to quit the world and wander.

It was an oddity of many of these people that they brought with them vestigial Polonius- or headmaster-inspired wisdoms, so that many felt compelled, especially after a dinner served on their boat, to clear their throats over a glass of brandy and ask Nicholas and his friends when they were going to settle down, get with the programme, start on their careers. They evidently detected no irony here. They may have been provoked to counsel by Nicholas's vague version of his recent history and his plans. He was less than forthcoming with newly met friends about the title to *Blackwing*; when asked who owned her, he knew he couldn't say he did, or he'd be mistaken for a drug dealer or—worse!—a rich kid. He also wouldn't confess the plain fact, *my daddy let me have the keys*. So he'd take on a cryptic mien, shrug, look at the night sky, say *some guy in Jamestown asked us to bring her south*.

We met dozens, scores, of people along our way who told of kindnesses done them by our son and his friends (without telling us of the kindnesses they returned). We heard stories of Nicholas's ingenuity with tools, his eagerness to lend a hand, his seamanship, his curiosity, his friendliness.

The fellow in the dinghy, a long way from home in Tulsa, declined our invitation to come aboard. He said to tell Nick he'd really done it this time.

'This one's worse than Wax Cay Cut; he'll know what I'm talking about. We screwed the pooch this time.'

What happened: the sailor and his wife had bounced across the bar of Little Harbour lagoon at high tide of a full moon. Now they'd have to wait for the next full moon to bounce back out.

Sailing the southern Abacos was a trial of attention. To sail is to attend: in New England the eye strains to pick out a buoy or the loom of a light. Here we watched the sea's surface for the tell-tale ripples of a shifting wind, and studied the sky for its lessons and warnings. But now we looked down as well as up; it is said of the Bahamas' shoals that the most valuable skill a navigator can bring to their successful circumvention is an aptitude to 'read' the water. By this is meant an ability to distinguish between the dark blue of deeps, the turquoise and aquamarine of adequate depth, the green of a grassy bottom, the milky pale yellow of sandy shoals, the white of a sand bar dry at low tide, the dark patch that looks like coral but is only a shadow cast by a cloud, the brown of coral that can tear a hole in a boat's bottom (not to be confused with the harmless brown of 'fish muds', caused by bottom-feeders eating dinner, stirring up the marl). Nicholas, who is colour-blind, nevertheless learned to read the water from *Blackwing*'s bowsprit, or in especially perilous waters from up her mast. The downside of that upside, he told us, was a clear view of sharks working the bottoms.

Learning to read thin water is an incremental adequacy; the apt scholar of shoals depends not only on memory and common sense, but on sunlight from above and behind. Sailing into the sun it is impossible to differentiate between the shades along the sea's spectrum. So we had to plan our passages, which demanded snaky course changes through erratic channels, according to the sun's declination, which often warred with felicitous tides. We trained ourselves to disregard our terror, to pretend to know better, to smile as we sailed into what seemed to be five feet, four, two. But I'd reach the end of an Abacos passage, strike the sails, line up a casuarina with a church steeple, triangulate that line with a line bearing 287 degrees to the butt of a dirt road, dodge a sand bar, home in on a water-tower (looking sharp for the submerged pilings of a wrecked pier), drop the anchor and uncramp my white-knuckled hand from the wheel and a dumb unfelt grin from my face.

But what if the worst had happened, if we'd been holed up for a week or two in one Eden in place of another? Or the other worst: we had had to spend a night at sea, floating two and a half miles above the bottom of Northeast Providence Channel? After all, I wasn't a single-handed Joshua Slocum dodging growlers, icebergs and pirates in the Roaring Forties. I wasn't commanding a convoy escort on the Murmansk run. Seen from above we must have made a dandy picture, sailing like gangbusters through pristine water under a warming sun. This was the Bahamas, as in the Sunday newspaper supplement ads. And if my keel hit sand? *Blackwing* would float off on a rising tide. And if she didn't? We'd wade ashore and phone Allstate.

As these verities sunk in, we settled into what became (for a time) a tranquil routine. The sun would wake us; we'd drink coffee and orange juice; we'd laze in the cockpit waiting for the tide to do the right thing. We'd make a shopping list; we'd take the dinghy ashore to search for ice and bread and beer and fruit and cheese;

we'd find what we came for. We'd take the dinghy back to
Blackwing and laze in the cockpit; we'd observe that it sure was a
nice day; we'd think aloud that it was almost warm enough to
swim; we'd say we were thinking about taking a swim; we'd swim;
we'd sit in the cockpit, letting the warm air dry us; we'd notice it
was coming on towards the lunch hour; we'd discuss lunch; we'd
make lunch; we'd eat lunch; we'd say we were considering a little
nap; we'd take a little nap; we'd pull up anchor and sail a few
hours to the next pretty beach; we'd drop anchor; we'd make rum
drinks; we'd take the dinghy ashore for a dinner of fried or sautéed
or grilled grouper or flounder; we'd bring the dinghy back to the
Blackwing; we'd put a tape in the deck, maybe Dave McKenna,
maybe Thelonius Monk; we'd sit in the cockpit, looking at the
night sky; we'd go below to our berth; we'd lie on our backs
talking, looking at the night sky. We'd sleep.

4

It was time to get out of the Abacos and across the Gulf Stream
to Florida. North of Green Turtle Cay casual yacht traffic thins
almost to vanishing, except for live-aboards transiting from north
of Palm Beach into the Bahamas in the late fall and early winter,
and back home in the spring. The northern Abacos are mostly
uninhabited, with a desolate end-of-the-world atmosphere,
especially on a cloudy day during a blustery north-west passage
of twenty-five miles, driven by a north-east wind of twenty knots
to Allan's-Pensacola. This was an abandoned Air Force missile
tracking station, populated by moray eels in its reefs and
barracuda in the mangrove flats. Oh, and sharks. Did I forget to
mention sand fleas? Sand fleas weren't a worry when the wind
gusted to thirty knots, but anchoring was.

I use a heavy anchor called a plough, made in England by
CQR (*secure*: get it?). I swear by it; I swear by anything weighing
twenty-five pounds that can arrest the drift of another something
weighing ten thousand pounds when that other something is being
hammered by a great north wind. The holding power of an anchor
is a function of physical properties that can be mathematically
calculated, once that anchor is set. To set an anchor—that is an

art; I believed it was an art I had mastered. Priscilla would bring *Blackwing* into the wind under power, and slow her till she was dead in the water, and I would nonchalantly, imperturbably lower the anchor to the bottom (no undignified heaving, no tangling myself in chain); I would then aloofly pay out anchor rope (called *rode*), while *Blackwing* drifted astern. When five times the water depth had been unflappably paid out in rode (I had marked it in twenty-foot increments), I would snub the rode to a cleat, and observe diffidently how, as usual, the anchor had CQRly bit into the bottom. I would then nod to Priscilla an almost imperceptible nod (no wild oaths, please, no despotic commands, no assholery) to shut the engine down and start chipping ice for the rum drinks. I would sit quietly in the bow, triangulating lines of sight on various objects ashore, casuarinas, say, or maybe palm trees. Meantime I would casually pay out more rode as *Blackwing* drifted astern, till I had achieved the desired ratio of seven to one, rode to depth.

Except at Allan's-Pensacola Cay. We were dressed in oilskins, weary, lonely, wet and cold from the front's spill of rain. It was late in the day, and the sun was too low to light the reefs that ringed both shores of the harbour, the only harbour within reach, a harbour said to be marginal in a northerly. Two boats were anchored close to each other, further up the harbour, where we would like to have been. Priscilla brought *Blackwing* into the wind; I lowered the anchor; *Blackwing* drifted fast astern; the anchor bounced uselessly along the hard-pan sand bottom. I could see it bouncing. It made me angry to see this, and to haul in rode and chain and twenty-five pound plough also made me angry, and made me reflect on how lucky was Priscilla to have in her hands a varnished teak steering-wheel instead of a muddy length of chain. This process was repeated for the next hour or so: the helmsperson, following the anchorperson's despotic commands, manoeuvred *Blackwing* into the wind; the anchorperson lowered the anchor, which skipped along the hard-pan bottom, provoking from the anchorperson wild oaths.

This routine did not proceed in solitude, unobserved. To watch a couple anchor a boat is one of the sea's great amusements, way more entertaining than a world-class sunset or moonbeams filtered through casuarinas. It is proof of one's superiority to observe—from the CQRity of one's own steady state, with one's own vessel tugging fruitlessly at what holds it, with a beverage cooling one's hand and perhaps a dish of beernuts nearby on one's cockpit table—a couple less evolved hurling oath, command and anchor. The world at such a moment is starkly binary, split between the anchored and the would-be anchored. Up at the head of the harbour were two boats, one of the anchored was pretending not very successfully to be not watching us. He was smoking a pipe! This pipe-smoking shook me to my rubber wellingtons. It was not right. And then, as though that were not enough, the pipe-smoker turned towards *Blackwing*, languidly, and motioned *my* helmsperson, to whom *I* gave despotic orders, to approach. And then, as though that weren't enough, she did his bidding.

'Holding's bad down there,' said the skipper of *Inshallah*, a heathen corruption of *que será, será*. 'Anchor here, between us.'

Priscilla commanded me, tyrannically, to lower the anchor, and I did, and it held. There was marginally room enough for our three boats to swing, if they swung together, without hitting. The skipper of *Inshallah* had violated a first principle of the Law of First Anchored: he had welcomed us to his sanctuary. This generosity was a breach of all anchoring protocols. I didn't know what to say, so I sulked. Priscilla said, 'Thank you.'

The skipper pulled on his pipe, which he smoked upside-down. 'I'd dive on that anchor,' he said. 'To make sure it's set.'

To examine an anchor in the Bahamas was always advised, because in the clear shoals it was an easy chore, sometimes even fun. (No one dives into Block Island's New Harbour to counterfeit study of his anchor dug into mud and beer cans and shit.) I eyed the mangroves seventy yards from my bow, and mused on the barracuda feeding there, in competition with sharks. I wondered whether the little food fish that lived among mangroves ever toured seventy yards to sightsee a plough anchor, and whether the bigger diners followed them on such a safari.

'You think it's a good idea to dive on that anchor?' I said.

'Well, I do think it's a good idea,' said the master of *Inshallah*.

'I think it's a good idea,' Priscilla said.

'You want to dive on that anchor?' I asked Priscilla.

Priscilla looked at me; she cocked her head; she shook her head slowly. I had a hunch she was thinking about where she was spending her sabbatical, and with whom.

'What I think I'm going to do,' I said to Priscilla and to her pipe-smoking friend on *Inshallah*, 'I think I'm going to slip down there in the water and have a look at that anchor.'

So I did. The water was warmer than the air, and the wind was blissfully uninteresting below the troubled surface. I stayed down there, looking sharp for predators, glancing behind toward the reefs and eels. A dozen feet down the anchor rested on rather than in the bottom; its flukes were tangled in a furze of eel-grass, and each time the wind blew *Blackwing* astern, the rode went taut, and the flukes strained at the grass, and held. I dove, and laboured to dig the flukes into the bottom, and it was like trying to dig them into the surface of a parking lot. So I tangled them thoroughly in the grass, and broke the surface gasping, and told Priscilla and her best friend that I wasn't all that impressed by what I'd seen. I didn't want to lean too hard on this, because night was coming on, and I couldn't imagine anything I less desired than to raise anchor, go elsewhere and try again. This was weak of me, and imprudent, and in violation of all maritime usage and decorum, but I was of a mind to say *what the hell*, to say, as it were, *inshallah*.

Our neighbour pulled at his pipe and remarked that he had been in this very spot four days, diving among fish, and he sure hadn't dragged. 'I'm dug in so deep I'll have to blast my way out.'

I would have responded with appropriate awe, but his other neighbour, his friend, had just arrived at *Inshallah* for cocktails, having rowed a little dink into what was now a thirty-knot gale.

That night, all night, while the wind gave *Blackwing* a battering, shaking her mast, rattling her rigging, bringing her to the end of her anchor rode with a jarring shudder, I stood anchor watch. I didn't have fun. I wished I'd never examined the anchor on the bottom; faith thrives on blindness. I had lit an anchor light, in deference to doctrine, so we wouldn't be run down by anyone coming on Allan's-Pensacola by night, which of course nobody would. Our nearby neighbours also showed anchor lights, and a few hours after midnight I saw *Inshallah* move to leeward, further and further astern. I watched, and wondered what to do. The pipe-smoking, among-man-eating-fish-diving, anchor-dug-in skipper surely knew what he was doing; he was no doubt paying out more anchor rode. He was not; he was dragging down on the reef, and as soon as I realized this, his neighbour began to shout and to blow a foghorn at his friend. The skipper of *Inshallah* was standing at his bow. No, that was the skipper's wife; the skipper was rowing his anchor and chain back upwind. It was an extraordinary feat, and he got it done, and got his anchor down in time, and did not lose his boat on the reef. No thanks to me. I made a mental note: next time you see an anchor light move, holler, the way Nicholas would.

5

Tomorrow dawned. We crossed a Gulf Stream as untroubled as a goldfish pond. Piece of cake. There was no confusion about the boundary of the Stream. If the unlikely transparency of Bahamian reef water is a hundred feet, the Gulf Stream allows visibility of three hundred; it is a warm (eighty degrees) river rushing north from the Yucatán Channel, gathering speed from the Coriolis force and from prevailing winds, bottle-necked between Florida and Bimini, crowded with sea creatures. I remembered reading the observation of a *National Geographic* photographer whose dives had been frustrated by sharks: 'When man enters the Gulf Stream, he enters the food chain. And he doesn't enter at the top.'

Our worry—and we had to have a worry or it wouldn't have been a day on the water—was being pushed so far north by the Gulf Stream that we couldn't make (or *lay*, as navigators say) Palm Beach. To take the effect of the current into account, I had charted a vector course, pointing our nose way south of Palm Beach in order to be crabbed north, and hit Lake Worth Inlet on the money, which is the only thing you can hit if you hit Palm Beach. The accuracy of this vector course depended entirely on a constant speed forward through the water. If something slowed or stopped us, we'd miss our landfall.

I was the alpha wolf in a pack of three fools; the other two boats depended on the accuracy of my loran read-outs, and on my navigational shrewdness. One skipper decided he didn't believe we had to point so far south, and so he veered off my course, heading closer to the rhumb-line (straight line, loxodrome, least distance between two points); he drifted north of Palm Beach and was last seen bobbing towards Labrador. (We were in radio contact until he declared he was resigned to his destiny; *inshallah*.)

There was lightning on the western horizon, but I didn't care about lightning. I cared about the United States Coast Guard. Let me tell you, sailing in the Gulf Stream is like sailing into a war zone. Coast Guard vessels were evident at all points of the compass. I mean big ships, ghostly white, with anti-aircraft batteries, and machine-guns and cannons. My dread was to be approached, stopped, boarded and searched. Not that I was running cocaine or weed or guns or—bank on it—money: if we were boarded near the axis of the Gulf Stream we'd be driven north at six nautical miles per hour, and that would make us sad. *Blackwing* is black (which is why she's a *Blackwing* rather than a *Redwing* or a *Snowball* or a *Flamingo*); a black boat is a red light to a white boat. I tried to make us inconspicuous, nonchalant; I did this by looking casually in the direction of the Coast Guard vessels—on the theory that they'd be suspicious if we pretended not to notice them—and by talking to Priscilla about poetry. I assumed they could hear us through their directional microphones, and I'd never heard drug dealers discuss poetry with Sonny and Rico on *Miami Vice*. I deduced that it was a mark of drug dealers that poetry was one thing they did not discuss. Live-aboard sailors had ascribed to the Coast Guard and DEA uncanny deductive powers, and I hoped that the Coast Guard had deduced that drug runners would on no account discuss poetry while running drugs across the axis of the Gulf Stream.

We'd been boarded and searched leaving Governor's Harbour by the Royal Bahamas Defence Force. Half a dozen uniformed men bearing automatic weapons had materialized in a fast inflatable runabout. They'd made a thorough search, opened a few tins of food, studied the bilges, looked through our duffle bags. This had been courteous; the enlisted men had joked with Nicholas about the Boston Celtics; when they left, the officer in charge had wished us *bon voyage*. Courtly, but with locked and loaded fire-power at port arms.

We knew we were watched. Unmarked planes flew frequently and low over our anchorages; it was conventional wisdom that the blimps we saw every day were equipped with high-resolution cameras of the kind used in satellites, and that if we were questioned by the Coast Guard where we had cruised, it was best to remember exactly, since the Feds had our itinerary thumbtacked to their bulletin board. Drug stories shouldered aside a more human-scale island mythology. We wanted to hear sweet stories, funny stories, instead we were warned about yachties being shot or burned to the water-line for poking a bow into the wrong cove, and we were told of hijackings and unsolved murders and beatings.

We would stand four-square against the drug scourge, but pretty please not along the axis of the Gulf Stream. In the event, we were left in peace until we were coming through Lake Worth Inlet in a thunderstorm, zero visibility, and a Coast Guard patrol boat radioed us and the other boat in our mini-convoy (the third having been set a little north of Greenland by now). We were naughty: we had entered the territorial waters of the United States of America without flying a quarantine flag, which is a little yellow triangle beseeching the Coast Guard to come aboard and rummage for contraband. Nicholas had warned us to fly that flag, and now the Coast Guard was cross with us even before we'd touched home plate.

Life is a crapshoot: the Coast Guard decided to search one rather than both of us. In the rain. And the wind. Under thunder. And lightning. Half an hour before night. The pointer pointed to our companion. *¡Adiós amigos!* We were out of there. Home. Home?

Come what came, we were safe. Snugged down below, drinking tea, we felt as smug as Magellans. We'd mounted a snapshot of Nicholas and his friends just above the loran read-out to remind us of three substantial reasons why we were where we were.

Priscilla was reading Nicholas's log of his passage down the Intercoastal Waterway, a 1,100 mile sequence of rivers, lakes, bays, and land cuts vulgarly titled The Ditch, an inland waterway (protected from the Atlantic mostly by barrier islands) from Norfolk, Virginia to Miami. We were eighty-three statute miles north of north of Miami, at Mile 1017. Powering at five knots (the Waterway is too narrow and tortuous most places to sail), we had two hundred hours of travel ahead of us. And that was just to Virginia. Beyond Virginia lay Chesapeake Bay, Delaware Bay, the New Jersey Coast, the East River, Long Island Sound, Fishers Island Sound, Block Island Sound.

It was raining hard now, and I'd lit the kerosene lamp to give us some light and warmth. *Blackwing* has a fireplace, a wood-burning stove that extends the cruising season in New England, but here in Florida a candle cut the damp cold. I liked being below. I thought we'd feathered our nest quite well, thank you. Our house is a rambling Victorian, too big for us, with spare rooms and redundant outbuildings; the place is stuffed with stuff: book cartons that haven't been opened since the mid-sixties, tools and machines to maintain the yard, closets of clothes held like Confederate war bonds in a profitless speculation that they might make a comeback (bell-bottoms, wide ties, white flannels); I've stored variant versions of manuscripts, students' short stories and essays and grades; I've stored empty shoeboxes in case they might be useful for storing something smaller than empty shoeboxes. You know; who doesn't know? But down here, below on *Blackwing*, the concept *necessary* was subject to ruthless revision. What I brought aboard, Priscilla would trip over; things stood trial for their lives. It was comfortable, and comforting, to strip down, to experience what could be lost in a burglary or foreclosure without diminishing us. As the weeks had passed, we had cleaned up our act, and we had learned the acrobatic tricks that made it possible to move with a show of practised grace from the forward vee-berth (as big and as comfy as a queen-sized bed), through the main cabin (with opposing settees, a drop-leaf table between them, a small galley aft on the port side), to the head (tucked tight behind the companionway steps, and under the cockpit's bridge deck). The main cabin was white and clean, with varnished cherry doors and trim, a varnished teak and holly cabin sole, plenty of light. We knew the inches and dark corners of the place we lived, and cleaned what was dirty, fixed what was broken, polished what was dull. Most of Nicholas's friends on the Waterway and in the islands lived aboard bigger and more complicated boats: clunky, over-rigged forty- and fifty-foot ketches equipped with generators to drive the electric refrigerator and freezer (we used block ice), to heat water (we used a kettle), to power the pressure water system (we pumped). Their boats slept six or eight, and four in comfort. *Blackwing* had four berths, but two of us made a crowd. Our boat was simple, and within the tiny universe we inhabited on *Blackwing* we had the experience rather than the dream of control and competence and— sometimes, now, protected from the driving rain—perfection.

We'd expected, living days and weeks in close quarters, that we'd get on each other's nerves. Nicholas had confessed to feeling cramped and corked, and so had his crew. Three had made a good number of friends to share confinement; one could always break off from two to brood, or sulk, or silently scream at the a) inconsideration, b) incompetence, c) imperfect hygiene of the other two, who would not notice, or could pretend not to notice, the absence of the other. Pretty soon the surly one, the tired one, the furious one would pop a cold beer, or tell a joke, or see a funny sight, and the little storm was dead. Now, silent below, watching Priscilla read, no place to go other than the place we had chosen as our comfy prison cell, I wondered how we'd do.

'We'll go right where he went,' Priscilla said. 'It's all here in the log; he'll tell us what to do. It'll be perfect. If we follow where Nick leads, we'll do just fine.'

It was so. He'd been where we were going. Talk about displacement, reversal of customary order. A father says, 'Here are the keys. Drive carefully.' Nicholas, in Governor's Harbour, had said, 'Here are the keys, be careful with the boat.' In fact, Nicholas's log was more explicitly cautionary than most fathers would dare: a father might say, 'Watch out for speed traps in Connecticut.' Nicholas's log said: 'The chart shows that Green #45 should be left to port northbound; the chart is *wrong*; beware a shoal spot fifty feet north-east of #45.' If we didn't beware, we'd hit it, and that was a fact. There were encouragements, too: 'Went to old hotel near Cocoa Beach Bridge and had a few. Funky joint, like hotel in *The Shining*. Check it out, but don't try to write a book there.' It was pure pleasure, taking Nicholas as our guide. I could invoke Beatrice leading Dante through Paradise, but I'll settle for modest scale: it was relaxing to let the son become the father, not to resist this inversion. He had been where I had not been, and he knew what I did not know: where to anchor, what bridge tender would open the draw on request, who grills a good hamburger, where to keep an eye open for otters, or laughs, or beauty. From this place forward, Palm Beach to Jamestown, we were in his hands. How did we feel to follow rather than lead? We felt swell.

BEVERLY LOWRY

PATRICIDE

By now, the shooting is old news, and Rush Springs, Oklahoma, has had its five minutes of notoriety. The story has been all over national magazines and newspapers and featured on prime-time television news—how, on a blistering day last July, Lonnie Dutton's two elder children, Herman, fifteen, and Druie, twelve, took a .243 deer rifle into the living-room of the trailerhouse where they lived, set the barrel of the gun against their sleeping daddy's head, just below his right ear, and blew him away, right there on the couch, a can of beer on the table beside him. How they killed him together, Herman steadying the gun while Druie pulled the trigger. How they had decided to do it—'kill Daddy'—that afternoon, when their sister, Alesha, who is ten, came out of the house crying and told them that their daddy had molested her. How the two boys were working in the field next to the trailerhouse that day—105 degrees and they'd been sent to chop and hoe—and decided that while they'd been putting up with their daddy's cruel mistreatment for years, this was different.

By mid-afternoon, all hush-hush to keep it secret from Alesha and their baby brother, Jake, eight, Herman and Druie Dutton had figured out what they had to do: their daddy had always told them that, if they ever discovered anyone fooling with their sister, they should pick up the .243 and shoot the son of a bitch in either the head, just below the ear, or the heart. Their daddy then poked the side of his head, to show where the bullet should go, then slapped the left side of his chest, to show them the heart, and then poked both boys in the side of the head, repeatedly and hard, and then slapped their chests. He wanted to be sure they understood. Herman and Druie were good children; they did what they could to keep their daddy calm, including stealing, calling their mother names, biting her and throwing darts at her. And so they waited until they were sure that their daddy was good and asleep, so that he wouldn't draw out the nine-millimetre from underneath his overalls bib and shoot them first. Then they went inside the trailerhouse and killed him with the .243, which had been stolen from somebody in Lawton, Oklahoma, some eight years earlier.

In October, three months after the shooting, the Oklahoma sun still beats down like emergency floodlights. People in Grady County are used to it. The ones I've met are friendly, plain and very white, with flat, twangy accents. The women grow their hair long and leave it; the men drive pick-ups. The economy is down the tubes, politics what you would expect. On the turnpike between Oklahoma City and Chickasha, I pass a billboard saying SOCIALISM IS WRONG.

In Grady County, a woman on her own gets company fast. While driving, I watch as car after car pulls alongside, slows down, revs up; the drivers look over, I go on. It's a world in which bars are windowless and dark, their parking lots filled with pick-ups and the occasional Ranchero. My first night in Rush Springs, I stepped outside my motel to go for a short run. It was early evening, the sun was low, but there was plenty of light. A pick-up came by, slowed down; there were three men inside, raising cans to their lips. A couple of minutes later, a woman and a young girl in a brand-new, extended-cab pick-up stopped, and the woman asked where I lived and if I had seen the three men who were parked at the top of the road, waiting for me. She offered to take me back to the motel.

Eighteen miles south of Chickasha, at a yellow blinking caution light, I turn right off US 81, away from downtown Rush Springs. The telephone book gives 'N of city' and 'SW of city' as addresses. The house I am heading towards, the home of Luther Dutton, the dead man's father, is on a road with no name, 'W of city'.

When I spoke to Luther Dutton on the phone, he said he had no problem talking to me or anybody else. He wanted the story told right, and for that to happen, 'There's only one way.' Just so long as it wasn't for a book. He didn't go for that book stuff. 'We're the only ones who know,' he assured me. And he told me how to get to his house.

South-west Oklahoma is farming country, water melons and peanuts mostly—Rush Springs calls itself Water Melon Capital of the World. There are cattle, some sheep, some goats. The rolling countryside lies between mountains to the east and dry plains not that far to the west; and it is lush, green and wet, with heavy-headed oak and pecan trees and thick, webby undergrowth.

Scrub oaks line the road to the Dutton house. Mustang grapevines grow over the tops of the stunted trees like a shroud. Beyond them, all you can see is more scrub, denser brush. Just before the Dutton mailbox, there is a beat-up locked gate with a rusted sign hanging on it saying PRIVATE PROPERTY. Over the gate, five huge, dark, withering catfish heads swing in the breeze.

Luther Dutton's new mailbox is shaped like a barn. It is festooned with blue bows. There are bows on the fence and across the top of the gate.

The red clay road leading to the house slants down a little in a tunnel of overhanging trees, then curves to the right. The landscape opens up and there is a big house with a wide front porch set on a cleared, very pretty rise in the land. There is a refrigerator on the porch and a couple of nonfunctioning cars out front, but it isn't trashy. The trees are big, and the grass a deep green. Lonnie Dutton and his children lived on this same piece of land, back in the scrub oaks and underbrush, with nothing but a rutted cow path for a way in or out. Nobody lives in the trailerhouse now.

It is six o'clock on a Friday evening. The season's first crop of peanuts has come in. The governor of Oklahoma is under investigation for illegal campaign funding. At seven o'clock that night, the unbeaten Rush Springs Redskins will take on the Hinton Comets in a Homecoming football game.

When I ring the doorbell, Luther Dutton answers. He is wearing jeans and a saggy white T-shirt. He has a kind of potato face, lumpy and uneven, a droopy lower lip and a bulbous nose. His hair is grey and thinning, uncombed. He is in his sixties, but he looks a good ten years older.

He invites me in, and we go through to a large room, kitchen, dining-room and living-room all in one. The room is clean and plain with fake wood panelling. There are little pictures on the wall, including a child's 'I-Love-You-Daddy' drawing which Luther says one of the kids made for Lonnie. A flyer is tacked on the refrigerator, announcing the town meeting in support of Herman and Druie held three months earlier, at which blue bows were sold to help pay legal expenses. The house is easy to keep and serviceable, with built-ins and new appliances.

We sit at a round table. Luther spits tobacco into a styrofoam cup, staring off in the general direction of the opposite wall and meeting my eyes only when it suits him.

He introduces me to his wife, Nancy. In rural areas, middle-aged women tend to fall into one of two categories: the chunk and the rail. The chunk puts on weight and acquires a bosom, hips, dimples, a double chin, a rolling gait; she has a girlish look and loves her food. The rail shrinks, her skin clings to her bones, her behind flattens, her neck turns into a column of folds. The rail usually chain-smokes, preferring cigarettes to food. A rail still in the ball game may cover up the damage with ice-blue eyeshadow and frosted pink lipstick; her hair will be dyed: black, yellow or red.

Nancy Dutton is a rail and has not been in the ball game for years. She could be eighty; it turns out she's sixty-one. In her thirties, she was institutionalized for mental and emotional problems and had shock treatments for more than a year; her daughter, Linda Munn, says that's why Nancy has a hard time remembering and sometimes seems so . . . flat. She sits on a bar stool next to the breakfast bar, smoking steadily, and lets Luther do most of the talking.

Lonnie Dutton lived on his father's property for nine years. Records list him as an unemployed roofer, but no one can remember him ever doing a day's work for wages. He lived on the dole, getting food stamps and money from government programmes and making his kids steal. When social services people came out for a home study, Lonnie pretended to live in Luther's house, and Luther and Nancy covered for him. The electricity in his trailer was illegally tapped from his father's line. His water supply came from his father's well. He would neither allow his parents to enter his trailerhouse, nor leave his own children with them when he went out. Wherever Lonnie Dutton went, his children went too. When he went to bars, they stayed in the truck until he was ready to go, no matter what the temperature or the hour. If Lonnie came out drunk at two or three in the morning, fifteen-year-old Herman drove home.

Lonnie graduated from high school in Sterling, Oklahoma, one of only three boys in a class of thirty, and so he was elected Class Favorite, Most Handsome and Best Dancer, the other two boys being pretty squirrelly-looking. He had two elder sisters, Linda, now forty-three, and Dina, who is forty-one. Lonnie died four days short of his fortieth birthday. Nancy says his kids were planning a surprise party for him, and that Druie had asked her to make a cake with candles.

'He was a hard-working boy,' Luther says of his son. 'All his life he worked hard. He had a deformed heart you know . . . He raised registered hogs.'

Luther makes statements like this, statements that clearly—to him—have some kind of resonance. And then he will pause, waiting for a response, I can't tell to what. After a beat, he goes on.

'Won nearly every prize in the county.'

And he describes his son, the hard-working, all-American farm boy, and Nancy tells me about Lonnie's deformed heart with the oversized valve and his high blood pressure.

As for school, 'He didn't do no good. But he was a damned fine carpenter.'

Luther Dutton backtracks, rethinks his story, checks himself. Nancy Dutton adds details, corrects small errors and contributes to Luther's main thrust, which is to let the world know that nobody understands what it has been like for him all these years, nobody. He is cagey, deft, sly, and thinks he can put one over on anybody. Luther and Nancy rarely use their son's name, but when they say 'he', I always know who they mean.

Yes, Luther will admit, he did thrash his son with a belt from time to time, but that's what people did in those days, striped their sons' backsides. He was trying to straighten him out, that was all; of course it didn't do any good.

I go over some of the stories I have heard: how Lonnie made his wife, Marie, stand against the wall, then told his kids to throw darts at her; how he poured jalapeno pepper juice in her eyes; how he chased Herman with a two-by-four and kicked him between the legs with a steel-toed boot; how he used to shoot at the chicken coop while Herman and Druie were inside; and how he played William Tell with Druie by making him stand against a wall, then shooting bullets in a circle around his head. I ask him, have any of these stories been exaggerated?

Luther thinks a long time. When he shakes his head and says simply no, there is no knowing what his attitude is. When cornered, he has a mantra which goes: 'I loved my son. I love my grandkids. My grandkids killed my son. And I have mixed emotions about that.' At first, I thought by mixed emotions he meant he was confused, then later on I decided he meant exactly what he said.

Luther has been interviewed a lot. He often asks and answers his own questions.

'Were those children abused? I'd have to say, yes. Those children were belittled, berated, beat on, abused, called everything in the book. But you know, I never heard those boys use a cuss word.'

Nancy shakes her head.

'They killed their daddy, yes. But they never used foul language.'

And he waits a beat or two and then restates his theme: 'Nobody knows what it was like, being a prisoner in your own home for years, nobody. But he was my son and I loved him. When you love somebody, you love them. Don't make no difference what they do.'

Luther pulls up his shirt sleeve. 'He cut me. Here.' Traces a scar on his bicep. 'Here.' Touches his arm close to the wrist. 'He shot me once—just birdshot, but I would have gone after him with my gun if my wife hadn't stopped me.'

Luther says Lonnie never should have got married, and that on his wedding night he said he'd rather go coon hunting. 'He hated women. He used to say, there's only one good woman in the world and that's her'—nods in Nancy's direction—'and all the rest are whores and liars.' Thinking about why Lonnie believed this, Luther goes to the sink, paces, starts to say something, then stops, mentions family secrets, things he can't talk about. 'But I'll tell you this,' he finally says. 'He was jilted and that's all I'll say. It was when he was a senior. He was always a man to hold a grudge, and that did it.' As for his sisters, he probably hated them most of all. 'But then,' Luther says darkly, 'he knew the things they did.'

And so, at twenty-two, Lonnie married Rosemarie Standford, even though he didn't want to—'It was her wanted to,' Nancy declares—and Luther says he would be the first to take the stand and say that, yes, Lonnie abused her and beat her up so bad you couldn't tell who she was. But as for the question of whether he molested Alesha, Luther Dutton says that's hard for him to know. 'I'll tell you this, Lonnie hated a pervert. He had no use for homos. He hated a queer. And I ask myself, would he molest his own child? I have a hard time with that, you see. I have mixed emotions about that. But to answer your question, I'd have to say I don't think he ever did. Or not that I ever knew of.'

At one point, Luther leaves the room and comes back in carrying a three-foot length of hard rubber tubing and a pistol in a holster. He puts them on the table.

'Now, ma'am,' he says, 'I don't meant to disrespect you, but you know what that is.' He nods at the tube. 'It's a tube from a pump to air up your tyres.' He pauses. 'That's what he used to beat them with.' He takes the pistol out of the holster. 'Ma'am. I don't mean to disrespect you.' The gun is an automatic. He takes the clip out. 'This was his gun. He was left-handed. A left-handed man.' He puts the nine-millimetre back in the holster. 'He wore it here.' He lays his hand across his heart. 'In the bib of his overalls. Always.'

Marie left Lonnie in 1989 and went to Texas to live with her mother. She took her children with her. A few months later, Lonnie went down there and made it up with Marie, saying he would change, they'd all move and make a life in Texas. Then things happened. Lonnie beat Marie up, Marie's mother called the police and Lonnie was thrown in jail. When he got out two weeks later, he went back home to Oklahoma. Soon afterwards, Herman and Druie asked to go back to live with their dad. This was before he started beating up on them, and anyway they didn't really trust their mother, especially after Lonnie had drilled certain facts into their heads and made them call her pig and whore dog. Lonnie filed a custody suit, which he won. Most people believe Luther helped his son pay for a good lawyer. Marie didn't have one.

Oklahoma has a law stating that, if a parent is absent from a child for twelve consecutive months and provides no support, then the parent's rights can be terminated without notice. As Marie Dutton has not seen her children in at least three years, she is no longer legally considered their parent. And one day recently, when the boys were in court, they were given the chance to see Marie. They refused. Druie eventually gave in and talked to her, but Herman stood firm.

L uther Dutton says he called the social services on 'this very phone—so many times,' and he gets out old telephone bills showing calls to a Chickasha number. As for the police, Luther says, 'The police are thirty-five miles away. You know what happens. Time they get here . . . And it's complicated. I mean, if you file charges, you have to stop and think, what's going to happen to the kids? We'd get into it over those kids. I'd see Herman with his head swollen up, Druie with a black eye, and we'd get into it. He'd tell me to mind my own damned business, those kids were his and he'd do what he damned pleased, and nobody better try to come between him and his kids. So . . . '

He shows me Lonnie's photograph album. There are diamond-shaped cuts in many of the snapshots, where Lonnie gouged out the face and body of Marie. One picture is of Lonnie on his wedding night, standing by a dog-pen, holding his arm over the coon hounds' heads to get them to jump up. He is trim, of medium build, a fairly good-looking young man. His smile is rascally, but not mean. In later photos, he is big and burly and will not look at the camera. In most of them, he is wearing a shapeless hat with a big brim, and you can see the gun holster sticking out of his overalls bib. I hold the pictures up in Nancy's direction. I would not have known, I say, that these were of the same person. She nods.

In one picture, it is Christmas, and Lonnie's four children and Nancy are lined up inside Luther and Nancy's house. Nancy is in the middle, looking pathetic in a droopy dress. The four children all hold rifles on their shoulders, like soldiers. Herman stands at one end, chin tucked in like a Marine, shoulders severely squared.

'See there,' Luther points at the right side of Herman's head. 'You can see how swollen up it is. And look at his mouth.'

Herman's head looks soft and melonish on one side, and his mouth is twisted and off-centre. Druie has a black eye.

'That's the gun they shot him with.' Luther taps the photo. 'Right there.' He points to the gun Herman has on his shoulder. 'That's the .243.'

Linda Munn, Lonnie's elder sister, has not lived in Rush Springs for ten years. But she has come back to Oklahoma to testify to her brother's brutality; there are pictures of her in the middle of the main street of Rush Springs, holding up a sign saying BRING OUR ANGELS HOME.

When I spoke to her later, her first words were, 'You didn't believe everything Daddy said, did you? That's what scares me. That people will go out there and take everything he says at face value.'

Linda Munn says her daddy beat up on her as far back as she can remember, once so badly she had blood streaks from the back of her neck to her ankles, and on Lonnie too—one time in the barn, so brutally that everybody went and hid so they couldn't hear. She also says that Lonnie didn't have a deformed heart or high blood pressure. 'That's bull poop. He was lazy. If those little boys are going to have to tell the truth about what went on, then we should too. That place he says Lonnie cut him? My brother didn't cut Daddy there. He did that himself, welding. I told him I knew that, but he just said, "Well, *they* don't."'

When Linda Munn was fourteen, she got pregnant, got married and came home to her parents' house to live with her new husband. Those were bad years. Nancy was in hospital getting shock treatments, and Luther was beating up on all of the kids.

Linda says that no girl was ever going to be good enough for Lonnie in her mother's eyes. 'If she didn't use the recipes my mom used or clean house the way my mom did, she was ridiculed. Marie never had a chance.'

Linda Munn says that she is prepared to believe just about anything that's said about her brother, and wonders about his sexual problems. She says he wouldn't let Marie change Alesha's diapers if anybody else was in the room, in case some man saw the baby's genitals and started getting ideas. When his daughter was a toddler, he used to introduce her as 'my nigger' and 'my little slut.' Once, when Alesha was about four, she fell off the porch and cracked her head. Linda's son Wayne picked her up and held her on his lap to see if she was badly hurt, and Lonnie came running up, waving his pistol, and told Wayne to take that child off his lap; he knew what Wayne was thinking—Linda says, because Lonnie was having those thoughts himself. And there is the story about Lonnie beating up Marie to make her have sex with another man, then, when she wouldn't, pouring alcohol down her throat until she did, then beating her up worse afterwards because she did it, and everybody blaming Marie because she didn't after all *have* to do it. Linda says she remembers her brother bragging that there was one thing he could say about Marie: she took an ass whipping better than any man he knew.

There are other houses on the road with no name, 'W of city'. Karen Caveny and her family live in a trailerhouse on the front part of their land, where they are building a home and share a fence line with the Dutton place. The living-room of the trailer is warm and comfortable, the walls covered with family portraits. Karen Caveny is a pleasant-faced woman in her mid-forties, smart and plain-spoken as a stop sign. She has a lot to say about what she heard out there. From 1984, when Lonnie moved his trailer on to his father's land and settled down with his pregnant wife and their three kids, she and her family never felt safe.

'Lonnie liked to shoot. My kids have dodged his bullets; we have bullet holes in the side of our house. When Lonnie and Marie first moved in, they had six white dogs. Those dogs were chasing livestock, and I sent my daughter Jodi to tell Herman to tell his daddy he had to do something about them. Next day, Herman told Jodi, "Daddy says you don't have to worry about those dogs any more. He stepped out on the front porch and shot them all."'

Karen Caveny caught Lonnie Dutton peering in her windows at least twice, and one time he stalked a neighbour who complained about goats in her yard, following her car in his pick-up and parking alongside it while she went to church.

'What you have to understand about Lonnie is, he liked intimidating people. And when you're doing the kinds of things he was doing and enjoying them, then I'd have to say that was evil.

'Marie?' Karen Caveny's eyes fill. 'Just after they moved in, we were in the house, the television was on, the washing-machine was going, it was night, and on top of all that noise I heard screams. I thought it was one of the animals, but when I went outside, I knew it was a person. It went on for forty-five minutes.

She was screaming his name out loud, begging him to stop.'

Karen Caveny eventually went back inside and turned up the television so she couldn't hear any more. At a quarter to six the next morning, there was a knock at the door and there stood Marie, holding Druie by the hand with Alesha on her hip. She was pregnant with Jake. 'That child was so big she was waddling. Her face was out to here, her eyes were black, and there wasn't a part of the whites of her eyes that was white; they were completely red. The blood-vessels had all burst, I guess. Her mouth was busted and one ear was torn. She had black-and-blue marks all over her. She needed a ride into town, and so we took them and put her and the children on a bus to Texas. Next thing I knew she was back. She came to us lots of times. Nancy would call me and I'd lie: Oh, I haven't seen Marie, haven't seen her in a long time. Marie would hide the children, lay them down under some bushes and wait for the right car to come along and she'd get up and put them in the car and get a ride where she needed to go.'

Karen Caveny says that she called the social services 'between thirty and fifty times' but that 'nobody came.' She made the reports anonymously because for a long time she and her family were Lonnie Dutton's only neighbours. 'He would know it was me turning him in. I had children of my own to think of. If he was doing the things he was doing to his own children, what would he do to mine?'

Lonnie liked to set fires on other people's land, and one time a dozen or so people who lived in the area got together and called the sheriff. Nobody came out until eventually someone from another county told a friend, who was a special investigator from yet another county, about what was going on, and that person roused some members of the Grady County Sheriff's Department. And when they arrived, Karen Caveny told them the whole story, about the screams and about Lonnie being a peeping Tom. 'They told us there was nothing they could do unless we caught him red-handed and held on to him until somebody came. Now can't you just see me saying, "Lonnie, will you wait right there while I call the sheriff?"' And while this was not said outright, the message Karen Caveny got from the Sheriff's Department was: be your own vigilante; do what you have to do.

People who live outside the city limits don't always live there from necessity or because they are farmers. They live there because they get a kick out of having their own way, by God; and living where they don't see, by God, anybody else; and having, by God, beaten the system. The Cavenys never thought of moving because of, 'Oh, the pioneer spirit. You don't let people run you off your property. You just don't.'

On 12 July, some time between four and five in the afternoon, Karen Caveny heard there had been a shooting on the Dutton place, and she was not surprised. But she thought Lonnie had shot his dad. Why? 'Because Lonnie was just that crazy and his dad was just that scared.' When she heard what had really happened, she says it was the last thing she would have imagined. 'I had a mental picture of those two little boys—you know, they're small; they look more like ten and twelve than twelve and fifteen—and I could see them holding that gun and praying to God that Lonnie wouldn't wake up before they pulled the trigger and I felt terrible for them. I wish they hadn't had to go through that. Nobody deserves to live the way they lived. They didn't just haul off and shoot their dad. He was a demon. He was living hell.'

There are constant and hurtful questions in Grady County these days: who saw the bruises or heard the screams; who called the social services or the child-abuse toll-free number to make reports; who was responsible for the fact that, while there were a lot of people who thought that Lonnie Dutton was a man in need of a good killing, his kids were the only ones up to doing it?

Employees of the Department of Human Services can't talk about individual cases. The Sheriff's Department will only say that, if a child won't talk, there's nothing they can do. A math teacher at Herman's school once took the boy aside and asked him about the bruises and abrasions on his face. Herman made up some tale about the limb of a tree hitting him and, even when the teacher said he didn't believe him, held fast to his story. And people in Rush Springs want to make it clear, they didn't know what was going on, they didn't even know Lonnie Dutton, he never came into town.

Everybody thinks something had to go wrong for those children to have fallen through the cracks of the system, but nobody knows exactly what. And I find myself wondering if *anything* could have been done to stop Lonnie Dutton's bullying, short of his children rising up and shooting him. The Dutton family was isolated and secretive. Nobody much knew where the trailer was, and Lonnie had installed motion detectors in his yard, connected to lights. He slept on the couch, surrounded by guns. If the lights came on in the night, he started shooting. It didn't matter what was out there. He didn't wait, he didn't aim. He just shot.

As I leave 'W of city', the sky is blood-red along the horizon. I keep thinking about Herman. Herman was the caretaker child, the one in charge; it was up to him to keep things on an even keel, take the hits for his brothers and sister, lie when anyone asked him about his bruises, run round at lunch-time to make sure the other kids were OK. Herman never quit trying to be the good child and please his dad. When Lonnie took them all shoplifting, Herman knew he would beat up on whoever didn't steal enough and so he cut back on his take. Last year, after Herman had failed to do a chore exactly right, Lonnie went after him with a two-by-four and knocked him out cold in the backyard; there is a declivity in Herman's skull now, big enough to lay your finger in.

Herman is the smallest boy in his class—I have seen his school group picture. He is in the front row, sparky-looking, perfectly proportioned, wiry. He is standing at an angle to the camera, one hand loosely curled on his thigh. His blond hair is in big waves, dramatically dipped to one side, and he is wearing a bright western shirt, a black belt, tight jeans and cowboy boots. He may be tiny, but his body is taking an adult shape, and he has a great sense of style.

That July afternoon, Herman told Druie he would be the one to shoot their daddy, but when they got in there, he couldn't do it. At fifteen, Herman was old enough to know the consequences, legal and otherwise. So the younger, more concrete-thinking Druie took the gun, but he couldn't do it either, although he said that if Herman could steady the rifle, he thought he could pull the trigger. Lonnie wore a droopy moustache, sometimes a forked beard and had had his head shaved to give him a meaner look. I imagine the two boys standing beside him, passing the rifle between them, keeping a careful eye on the bald head, the moustache, the chin, the bulked-up body of their two-hundred-plus pound dad in his overalls, the nine-millimetre automatic in a holster beneath the bib.

And so Herman aimed the .243 and put his finger on the trigger again, and just as he was about to lower the barrel once more, Druie pushed the trigger back. The bullet made a neat three-quarter-inch entry hole, then exploded inside Lonnie Dutton's skull. It did not exit. There was a lot of blood. Lonnie died instantly.

Herman and Druie ran out the front door. Alesha and Jake were playing in the back yard, Herman had made sure of that because he didn't mean for them to see; but Alesha heard the noise and ran in the back door, saw her daddy lying dead on the couch and started screaming.

Herman herded his brothers and sister together, and all four children ran down the rutted cow path to their daddy's pick-up, bawling. They were heading down to the main road, going God knows where, when their cousin, Linda Munn's son Wayne, who until a week before had been a Rush Springs policeman, drove in. Herman told him, 'I think Daddy's dead.' Wayne was not surprised; people had been expecting a shooting out there for years; they just didn't know who would end up dead. But he thought it would be Luther or one of the kids, not Lonnie.

The first police officer on the scene was Guy Huggins, the deputy Sheriff. He said that the trailerhouse was swept up and fairly clean, and that there were no illegal drugs on the premises. Later on, he went to pick up Herman and Druie at a relative's house, and all four kids were still bawling. Herman said that he was the one who shot his dad; then, when Huggins got the boys to the Sheriff's annexe in Chickasha, where they were questioned separately, Druie said that Herman held the gun but that he pulled the trigger. Both boys knew what they had done and said they loved their daddy. When was the funeral? Could they go?

It is dark now. In Rush Springs, the Homecoming game is in progress. The scoreboard lights say ten minutes left in the second quarter, the Redskins leading by two. I park on the highway. The stadium lights up the pitch-black night. Everybody's there: men with their feet up on a fence rail, smoking; women selling tickets, talking to their daughters. Let loose in the warm night air, kids run around like wild things.

At half-time, I drive into the parking lot and buy a ticket. The band—mostly white children in red and black uniforms—has marched out and plays 'Ebb Tide'. Convertibles circle the field, as Homecoming maids perched atop the back seats smile and wave. They have a lot of hair, frizzed up, fanned out, shiny with goo. Their cars stop at the fifty-yard line, where each maid is escorted through a flower-decked arbour. The queen and king are crowned, flash bulbs pop.

The Dutton compound is only five miles off, but it's a long way from there to here. As the band and the Homecoming court leave the field, and the Redskins roll back on, I think about the boys, what might have been happening to them, right now, this minute, if they hadn't killed their father.

All four Dutton children have been made wards of the court, a ruling that Marie Dutton is still fighting. Alesha and Jake have been put into the temporary care of a relative. Herman and Druie were sent to the Oklahoma Juvenile Diagnostic and Evaluation Center, which recommended unequivocally that they be put in therapeutic foster care with two adults as role models, and should receive long-term counselling and therapy with their siblings. It was strongly recommended that a court trial be avoided. If Herman and Druie stay out of trouble until April 1996, their records will be clear.

Nobody knows when the four children will be together again. The court has ruled that any member of the Dutton family seeking custody must first agree to therapy.

Back on US 81, heading north, I wonder what secrets are buried with Lonnie Dutton and what Luther Dutton was making up. I wonder how all four kids will turn out. I think about Herman. Herman has his own room now, his own things. I wonder what his nights are like, what he thinks about, what kind of plans he is making.

Later that night I wake up screaming. A rat is at me, biting and biting me, and I cannot move.

CHRISTIAN MCEWEN

THE BUSINESS OF
MOURNING

Christian McEwen

One of us is missing.
One or maybe two.
I count us on the fingers of one hand.

I was the eldest of six children. Please God, bless Mama and Papa and Katie and James and Helena and John and Isabella and me. It was important to me that we were six. It was important to all of us. 'How many children are there in your family?' We were competitive about it, slightly superior.

Somebody is missing.
Which of us is gone?

James is gone, and Katie. James shot himself in June, and in September Kate was drowned.

The news that someone is dead is a tiny tragedy all of its own. It is devastating when you hear it, and it stays potent for a long time afterwards. I do not cry about my father any more, but if I want to miss him (and I sometimes do) I tell myself he's dead in the words my mother used, three and a half years ago.

'Darling, Papa has died—'

In the same way I tell myself the news of James and Katie.

'It's not good—James has killed himself.'

'Another horrible tragedy. Your mother's on the phone.'

For a single moment I believe they're dead. Then my attention skitters back to normal. There are six of us, and I'm the eldest. It is in the nature of things that I should die first. Kate is twenty-five. James is twenty-two. I am twenty-seven and there is nothing to worry about.

When my father died, Kate looked for him all over the house. She went into his study calling for him, 'Papa—'

He had a heart attack and died at fifty-three.

Kate was twenty-five. James was twenty-two.

It is the end of the third week in June, and I have just arrived back from the States, where I've been living for the past four years. James's funeral is the day after tomorrow, and James is nowhere to be found.

THE BUSINESS OF MOURNING

I want to look for him, but I don't know where to start. He was wild this year, crazy, maverick, out of control. Everybody tells me so. He has painted a gigantic mural on the kitchen wall. There are bullet holes through the windows of the flat.

Two and a half months later, Kate is drowned. I do not look for her. Her body is in Africa, and I am on the phone to British Airways. We talk, flatly, about the carriage of human remains.

When a grown-up dies, a grandmother or a grandfather, a parent even, or a friend, it is a single death, a relatively simple thing. When a child dies, or someone you have known as a child, it's not so simple. I knew James and Kate for all their lives. I am who I am, in part because they were who they were. For twenty years we divided the world between us. I don't know how to talk about this. I feel I've lost so many people, and some of them are me.

The day before Kate's funeral, my cousin Sam gives me a massage. I am very frightened. I drive with Mama to the hospital to see the body.

After Mama had gone, I knelt down beside the coffin and looked at Katie for a long time. The bruising shone dull grey across her nose, like the smudge of a BB pencil. There was another, blacker bruise on the left side of her face, and a dark mark on her left cheek, and also on her chin. I touched her all over and I talked to her a little, very softly. Her skin still had that Katie softness, very, very cold—

James killed himself. There is no doubt about that. He locked himself in John's bedroom and he lay down on the bed. He wedged the shotgun between his legs, reached down with his long arms and pulled the trigger.

And Katie? Katie drowned. But no one knows the circumstances of her death. She disappeared early one Thursday morning, and was found next day by the police, washed up above the high-tide mark, ten minutes from the house where she'd been staying.

What did she do the day before she died? The Kenyan authorities do not care to investigate.

For a while there are rumours that she'd been attacked, that she'd taken an overdose, that she too had committed suicide.
For a while there are a hundred stories on the go.

It is June, it is July, it is August and September. Isabella has twelve packets of photographs. We look at them for James, and then we look at them for Katie: blurred faces, fat orange wallets. We look at pictures and we go on talking.

James on heroin, James manic, James stampeding around London and New York, doing deals and picking people up. James denouncing Mama to the papers. I thought I knew those stories. I thought I knew them all. But everyone I talk to has a different version.

James was a junkie. He needed to get settled. If he'd only had a girlfriend. If Papa were alive.
I ask more questions and I listen to more answers. If I listen long enough will I believe he's dead?

I take James's diary and I read it from cover to cover. He was a good writer, better than any of us, and I hear him teasing as I turn the pages. I sit on the tops of buses and I try to make space for him inside my head: to become a little of what he was— funny, loving, generous. The desperation and the gossip drop away. Then Kate is dead, and everything begins again.

James and I were in the States together. We wrote letters to each other, often. I loved him as a grown-up friend, not simply as a brother. With Katie, things are different. I knew her best when we were in our teens. Since then, we've gone our separate ways. She was the beautiful one, I was the tomboy. She was the artist, I was the academic. Without quite realizing it, we were defined in opposition to each other. Now she is dead, and I don't know who she was, or how to mourn.

I visit Katie's lovers and her friends. I hear their stories too. Kate and housing crises, Kate and painting, Kate and problems with her business deals. Sometimes I think there are no happy stories. James and Kate: two miserable people. Then I meet other friends, hear different stories, and they're alive again. They're both alive and well.

When I went with Mama to the hospital to see Kate's body, I thought I'd learn something. Whatever happened after that, I'd know that she was dead. But all I did was add a dead face to the crowd of living ones: Katie faces in the photographs and drawings, Katie faces from this summer, and all through our growing up.

After Katie dies, I dream I am to blame. I don't know how exactly, but I feel very uneasy. Then a parcel arrives from Papa: lots and lots of sheets of paper, a long, long letter—and I know it isn't my fault after all.

Faces, faces, and a shaky sense of guilt. Everybody had it, fumbling, as if guilt were somehow a relief, easier to admit to than those blazing absences. So many conversations started with, 'If only—'. Running through them was an almost messianic regret: 'I should have saved them—'

It is difficult to acknowledge that people have their own lives, their own deaths, their own integrity. You cannot save them. After James died, Katie had a dream in which she said to him, in the words we all were thinking, 'I just wish you hadn't done it—'

James looked over at her, teasing, scornful, utterly successful. 'I *know* you do,' he said.

We wished all summer that James hadn't done it. We wished all autumn that Kate hadn't drowned. At the same time we fought to understand that they were dead, to school ourselves to that, to know it well.

'It's not good, James has killed himself—'

'Another horrible tragedy—'

I write to everyone I know, as though by that repeated telling I could tell myself, thoroughly once and for all. But James and Kate come back again, they will not go away. I see them in the pub and on the street. They're not here at this moment, not right now. But they'll be in. James is visiting some friends of his, and Kate, she's working over at the flat.

You try to tell yourself, 'They won't come back,' and still, you cannot know it. Your body knows it, in its tears and restlessness, its absolute exhaustion. The rest of you takes time to understand. You do the washing up, you go on coping. You drink and talk. You cry, sometimes you scream.

Only much later does all this come into focus: as a time without perspective, a strange, lost time without a future. I remember being genuinely surprised when someone asked me to a party. I had forgotten there would ever be parties again.

Friends help, and so do all those letters of condolence. Friends know about ordinary life. They know about parties. They can remind you that the pain won't last for ever, that now *is* extraordinary, and things will change.

In the meantime, there is mourning, which is complicated business. From the outside it looks simple—you're in pain, you miss someone, you cry. But mourning isn't simple in that way. Whatever you do or feel, whether you go to pieces or you cope, you always have the sense that you're pretending. If you are brave, then really you are showing off. If you scream, it means you want attention.

I thought about all this, and wondered why. In part it is to do with other people, shifting expectations. You 'ought' to be brave. You 'ought' to express your feelings. The rules are contradictory. But mourning is complicated, even without pressure from outside. Sometimes you can't do it, even if you want to. Sometimes you do it intolerably well, and are overwhelmed with feelings—fear and anger, jealousy and hate, and a whole range of things which hardly seem to qualify as feelings—muddle, numbness, even boredom.

But even at its worst, no grief is constant. It does let up sometimes, and when it does, there can be moments of extraordinary clarity, or real happiness.

In the week between Kate's death and her funeral, some friends of hers came up to stay in Scotland. We played football, we danced, we went for walks and climbed trees. We picked mushrooms and made a huge cauldron of mushroom soup. These were distractions, it is true. But they were also celebrations, tributes to the ordinary, acknowledgements of the spaces that exist: the gaps inside the pain.

From the outside, James's death and Kate's are labelled 'tragic'. We, the family, the survivors, are to be pitied.

I do not want that pity, or that version of events. I do not want a story of James's life which brings him 'inevitably' to suicide, a story which starts from Katie's drowning and works backwards into fate. 'She was too talented, too beautiful to live. She was a Botticelli angel, born for Paradise—'

Kate was not an angel. She was a human being like the rest of us. She drowned. It was an accident. The currents pulled her down.

All summer I fight to keep things separate and difficult, to resist the 'therefores' and 'of courses'.

James killed himself. That was a choice he made. He might have made other choices. Yes, he might.

Kate has been dead for nearly two months, James for just over four. It is Hallowe'en, it is Guy Fawkes Day, and the intolerable present has heaved itself back into place. The summer is over, that strange hot summer. It has come to an end. I still cower against the future and its unknown blows, but for the moment it is nice to be inside, to be sitting at a desk again, protected, somehow, by the winter and the cold.

Meanwhile the summer's legacy is still not sorted out. There are death duties to pay because of James. There are old debts, old difficulties that Katie left. This month my mother is moving house, leaving the upstairs bedroom where James shot himself. She has already collected and distributed his things. At some point in the future she will drive down south for Katie's.

In my head are pictures of them: James and Katie. One dead face and many living ones. They are little children, and I look down on the curly tops of their heads. They are great big people far taller than I am. I stare at them, and up beyond them into the sky, where in a dream I saw them both, their faces made of clouds.

They have left me their letters and a few bits of clothes. They have left me their friends, an enormous number. And they have left me alone, as they've left each of us alone. I look up, and I look down. There is a gap below me, where they used to be.

MIKAL GILMORE

FAMILY ALBUM

I am the brother of a man who murdered innocent men. His name was Gary Gilmore. After his conviction and sentencing, he campaigned to end his own life, and in January 1977 he was shot to death by a firing-squad in Draper, Utah. It was the first execution in America in over a decade.

Many people know this part of the Gary Gilmore story. It was an international news item in 1976 and 1977, and it became the subject of a popular novel and television film. What is less well known, what has never been documented, is the origin of Gary's violence—the history of my family. It isn't a comforting story to tell, nor has it been an easy legacy to live with. Over the years, many people have judged me by my brother's actions as if in coming from a family that yielded a murderer I must be formed by the same causes, the same sins, must by my brother's actions be responsible for the violence that resulted, and bear the mark of a frightening and shameful heritage. It's as if there is guilt in the fact of the blood-line itself. Maybe there is.

Mormon Utah in the early twentieth century was a nation within a nation. The Mormons had been persecuted horribly in the early nineteenth century. They had been driven across the country to the western desert. They had come to believe in violence, not just for protection, but for punishing abuses and betrayals, for vengeance. The early Mormons formed vendetta squads—such as the bloody Sons of Dan—to deal with enemies and traitors.

The Mormons developed a doctrine of blood atonement: if you took life, then you must lose your own (a prescription never applied to the Church's official assassins). They believed in capital punishment. The bloodier the execution, the better. Atoning for murder required a sacrifice: there should be ritual, blood, witnesses. Mormons favoured death by firing-squad or by hanging; these were—and today remain—the only options available to the condemned in Mormon law. Hangings were public. The gallows were placed in meadows or valleys, and Mormons brought their families to watch.

Bessie Gilmore was born Bessie Brown in 1913, the fourth of nine children, in the strict Mormon community of Provo, Utah. She often told us that she remembered being loaded by her father into the family wagon one winter morning, along with her brothers and sisters, and being driven in darkness to a hanging ceremony. She watched the man being led up the stairs to the noose and the executioner. She would not watch the hanging but shut her eyes tight and buried her face in her father's side. She heard the trapdoor crack open, then a horrible snapping sound as the man's weight hit the end of the rope's length and his head was yanked loose from his body. She heard cheers and applause. On moving away from the site, she turned back and saw the man's body dangling and swaying. Men around her were holding the hands of their children, pointing at the corpse, admonishing their brood to remember the moment and the lesson.

Bessie Brown remembered. The event haunted and terrified her for the rest of her life. She began to hate her own people—or at least the beliefs that would allow them to participate in hanging. When I was a child, and we were living in Portland, Oregon, she anxiously followed the news of impending executions. She wrote letters to the governor, arguing against the death penalty on moral grounds, asking the state to commute the condemned person's sentence. She asked me, or any of my brothers who might be around, to join her at the dining-table and write our own letters to the governor. She explained that these were the only killings we *knew* were going to occur and the only killings we could prevent.

She called the men who had arranged the public hangings the dead-makers. Mormon law had made it permissible for those watching to enjoy the deaths: the executions unleashed the demons of the hanged murderers—demons that flew from the gaping mouths of the men as their necks snapped and their souls departed, and then, once loose, were free to find new victims and haunt the witnesses to the deaths.

When she got older, Bessie began to drink and smoke—two habits forbidden to Mormons—and to flirt with boys. She wore pretty dresses to the Church dances and stayed out all night. One morning, sneaking back home, her father caught her. He called her terrible names and beat her. She ran away; her parents found her living in San Francisco; they dragged her home. A few months later, she ran away again.

Eventually, she ran away for good. One afternoon in Salt

Lake City she was visiting some girlfriends at one of the city's best hotels when she saw a beautiful man stroll into the lobby. Frank Gilmore was dressed in a fine suit and wore spats and carried a cane. She was dazzled. He was the most debonair person she had ever seen. She met him; he charmed her. He was not a Mormon.

My father was born in the late 1890s and grew up among spiritualists, vaudevillians and circus performers. His mother Fay La Foe had worked for many years as a medium, holding seances, telling fortunes, acting as a broker between the living and the dead. It was rumoured that in her younger days she had an affair with an up-and-coming magician, Erich Weiss—later famous as Harry Houdini. One of the family legends was that my father was their offspring, that he was Houdini's bastard son. According to my mother, my father's real name was Francis Weiss. She did not know where the name Gilmore came from. It was one of the many surnames he used during his life.

Frank Gilmore was a ladies' man. He was handsome and intelligent, he dressed splendidly and told captivating stories. He had been a stunt man for the actor Harry Carey and others in the silent-film era, and for years worked as a tightwire-walking clown in the Barnum and Bailey Circus under the name of Laffo, until a long fall without a net left him with a severely broken leg and injured back. He claimed that he had been a drinking buddy of Frank James and Buffalo Bill, in the Wild West's closing days. The only item of self-mythology he never vaunted was his possible relation to Harry Houdini; it was his mother who made that boast, to his irritation. He did not want to be the son of a man whom he would never know.

Frank Gilmore was twenty years older than my mother. He was married, with two children, when she met him. But she wanted to marry him. Frank Gilmore left his wife and in 1939 was married to Bessie Brown in a service conducted by his mother, who had a clergyman's licence in the Spiritualist Church. Her father was outraged and ashamed.

Whatever enjoyment Frank and Bessie may have had, it did not last long. By the time Frank Jr was born, my father was sullen and drinking heavily, and he and my mother bickered about money, family and religion constantly. My mother tried to keep pace with his drinking, making the nightly rounds of taverns with him as a way of forging a truce, but when she became pregnant again, she stopped drinking.

My father did not want a second child. He claimed the child was not his. He demanded that my mother have an abortion. One night, drunk, he beat her. He beat her again a few nights later. She left with Frank Jr and went to her father's farm. My father brought her back. They made a peace. Gary was born in 1941. My father neglected his second son; over the years, the disregard would turn to mutual hatred.

Pictures in the family scrapbook show my father with his children. I have only one photograph of him and Gary together. Gary is wearing a sailor's cap. He has his arms wrapped tightly around my father's neck, his head bent towards him, a look of broken need on his face. It is heart-breaking to look at this picture—not just for the look on Gary's face, the look that was the stamp of his future, but also for my father's expression: pulling away from my brother's cheek, he is wearing a look of distaste.

When my brother Gaylen was born in the mid-forties, my father turned all his love on his new, beautiful brown-eyed son. Gary takes on a harder aspect in the pictures around this time. He was beginning to keep a greater distance from the rest of the family. Six years later, my father turned his love from Gaylen to me. You don't see Gary in the family pictures after that.

Gary had nightmares. It was always the same dream: he was being beheaded.

In 1953, Gary was arrested for breaking windows. He was sent to a juvenile detention home for ten months, where he saw young men raped and beaten. Two years later, at age fourteen, he was arrested for car theft and sentenced to eighteen months in jail. I was four years old.

When I was growing up I did not feel accepted by, or close to, my brothers. By the time I was four or five, they had begun to find life and adventure outside the home. Frank, Gary and Gaylen signified the teenage rebellion of the fifties for me. They wore their hair in greasy pompadours and played Elvis Presley and

Fats Domino records. They dressed in scarred motorcycle jackets and brutal boots. They smoked cigarettes, drank booze and cough syrup, skipped—and quit—school, and spent their evenings hanging out with girls in tight sweaters, racing souped-up cars along country roads outside Portland, or taking part in gang rumbles. My brothers looked for a forbidden life—the life they had seen exemplified in the crime lore of gangsters and killers. They studied the legends of violence. They knew the stories of John Dillinger, Bonnie and Clyde, and Leopold and Loeb; mulled over the meanings of the lives and executions of Barbara Graham, Bruno Hauptmann, Sacco and Vanzetti, the Rosenbergs; thrilled to the pleading of criminal lawyers like Clarence Darrow and Jerry Giesler. They brought home books about condemned men and women, and read them avidly.

I remember loving my brothers fiercely, wanting to be a part of their late-night activities and to share in their laughter and friendship. I also remember being frightened of them. They looked deadly, beyond love, destined to hurt the world around them.

One hot summer afternoon, I was sitting in the living-room watching television when my brother Gaylen walked through the front door. He was bare-chested and covered with blood. He had tried to join a local gang. For the initiation, the gang-lord had stripped him and tied him up, then shot him repeatedly with a pellet rifle. Gaylen sat in a chair at the kitchen table as my mother washed the blood from him and picked the pellets from his arms and chest. She cried and talked about calling the police, but Gaylen made her promise that she wouldn't.

Gary came home from reform school for a brief Christmas visit. On Christmas night I was sitting in my room, playing with the day's haul of presents, when Gary wandered in. 'Hey Mike, how you doing?' he asked, taking a seat on my bed. 'Think I'll just join you while I have a little Christmas cheer.' He had a six-pack of beer with him and was speaking in a bleary drawl. 'Look partner, I want to have a talk with you.' I think it was the first companionable statement he ever made to me. I never expected the intimacy that followed and could not really fathom it at such a young age. Sitting on the end of my bed, sipping at his Christmas beer, Gary described a harsh, private world and told me horrible, transfixing stories: about the boys he knew in the detention halls, reform schools and county farms where he now spent most of his time; about the bad boys who had taught him the merciless codes of his new life; and about the soft boys who did not have what it took to survive that life. He said he had shared a cell with one of the soft boys, who cried at night, wanting to disappear into nothing, while Gary held him in his arms until the boy finally fell into sleep, sobbing.

Then Gary gave me some advice. 'You have to learn to be hard. You have to learn to take things and feel nothing about them: no pain, no anger, nothing. And you have to realize, if anybody wants to beat you up, even if they want to hold you down and kick you, you have to let them. You can't fight back. You *shouldn't* fight back. Just lie down in front of them and let them beat you, let them kick you. Lie there and let them do it. It is the only way you will survive. If you don't give in to them, they will kill you.'

He set aside his beer and cupped my face in his hands. 'You have to remember this, Mike,' he said. 'Promise me. Promise me you'll be a man. Promise me you'll let them beat you.' We sat there on that winter night, staring at each other, my face in his hands, and as Gary asked me to promise to take my beatings, his bloodshot eyes began to cry. It was the first time I had seen him shed tears.

I promised: Yes, I'll let them kick me. But I was afraid— afraid of betraying Gary's plea.

My father had taken his love from everybody else in the family and came to favour only me with it. This was another reason I felt apart from my brothers and I have never been comfortable admitting it. I was held up to them as the example of worth and goodness that they were not. Before I was born, Gaylen had been the favoured one. After I arrived, my father shunned Gaylen, made fun of him, called him fat, hit him, accused him of heading towards Gary's criminal life—which he accordingly did. My father never brutalized me, as he had brutalized Gary and Gaylen. Maybe he saw me as his last chance at successful love.

303

I remember my father finishing one tirade by taking Gaylen's pearl-handled, nickel-plated toy revolver, one of Gaylen's favourite possessions, and giving it to me. A day or two later, after my father left town on business, Gaylen dragged all my toys into the side yard and locked me in the house. I watched out of the dining-room window as he smashed toy after toy with an axe. He tossed the shattered heap of plastic in the trash can. When he came back in, he was crying. 'Someday,' he said in a voice thick with pain, 'he'll hate you too.'

Then there was the incident on Christmas Day.

I don't remember how it started, but my father and Gary became embroiled in an ugly confrontation. Each tested the other's toughness. Then they threatened to kill each other. My mother pleaded with them to stop, but the moment was too tense. Gaylen stepped in and asked my father to leave Gary alone. My father—already an old man, but still amazingly strong—made his fist and punched Gaylen in the stomach. I have never forgotten the awfulness of that blow. Gaylen doubled over in pain, and Gary went over to help him. My father grabbed me and said that we were leaving and would spend Christmas in a hotel. I did not want to go, and I said so. 'Don't *you* turn against me too,' he said, and the look of rage and hurt on his face was enough to make me go with him. I was afraid of what he might do to us all if I stayed.

My mother begged my father to remain, to apologize to Gaylen and Gary and try to repair the Christmas, or at least to let me spend the holiday with my brothers. My father would hear none of it. As he and I were in the car, pulling out of the driveway, I looked up at my mother and brothers, who were gathered on the porch, watching us leave. I could tell from the way my brothers were looking at me that they would never forgive me, would never let me into their fraternity.

I felt like a traitor. I wanted to join my brothers—to be standing with them on the porch, watching as the source of their hurt left them—but I knew I never could. I was eight, maybe nine, years old.

In 1960, my family moved from the semi-rural, semi-industrial outskirts of Portland to an upper-middle-class area nearby, known as Milwaukee. My father had settled down, as much as he knew how to. He had become a self-styled publishing entrepreneur: he compiled the numerous residential and business building-codes for the areas of Seattle, Tacoma and Portland, and published them in seasonal manuals in which he sold advertising spaces to local architects and contractors. It proved a lucrative business. We bought a big four-bedroom house with a tear-drop-shaped driveway, perched at the top of a hill that afforded a remarkable view of the entire stretch of the Willamette Valley. On clear days, you could view the fast-changing, oddly lopsided skyline of downtown Portland.

My mother saw the relocation as a new start. This was the home she had always wanted, she said, and she set about landscaping the yard with elaborately-patterned flower gardens and filling the house with fine furniture imported from Europe and Japan. I think she hoped that a new, better home would rehabilitate the family, give my wayward brothers new pride and win back my father's faith and support for his sons.

But Gary was drinking and popping pills. He began hanging out with the friends he had met in jail. He brought home guns. But he proved more a fearless crook than a clever one; he was arrested often, and each new sentence stretched longer than the one before. He had lived most of his adolescence and young adulthood in Oregon's city and county jails and had acquired a reputation as a hard-ass—somebody the other prisoners were not likely to go up against and the jailers would watch warily. He spent over half his jail time in isolation, for defying the institution's rules or for provoking or hitting guards. Many times he found himself in the jail hospital, following beatings by guards. He escaped twice—once by jumping from a second-storey window at a pre-trial hearing. It was that escape, I think, that produced his longest free time; he was gone for nearly two years, travelling around the country. One day, we got a call from Texas—the state where Gary had been born. He needed money; he had met a woman he wanted to marry, and they were going to have a baby. Reluctantly, my father sent the money. That was the last we ever heard of wife and baby.

Gaylen had his own litany of misdeeds. He was suspended from the local junior high and high schools, and eventually expelled. He stole cars and committed thefts and he drank a good deal more than Gary. By the age of sixteen, Gaylen was a fully-fledged alcoholic. In time, he developed his own criminal speciality—forging signatures and writing bad cheques—and, like Gary, spent much of his time in local jails or in flight, skipping bail and violating probation or parole. He joined the navy. He lasted six weeks. After he had gone AWOL five times, the base commanders concluded that Gaylen did not have a military career ahead of him and shipped him back home with an honourable discharge.

If my family sounds like white trash—as many have asserted—well, perhaps it was. Yet we were unusual white trash. Gary was an artist: I don't mean simply that he could draw well, or that he had pretensions, but that he could draw and paint with remarkable clarity and empathy. The best of his work had the high-lonesome, evocative power of Andrew Wyeth's or Edward Hopper's, though it was more openly haunted and death-obsessed. Gaylen read Poe, Rilke, Nietzsche, Kant, and memorized pages from Shakespeare, Thomas Wolfe and Edwin Arlington Robinson. He also wrote poetry, and it was startling. Like Gary's art, it spoke about being on the outside of life, heading for a self-willed inferno.

Where did this odd mix of raw talent, uncanny intelligence and wasteful ambition come from? Why did their gifts mean so little to my brothers? Why did they prefer a life of crime over a life in art?

I tried to talk to my brothers about their artistic interests, but they didn't want to talk. One afternoon, when Gary and I were sitting around the house, I tried to get him—for the umpteenth time—to show me some basics about drawing. He was drinking cough syrup and laughed in a polite but firm way that announced: *No dice*. I tried to crack Gary's indifference, to tell him I thought he could be a successful artist if he wanted to. Why didn't he make art his life—or at least his vocation? He chased his cough syrup with a swig of beer, then looked at me and smiled. 'You want to learn how to be an artist?' he said. 'Then learn how to eat pussy. Learn that, and it's the only art you'll ever need.'

Gary and Gaylen weren't at home much. I came to know them mainly through their reputations, through the endless parade of grim policemen who came to the door trying to find them, and through the faces and accusations of bail bondsmen and lawyers who arrived looking sympathetic and left disgusted. I knew them through many hours spent in waiting-rooms at city and county jails, where my mother went to visit them, and through the numerous times I accompanied her after midnight to the local police station on Milwaukee's Main Street to bail out another drunken son.

I remember being called into the principal's office while still in grammar school, and being warned that the school would never tolerate my acting as my brothers did; I was told to watch myself, that my brothers had already used years of the school district's good faith and leniency, and that if I was going to be like them, there were other schools I could be sent to. I came to be seen as an extension of my brothers' reputations. Once, I was waiting for a bus in the centre of the small town when a cop pulled over. 'You're one of the Gilmore boys, aren't you? I hope you don't end up like those two. I've seen enough shitheads from your family.' I was walking down the local main highway when a car pulled over and a gang of older teenage boys piled out, surrounding me. 'Are you Gaylen Gilmore's brother?' one of them asked. They shoved me into the car, drove me a few blocks to a deserted lot and took turns punching me in the face. I remembered Gary's advice—'You can't fight back; you *shouldn't* fight back'—and I let them beat me until they were tired. Then they spat on me and got back in their car and left.

I cried all the way back home, and I hated the world. I hated the small town I lived in, its ugly, mean people. For the first time in my life I hated my brothers. I felt that my future would be governed by them, that I would be destined to follow their lives whether I wanted to or not, that I would never know any relief from shame and pain and disappointment. I felt a deep impulse to violence: I wanted to rip the faces off the boys who had beaten me up. 'I want to kill them,' I told myself, 'I want to *kill* them'—and as I realized what it was I was saying, and why I was feeling that way, I only hated my world, and my brothers, more.

Mikal Gilmore

I've come to understand better why my brothers didn't seem to mind spending so much time in jail: it was preferable to being at home. My parents fought bitterly and often. In the worst fights my father would taunt or insult my mother until, driven by his sure-handed meanness, she would attack him physically. Many times I threw myself between them, trying to stop the fighting, begging them to forgive and love one another (my brothers, when they were home, refused to interfere in these fights; they said the battles had been going on for too many years, and there was no longer any point in becoming involved). Sometimes I succeeded in calming my parents, but the wounds were deep, and my mother would usually end up standing in front of my father, her face contorted in humiliation and fury, swearing that she would knife him in the throat during his sleep for all the pain he had made her feel. My father would fold out the sofa in the living-room and surround it with a fortress of chairs, so he could hear my mother tripping over them if she came to kill him. He would lie down on the sofa to sleep, and he would keep me next to him. Many nights I would lie there, next to my sleeping father, waiting for the sound of footsteps, the creak of floorboards, the glint of the knife. I would lie there watching the darkness. I would not fall asleep until dawn.

Sometimes, the fights were about me: who would have custody if they divorced or should I stay with my mother or go with my father when he made his trips between Portland and Seattle. My parents insisted that I choose between them. I felt awful no matter what choice I made. This is the way I learned how to love.

The time I spent with my father in Seattle was more peaceful than the time I spent at home in Portland. My father was busy and left me to myself. He didn't care if I stayed home from school for days on end. Because my brothers did not play with me much as a child, I was accustomed to keeping to myself. I filled the day by walking to the zoo, or catching a bus downtown, where I'd hang out in bookstores and movie theatres, or spend hours exploring abandoned Victorian houses in the Queen Anne district.

In the evenings, I sat in the apartment, reading the fantasy fiction of Edgar Rice Burroughs and Jules Verne, the horror

stories of Edgar Allan Poe, the epic comic-book tales of Carl
Barks or the EC crime and horror tales. Then I would huddle
close to my father when he arrived home, and we would watch
television together until late at night. We liked the westerns and
police dramas. We would watch *Maverick, Have Gun Will Travel,
Dragnet* or *The Untouchables*, one evening after another, far away
from the tumult of the home back in Oregon.

It was during one of these stays in Seattle, in the early
months of 1962, that I learned that my father had lung cancer
and would die within months. He never knew what was coming.
One day he had been old—in his late sixties—but still strong and
active, and then he was horribly tired and sick, confined to the
bed where he spent the last few months of his life coughing
sputum into a bowl. I remember the smell of it, because I lived in
the same room with it until the day my father died. It was sickly-
sweet, like a spoiled flower. I was surprised that death could be
fragrant.

My mother was grief-stricken. She tried to show him
tenderness and care, but the years of abuse had taken their toll.
As my father slept in the next room, my mother talked about
how he had hurt and betrayed her and how she had come to hate
him—she hated him more now that he was going to leave her
alone with the family, with little money. I had never heard her
sound more bitter. I left the room and walked past my father's
room and looked in on him. He was sitting on the side of his
bed, holding his head in his hands, and when he looked up at
me, I saw agony on his face. I went back to my mother and told
her that he had overheard what she had said. 'Good,' she replied.
'I wanted him to hear.' Later that night, I found my parents
sitting at the kitchen table, holding hands, talking softly. My
father was crying, and my mother was petting his hand. I had
never seen my parents hold each other's hands before.

Gary stole a car in Portland and drove it up to Seattle to see
my father; I think he was hoping for a last chance at
reconciliation. On the drive back, Gary was arrested as he
crossed the Washington–Oregon border. He was sentenced to a
year and a half in the county jail.

Frank Gilmore, Sr died on 30 June 1962. Gary was in
Portland's Rocky Butte Jail, and the authorities denied his

request to attend the funeral. He tore his cell apart; he smashed a light-bulb and slashed his wrists. He was placed in 'the hole'—solitary confinement—on the day of father's funeral. Gary was twenty-one. I was eleven.

I was surprised at how hard my mother and brothers took father's death. I was surprised they loved him enough to cry at all. Or maybe they were crying for the love he had so long withheld, and the reconciliation that would be forever denied them. I was the only one who didn't cry. I don't know why, but I never cried over my father's death—not then, and not now.

Frank Gilmore had not planned for dying. He had not made adequate preparations for his family: there was no will and no money. He left a large house that was still not paid for, and a business that neither my mother nor brothers knew how to operate, though we all tried our hands at it. It wasn't clear who held the copyright on my father's publications, and within a few months, competitors moved in and claimed that he had promised the business to them. Eventually my mother lost control over the publishing; when she did, the family was without solvency and without a financial future. To save the house, and to keep me in school, my mother took a series of menial jobs—working as a crew leader during the summer for children picking berries and beans in local fields, and eventually settling into a job as a waiter's assistant at a local restaurant in downtown Milwaukee. She worked long hours and developed a form of arthritis that proved progressively crippling. She dreamed of the day when she would receive social security payments that were large enough to allow her to quit her job. In time, the work and expenses proved too much. My mother lost her job at the restaurant when her hands and legs became too stiff and enfeebled for her to work. After that, there was never much money. For a while we went on welfare. My mother felt humiliated.

With my father's death Gary's crimes became more desperate, more violent. He talked a friend into helping him commit armed robbery. Gary grabbed the victim's wallet while the friend held a club; he was arrested a short time later, tried and found guilty. The day of his sentencing, during an afternoon when my mother had to work, he called me from the Clackamas

County Courthouse. 'How you doing partner? I just wanted to let you and mom know: I got sentenced to fifteen years.'

I was stunned. 'Gary, what can I do for you?' I asked. I think it came out wrong, as if I was saying: I'm busy; what do you *want*?

'I . . . I didn't really want anything,' Gary said, his voice broken. 'I just wanted to hear your voice. I just wanted to say goodbye. You know, I won't be seeing you for a few years. Take care of yourself.' We hadn't shared anything so intimate since that Christmas night, many years before.

My brother Frank had converted to the Jehovah's Witnesses; he'd had enough of both Catholic *and* Mormon theology. In 1966, he was drafted, but refused to learn how to fire a rifle in basic training; his church would not allow its members to carry or use arms in the nation's name. Frank was court-martialled and served three years at Leavenworth Federal Penitentiary. One brother jailed for his tendency to violence; another for his refusal to participate in sanctioned violence.

Gaylen got into progressively worse scrapes. One night, my mother and I were sitting in the kitchen when a car pulled into the driveway and several men piled out. My mother quickly locked the door and dragged me up the stairs, into my father's old office. From downstairs, we could hear the men kicking and pounding on the door. 'If you make us come in there to find you, Gilmore, we're going to kill you.' My mother did something I had never known her to do before: she called the police. The pounding and threats continued for several minutes until the sound of a police siren's wail began to make its way up the hill. The men jumped in their car and were gone. A few days later, when Gaylen returned home, my mother told him about the incident. He sat quietly for a while, then asked my mother if she could lend him a hundred dollars; there was something he needed to do. She opened her purse, gave him the money, and Gaylen walked out of the door without saying a word. The next time we heard from him, he was in Salt Lake City, visiting an old friend. He had no plans to return home, he said. Then, a few months later, we heard he was in the hospital, in critical condition. His friend had found him in bed with his wife and stabbed him.

Gaylen recovered and went to Chicago to visit some friends.

In 1970 he returned home. He had changed. He was pinched and emaciated. His speech was broken. He still drank too much and was taking painkillers. He seemed to have lost much of his wit and intelligence. He knocked on my door at two in the morning, in a drunken stupor, and stumbled in and dropped on the sofa, talking incoherently. I put a blanket on him and sat with him until he passed out.

Gaylen persuaded his girlfriend from Chicago to join him in Portland. In November 1971, they were married. Two weeks after the wedding, he woke up one night in severe pain; the knife wounds in his stomach and bowel had reopened. He went into the hospital and a few nights later at three in the morning, his wife called me. Gaylen was dead. He was twenty-six years old.

The next morning, my brother Frank and I visited Gary at Oregon State Penitentiary to tell him the news. As he entered the visitors' room, he looked unusually old and tired for a man of thirty. He knew that something was wrong.

'We have bad news for you, Gary,' Frank began.

The warden at Oregon State allowed Gary to attend the funeral. It was the first time the family had gathered together in nine years. It was also the last time.

I didn't have much talent for crime (neither did my brothers, to tell the truth), but I also didn't have much appetite for it. I had seen what my brothers' lives had brought them. For years, my mother had told me that I was the family's last hope for redemption. 'I want *one* son to turn out right, one son I don't have to end up visiting in jail, one son I don't have to watch in court as his life is sentenced away, piece by piece.' After my father's death, she drew me closer to her and her religion, and when I was twelve, I was baptized a Mormon. For many years, the Church's beliefs helped to provide me with a moral centre and a hope for deliverance that I had not known before.

I think culture and history helped to save me. I was born in 1951, and although I remember well the youthful explosion of the 1950s, I was too young to experience it the way my brothers did. The music of Elvis Presley and others had represented and expressed my brothers' rebellion: it was hard-edged, with no apparent ideology. The music was a part of my childhood, but by the early sixties the spirit of the music had been spent.

Then, on 9 February 1964 (my thirteenth birthday, and the day I joined the Mormon priesthood), the Beatles made their first appearance on the *Ed Sullivan Show*. My life would never be the same. The Beatles meant a change, they promised a world that my parents and brothers could not offer. In fact, I liked the Beatles in part because they seemed such a departure from the world of my brothers, and because my brothers couldn't abide them.

The rock culture and youth politics of the sixties allowed their adherents to act out a kind of ritualized criminality: we could use drugs, defy authority, or contemplate violent or destructive acts of revolt, we told ourselves, *because we had a reason to*. The music aimed to foment a sense of cultural community, and for somebody who had felt as disenfranchised by his family as I did, rock 'n' roll offered not just a sense of belonging but empowered me with new ideals. I began to find rock's morality preferable to the Mormon ethos, which seemed rigid and severe. One Sunday in the summer of 1967, a member of the local bishopric—a man I admired, and had once regarded as something of a father figure—drove over to our house and asked me to step outside for a talk. He told me that he and other church leaders had grown concerned about my changed appearance—the new length of my hair and my style of dressing—and felt it was an unwelcome influence on other young Mormons. If I did not reject the new youth culture, I would no longer be welcome in church.

On that day a line was drawn. I knew that rock 'n' roll had provided me with a new creed and a sense of courage. I believed I was taking part in a rebellion that mattered—or at least counted for more than my brothers' rebellions. In the music of the Rolling Stones or Doors or Velvet Underground, I could participate in darkness without submitting to it, which is something Gary and Gaylen had been unable to do. I remember their disdain when I tried to explain to them why Bob Dylan was good, why he mattered. It felt great to belong to a different world from them.

And I did: my father and Gaylen were dead; Gary was in prison and Frank was broken. I thought of my family as a cursed outfit, plain and simple, and I believed that the only way to escape its debts and legacies was to leave it. In 1969, I graduated from high school—the only member of my family to do so. The next day, I moved out of the house in Milwaukee and, with some friends, moved into an apartment near Portland State University, in downtown Portland. A short time later, encumbered by overdue property taxes, my mother gave up the nice home on the hill that she had struggled to hold on to. She and my brother Frank bought a small trailer and settled into a trailer camp.

Gary and I exchanged letters, but whole worlds separated us. In Oregon inmates weren't allowed visitors under the age of eighteen. I felt too guilty to write to Gary about what I was doing in school or about friends and pastimes, because to Gary these existed on the 'outside'. After Gaylen's death, Gary seemed to change. He had lost two members of his family without the opportunity for final reconciliation, and he wanted desperately to be free. In his letters, he began to express more concern for me, more curiosity about what I was doing, who my friends were. He was trying to be my brother. But I told myself I didn't have time for the long trek down to Salem, Oregon, to visit him. I think I was trying to forget him, trying to leave him and our past life behind.

But Gary didn't want to be forgotten.

In the fall of 1972, Gary was granted a 'school release' to attend a community college in Eugene, Oregon, and study art, on the condition that he return to a dorm facility every evening and never leave the Eugene area without the consent of his counsellors. Our family saw it as a turning-point.

But on the morning of his release, Gary showed up at my door, a six-pack of beer in his hand. He explained that he wanted to visit friends and family in Portland. 'I'll go back before the night,' he said. 'I can still register tomorrow without getting in any trouble.'

The next afternoon, he showed up again. He was wearing a long black raincoat and a pork-pie hat. With his half-grown goatee he looked like a hick hipster. He had a red glare about his eyes. He had not returned to Eugene as he said he would. For his failure to do so he could not only lose his scholarship but be sentenced to additional jail time.

'Gary, what are you doing here?'

He skirted the question. 'Let's get lunch some place. Know any good places?' I said that there was a restaurant within walking distance, but Gary didn't want to be seen on the streets. He wanted to go by taxi. My anger began to turn to dread. We ended up at a topless bar. As Gary studied the girl on stage, he seemed to be in a trance. I asked him why he wasn't going to school.

He was silent for a long time and stared at the table. When he spoke, it was with his slow, countrified drawl. 'I'm not cut out for school. Man, they can't teach me anything about art that I don't already know. Besides, there are more important things.' He leaned towards me and locked his stare into mine. 'A friend of mine from the joint is being brought up to the dental school here next week. A couple of guards are bringing him up and I want to go see him. Uh, I need a gun. Can you help me?'

I told him he was throwing away his life.

He narrowed his eyes. 'It's a matter of dignity,' he said. Gary stared at me for a long time without expression. He fidgeted with a book of matches. 'I'd do it for *my* brother,' he said.

I saw him only two more times that month. He visited me while I had a girlfriend over and asked me to play Johnny Cash records for him. He was sober and charming. When we were alone, I tried to prod him about his plans. 'Let's just say they've changed,' he said. 'Don't you worry about it. The less you know, the better off you are.'

A few days later I came out of a class at Portland State, and Gary was waiting outside. He had borrowed a car and wanted me to meet some friends. We drove out, Gary drinking beer and conversing in a friendly manner. At his friends' house, Gary showed me a collection of his drawings and paintings: drawings of children, studies of ballet dancers and bruised boxers, an occasional depiction of violent death. 'Here,' he said, 'take what you want.' To him, pictures were drawn then given away.

His friends enjoyed luxury that he had never known. While

showing me the indoor swimming-pool, Gary opened his jacket, took out a pistol and handed it to me, handle first. 'Think you could ever use one of these?' he asked in his best Gary Cooper fashion.

I felt awkward and vulnerable: it was the first time I had ever held a gun. I kept the barrel pointed towards the pool and lifted my finger from the trigger. He took the gun and returned it to his jacket pocket. 'C'mon,' he said. 'I'll drive you home.' We drove back in silence. He seemed angry.

Two nights later I watched a news report of his arrest for armed robbery. My mother and I were unable to visit him in jail, but we attended his trial. Handcuffed and on the verge of tears, Gary acted as his own defence and pleaded for a reprieve. 'I have done a lot of time and I don't think it would do me good to do any more,' he told the judge. 'I have been locked up for the last nine-and-one-half calendar years consecutively, and I have had about two-and-a-half years of freedom since I was fourteen years old. I have always gotten time and have always done it, never been paroled, only had one probation. I have never had a break from the law and I have come to think that justice is kind of harsh and I have never asked for a break until now.'

The judge sentenced Gary to an additional nine years. The next time I saw him was six days before his execution.

In the summer of 1976, I was working at a record store in downtown Portland, making enough money to pay my rent and bills. I was also writing freelance journalism and criticism, and had sold my first reviews and articles to national publications, including *Rolling Stone*.

On the evening of 30 July, having passed up a chance to go drinking with some friends, I headed home. *The Wild Bunch*, Peckinpah's genuflection to violence and honour, was on television, and as I settled back on the couch to watch it, I picked up the late edition of *The Oregonian*. I almost passed over a page-two item headlined OREGON MAN HELD IN UTAH SLAYINGS, but then something clicked inside me, and I began to read it. 'Gary Mark Gilmore, 35, was charged with the murders of two young clerks during the hold-up of a service station and a motel.' I read on, dazed, about how Gary had been arrested for killing

Max Jensen and Ben Bushnell on consecutive nights. Both men were Mormons, about the same age as I, and both left wives and children behind.

I dropped the paper to the floor. I sat on the couch the rest of the night, alternately staring at *The Wild Bunch* and rereading the sketchy account. I felt shocks of rage, remorse and guilt—as if I were partly responsible for the deaths. I had been part of an uninterested world that had shut Gary away. I had wanted to believe that Gary's life and mine were not entwined, that what had shaped him had not shaped me.

It had been a long time since I had written or visited Gary. After his resentencing in 1972, I heard news of him from my mother. In January 1975, Gary was sent to the federal penitentiary in Marion, Illinois. After his transfer, we exchanged a few perfunctory letters. In early April 1976, I learned of the Oregon State Parole Board's decision to parole Gary from Marion to Provo, Utah, rather than transfer him back to Oregon. The transaction had been arranged between the parole board and Brenda Nicol (our cousin) and her father, our Uncle Vernon Damico, who lived in Provo. I remember thinking that Gary's being paroled into the heart of one of Utah's most devout and severe Mormon communities was not a great idea.

Between his release and those fateful nights in July, Gary held a job at Uncle Vernon's shoe store, and he met and fell in love with Nicole Barrett, a beautiful young woman with two children. But Gary was unable to deny some old, less wholesome appetites. Almost immediately after his release, he started drinking heavily and taking Fiorinal, a muscle and headache medication that, in sustained doses, can cause severe mood swings and sexual dysfunction. Gary apparently experienced both reactions. He became more violent. Sometimes he got rough with Nicole over failed sex, or over what he saw as her flirtations. He picked fights with other men, hitting them from behind, threatening to cave in their faces with a tyre iron that he twirled as handily as a baton. He lost his job and abused his Utah relatives. He walked into stores and walked out again with whatever he wanted under his arm, glaring at the cashiers, challenging them to try to stop him. He brought guns home, and sitting on the back porch would fire them at trees, fences, the sky. 'Hit the sun,' he told Nicole. 'See if you can make it sink.' Then he hit Nicole with his fist one too many times, and she moved out.

Gary wanted her back. He told a friend that he thought he might kill her.

On a hot night in late July, Gary drove over to Nicole's mother's house and persuaded Nicole's little sister, April, to ride with him in his white pick-up truck. He wanted her to join him in looking for her sister. They drove for hours, listening to the radio, talking aimlessly, until Gary pulled up by a service station in the small town of Orem. He told April to wait in the truck. He walked into the station, where a twenty-six-year-old attendant, Max Jensen, was working alone. There were no other cars there. Gary pulled a .22 automatic from his jacket and told Jensen to empty the cash from his pockets. He took Jensen's coin changer and led the young attendant around the back of the station and forced him to lie down on the bathroom floor. He told Jensen to place his hands under his stomach and press his face to the ground. Jensen complied and offered Gary a smile. Gary pointed the gun at the base of Jensen's skull. 'This one is for me,' Gary said, and he pulled the trigger. And then: 'This one is for Nicole,' and he pulled the trigger again.

The next night, Gary walked into the office of a motel just a few doors away from his Uncle Vernon's house in Provo. He ordered the man behind the counter, Ben Bushnell, to lie down on the floor, and then he shot him in the back of the head. He walked out with the motel's cashbox under his arm and tried to stuff the pistol under a bush. But it discharged, blowing a hole in his thumb.

Gary decided to get out of town. First he had to take care of his thumb. He drove to the house of a friend named Craig and telephoned his cousin. A witness had recognized Gary leaving the site of the second murder, and the police had been in touch with Brenda. She had the police on one line, Gary on another. She tried to stall Gary until the police could set up a roadblock. After they finished speaking, Gary got into his truck and headed for the local airport. A few miles down the road, he was surrounded by police cars and a SWAT team. He was arrested for Bushnell's murder and confessed to the murder of Max Jensen.

Gary's trial began some months later. The verdict was never in question. Gary didn't help himself when he refused to allow his attorneys to call Nicole as a defence witness. Gary and Nicole had been reconciled; she felt bad for him and visited him in jail every day for hours. Gary also didn't help his case by staring menacingly at the jury members or by offering belligerent testimony on his own behalf. He was found guilty. My mother called me on the night of Gary's sentencing, 7 October, to tell me that he had received the death penalty. He told the judge he would prefer being shot to being hanged.

On 8 November I heard that Gary had waived all rights of appeal and review. He wanted to be executed. Fourth District Judge J. Robert Bullock had complied, setting the date of execution for Monday 15 November. Gary's attorney filed for a stay of execution—against his protests—and the Utah Supreme Court granted one.

I decided to confront Gary about his decision. The next day I called Draper Prison, where he was being held. Our first exchanges were polite and tentative. Gary became impatient. 'Something on your mind?'

I asked if he was serious about requesting execution.

'What do you think?'

'I don't know.'

'That's right. You don't. You never knew me.' Gary had thrown down a barrier I couldn't leap over. I was lost for a reply. 'Look,' he continued, in a softer tone, 'I'm not trying to be mean to you, but this thing's going to happen one way or the other; there's nothing you can do to stop it and I don't particularly want you to like me for it. It'll be easier for me if you don't. It seems the only time we ever talk to each other is around the time of somebody's death. Now it's mine.'

I felt helpless. I asked him to consider mother.

'Well, I want to see mother before all this goes down,' Gary said. 'I want to see all of you. Maybe that will make it easier. But I don't want you or anybody else to interfere. It's my affair. I don't want to spend the rest of my life on trial or in prison. I've lost my freedom. I lost it a long time ago. I don't want you

319

to think I'm some "sensitive" artist because I drew pictures or wrote poems. I killed—in cold blood.' A guard told Gary that his time was up. I asked him to tell his new attorney, Dennis Boaz, to call me. Boaz phoned that night. He said that he supported Gary's right to die and that on the following day, 10 November, he and Gary would appear before the Utah Supreme Court and ask them to lift the stay. I asked Boaz to call me as soon as the court made its decision. He promised to call me by four o'clock the next day. His closing line stayed with me. 'Is it OK if I call you collect? I'm a poor man.'

He didn't call. I learned of his and Gary's successful appearance before the court on the network news, which showed clips of my brother being led from the courtroom in shackles, with his wary, piercing stare. Overnight, the most painful and private part of my family's history, a past that I had tried for years to escape, was everywhere. Gary was on the national news nearly every evening of the week; he was on the front page of every newspaper I saw; he was staring out at me from the cover of *Newsweek*. Inside the magazine, I found pictures from my family's photo albums. There was a picture from a distant Christmas with my father, Gary, Gaylen and me, standing in a line. Nobody in the picture looked happy.

Utah governor Calvin Rampton ordered a stay of execution, referring the matter to the state board of pardons and earning the epithet of 'moral coward' from Gary. I received a call on the night of his order from Anthony Amsterdam of Stanford Law School, a well-regarded opponent of the death penalty and a member of the bar of the United States Supreme Court. He outlined a possible course of action for the family: a family member could retain counsel to seek a stay from the US Supreme Court, the duration of which would be determined by the Court's willingness to review the case and the subsequent decision of that review. This meant that Gary would be entitled to a new trial. I passed the information on to Mother, who also spoke with Amsterdam. We agreed to retain him pending the pardons-board decision. On Tuesday morning, 16 November, the day after Gary's scheduled execution, Amsterdam called me with the news that Gary and Nicole had attempted suicide with an overdose of sedatives.

On 30 November the pardons board decided to allow the execution to go forward. On 3 December the US Supreme Court granted a stay of execution. Our calls to the prison were turned away. Gary issued an open letter asking my mother to 'butt out'. During this time neither Gary nor his legal representatives attempted to contact any members of the immediate family.

On the morning of 13 December, the Supreme Court lifted its stay, declaring that Gary had made a 'knowing and intelligent waiver of his rights'. The next day Judge Bullock reset the execution for 17 January. Gary was confined to a 'strip cell' and denied visits, even from family members.

By Christmas I told myself and anyone who asked that I didn't care about what might happen. I spent the holidays drunk or drugged. My girlfriend went home to visit her family, and I was with a different woman every night she was gone. I took sleeping-pills because I couldn't sleep. When I couldn't sleep, I walked around my house, throwing and breaking things. One night, I dreamed of Gary being tied to a stake and bayoneted repeatedly, while I stood on the other side of a fence, unable to reach him. In the morning, I heard of another, nearly fatal suicide attempt by Gary.

I desperately wanted to see him, to reach out to him at last, to achieve a reconciliation. I was not resigned to his execution.

Draper Prison is located in the Salt Lake Valley at a place known as the 'Point of the Mountain'. The valley is heavily polluted, and one doesn't become aware of the surroundings until the final, winding approach to the prison. Draper rests at the centre of a flat basin, surrounded by tall, sharply inclined snowy slopes. It offers the most beautiful vista in the entire valley.

My brother Frank and I were led into a triangular room in which no guards were present. Gary strolled in. He was dressed in prison whites and in red, white and blue sneakers. He twirled a comb and smiled broadly. I'd seen so many photos and film clips that showed him looking grim and cold-looking that I'd forgotten how charming he could be. 'You're looking as fit as ever,' he said to Frank, 'And you're just as damn skinny as ever,' he said to me. He rearranged the benches in front of the guardroom window. 'So those poor fools can keep an eye on me,' he said.

For the first few minutes we exchanged small talk. Then I spoke of the prospect of intervention, but Gary cut me off. 'Look, I don't want anybody interfering, no outside causes, no lawyers like Amsterdam.' He took hold of my chin. 'He's out of this, I hope.' Before I had a chance to reply, the visitors' door opened and Uncle Vernon and Aunt Ida entered. The visit became an ordeal, Gary and Vernon did most of the talking, discussing the people Gary wanted to leave money to and cracking macabre jokes. Vernon had brought along a bag of green T-shirts adorned with a computerized photo of Gary and the legend, 'Gilmore—death wish'. Vernon and Gary discussed the possibility of Gary wearing one on the morning of the execution, and Vernon auctioning it off to the highest bidder.

As we were leaving, Gary offered me a T-shirt. I didn't accept it.

'Well,' he drawled, smiling, 'it's a little big for you, but I think you can grow into it.' I took the shirt.

I visited Gary again. I forced myself to ask the question I'd been building up to: 'What would you do if we were able to stop this?'

'I don't want you to do that,' he said gravely.

'That doesn't answer my question.'

'I'd kill myself. Look, I'm not watched closely in this place. I could've killed myself any time in the last two weeks. But I don't want to. Besides, if a person's dumb enough to murder and get caught, then he shouldn't snivel about what he gets.'

Gary went on to talk about prison life, describing some of the brutality he had witnessed and some that he had fostered. He was terrified of a life in prison. 'Maybe you could have my sentence commuted, but you wouldn't have to live that sentence or be around when I killed myself.' The fear in his eyes was most discernible when he spoke about prison, far more than when he spoke about his own impending death—maybe because one was an abstraction and the other an ever-present concrete reality. 'I don't think death will be anything new or frightening for me. I think I've been there before.'

We talked for hours, or rather Gary talked. This was the first real communication we had had in years; neither of us wanted to let go. I told Gary that I was supposed to leave that night, to go back home and spend the weekend with mother. 'Can't you stay for one more day?' he asked. I agreed to return the next day.

I reached our lawyer and told him that I had decided not to intervene to block the execution. Telling him was almost as hard as making the decision. I could have sought a stay, signed the necessary documents and gone away feeling that I had made the right decision, the moral choice. But I didn't have to bear the weight of that decision; Gary did. If I could have chosen for Gary to live, I would have.

On Saturday 15 January, I saw Gary for the last time. Camera crews were camped in the town of Draper, preparing for the finale.

During our other meetings that week, Gary had opened with friendly remarks or a joke or even a handstand. This day, though, he was nervous and was eager to deny it. We were separated by a glass partition. 'Naw, the noise in this place gets to me sometimes, but I'm as cool as a cucumber,' he said, holding up a steady hand. The muscles in his wrists and arms were taut and thick as rope.

Gary showed me letters and pictures he'd received, mainly from children and teenage girls. He said he always tried to answer the ones from kids first, and he read one from an eight-year-old boy: 'I hope they put you some place and make you live for ever for what you did. You have no right to die. With all the malice in my heart. [*name*.]'

'Man, that one shook me up for a long time,' he said.

I asked him if he'd replied to it.

'Yeah, I wrote, "You're too young to have malice in your heart. I had it in mine at a young age and look what it did for me."'

Gary's eyes nervously scanned some letters and pictures, finally falling on one that made him smile. He held it up. A picture of Nicole. 'She's pretty, isn't she?' I agreed. 'I look at this picture every day. I took it myself; I made a drawing from it. Would you like to have it?'

I said I would. I asked him where he would have gone if he had made it to the airport the night of the second murder.

'Portland.'

I asked him why.

Gary studied the shelf in front of him. 'I don't want to talk about that night any more,' he said. 'There's no *point* in talking about it.'

'Would you have come to see me?'

He nodded. For a moment his eyes flashed the old anger. 'And what would *you* have done if I'd come to you?' he asked. 'If I had come and said I was in trouble and needed help, needed a place to stay? Would *you* have taken me in? Would you have hidden me?'

The question had been turned back on me. I couldn't speak. Gary sat for a long moment, holding me with his eyes, then said steadily: 'I think I was coming to kill you. I think that's what would have happened; there may have been no choice for you, no choice for me.' His eyes softened. 'Do you understand why?'

I nodded. Of course I understood why: I had escaped the family—or at least thought I had. Gary had not.

I felt terror. Gary's story could have been mine. Then terror became relief—Jensen and Bushnell's deaths, and Gary's own impending death, had meant my own safety. I finished the thought, and my relief was shot through with guilt and remorse. I felt closer to Gary than I'd ever felt before. I understood why he wanted to die.

The warden entered Gary's room. They discussed whether Gary should wear a hood for the execution.

I rapped on the glass partition and asked the warden if he would allow us a final handshake. At first he refused but consented after Gary explained it was our final visit, on the condition that I agree to a skin search. After I had been searched by two guards, two other guards brought Gary around the partition. They said that I would have to roll up my sleeve past my elbow, and that we could not touch beyond a handshake. Gary grasped my hand, squeezed it tight and said, 'Well, I guess this is it.' He leaned over and kissed me on the cheek.

On Monday morning, 17 January, in a cannery warehouse out behind Utah State Prison, Gary met his firing-squad. I was with my mother and brother and girlfriend when it happened.

Just moments before, we had seen the morning newspaper with the headline EXECUTION STAYED. We switched on the television for more news. We saw a press conference. Gary's death was being announced.

There was no way to be prepared for that last see-saw of emotion. One moment you're forcing yourself to live through the hell of knowing that somebody you love is going to die in an expected way, at a specific time and place, and that there is nothing you can do to change that. For the rest of your life, you will have to move around in a world that wanted this death to happen. You will have to walk past people every day who were heartened by the killing of somebody in your family—somebody who you knew had long before been murdered emotionally.

You turn on the television, and the journalist tells you how the warden put a black hood over Gary's head and pinned a small, circular cloth target above his chest, and how five men pumped a volley of bullets into him. He tells you how the blood flowed from Gary's devastated heart and down his chest, down his legs, staining his white pants scarlet and dripping to the warehouse floor. He tells you how Gary's arm rose slowly at the moment of the impact, how his fingers seemed to wave as his life left him.

Shortly after Gary's execution, *Rolling Stone* offered me a job as an assistant editor at their Los Angeles bureau. It was a nice offer. It gave me chance to get away from Portland and all the bad memories it represented.

I moved to Los Angeles in April 1977. It was not an easy life at first. I drank a pint of whiskey every night, and I took Dalmane, a sleeping medication that interfered with my ability to dream—or at least made it hard to remember my dreams. There were other lapses: I was living with one woman and seeing a couple of others. For a season or two my writing went to hell. I didn't know what to say or how to say it; I could no longer tell if I had anything *worth* writing about. I wasn't sure how you made words add up. Instead of writing, I preferred reading. I favoured hard-boiled crime fiction—particularly the novels of Ross Macdonald—in which the author tried to solve murders by explicating labyrinthine family histories. I spent many nights listening to punk rock. I liked the music's accommodation with a merciless world. One of the most famous punk songs of the period was by the Adverts. It was called 'Gary Gilmore's Eyes.' What would it be like, the song asked, to see the world through Gary Gilmore's dead eyes? Would you see a world of murder?

All around me I had Gary's notoriety to contend with. During my first few months in LA—and throughout the years that followed—most people asked me about my brother. They wanted to know what Gary was like. They admired his bravado, his hardness. I met a woman who wanted to sleep with me because I was his brother. I tried to avoid these people.

I also met women who, when they learned who my brother was, would not see me again, not take my calls again. I received letters from people who said I should not be allowed to write for a young audience. I received letters from people who thought I should have been shot alongside my brother.

There was never a time without a reminder of the past. In 1979, Norman Mailer's *The Executioner's Song* was published. At the time, I was living with a woman I loved very much. As she read the book, I could see her begin to wonder about whom she was sleeping with, about what had come into her life. One night a couple of months after the book had been published, we were watching *Saturday Night Live*. The guest host was doing a routine of impersonations. He tied a bandanna around his eyes and gleefully announced his next subject: 'Gary Gilmore!' My girlfriend got up from the sofa and moved into the bedroom, shutting the door. I poured a glass of whiskey. She came out a few minutes later. 'I'm sorry,' she said, 'I can't live with you any more. I can't stand being close to all this stuff.' She was gone within a week.

I watched as a private and troubling event continued to be the subject of public sensation and media scrutiny; I watched my brother's life—and in some way, my life—become too large to control. I tried not to surrender to my feelings because my feelings wouldn't erase the pain or shame or bad memories or unresolved love and hate. I was waiting to be told what to feel.

I tried to leave the reality of my family behind me. I visited my mother in Oregon a couple of times a year, but the visits were always disturbing. She talked incessantly about the past—about her childhood in Utah, about Gary's death, about the family curse—and her health was bad. After Gary's death, she refused to leave her trailer, and my brother Frank and I could not convince her to see a doctor.

In the last few years of her life, my mother began to tell my brother Frank and me stories that were like confessions. She told us how she had hated her father: he had been a cruel and authoritarian Mormon patriarch; he had beaten his children with a whip; he had tormented and humiliated her brother George terribly. She never forgave him for dragging her to the hanging in the meadow. She had not, in fact, managed to keep her face buried in his side that morning. In the instant before the trapdoor was pulled, her father grabbed her by the hair and yanked hard, forcing her to watch the man as he dropped to death. On the ride back, she decided that she would never forgive her father, and that she would live a life to spite his hard virtue.

In June 1980, her stomach ruptured. She was sitting in the small front room of her trailer, talking to my brother about all the pain her father and her husband had left her with, and she started to lose blood. We brought her to the hospital. She fell into a coma, and a few days later she died.

I helped my brother bury her. Frank was forty years old, and he seemed lost without her.

The night of her funeral, Frank and I stayed at a friend's house. I had to fly back to Los Angeles the next day. I told Frank to come to California and stay with me for a while. In the morning we said goodbye. I watched him turn and walk away. I wrote to him as soon as I got back to LA. Within a few days, the letter came back. It was marked: NO LONGER AT THIS ADDRESS. NO FORWARDING ADDRESS. For a long time I tried to find him, but I never did. I have not seen him since that morning we said goodbye to each other on that haunted stretch of Oregon highway. He seemed to have walked into the void with all the other ghosts.

A few months after my mother's death, I fell in love. Like me, she came from a family with a history of death and brutality. We believed we could help each other make up for our losses and in August 1982 we were married.

The marriage did not last—how could it? My wife and I brought along too many family demons for one house. I hadn't so much loved her as tried to save her, in order to atone for my failure to save my brother. I went on to pursue one vain relationship after another, in a desperate attempt to discover or build the sort of family that had not been present in my childhood. I sometimes sabotaged my relationships, as a way of never having the family life I claimed I wanted so much—of *not* passing to my children the inheritance of violence and ruin that I feared might be genetic. For far too long, I stopped wanting any home or family, because it hurt too much, felt too much like irredeemable failure, to want those things and yet feel I would never have them, or might damage them once I did have them.

And then, a few years ago, I decided I was ready to move back home. I believed I could live again in the place where so much ruin had occurred and simply ignore all that ruin; I thought I might seize those dreams I had wanted for so long. But I came face-to-face with that damn family spectre, and it devastated my life and also my hope, and I returned to my friends and life in Los Angeles.

Can murder's momentum end? It has been fifty years since Gary was born. It has been over fourteen years since he committed his murders and died for them. You would think that would be enough time to forget, to redeem. But the past never stops.

Early one evening a few months ago a friend called to tell me that *A Current Affair*—a nationally syndicated programme that takes real-life scandal and repackages it into a news-entertainment format—would be running a segment that night on my brother. The show's producers had tracked down Nicole and persuaded her to grant an interview about Gary and his murders and execution—the first lengthy television interview she had ever agreed to do.

It came as a bit of a surprise to me that, after well over a decade, Gary's relationship with Nicole and his death would still be hot news. Maybe it was a slow day for scandalmongering. I tuned in to the programme, expecting something tasteless, and what I saw was certainly that. But it was also strangely affecting in ways I had not expected: there was news footage of Gary being led to and from court during the many hearings of those last few months, handcuffed and dressed in prison whites, his wary, appraising eyes scanning the cameras that surrounded and documented him. I remembered watching this footage back in the daze and fury of 1976. Fourteen years later he looked cold-blooded, arrogant, deadly. He also looked plain scared, and he looked like *my* brother. That is, like somebody I both loved and hated; somebody who had transformed my life in ways that could never be repaired; somebody I had missed very much in the years since his death and I wished I could talk with, no matter how painful the talking might be.

The programme's message was sordid and mean-spirited. The point, it seemed, was to try to hang much of the blame for Gary's murders on Nicole. Nicole described the last time Gary had hit her. 'I had been hit before by men,' she said, 'and I told myself, "I'm leaving." No matter what I did, I did not deserve that. He knew that was how I felt. And when I looked at him, I knew that when I went, he would kill someone. I knew that if I left him, somebody would die for it.'

'And yet you left anyway?' the interviewer asked.

Nicole looked off camera for a moment. 'One of the greater regrets of my life,' she said.

The interviewer's implication couldn't have been plainer: Nicole shared in the blame. 'How could you say you loved somebody so cold-blooded?' he asked at the end.

'There isn't a day goes by,' said Nicole, 'his name doesn't go through my head. He came into my life, he loved me, and he destroyed all the good that was there.'

'If you could erase Gary Gilmore from your life, would you?'

Again, another glance away, and she shook her head.

'And you say that,' the interviewer asked, 'knowing that if you erased Gary those two men would still be alive, those men's children would still have their fathers . . .'

Finally, Nicole closed off the question. 'Yeah,' she said, nodding. 'Yeah, then I would.'

The camera cut to the programme's host, who had an expression of smug disgust. 'Tough to shed a tear for her,' he said.

I turned off the television and the lights in my front room, and I sat in the dark for hours.

Only a few months before, I had gone through one of the worst times of my life—my brief move to Portland and back. What had gone wrong, I realized, was because of my past, something that had been set in motion long before I was born. It was what Gary and I shared, more than any blood tie: we were both heirs to a legacy of negation that was beyond our control or our understanding. Gary had ended up turning the nullification outward—on innocents, on Nicole, on his family, on the world and its ideas of justice, finally on himself. I had turned the ruin inward. Outward or inward—either way, it was a powerfully destructive legacy, and for the first time in my life, I came to see that it had not really finished its enactment. To believe that Gary had absorbed all the family's dissolution, or that the worst of that rot had died with him that morning in Draper, Utah, was to miss the real nature of the legacy that had placed him before those rifles: what that heritage or patrimony was about, and where it had come from.

We tend to view murders as solitary ruptures in the world around us, outrages that need to be attributed and then punished. There is a motivation, a crime, an arrest, a trial, a verdict and a punishment. Sometimes—though rarely—that punishment is death. The next day, there is another murder. The next day, there is another. There has been no punishment that breaks the pattern, that stops this custom of one murder following another.

Murder has worked its way into our consciousness and our culture in the same way murder exists in our literature and film: we consume each killing until there is another, more immediate or gripping one to take its place. When *this* murder story is finished, there will be another to intrigue and terrify that part of the world that has survived it. And then there will be another. Each will be a story; each will be treated and reported and remembered as a unique incident. Each murder will be solved, but murder itself will never be solved. You cannot solve murder without solving the human heart or the history that has rendered that heart so dark and desolate.

This murder story is told from inside the house where murder was born. It is the house where I grew up, and it is a house that I have never been able to leave.

As the night passed, I formed an understanding of what I needed to do. I would go back into my family—into its stories, its myths, its memories, its inheritance—and find the real story and hidden propellants behind it. I wanted to climb into the family story in the same way I've always wanted to climb into a dream about the house where we all grew up.

In the dream, it is always night. We are in my father's house—a charred-brown, 1950s-era home. Shingled, two-storey and weather-worn, it is located on the far outskirts of a dead-end American town, pinioned between the night-lights and smoking chimneys of towering industrial factories. A moonlit stretch of railroad track forms the border to a forest I am forbidden to trespass. A train whistle howls in the distance. No train ever comes.

People move from the darkness outside the house to the darkness inside. They are my family. They are all back from the dead. There is my mother, Bessie Gilmore, who, after a life of bitter losses, died spitting blood, calling the names of her father and her husband—men who had long before brutalized her hopes and her love—crying to them for mercy, for a passage into the darkness that she had so long feared. There is my brother Gaylen, who died young of knife wounds, as his new bride sat holding his hand, watching the life pass from his sunken face. There is my brother Gary, who murdered innocent men in rage against the way life had robbed him of time and love, and who died when a volley of bullets tore his heart from his chest. There is my brother Frank, who became quieter and more distant with each new death, and who was last seen in the dream walking down a road, his hands rammed deep into his pockets, a look of uncomprehending pain on his face. There is my father, Frank Sr, dead of the ravages of lung cancer. He is in the dream less often than the other family members, and I am the only one happy to see him.

One night, years into the same dream, Gary tells me why I can never join my family in its comings and goings, why I am left alone sitting in the living-room as they leave: it is because I have not yet entered death. I cannot follow them across the tracks, into the forest where their real lives take place, until I die. He pulls a gun from his coat pocket. He lays it on my lap. There is a door across the room, and he moves towards it. Through the door is the night. I see the glimmer of the train tracks. Beyond them, my family.

I do not hesitate. I pick the pistol up. I put its barrel in my mouth. I pull the trigger. I feel the back of my head erupt. It is a softer feeling than I expected. I feel my teeth fracture, disintegrate and pass in a gush of blood out of my mouth. I feel my life pass out of my mouth, and in that instant, I collapse into nothingness. There is darkness, but there is no beyond. There is *never* any beyond, only the sudden, certain rush of extinction. I know that it is death I am feeling—that is, I know this is how death must truly feel and I know that this is where beyond ceases to be a possibility.

I have had the dream more than once, in various forms. I always wake up with my heart hammering hard, hurting after being torn from the void that I know is the gateway to the refuge of my ruined family. Or is it the gateway to hell? Either way, I want to return to the dream, but in the haunted hours of the night there is no way back.

SOUSA JAMBA

BROTHERS

'Please, do whatever you can to help me get out of here.' It was Davide, my younger brother, his voice faint on the telephone from Angola. Then a man who spoke Portuguese with a strong French accent came on the line and said, 'Either you help your brother get out of the country or he will be dead. They are recruiting men his age.' A day later, Davide, whom I had not seen for eight years, managed to call again. This time he told me that he had just spent three months in prison.

I knew that getting Davide out of Luanda was not going to be easy. Angola was now back at war, and the authorities were ensuring that no man eligible for military service slipped through their net.

This was June, last year. Nine months earlier, in September 1992, Angola had been a very different place; a peace accord had been signed and had, despite a few glitches, endured, ending the eighteen-year civil war; Angolans were going to vote for the first time; from London I could phone and speak to my relatives in Luanda without fearing that the Angolan security services were listening in.

The elections themselves were remarkably peaceful, but after the results were announced Unita, the main opposition party, claimed that they had been fraudulent. The MPLA, which had won most of the seats, insisted that they had been free and fair, and the international observers and the UN concurred. A battle ensued between the government and Unita forces, and the vice-president of Unita, Jeremias Chitunda, was killed. He had been part of a Unita delegation in Luanda which, with the help of United Nations mediators, was trying to negotiate a settlement to the post-election crisis. His car was hit by a rocket as he and other high-ranking Unita officials were trying to leave the city.

Unita installations all over the country were destroyed, and hundreds of Unita activists were thrown in jail; many thousands were killed. Davide was working in Namibe, a small town in the southern Angolan desert near the Namibian border, where he had been part of a Unita team monitoring the elections. I had heard reports of fighting in Namibe and was worried about Davide. I also knew that captured Unita soldiers were being imprisoned or forced to fight on the government side. The idea of Davide marching against Unita with a rifle horrified me. Now I had heard from him: at least he was still alive. I had to get him out of Angola.

The civil war had scattered my family. I had last seen Davide for six hours in 1985 when he was thirteen, and I was passing through Zaire on my way to Angola. Before that, I had not seen him for ten years. In my memory, Davide was still a baby.

As I sat in London, trying to work out how to rescue my brother, I kept thinking of my childhood. I come from a family of eleven; I am the tenth, Davide is the eleventh. In our ethnic group, the Ovimbundus, last-borns—*kuasualas*—are fêted like first borns. When I was a child, the elders gave me presents and held me on their laps, but I was dethroned in 1972, when Davide was born. I was six years old. Davide was a sickly baby who cried a lot and needed my mother's constant attention—I felt that she loved him more than she loved me.

After the Portuguese left Angola in 1975, the three liberation movements—the Popular Movement for the Liberation of Angola (MPLA), the National Union for the Total Independence of Angola (Unita) and the National Front for the Liberation of Angola (FNLA)—came to our home city of Huambo in the central highlands on recruiting drives. Most of my family joined Unita, which was led by Jonas Savimbi who, like us, was not only an Ovimbundu but also a Protestant. Joining Unita was something we did as naturally as attending church.

Political analysts both in and out of Angola have often characterized the civil war in terms of the cold war—as a struggle between competing ideologies in which the ruling MPLA was the defender of communism and Unita its arch-enemy. The truth is far more complex: what was really at stake was which ethnic élite would prevail in Angola. The MPLA drew most of its support from urban Mbundu people from Luanda and people of mixed race. It was backed by the Soviet Union and Cuba. The FNLA was mainly Bakongo and had its roots in a movement founded in the sixties by Angolan exiles in Zaire who hoped to revive the famous Bakongo Kingdom. It was backed by the United States. Unita was an offshoot of the FNLA and drew most of its recruits from the Ovimbundu. At first it received assistance from China, then later from the United States and South Africa.

In 1975 my mother joined the Unita Women's League. Until then she had been a full-time housewife, but now, to the consternation of my father, she started travelling around Angola, dressed in trousers made of Unita flags, attending rallies and addressing meetings through a megaphone. My father believed that a woman should stay in her adobe kitchen. He was further incensed by the news that she had taken to putting her hands in her pockets—grossly unfeminine behaviour.

My mother often took Davide along with her on these trips. I still recall her description of the *welwitschu mirabilis* that she had seen in the Namibe desert, a woody plant with a long tap root which can live up to a hundred years; I had often heard the elders repeat the legend that this plant could eat people, and I was jealous that my mother had taken Davide to see it, not me.

In 1976, as hundreds of Cuban troops approached Huambo with tanks and planes, most of my family fled. I got into a car with my sister Noemia and her husband. Davide and my mother (now separated from my father) went with Jaka, one of my older brothers, and his wife. We thought we would only be away for a couple of days—the Unita activists had told us that the Cubans would soon be forced out; that there was a large shipment of arms coming from China for the Unita soldiers; that the Unita men were invincible. We believed them. But as it turned out, the members of my family were to be separated for more than a decade.

Noemia, her husband and I reached Menongue, a town in Eastern Angola on the banks of the Cubango river. Here we met my mother and Davide, who had also ended up there with Jaka. During Portuguese rule, Menongue was a prosperous resort, but by this time the walls of the plush hotels had been sprayed with bullets, and the rooms were full of refugees. Everyone was panicking. Jaka managed to get my mother on a plane to Zaire. Davide went with her. Jaka then joined the Unita army and went for military training deep in the bush. I stayed with my sister and her husband, and we joined a large group of about a thousand people who were planning to walk through the Angolan jungle to Zambia. Our only guidance was provided by an old map someone had plucked from a classroom wall. The map proved on many occasions to be disastrously inaccurate; what was marked as a river often turned out to be a huge, impassable swamp. We were trying to avoid the main roads because we thought they would be filled with Cubans and MPLA troops. Many people died of starvation and disease; others got lost in the jungle and were attacked by wild animals. Of the original group, only fourteen of us made it to the Zambian border. We survived by eating mushrooms and caterpillars. One rainy night, I remember shivering under my wet, cold blanket, crying, wanting my mother, imagining her and Davide sitting somewhere having hot chocolate with bread and jam.

I spent most of my childhood in Zambia; I couldn't join my mother and Davide in Zaire because no one knew where they were. I went to primary school in Lusaka, the Zambian capital, and then to a secondary school in Mwinilunga in the north. Noemia did everything she could for me, sometimes going without shoes herself to support my studies.

I left school when I was nineteen and returned to the part of Angola under Unita control. I had finally made contact with my mother through a businessman who travelled between Zaire and Zambia, and on my way home I managed to meet up with her and Davide; he was now thirteen, spoke fluent French and Ligala and was obsessed with break-dancing. He was fascinated by me and kept asking my mother questions: why I didn't look like him? Why was my hair so long? My mother would not stop apologizing for having left me behind eight years before; she seemed to feel both guilty and nervous. In the short time we spent together, she tried to say a great deal, but I was a very different person from the child she had known. I now spoke Portuguese and Umbundu with a slight Zambian accent, which she found very strange. One thing hadn't changed; I still envied Davide his closeness to her.

I spent a year in the Angolan bush where I worked in the Unita propaganda section, spending most of my time writing pro-Unita articles which were then broadcast on Unita radio, known as the Voice of the Black Cockerel. Then, in 1986, I was sent to Britain on a scholarship.

Two years later, my mother decided to return to Angola with Davide. She had been very homesick in Zaire, and the Unita-controlled area was now very large and very safe. Davide studied at the Unita school in southern Angola and had a job sorting diamonds, one of the major sources of Unita's income.

After the 1991 peace accord, Unita moved into the main cities, and the party leaders sent Davide to Namibe to help campaign for the elections. When war broke out, Davide was trapped.

To get Davide out of Angola, I had first to go to Portugal. Although there were still flights out of Luanda to other parts of Africa, there were so few passengers that it was easy for officials to spot people who were trying to flee the country. Portugal was a much more popular destination, especially for young people, which made it easier for Davide to slip through the Angolan controls. I had several Portuguese friends, including the novelist Pedro Paixao who offered at once to serve as Davide's guardian, and the Angolan emigré community in Portugal had created networks to support new arrivals. The real problem was getting a visa for Davide. Since the peace accord had collapsed, the Portuguese authorities, mindful of the large numbers of young men who would be trying to escape from Angola, had clamped down on immigration.

I called Davide in Luanda: I could tell he was nervous; he was often afraid to go out because the army recruiters were picking up every young male they came across. I tried to keep his spirits up, telling him to be strong. I told him that if he got the chance to get to some other country—Namibia, or Brazil, or South Africa—he should seize it, and not count on making it to Portugal.

For more than two years I had been writing a weekly column in *O Independente*, a large-circulation Portuguese weekly. The paper was also widely read in Angola, which was how my brother made contact with me in the first place—he spotted my byline. I frequently criticized the way in which Unita members were being treated by the government, which I later learned had led to members of my family still in Luanda receiving threats. Davide had managed to keep our relationship secret, but I was very worried that the authorities would work it out. When we spoke on the telephone, we talked in code.

In the early hours of a Thursday morning in September 1993, Pedro Paixao and I were at Lisbon airport awaiting Davide's arrival. I had not slept the previous night. I knew that the immigration officers in Luanda were on full alert; if they found out who Davide was or realized that he was fleeing the country they would send him straight to prison and from there to the army.

After an hour's delay, the plane from Luanda landed, and eventually Davide came through the gate. He was taller than me, but very thin—to me it looked as though he was suffering from malnutrition. His hair was red; his eyes were slightly bulgy. As I hugged him, I tried hard to hold back the tears. My own brother looked almost like the starving Africans I had seen in photographs. He was carrying a small black bag which contained a tattered track suit. He wore a white shirt, jeans and a pair of ill-fitting boots. As we drove to Estoril, where Pedro lived, Davide looked around at the beauty of Lisbon; he could scarcely grasp that he was really here.

When we arrived at Pedro's house, Pedro's first act was to throw open his wardrobe and invite Davide to choose whatever he wanted. Davide could not believe his luck, faced with so many clothes, but I kept telling him to take the oldest things so as not to abuse our host's generosity. This was the beginning of some tension between us; Davide could not see why he should hold back—Pedro had told him to take what he wanted—and thought that I was being difficult.

Later that morning, we went out to buy Davide some shoes. I thought he should buy a sensible pair; he wanted something snazzy and felt that I was imposing my taste on him because I was paying. I insisted that I knew what was best for him. He insisted that I was treating him like a child. I tried to reason with him; he threw a tantrum. We had different ideas about what being brothers meant. He was still the *kuasuala*, the last-born, and he expected me to indulge his every whim; I wanted to help him become as independent as he could.

As time went on, I sometimes did not know exactly how to deal with Davide. I had never had a younger brother. I kept wondering what brothers did with each other. How much, for instance, could I tell him of my private life? Were there special things I had to do to keep his respect? We did agree on one matter—the importance of food. We went to restaurants and ordered huge meals; I wanted Davide to put on weight.

We spent so much time with other people that we scarcely had a chance to talk. I also sensed that Davide did not really want to dwell on what he had been through. He was more interested in how he could get to study business management. But he still bore the marks of someone who had been living in fear: in restaurants he would suddenly begin to whisper to me if there was a black person within earshot. We shared a room, and he talked in his sleep—he just couldn't escape from his past. I tried everything to distract him; I bought him the Portuguese translation of Mario Vargas Llosa's novel *Aunt Julia and the Scriptwriter*, but it became clear that Davide didn't really enjoy fiction—he said that life was too short. He preferred reading Edgar Morin, the French sociologist.

One evening, we were sitting in a seaside restaurant, when suddenly Davide said, 'You know, sometimes I wish I wasn't Angolan.'

'Why?'

'Oh, some of the things we do to each other. I have seen so much in Angola. I was almost killed. I was saved by some women who kept pleading with the policeman who was about to pull the trigger. I am very lucky to be alive. I saw a man being forced by the police to eat a Unita flag. He was vomiting and shitting all over while his children were watching.'

I asked him what prison had been like. Davide shook his head. 'I will tell you all about it some day. All I can say is that I know what hell is like.'

'How did you survive?'

'We got into the wrong lorry. After all the Unita supporters were rounded up, they started sorting out who was Ovimbundu and who was Mucubal. Four of us got into a lorry filled with Mucubal people, and luckily no one denounced us. The Ovimbundus were all taken to Bentiaba and shot.'

Davide was weeping. I said that Unita too had committed human rights abuses, and that no party in Angola was beyond reproach. Davide agreed, looking straight out at the yachts on the sea. The waiter brought us large sirloin steaks with salad, and we dug in.

Davide found a place in college to do a diploma in business studies. I left Lisbon for London feeling relieved.

I returned to Portugal six months later, and Davide met me at the airport, accompanied by his new girlfriend. He had put on so much weight I found it hard to believe that this was the same person I had met off the plane from Luanda. He was bubbling over with excitement, telling me all about a college trip he had taken to Spain.

Davide had made many friends. He took me to his college, where his lecturers told me that he often came top of his class. I noted that he had already adopted some Portuguese traits, including a passion for football. He slept with a small Benfica flag next to his pillow. Flashy shoes and baggy trousers no longer interested him—he now wanted to look as dowdy as any other Portuguese student, dressing in black jeans, canvas boots and T-shirts.

The sight of my own brother transformed from a difficult, emaciated youth to a zestful, curious student brought home to me the depth of Angola's tragedy. There were hundreds of young men who could be busy at school and at college, preparing for the future. Instead, they were in prison or on the front line.

For more than three months now, the Angolan government has been meeting with Unita in the Zambian capital, Lusaka, to try and negotiate a solution to the Angolan imbroglio. Nothing has come of the negotiations so far. There will only be peace if the powerful élites from the many regions of the country are allowed to exist in their own spheres of influence. Angola will only survive as a federal state in which power is not concentrated within an élite from a specific area. For years, each of the two warring sides had convinced itself that it could crush the other. In truth, they will have to learn to coexist.

TODD MCEWEN

A VERY YOUNG DANCER

Ihave a snapshot of the two of us: late on a summer afternoon we're playing in an inflatable wading-pool. You can see in our faces that the water has gone cold, the sun too low now. I remember the day: my sister Moira, in the risible frilled bathing-suit of 1959, had deliberately leaned on the side of the pool and let the water out. After she'd done this ten times, I tried to drown her. That night I found my bed had been filled with giant rusting nails.

Between Moira and me there is love and fear and crankiness. And always her stubbornness. Before her stubbornness unfolded, gigantic, we played happily together. She Felix and I Poindexter.

At times I had to protect her.

The O'Gradys lived next door. Loud and knockabout, they were a large share of the pool of playmates. It wasn't possible to tell what 'play' with the O'Gradys might mean. It might be lots of fun or an O'Grady might hit you in the stomach as hard as he could. You might be building a magic fort, Mighty Mouse's redoubt itself, only to watch an O'Grady suddenly run into your own house and break something on your mother's vanity table. I have a picture of Moira with a huge scarf tied round her neck (she was Mighty Mouse that day), standing on the front porch with Kelly O'Grady. Later that day Kelly's brother Joe pushed Moira down on the rough driveway. She scraped her knee open, and I socked him in the belly, and another of Mrs O'Grady's Maginot Lines went up between our yard and theirs. She made them out of clothes-line, wheelbarrows, tampon boxes and rickety laths.

Here, another picture, 1961: a portrait in a cardboard frame stamped in gold, *La Playa Dance Studio*. There were many times in Moira's life when she wanted to be a dancer. The first was when she was a chubbette—as JC would say (JC is one of those men who met my sister in the 1970s and never forgot her). In this picture, she has glitter in her hair and is wearing a black leotard and blue tights; she's holding a spray of plastic flowers; behind her is a parasol. I can see Moira is already *away from the family*. She is doing things for her own secret reasons. Moira wouldn't have danced because others did, nor would she have taken any pleasure in its physicality.

Her reasons were deep, theatrical, almost religious.

But it was after she had given up dancing for the first time

—had not danced for many years—that Moira's stubbornness really bloomed tough and rooty. She had fallen in love with beauty. And then she added death. Death she liked.

She was getting attention as a poet in high school. She wrote beautiful, dark sonnets, contrasting love and pain or, really, filling love with pain. Sonnets, however, brought praise from teachers, and good marks brought praise from Father. This Moira didn't want.

She wanted to do things she thought he could never really understand, so she would never need his approval. Father, an only child from the country, shy in school and not knowing how to handle girls, has tried to protect her from her earliest days. She, fierce, has always felt this as the big pillow of a smothering movie fiend. They have now made a certain floating peace, though if Father approaches Moira her eyes dilate and she breathes apprehensively: fight or flight.

She's often said, *I was made to lie on couches, smoking cigarettes and reading Russian novels.*

I saw her one day sitting on top of the back seat of someone's MG, a very un-Californian scarf whipping in the wind. He was driving fast, and Moira was laughing. Aside from the danger (I have always feared for her life), this picture seemed *outré* for our town. Who did she think she was?

An open patio door day in early summer when Grandfather was still alive. He was beaming at a Tiffany carafe in the china closet which caught the light, and was humming to himself, as he would do at lunch. I remember his gaze turning slowly to goggle at the arrival of Moira and Babette, her fellow bohemian. Babette was a Bad Girl, the other rider on the MG trunk. Her black hair had flapped, raven-like, a death-warning in the breeze.

Moira and Babette arrived with suddenly thrusting prows: the first brassière-less day of a life in which they finally had something to be bra-less about. Grandfather giggling. Smiling, but only as he smiled at any member of the family. We made him so happy. Father choking really and turning red and giving up any pretence at smiling, staring sidewise at the mobile and insistent breasts of Babette. It was interesting to watch him try to formulate a Question for the Girls, while gagging and levering out of his mouth the large bite of pickle that had almost killed him.

Well hello, girls—where'd you get the sweaters?

This a genius bit of Fatherdom: the way he used his basso on *sweaters* maddened Moira because of course they weren't *sweaters* at all but blinding, breast-clinging leotards of turquoise and canary. Father's growl and bulging eyes told her she was living the last seconds of her unbra'd idyll. Moira and Babette to Moira's room. Grandfather smiling at me as we sat, briefly by ourselves, at the table. Insistences and fiats of undisguised rage and anguish, Father to Mother in the kitchen.

Moira decided to be a dancer—for the second time. By dancing, you can really die. Die for art and look like a pre-Raphaelite corpse at your suburban funeral, which will mock you. It's the beauty of consumptives. Death so near. Dancing, you whittle yourself down into something painful and fragile and then you smash it into a million pieces. On each shard is written a lot of things: Diaghilev, iced coffee, lower back pain.

TB is really the look—use kohl on your eyes and stop consuming everything but Diet Coke, Bubble Yum and Marlboro Lights. Stop feeding your brain. Rebel and rebel, against anything you might have learned while dramatically dying along with the Rossettis in that stifling high school.

A slow death may be exotic. It depends on the amount of eye make-up used. The whole idea of tragedy and art angers fathers.

Moira decided to defy Father in the things he stood for. She rocketed off from the reason and order accepted as the Way in our peacefully paranoid family. Spun away into bunkum, became the beautiful prey of the insights of the supermarket and men and women who have to invent and fib up everything in the world, so alone and left behind are they.

George Washington made bedspreads out of marijuana, she told me once.

Idly one day I opened a plastic Easter egg I found on her bureau. Inside was a suspect-looking pill. Mother was there. Doubt, denial, amphetamine followed; involvement of a blamed friend and then the blamed friend's parents. Mother and Father had looked into the abyss now. That a rogue pill was to be found in our house!

At sixteen she had an involved and highly secret affair with a defrocked minister and frocked kook with long blond hair and one of the original water-beds.

Moira I knew had gone her own way entirely. I knew there would be unimaginable men and locales, cars hinted at in crime dramas. No matter how sunny Moira would sometimes be, she had already left me and I knew I wouldn't be having her back.

Just yesterday I passed by the church where Moira married for the first time. It was not 'our' church, nor of our ostensible denomination, but in California anyone with a collar and an altar will marry you. A small pine hexagon on a quarter acre, it reeked of computer-land liberalism.

Moira's wedding was memorable in that I, as usher, seated everyone wrongly. They were pretty mad about it too. Though I had never had to calculate how to seat people in a hexagon.

Before the ceremony I wandered through the hall, which wrapped round the chapel like a ring box. Unexpectedly (all things were already out of my control), I came upon Ricky, the husband-to-be, and his best man Pierce. They were smoking Luckies (American courage?), and Pierce sheepishly pocketed a flask of something as I came up. They had used something else too. I tried to look into them, to see what it was that allowed people to experience fully moments like this.

I said something silly, like, *Ready gentlemen?* and went out into the chapel to face the sore clumps of guests I'd mismanaged.

No one believed in this, even the minister. The whole thing had an air of *shotgun* about it. Though who was aiming at whom?

Live together? With her friendly, naïve little lover, both of them a month out of high school?

You must think I'm crazy, Father had said.

If they had simply lived together, they would have parted friends. Instead, thanks to Moira's stubbornness, they built a Hell in Heaven's despite, and foundered.

Moira suspected Father of forcing them to marry in order to keep them apart. Very well—she would get married and keep house (expensive in our little town). By accepting Father's dare, she would win. It would be as sweet as living in sin. She knew it would bother him immeasurably, constantly, that she had married at an inappropriate age, clouding her future with short-sighted decisions.

Moira and Ricky sighed romantically over their collection of

Rudy Vallee records. Ricky took a job in a furniture store. Moira began working for a sullen pharmacist. They paid their rent and acted a little smug towards Father, who seethed but, thwarted, could do nothing. They wondered what had happened to Art, ambition. Wondered if they'd ever had any. Moira crammed her personality into a kind of 1930s exoticism. She bought old lamps with fringes on the shades and took up *Sobranies*.

Los Angeles began to loom over them. Los Angeles, which sounds like Heaven until you say it out loud. Los Angeles, where people daily burn out like so many cigarettes smoked on *Dragnet*. Los Angeles, which loomed over Ricky who dreamt of acting and singing. Loomed over Moira, the exotic, the *danseuse*, the rebel. Los Angeles of the thirties, the bungalows, the palm trees. Life there would be what they enjoyed on their records. *Down there*.

Invent for yourself a map of *Duarte*, or some equally hapless Southland place: make half-dark plots under the off-ramps of freeways. See if you could live there.

Of these places and Moira's life there I have no understanding. Of these places and Moira's life there I have no pictures. I did not want to know the reasons Moira and Ricky had gone to Los Angeles. I assumed they thought the exotic would be found there.

Once I visited her; it was like viewing a diorama. It was a visit more with her apartment than with herself. Their Rudy Vallee furniture was there, but the fun, the play was gone. I could see Ricky's heart had gone out of everything. I could see there was nothing there.

I began to get severe, typed letters from Mother (she changed now from carefree script ball to lawyerly Courier) about Difficult Times and desperate little money-making schemes (Amway and worse) and how Moira and Ricky Still Loved Each Other Though. Which couldn't have been true: they were friends and young, and hadn't wanted, or expected, love. Or got it.

Moira's letters dried up entirely. Now when I do not hear from her I am fearful, fearful as can be. She goes from voluminous correspondence to silence, by decade it seems, or according to whom she is leaning on.

That year another bureau egg was opened and another grim little secret came out, or a few secrets, parts of an LA puzzle no one wanted to put together: I had a letter from Father. He had been to visit Moira. She was dancing, yes, in a nowhere-going studio with no connections to the larger, the real. To the *financial* world of dance, as he might have put it. Small studio under an off-ramp. And there was a man about, an older South American man no one liked the sound of.

Being South American was charming to Father, who fell down at the exact moment he should have been bringing his savage judgement to bear. On Los Angeles, on Moira, on the studio under the off-ramp, on South America. But if he must confront something he feels to be bad, he often shrugs and thinks the best of it. Of this older, not-good-seeming man. Who eventually backed my sister into a corner in her kitchen and did something very wrong. Hospital, phone calls, regrets, drinks, promises. We weren't capable of helping her.

In the spring I was told in a very roundabout way that Ricky had left. And that Moira was bound for New York! A *Footlight Parade* montage: train, telegraph wires, newspapers and calendars riffled by the unseen hand of fate. I could feel her being swept along by her unhappiness. Even though she had accomplished nothing, she would be elevated by the *act* of going to New York, she'd be a Star. But it wasn't as if they had invited her.

It seems hard to believe now, seems cruel and wrong that I was in New York when Moira was there, and almost never saw her. Seems like school, where we used to pass each other as if we were strangers; once in a while Moira would sing out my name, if she were in high spirits, but that was seldom. For my part I was secretive, pimpled, made speechless by the beauty and vivacity of her gang.

Some days in New York it seems there are friends in every street, but I never ran into Moira. Sundays I would walk from Riverside Drive down Broadway to the Battery—a strange walk of which I never tired. Often around 14th Street, or sometimes at City Hall, I felt myself in a kind of tunnel. Tunnel through the city which felt empty of her. I would wonder where in the world she was and then remember, with a pang, that she was here. Somewhere.

I wondered what romance out of New York's many romances

Moira was finding. On my walks, which I could have taken with her, I found romance in funny places; she and I are quite the same. The dark elevator banks in the RCA Building; outside the Wilke sisters' pipe shop on a rainy Madison Avenue Sunday; Fulton Street around two in the afternoon.

But what of exoticism? New York hasn't much to offer— except for money.

With her anti-heroine Babette, Moira shared a studio on the East Side, above a would-be jaunty nautical bar. The Old Rum Dog, filled most nights with the ordinary people of the commercial East Side of cake shops, expensive dry-cleaners and tiny hardware outlets. Moira and Babette had a sofa, a plant and a cat, Babette's from California. The few times I was in their apartment, the cat and I studied each other. She looked Californian: I wondered if we all did. She obviously felt ill at ease in the city, but she was *handling* it.

Moira's and Babette's was an apartment where it always seemed to be summer. Night noise from the Old Rum Dog and the permanently skewed bamboo blind which flapped in the open window, in the noisy breezes of August or the mad heat of the February radiator. Babette and Moira must have walked through the winter streets in stunned silence.

The exotic? Their apartment smacked more of 'That Girl' than Paris in the twenties.

Sitting with their cat, I used to think to myself, this is an apartment where men come. What men? For Babette, lanky Jewish actors and medical students. Babette meant to study acting. She had been to a studio under an off-ramp. For Moira? I didn't know—urban hippies perhaps, or cute disco guys with dog-shaped heads. Maybe Moira and Babette only socialized in the Old Rum Dog and never brought anyone up. The place was small and Moira always got ready to go out as soon as I arrived.

Moira danced. Moira was dancing and she was in New York: these were the facts with which she decorated her proscenium. Externally true, it was something she could say to people she might meet (in the Old Rum Dog?) or to Mother and Father or to irritating people from our town whom she encountered in her imagination. But she was not a professional dancer. Every morning she filled her dance bag with socks and cigarettes and got on the subway along with a thousand others and *took class*.

It was by the Ed Sullivan Theater; I met her there sometimes. I would have a sandwich or a frigid coffee-shop salad; Moira would have only coffee—she was eating nothing. And in these little coffee-shops around Times Square, she would talk and talk, talk hugely, and I never learned a thing. She never revealed herself, her thoughts, her plans. I never heard her say what she thought was going to happen to her, or what she was doing there.

Ballet was really out of the question. When she began dance for the second time it was already so late that not even the most noxious, acaloric diet would put her in the ballerina's body. But this she refused to discuss: it was going to happen. Meanwhile the studio had connections enough—probably due to its location more than anything else; there was television work and the odd Broadway audition. Moira was in New York and Moira was dancing. Babette was in New York and Babette was an actress. Moira and Babette were each spending hundreds of dollars a week of their families' money and claiming to practise their professions.

Sometimes to our coffee-shop meetings I brought friends, guys I knew from college. Brought them along as tokens—or as evidence that there were people who didn't live on nicotine and chicle alone. Whereas they looked on Moira with admiration and interest, I was worried she could sniff them out as establishmentarians, no matter what they were wearing. I felt she looked painted and undernourished. Drawn. Pained. I like to think that meeting these men, if only for coffee and gum, kept Moira on some kind of track. At least reminded her there was a world that did not demand a pose.

Mitch, the painter, entertained her. *I really like that guy*, she said.

Now he always asks about her in a way which brings back the sharp chlorine taste of the icy glasses of water we'd have in those coffee-shops.

Jay, the actor, took her out once. They went all over town visiting tourist spots until Jay, suddenly tired of Moira's perpetual mystery, announced, *The wallet is closed*. Moira liked him but has quoted me this ever after. She was used to depending on her looks so that she never had to spend any money: modest doors, and wallets, opened for her.

Jules, a doctor, took her out to dinner. After kidding her for a while in his usual way, he fell silent and meditated on how different life must be in California. All the while gazing at Moira, her coffee and dance gossip and gum. What she wanted after dinner was gum.

I could go for that guy in a big way, said Moira in her Goils Together, *Stage Door* voice. She was always so sunny, so much the game girl when she was with my friends—well, perhaps I did fail: Moira views us all as shallow and straight, and saves her darker passions for men who are a bit dangerous.

Before the hormones came she enchanted Father. Or perhaps charm is a better word: she wouldn't put enough effort into really beguiling anyone. But what, as JC asked me recently, will happen when that no longer works? Simply—ends? She'll be just another person, perhaps not Moira at all. A person on whom exoticism hangs awkwardly and whose romanticizing will sound shrill.

I went away from New York, transferred to a rain and snow location because I had once been romantic enough to say I liked such weather. Moira was rescued by a policeman: rescued from the tedium of her behaviour, to which she was blind, and from the tedium of New York, of which she was beginning to tire.

Did they meet in the Old Rum Dog? It must have been there. A young policeman whose mind often wandered in the directions of more money, showbiz and girls. But also a handsome and affable policeman, and therefore an unusual policeman. Moira was writing to me then, in the 'designer' hand she had perfected on her ubiquitous graph paper. The grid she plans her whole life on. I began to get letters about 'Hubby'. These lacked the hints I had come to look for, hints of a darker side to Moira's life. She sounded quite bubbly. She must be awfully bored, I thought. Where's the exoticism in someone who is cheerful and affable?

In high school Moira once spat on a policeman.

Mother participated without shame in the romance of this romance. A suburban newspaper reader, she was filled with joy that her little girl in New York had a personal policeman to walk her to her door.

A VERY YOUNG DANCER

In my far posting I would come in from the rain and find letters from Mother and Moira. Moira stating in a frankly unbelievable way how life was good (Moira is ever unconvincing expatiating on outward things). Mother chirped about Moira's *beau* and reminisced in a frankly unbelievable way about Father. I would read these letters sitting by the fire, my only source of heat, and after pondering them, I would slowly push them into the grate. It all seemed remote, insincere. Reaganomic. Irritating, compared with the lush green field I could see from my window.

Moira wrote of a romantic weekend she spent with Hubby in the Poconos. Hubby's idea of romance (now Moira's?): the heart-shaped bath. Under my rain-clouds, I wondered what Moira looked like. I wondered if in-room adult movies and komplimentary champagne were now to her taste, if these would fill her metabolic need for the exotic.

I grieved that none of my family could tramp with me down my muddy road, that they had to write me of such things, that I found in them no joy of the news of home.

The second time I didn't go. Mother's and Moira's letters, bubbling over with wedding plans. In my rainy place I felt I could not bear to watch college town meet Flatbush. Such an American confrontation I couldn't bear to face.

I experienced the wedding at my fireside. According to the letters, Moira and Hubby laughed all the way across town, from wedding to reception, laughed all the way in their horse-drawn cab. Laughed at the drizzle, the traffic. Moira blew kisses to people. My sister charmed the whole of Second Avenue that day.

At the reception everybody covered their ears against the Texas swing band. Father recited an 'Encomium' he had written. It united love and genetic theory in a way which perplexed pretty much everyone. It brought tears to the eyes of the old family friend who was blind drunk and died soon after.

According to the pictures—group shots at table, chasms of incomprehension—there was a submerged battle here: between those who knew how to act at parties and those who thought parties a little bit low. Hubby's bruddas clapping him on the back. Insinuatingly handsome boys with eyes as if mascara'd. Their dates in all the finery of Thompson Street; fingernails to scratch the eye of God.

The old family friend's eyes rolled up into his head. Moira smiling with the tension of the ranks before her, with relief, with joy. This was to be a real marriage: she was having a real wedding. The tuxedos that were owned were confident and garish, the rented tuxedos sober and a little too earnest.

Hubby's family ran a little old restaurant on Bleecker Street. There were always soft lamps lit. Moira and Hubby went to live in the neighbourhood.

Hubby's eyes were green as Italian cypresses. Moira had found the exotic again. She had been looking for it on the East Side but it was not to be found among stewardesses.

What were the exoticisms of the West Village? Was Moira happily breathing in and out antique bohemianism? She and Hubby lived upstairs from a man who sold curious books. These weren't pornographic: their high prices coupled with their utter uselessness was what disturbed you. A pamphlet: *Use of the Killing Jar*. A catalogue of costumes *and* manacles used by Odd Fellows and Rebekahs. A mouldy album of photographs, all close-ups of the ankle straps on girls' shoes. But he was a very pleasant man.

On their street was a *frisson* of Mob; perhaps many 'love' this about the West Village. Perhaps Hubby's whispered talk was that, to Moira, of George Raft.

Moira had once told Hubby about South America and what he had done to her in the kitchen. Had weeping told him after one of their earliest tender moments. Not long after they moved to the Village, Hubby whispered to her one night that South America *had been taken care of*. Moira immediately made love to Hubby in a dark chill. It was exotic that Hubby could *say* that.

Hubby's trenchant sexuality she must have found exotic as well. Green eyes glowed on the Staten Island Ferry and they made their way to the rest room.

Poconos or no, marriage itself was exotic to Moira for a time; love lived and freely given and taken. Was the future really to become old? Moira never believed that. The old white-haired woman, who had married an Italian and lived out her life in the West Village?

Moira began to become Italian. Now was not the world of nightclub, now was learning street savvy. Now was learning to spend most of her time with other women, at vegetable stand and beauty parlour. Women you were now bound to; women you had bound yourself to be.

Everyone said she looked Italian (they meant she acted Italian).

I saw her briefly one Christmas. The Moira I recalled fondly as a pleasing, earthy girl was changed, thinner even than dancing thin (she was making excuses not to take class every day). Her voice had sailed high up her nose. She seemed to delight in low talk, recounting, as the other women did, the boasts and exploits of their men.

Did she know, as she parodied the lives of these people, that she was building a wall against them and not becoming one of them? That she must eventually offend them? Moira hadn't been absorbed; she hadn't adopted anything; it was the fun of being in a TV movie. She *thought* she loved them.

Take a boy born and raised in dazzle but not cold towards it like others of the city. Dazzled, off-kilter. Take the first, the tallest, the friendliest, the handsomest, the most loved by Ma. Start pushing him this way and that. Let him do well in school but remind him that it takes money to go on in school. Tell him how much the girls will like him; remind him that Catholics get married. But that Europeans fool around. Tell him he can do anything, anywhere, what do you want with this stupid showbiz anyway? Keep him tied so close to the house, the neighbourhood, that going to 14th Street for a guilty beer seems like going away to college. Take Hubby and his mother—please.

Sleaze puts everything in perspective. Hey, guys fool around, right? Sure. Everybody knows that. It's exciting. It's uptown. Sure, I meet plenty of girls like that on the job. The things they've done to me in the truck heading for the station. Let one or two slip away, you go around see 'em later. Hey.

Especially liked leggy ones with tight skirts and wet red lips. Liked them under the bridges, disarrayed against his bold cop car. Guys fool around, right?

What were the beginnings of Moira's suspicions? Hubby's clothes or Hubby's talk?

To better control the bruddas and to save money for their

Todd McEwen

loose moonlighting enterprises, Hubby suddenly moved himself and Moira into Ma's house. Exoticism was at a low ebb surely. It was impossible to make love there without being judged by the furniture, the attentive walls. Recreation became a few lines, for them both.

Now Ma had everyone within reach and she was happy that they were so miserable. Especially Moira, who may *pass* for Italian but I don't trust that girl—she's not like us, why did you marry a girl like that, Hubby?

Moira completely gave up saying she was going to dance. She would fill her bag and take the subway uptown, but only to meet some dancers in one of the coffee-shops near the studio. She dropped her ballet classes—claiming or admitting what to herself I don't know—and took only jazz. This was something she could do, and with Broadway and the television studios around the corner . . . She smoked more and starved herself—difficult at Ma's—to keep her figure. Being a dancer became looking like a dancer on the subway: gum, Diet Coke, bag—dancer. She began to take class twice a month. Hubby complained of the cost. Shades of Ricky.

This was sprained, that torn, another thing bruised. Finally Moira broke her toe and had to wear an ugly wrapping on it, like a Soviet summer shoe. Hubby complained about this too. A sick wife isn't glamorous. A sick wife is a drag on the family. Could he already see her limping around the neighbourhood at fifty with a cane and a few vegetables in her gnarled hands, Italian peasant death already upon her? Hubby had his own nightmares.

On her trips uptown Moira took to looking at jobs posted in windows, the windows of Times Square so often loved and hated. The zoo needed someone for the penguins. She got the job, even with the Soviet shoe. *Aw, hell, that's how penguins walk anyway*, the man said.

Here for Moira was freshness in the city. Times Square and the dirty jumble of the West Fifties had rejected her, had *broken her foot*. Here, if not romance or nostalgia, was a new, clean ethic. Perhaps she thought back on the beauties of California, on the kook and the water-bed big as Marin County. Sun and green hills, the stroking Pacific instead of John Calvin's Atlantic. Maybe Moira romanticized the whole ecosystem, revived the chubbette's love of animals, began to use it all as a weapon against Hubby and Ma and the lacquered wives of the bruddas. Against the cold, dirty, heaped-up slush which looked dirtier now without imaginary chase-lights.

I saw Moira at the zoo during a trip to New York. I got out of the taxi and soon found myself in a pen with a female walrus named Sitka. The walrus came at me with, it seemed, great difficulty. Huge thing, a moving, silting hill, with a breath that would wake the dead. That *was* waking them. Sitka rolled to a halt two feet from me and wobbled. She held her head up, regarding me sidelong, as a dog might.

She wants to shake hands, said Moira.

Stunned by Sitka's breath (which in fairness would be the breath of anyone who ate raw fish only and had two-foot-long teeth), I held out my hand, stiffly and high, as if it were a flipper. Sitka teetered and for a moment I thought she was going to fall on me; issued a huge blast of her mackerelly wind and there: she was touching her flipper to mine. She seemed happy.

In the taxi I worried whether Sitka had really been pleased to meet me. I thought, this is how Moira thinks.

Moira also got on very well with the penguins. One penguin, Moe, always stood high above the others, on top of their artificial ice cake. He would see Moira coming in the gate in the morning and bray like a donkey. The others would straighten up, organizing themselves, looking expectant. They loved Moira. Moira who one day made an awful mistake.

Under pressure, doing someone else's job, she became irritated at the penguins, who were taking a long time eating. She threw them some fish, and instead of eating it, they were goddamn *playing* with it. All over the place. It was the first day of spring and they were excited and happy. They threw the fishes, one to another, and hiccuped and brayed and laughed. They stumbled crazily around, the fish under their feet, giggling old ladies in a fun house. All the animals had to be fed at precise times, and Moira was running late.

I'm not going to give youse any more, she announced, *even though there's still some left. Your time's up. I can't fart around wit youse guys all day*. She always spoke to them in Brooklynese.

The penguins reeled back, surprised at being addressed so

sharply, but they were careful to pay attention when Moira spoke to them. They loved her and tried hard to understand what she said: you could see it in their eyes.

Moira turned to go. Some of the penguins which lived with more gusto began to bray for fish. Moira spun round and put her pail on the ground, straddling it. The penguins grew quiet and gathered round her. Coach and team; reporters and the Mayor.

Listen youse guys, she said. *All gone!*

As if to the family dog. And suddenly clapped her hands with a bang.

Penguins vomit when frightened, to lighten themselves for escape. And vomit they did to a man. At Moira's deafening handclap, echoing off the smooth walls of their enclosure, they opened up and let fly. All over their fake iceberg and Moira.

She had to burn her clothes, not an easy thing in a house on Bleecker Street. Ma and the lacquered ones complained for weeks that the building smelled. Hubby acted as though he thought Moira had done this, *worked with animals*, to get at Ma. Bleecker Street was not a place where you could discuss marine ecology, even casually.

I saw Moira again the next winter—a sad little weekend when she visited me at my hotel. Hubby was on duty. We hit the coffee-shops and took each other to some favourite places: the McAnn's where you go way downstairs, the lobby of the Woolworth Building. I showed her the outside of the Wilke sisters' place. She was drawn and adult. We talked in a dry way; I did not pitch my conversation at the level of concern I felt for her.

At one point she said, *This is a good marriage*. So insistent, yet so soft, so Moira looking out the window, that I was filled with pity.

Hubby had Ma to deal with, but the hardest thing he was up against was Moira's otherness. That is the rock upon which all men have founded their rebellion against her. Moira the poet, Moira the hugely silent, the more intelligent than thou. Moira who refuses to be told what to do or to be pinned down.

She was more and more alone as Hubby stayed out doing God knows what. I worried about drugs, alcohol. Moira was imprisoned in Ma's house with no one she could talk to; with several females intent on grinding Moira out of herself or—a more attractive prospect—on getting rid of her altogether.

Hubby took her to the Poconos, drank too much and abused her, in an even lower-rent heart-shaped bath than before.

Babette utterly fecklessly married an utterly feckless Jewish–Irish car salesman who really liked drugs. It seemed the four of them were to go on holiday together.

The idea of ordure at Key West. A tropical island paved from shore to shore, coral and pines dying daily; no beach to speak of but a dump of sand imported from Miami; the idea that *everything is available*: what do you want, man, what do you want? I got everything. Drug dealers, dipsomaniacs and dorks all crowded into the same heaving bars; music so loud it can't be heard. Dark looks from the island's underclass, hived off to shoot and stab each other in side-streets over who's first to please the tourists with deals, boys, girls. Unfamiliar yet temporarily pleasing drinks. Moira and Babette, the Goils, in new and tantalizing frocks and sudden tans: corners of their breasts unseen in New York. Buy straw hats and sponges and, half-smashed, make love under the midday air-conditioner, head back to the bar to meet up and score a few lines—what bad-kid bliss. Life is a breeze in the Florida Keys.

Moira had found a new moon to think about. A real tropic moon, framed by palms. Sultry nights in hut-like bars, rooms with ceiling fans. What was she communing with? Perhaps the whole place was becoming Havana. She liked the crowd she met in between fights with Hubby—who spent the whole time bombed—and watching Babette fight with her madman.

Were Moira and Babette, in the fortress of their togetherness, the cause of so much seeking of black holes by Hubby and the screwball? Wasn't Hubby reminded that Moira wasn't like him, the whole time he bought hats and drinks and drugs? Moira wasn't having a good time like she should. Like the girls in the neighbourhood would. Like the girls under the bridge against his steering-wheel.

Everyone agreed it was tremendous fun. Moira agreed tiredly, Babette sceptically, the nut madly, Hubby, depleted, angrily. His holiday stung him in the middle of La Guardia Airport: Moira was not playing along. She wasn't playing along with Ma and the other girls. He felt lonely with Moira. She isn't like us and she's driving me fucking crazy and so is Ma and everyone else.

Back through streets which were complicated with nostalgia and half-thoughts. Back to the house and the silences of Ma. Back to restraining themselves in every way in a place which was stifling, whatever the month.

Stifled: Moira's strange exuberances which were never about subjects that Ma and the girls understood. Stifled: dancing—far away now on some X-ray in a midtown file drawer. Stifled: Hubby's idea of himself, powerful at something, instead of being saddled with Ma and the bruddas and a growing *iconoclast* for a wife.

Hubby began to envy the dullest of his brothers, Paul, paid only enough for beer and cigarettes and a line or two, in cash, at the end of every day. Who gruntingly wolfed down Ma's pasta and was petted by her. Whose face was the simple one at the base of any totem-pole.

Moira's letters to me stopped completely.

A few weeks after fun in the sun, Hubby was more off his head than on, more under the bridges than ever before. He even picked up girls from outside the Tunnel. He spent his money on vodka and drugs.

Moira wasn't working. She seemed to need most of her time now just to be Moira, as if by spending time alone in her room, away from the others, she could somehow grow strong again.

All came to nought: a broken mirror, food all over the walls, Ma shrieking but in secret delight, Hubby drunk and more—standing frightened over Moira, crumpled and bleeding in the kitchen corner.

She moved out immediately—went uptown to a dancing friend. She didn't speak to Hubby and didn't go back. He arrived four or five times, soulfully addressing his side of the door, claiming to love her, claiming to have flowers. Moira never opened it. She never said a word. He would return, hours later, loud and abusive and raging, pounding the door with his fists and once attacking the hinges with a crowbar. The last time he said he had a gun.

He was a sick policeman with a mother who had killed the life in him, and he was going to learn about Moira's determination, that quality she had been putting in her storehouse for years—choosing not to use it in school, not being able to see it bear fruit in dance. She would go away from Hubby and never see him again. He had *interrupted* her.

The phone rang, next to the window on my rainy field. Nothing had happened to my field but rain successive to sun; it didn't seem as if enough time had passed in the field for these things to have happened to Moira.

Can't you come here and help me? she said. *I'm moving to Florida. Hubby's been hitting me. I'm sick now.*

The whole family had left the building on Bleecker Street. The restaurant was closed for the afternoon. I could see that the street, the halls and this room were echoing for Moira. I taped boxes together and she filled them.

You might think you would somehow recognize the *things* of someone of your own blood; I found myself unbelieving in the face of her kitchenware. *These* plates? The witnesses of Hubby's cruelty. Moira divided their material life down the middle: six tumblers each, six sets of flatware; she got the antique mirror and he got the sofa.

I watched her pack her clothes, clothes that were not Moira: vivid blouses, restrictive skirts, bright stuff with shoulder pads like Fallingwater. What sort of places had these evening gowns been worn to? Had they ever got above 14th Street? Was Moira happy when she stepped out in them? Or did the ends of evenings have scripts already?

These clothes were what they were trying to make her. What use would they be in Florida? She wasn't going to be that person now.

We waited for the movers. I dragged a heavy trunk across the floor, gouging the wood. From that point on, Hubby only talked about money: did she have to wreck the joint? Moira sat and smoked and kept cleaning up after herself until the last minute, the way she'd learned from the Women with Nothing Else To Do: picking up the tiniest flecks of ash with a licked fingertip. Life in this house, I thought.

The movers took away Moira's junk. The building was still silent, but I knew someone would be watching from across the street. In a drawer she found an unfamiliar lipstick and cried. It was startlingly red.

A dull day had turned a brilliant, warm blue. We drove uptown with a wacky cabby who flirted with Moira. He wore his dark glasses on a string and had a tropical shirt. She enjoyed it. Was she in Florida already?

Life is a breeze in the Florida Keys. Life is a breeze in the Florida Keys. Life is a breeze in the Florida Keys. Moira's mantra: she had begun saying it because she thought it was corny and funny; now she was clinging to it.

The day after moving Moira out, we took an awful series of short flights in the interest of economy. We were punch-drunk with the events of the week by the time we got on the plane. Moira sat in the back, near the tail, where she always feels safe. Wants to be *the last to go*. Sat in the back near the tail smoking and having bottled cocktails and even eating a little.

I couldn't bear to look at Moira so damaged and thin and hurt. She had that hopeful, hangy look children put on in times of great pain. They don't know everything can always get worse.

At Memphis, we stumbled off the plane and rambled along unfamiliar hallways and ramps. Moira chided me for buying a local paper. We sat down, stunned, in a coffee-shop and decided to eat. We were together now (having been apart on the plane) and Moira took up her slow, quiet diatribe: what had happened to her and Hubby, her *epic*. Full of it already, but listening, I got up for mustard. Moira's shocked face told me it wasn't a moment to leave the table. I registered this but felt caught in the act. *Well, goodbye!* I said, waving jauntily and hurrying away. She laughed loudly, and I thought, why, this *is* Moira that I have with me.

We laughed again at Miami. We laughed at a big red suitcase which was making the rounds of all the baggage carousels, like a dog looking for its forgetful mistress. Where are you a-headin', Big Red? How long will you wander?

Life is a breeze in the—

I hated Florida on sight. As soon as we stepped out of the plane at Key West I felt I had never washed my clothes. I felt as if I were zitted; I felt the way you do when you wear too much clothing to the theatre.

By taxi to Cap'n Spinney's Motel, agreeably crummy, with old-fashioned matchbooks of which we both approved. It was late but Moira was going to call her gang. She needed to walk in somewhere, surprisingly, beautifully, remarkably, upon these people where she'd determined she'd found a home.

At a big table heaped with Japanese food I took a step into Moira's life such as I had never done. Midnight: we were both loopy from the flight and the strain of the past week. Moira didn't seem relieved. Indeed, she was overwrought: she was still poised on New York's threshold, not Florida's. But after the airplane drinks and mixed nuts and things that blow dry air in your face, the food was restoring and the beer refreshing. Who was paying?

Moira was ignoring me now—that was fine. She needed to take her shoes off and sink, away, alone. I tried not to be sceptical of the ooze.

She has always assumed that anyone with a drink is *fine* anyway.

I found myself talking to some people from everywhere. People who had been kicked out, or had kicked themselves out, of every state, job, marriage and idea there is. These were people who had daily quelled their gorges, day after day battling unknowing as Moira had done, in some other place, off-island, off-key, and had vacationed here—stunned by the brilliance, the availability, the *pleasing drinks* of life once they had walked out of their offices, coffee-shops, off-ramp studios and on to the plane and Key West. A riot of availabilities. These are people you read about but would never want to know, people who after two weeks of pleasing drinks and erections decide to *move* to the place where they've had their holiday.

They had all run away and forgotten, easily or with help, everything about life. Each decided to build a little network of crimes and guilty pleasures and take that for the world. They do not know that pleasure does not have to be paid for. They do not know that there are people in the world who need them.

Words rot in Key West: the news is controlled by knobs next to the air-conditioner; it's something to be turned down, then off by the bartender when you shamble, blissful, in.

Moira was pale and intense and trembling a little. Japanese food was not for her. The beer seemed only to have magnified her needy state. She was talking ardently, worried, to a curly man named Willy. He had arrived at the restaurant half an hour after we did. Moira had been on the phone to him, and a few others, from Cap'n Spinney's. I remembered Willy's name; he had seemed expectant, hopeful, happy when he arrived. He looked a little sombre now that Moira had been talking to him for half an hour.

Here, she had brought him a whole planeful of New York, of the mad thoughts you have in limbo. The longings you feel, the loves, in airports and airplanes. Willy was going to find out what it was to be the particular focus of Moira. She was explaining it, if he but knew, through a miasma of hiding-places, cigarettes, Diet Coke, bubble gum, her first marriage, Xanax, sushi and beer. Explaining, tragic, quite beautiful. Pale and nervous side by side with the chubby complacency of all these people who had given up.

I figured I knew the score, now that I knew Moira had selected someone, that there was a partner with whom she'd dream up moon and palm. I supposed Moira would disappear into what trailer or boat or rotting apartment Willy had, and that I would have several humid days to myself with no one to talk with, and Moira speaking to me already from inside the Romance of the Tropics. But it wasn't like that: around one in the morning I saw Moira and Willy holding hands, at arm's length, looking at each other. He made to go and she pulled him closer, intent on kissing him, which he manoeuvred into lightly, on the cheek. She seemed happy enough with that and watched him leave. He seemed to know that something large and troubling had arrived for him.

Moira and I went back to Cap'n Spinney's, back to our refrigerated room. I got in bed and slept; Moira smoked for several hours and toyed with a bottled cocktail she'd been too preoccupied to drink on the Memphis–Miami flight. She sat by the air-conditioner and looked out at Cap'n Spinney's pool, which glowed murkily and suggested *organism*.

She began looking for a place the next day. Father had sent her some money but it wasn't a lot: not like the life's savings you saw people blowing on every corner. The humidity appalled me.

Just in walking from Cap'n Spinney's to the T-shirt shops, Cuban cafés and bars that constituted everyone's complete errands, I was oppressed, depressed and drenched. After three hours I felt *I* had lived the lives you saw oozing away and softening in the faces on Duval Street.

We began visiting realtors, New York women in severe, air-conditioned offices who hadn't any idea why someone would come to Key West, except that people were renting. Moira wanted a more tropical realtor. We found several—lounging at wickerwork desks in clean cut-offs and tropical shirts, and studying Moira. Eyes offered lower rents than mouths. I feared for her, but knew I had to let go of this. I would soon be back in my rainy place. Perhaps Willy was a good man and would look out for her. He didn't look ready to. Moira was phoning him rather more often than he'd anticipated. Willy kept the tropical boulevardier's extended night, but she wasn't sleeping at all.

Moira didn't want to share a house. There were two kinds of apartments: strange buildings from the 1930s, lino'd and fluorescent lighted in the 1950s into horror-movie sets, where echoes never quite stopped; and over-detailed efficiencies in poorly remodelled houses—inept tilework and cheap, ornate ceiling fans.

There is nowhere for normal people to live, I remarked to Moira on the street. She glanced at me, rueful and chastened by the rents.

She looked longingly at these overdone boxes while the hungry realtors watched her. Her money would not last long, especially as she was acting as though she were on holiday. Which is how everybody acts in Key West—until they run out of money. Then Key West loses interest in you. You become something tourists turn away from.

I have never had such a difficult parting. I had to go back to my rain. I felt I might expire in the shallows of Key West. For the first time I felt I was abandoning her, crabbed and mean. I felt resentful that Moira hadn't, couldn't have visited me in the rainy place. I wanted her to see that people can live with themselves. That they can love each other. That life can be believed.

We drank a bit, Moira and I, the night before I left. I was rocked in the taxi and knocked side to side in the little plane. When I got to Miami I ordered two Pepsis and two beers, and left the beers on the bar as if they had suddenly become giant combination breakfasts, greasy, steaming and odious.

Moira bloomed. This was one of her bloomings. Moira, whose body, speech and self change to suit the drama and the romance of the day. And the danger. Moira, who as I have grown to love her has gone from chubbette to feisty earth mother to strange, spooky, rickety dancer to a loud, over-toiletted, tough, scrawny Carmine Street cackler. To abused divorcee, drawn and introspective. To tropical flower: her wavy hair lustrous with coconut oil, vibrant colours on her eyes and lips. In the snapshots she has sent me from time to time, she and Willy in front of their motel room, I have seen her silky brown legs. Moira lovely, piquant and raw, shackled to something.

Along with everyone on Key West, Moira now worships the wrecked people: Isadora, Patsy Cline, Elvis, Judy Garland. We're wrecked too and we hear you singing.

Drugs. A hole down which I do not want to lose her. But what could I do from the rainy place? Really, drugs are the *jewel* of the Republican economy, not at all its nemesis. Drugs are the business of the place, not straw hats or pleasing drinks or sponges. Drugs. Perhaps: she is there and so are they and that is all there is to say.

She sank. About waist-deep, ran aground on the reef of the waiters, bartenders, hangers-on. Life is a breeze in the Florida Keys: this is what Moira now believes. The people she follows are as damaged and unworldly as a bunch of actors, and as theatrical in their comings and goings and weepings. Their little tragedies, seasonal matings, scenes of anger and regret.

So it was Moira on the phone this morning, alone again. *He's gone. Moving out. I feel sad.*

I told her I would go to see her. I pictured being rocked in the little plane, the air-conditioner at Cap'n Spinney's and the pleasing drinks and the dangers there.

I remembered Moira staring out all night at the murky pool, loved her, and did not say so.

LOUISE ERDRICH

THE NAMES OF WOMEN

Louise Erdrich

Ikwe is the word for woman in the language of the Anishinabe, my mother's people, whose descendants, mixed with and married to French trappers and farmers, are the Michifs of the Turtle Mountain reservation in North Dakota. Every Anishinabe *Ikwe*, every mixed-blood descendant like me, who can trace her way back a generation or two, is the daughter of a mystery. The history of the woodland Anishinabe—decimated by disease, fighting Plains Indian tribes to the west and squeezed by European settlers to the east—is much like most other Native American stories, a confusion of loss, a tale of absences, of a culture that was blown apart and changed so radically in such a short time that only the names survive.

And yet, those names.

The names of the first women whose existence is recorded on the rolls of the Turtle Mountain Reservation, in 1892, reveal as much as we can ever recapture of their personalities, complex natures and relationships. These names tell stories, or half stories, if only we listen closely.

There once were women named *Standing Strong*, *Fish Bones*, *Different Thunder*. There once was a girl called *Yellow Straps*. Imagine what it was like to pick berries with *Sky Coming Down*, to walk through a storm with *Lightning Proof*. Surely, she was struck and lived, but what about the person next to her? People always avoided *Steps Over Truth*, when they wanted a straight answer, and *I Hear*, when they wanted to keep a secret. *Glittering* put coal on her face and watched for enemies at night. The woman named *Standing Across* could see things moving far across the lake. The old ladies gossiped about *Playing Around*, but no one dared say anything to her face. *Ice* was good at gambling. *Shining One Side* loved to sit and talk to *Opposite the Sky*. They both knew *Sounding Feather*, *Exhausted Wind* and *Green Cloud*, daughter of *Seeing Iron*. *Center of the Sky* was a widow. *Rabbit*, *Prairie Chicken* and *Daylight* were all little girls. *She Tramp* could make great distance in a day of walking. *Cross Lightning* had a powerful smile. When *Setting Wind* and *Gentle Woman Standing* sang together the whole tribe listened. *Stop the Day* got her name when at her shout the afternoon went still. *Log* was strong, *Cloud Touching Bottom* weak and consumptive. *Mirage* married *Wind*.

Everyone loved *Musical Cloud*, but children hid from *Dressed in Stone*. *Lying Down Grass* had such a gentle voice and touch, but no one dared to cross *She Black of Heart*.

We can imagine something of these women from their names. The Anishinabe historian Basil Johnston notes that 'such was the mystique and force of a name that it was considered presumptuous and unbecoming, even vain, for a person to utter his own name. It was the custom for a third person, if present, to utter the name of the person to be identified. Seldom, if ever, did either husband or wife speak the name of the other in public.'

Shortly after the first tribal roll, the practice of renaming became an ecclesiastical exercise, and, as a result, most women in the next two generations bear the names of saints particularly beloved by the French. *She Knows the Bear* became Marie. *Sloping Cloud* was christened Jeanne. *Taking Care of the Day* and *Yellow Day Woman* turned into Catherines. Identities are altogether lost. The daughters of my own ancestors, *Kwayzancheewin—Acts Like a Boy* and *Striped Earth Woman*—go unrecorded, and no hint or reflection of their individual natures comes to light through the scattershot records of those times, although they must have been genetically tough in order to survive: there were epidemics of typhoid, flu, measles and other diseases that winnowed the tribe each winter. They had to have grown up sensible, hard-working, undeviating in their attention to their tasks. They had to have been lucky. And if very lucky, they acquired carts.

It is no small thing that both of my great-grandmothers were known as women with carts.

The first was Elise Eliza McCloud, the great-granddaughter of *Striped Earth Woman*. The buggy she owned was somewhat grander than a cart. In her photograph, Elise Eliza gazes straight ahead, intent, elevated in her pride. Perhaps she and her daughter Justine, both wearing reshaped felt fedoras, were on their way to the train that would take them from Rugby, North Dakota, to Grand Forks, and back again. Back and forth across the upper tier of the plains, they peddled their handworked tourist items—dangling moccasin brooches and little beaded hats, or, in the summer, the wild berries, plums and nuts that they had gathered

Louise Erdrich

from the wooded hills. Of Elise Eliza's industry there remains in the family only an intricately beaded pair of buffalo horns and a piece of real furniture, a 'highboy', an object once regarded with some awe, a prize she won for selling the most merchandise from a manufacturer's catalogue.

The owner of the other cart, Virginia Grandbois, died when I was nine years old: she was a fearsome and fascinating presence, an old woman seated like an icon behind the door of my grandparents' house. Forty years before I was born, she was photographed on her way to fetch drinking water at the reservation well. In the picture she is seated high, the reins in her fingers connected to a couple of shaggy-fetlocked draught ponies. The barrel she will fill stands behind her. She wears a man's sweater and an expression of vast self-pleasure. She might have been saying *Kay-goh*, a warning, to calm the horses. She might have been speaking to whomever it was who held the camera, still a novel luxury.

Virginia Grandbois was known to smell of flowers. In spite of the potato picking, water hauling, field and housework, she found the time and will to dust her face with pale powder, in order to look more French. She was the great-great-granddaughter of the daughter of the principal leader of the *A-waus-e*, the Bullhead clan, a woman whose real name was never recorded but who, on marrying a Frenchman, was 'recreated' as Madame Cadotte. It was Madame Cadotte who acted as a liaison between her Ojibway relatives and her husband so that, even when French influence waned in the region, Jean-Baptiste Cadotte stayed on as the only trader of importance, the last governor of the fort at Sault St Marie.

By the time I knew Virginia Grandbois, however, her mind had darkened, and her body deepened, shrunk, turned to bones and leather. She did not live in the present or in any known time at all. Periodically, she would awaken from dim and unknown dreams to find herself seated behind the door in her daughter's house. She then cried out for her cart and her horses. When they did not materialize, Virginia Grandbois rose with great energy and purpose. Then she walked towards her house, taking the straightest line.

That house, long sold and gone, lay over one hundred miles

due east and still Virginia Grandbois charged ahead, no matter what lay in her path—fences, sloughs, woods, the yards of other families. She wanted home, to get home, to be home. She wanted her own place back, the place she had made, not her daughter's, not anyone else's. Hers. There was no substitute, no kindness, no reality that would change her mind. She had to be tied to the chair, and the chair to the wall, and still there was no reasoning with Virginia Grandbois. Her entire life, her hard-won personality, boiled down in the end to one stubborn, fixed, desperate idea.

I started with the same idea—this urge to get home, even if I must walk straight across the world. Only, for me, the urge to walk is the urge to write. Like my great-grandmother's house, there is no home for me to get to. A mixed-blood, raised in the Sugarbeet Capital, educated on the Eastern seaboard, married in a tiny New England village, living now on a ridge directly across from the Swan Range in the Rocky Mountains, my home is a collection of homes, of wells in which the quiet of experience shales away into sweet bedrock.

Elise Eliza pieced the quilt my mother slept under, a patchwork of shirts, pants, other worn-out scraps, bordered with small rinsed and pressed Bull Durham sacks. As if in another time and place, although it is only the dim barrel of a four-year-old's memory, I see myself lying wrapped under smoky quilts and dank green army blankets in the house in which my mother was born. In the fragrance of tobacco, some smoked in home-rolled cigarettes, some offered to the Manitous whose presence still was honoured, I dream myself home. Beneath the rafters, shadowed with bunches of plants and torn calendars, in the nest of a sagging bed, I listen to mice rustle and the scratch of an owl's claws as it paces the shingles.

Elise Eliza's daughter-in-law, my grandmother Mary LeFavor, kept that house of hand-hewed and stacked beams, mudded between. She managed to shore it up and keep it standing by stuffing every new crack with disposable diapers. Having used and reused cloth to diaper her own children, my grandmother washed and hung to dry the paper and plastic diapers that her granddaughters bought for her great-grandchildren. When their plastic-paper shredded, she gathered them carefully together and one day, on a summer visit, I woke early to find her tamping the rolled stuff carefully into the cracked walls of that old house.

It is autumn in the Plains, and in the little sloughs ducks land, and mudhens, whose flesh always tastes greasy and charred. Snow is coming soon, and after its first fall there will be a short, false warmth that brings out the sweet-sour odour of highbush cranberries. As a descendant of the women who skinned buffalo and tanned and smoked the hides, of women who pounded berries with the dried meat to make winter food, who made tea from willow bark and rosehips, who gathered snakeroot, I am affected by the change of seasons. Here is a time when plants consolidate their tonic and drop seed, when animals store energy and grow thick fur. As for me, I start keeping longer hours, writing more, working harder, though I am obviously not a creature of a traditional Anishinabe culture. I was not raised speaking the old language, or adhering to the cycle of religious ceremonies that govern the Anishinabe spiritual relationship to the land and the moral order within human configurations. As the wedding of many backgrounds, I am free to do what simply feels right.

My mother knits, sews, cans, dries food and preserves it. She knows how to gather tea, berries, snare rabbits, milk cows and churn butter. She can grow squash and melons from seeds she gathered the fall before. She is, as were the women who came before me, a repository of all of the homely virtues, and I am the first in a long line who has not saved the autumn's harvest in birch bark *makuks* and skin bags and in a cellar dry and cold with dust. I am the first who scratches the ground for pleasure, not survival, and grows flowers instead of potatoes. I record rather than practise the arts that filled the hands and days of my mother and her mother, and all the mothers going back into the shadows, when women wore names that told us who they were.

BRET EASTON ELLIS

THE UP ESCALATOR

I'm standing on the balcony of Martin's apartment in Westwood, holding a drink in one hand and a cigarette in the other, and Martin comes towards me, rushes at me, and with both hands pushes me off the balcony. Martin's apartment in Westwood is only two storeys high, and so the fall is not that long. As I'm falling I hope I will wake up before I hit the ground. I hit the asphalt, hard, and lying there, on my stomach, my neck twisted completely around, I look up and focus on Martin's handsome face staring down at me with a benign smile. It's the serenity in that smile—not the fall really, or the imagined image of my cracked, bleeding body, that wakes me up.

I stare at the ceiling, then over at the digital alarm-clock on the nightstand next to the bed, and it tells me that it is almost noon, and I uselessly hope that I have misread the time by shutting my eyes tightly, but when I open them again, the clock still reads that it is almost noon. I raise my head slightly and look over at the small, flickering red numbers glowing from the Betamax, and they tell me the same thing the hands on the melon-colored alarm do: almost noon. I try to fall back asleep, but the Librium I took at dawn has worn off, and my mouth feels thick and dry, and I am thirsty. I get up, slowly, and walk into the bathroom, and as I turn on the faucet I look into the mirror for a long time until I am forced to notice the new lines beginning around the eyes. I avert my gaze and concentrate on the cold water rushing out of the faucet and filling the cup my hands have made.

I open a mirrored cabinet and take out a bottle. I take its top off and count only four Librium left. I pour one green-and-black capsule into my hand, staring at it, then place it carefully next to the sink and close the bottle and put it back into the medicine cabinet, and take out another bottle and place two Valium from it on the counter next to the green-and-black capsule. I put the bottle back and take out another. I open it, looking in cautiously. I notice there is not too much Thorazine left and I make a mental note to refill the prescription of Librium and Valium, and I take a Librium and one of the two Valium, and turn the shower on.

I step into the big white-and-black tiled shower stall and stand there. The water, cool at first, then warmer, hits me in the face hard and it weakens me, and as I slowly drop to my knees, the black-and-green capsule somehow lodged in the back of my throat,

I imagine, for an instant, that the water is a deep and cool aquamarine, and I'm parting my lips, tilting my head to get some water down my throat to help swallow the pill. When I open my eyes I start moaning when I see that the water coming down at me is not blue but clear and light and warm and making the skin on my breasts and stomach red.

After dressing I walk downstairs, and it distresses me to think of how long it takes to get ready for a day: of how many minutes pass as I wander listlessly through a large walk-in closet, of how long it seems to take to find the shoes I want, of the effort it takes to lift myself from the shower. You can forget this if you walk downstairs carefully, methodically, concentrating on each footstep. I reach the bottom landing and I can hear voices coming from the kitchen and I move towards them. From where I'm standing I can see my son and another boy in the kitchen looking for something to eat, and the maid sitting at the large, wood-block table staring at photographs in yesterday's *Herald Examiner*, her sandals kicked off, blue nail-polish on her toenails. The stereo in the den is on and someone, a woman, is singing, 'I found a picture of you.' I walk into the kitchen. Graham looks up from the refrigerator and says, unsmiling, 'Up early?'

'Why aren't you at school?' I ask, trying to sound like I care, reaching past him into the refrigerator for a Tab.

'Seniors get out early on Mondays.'

'Oh.' I believe him but don't know why. I open the Tab and take a swallow. I have a feeling that the pill I took earlier is still lodged in my throat, stuck, melting. I take another swallow.

Graham reaches past me and pulls an orange out of the refrigerator. The other boy, tall and blond, like Graham, stands by the sink and stares out the window and into the pool. Graham and the other boy both have their school uniforms on and they look very much alike: Graham peeling an orange, the other boy staring out at the water. I'm having a hard time not finding either one of their stances unnerving so I turn away, but the sight of the maid sitting at the table, sandals by her feet, the unmistakable smell of marijuana coming from her purse and sweater, somehow seems worse, and I take another swallow of Tab, then pour the rest of it down the sink. I begin to leave the kitchen.

375

Graham turns to the boy. 'Do you want to watch MTV?'

'I don't . . . think so,' the boy says, staring into the pool.

I pick up my purse which is sitting in an alcove next to the refrigerator and make sure my wallet is in it because the last time I was in Robinson's, it was not. I am about to walk out the door. The maid folds the paper. Graham takes off his burgundy letterman's sweater. The other boy wants to know if Graham has *Alien* on video. From the den, the woman is singing, 'Circumstance beyond our control.' I find myself staring at my son, blond and tall and tanned, with blank, green eyes, opening the refrigerator, taking out another orange. He studies it, then lifts his head when he notices me standing by the door.

'Are you going somewhere?' he asks.

'Yes.'

He waits for a moment, and when I don't say anything, he shrugs and turns away and begins to peel the orange, and somewhere on the way to Le Dôme to meet Martin for lunch, I realize that Graham is only one year younger than Martin, and I have to pull the Jaguar over to a curb on Sunset and turn the volume down and unroll a window, then the sun-roof, and let the heat from today's sun warm the inside of the car, concentrating on a tumbleweed that the wind is pushing slowly across an empty boulevard.

Martin is sitting at the round bar in Le Dôme. He is wearing a suit and a tie, and he is tapping his foot impatiently to the music that is playing through the restaurant's sound system. He watches me as I make my way over to him.

'You're late,' he says, showing me the time on a gold Rolex.

'Yes, I am,' I say, and then, 'Let's sit down.'

Martin looks at his watch and then at his empty glass and then back at me, and I am clutching my purse tightly against my side. Martin sighs, then nods. The *maître d'* shows us to a table and we sit down, and Martin starts to talk about his classes at UCLA and then about how his parents are irritating him, about how they came over to his apartment in Westwood unannounced, about how his stepfather wanted him to come to a dinner party he was throwing at Chasen's, about how Martin did not want to go to a dinner party his stepfather was throwing at Chasen's, about how tiredly words were exchanged.

I'm looking out the window at a Spanish valet standing in front of a Rolls-Royce, staring into it, muttering. When Martin begins to complain about his BMW and how much the insurance is, I interrupt.

'Why did you call the house?'

'I wanted to talk to you,' he says. 'I was going to cancel.'

'Don't call the house.'

'Why?' he asks. 'There's someone there who cares?'

I light a cigarette.

He puts his fork down next to his plate and then looks away. 'We're eating at Le Dôme,' Martin says. 'I mean, Jesus.'

'OK?' I ask.

'Yeah. OK.'

I ask for the check and pay it and follow Martin back to his apartment in Westwood where we have sex, and I give Martin a pith helmet as a gift.

I am lying on a *chaise longue* by the pool. Issues of *Vogue* and *Los Angeles* magazine and the Calendar section of the *Times* are stacked next to where I am lying, but I can't read them because the color of the pool takes my eyes away from the words, and I stare longingly into the thin aquamarine water. I want to go swimming, but the heat of the sun has made the water too warm, and Dr Nova has warned about the dangers of taking Librium and swimming laps.

A poolboy is cleaning the pool. The poolboy is very young and tanned and has blond hair; he is not wearing a shirt but he is wearing very tight, white jeans, and when he leans down to check the temperature of the water, muscles in his back ripple gently beneath smooth, clean, brown skin. The poolboy has brought a portable cassette-player that sits by the edge of the Jacuzzi, and someone is singing, 'Our love's in jeopardy,' and I'm hoping the sound of the palm fronds moving in the warm wind will carry the music into the Suttons's yard. I'm intrigued by how deep the poolboy's concentration seems to be, at how gently the water moves when he skims a net across it, at how he empties the net that catches leaves and multicolored dragonflies that seem to litter the water's gleaming surface. He opens a drain, the muscles in his arm flexing lightly, only for a moment. And I keep watching, transfixed, as he reaches into the round hole, and his arm begins to lift something out of the hole, muscles momentarily flexing again, and his hair is blond and wind-blown, streaked by sun, and I shift my body in the lounge chair, not moving my eyes.

The poolboy begins to raise his arm out of the drain and he lifts two large gray rags up and drops them, dripping, on to the concrete, and stares at them. He stares at the rags for a long time. And then he makes his way towards me. I panic for a moment, adjusting my sun-glasses, reaching for the tanning oil. The poolboy is walking towards me slowly, and the sun is beating down, and I'm spreading my legs and rubbing oil on the inside of my thighs and then across my knees and ankles. He is standing over me; Valium, taken earlier, disorients everything, makes backgrounds move in wavy, slow motion. A shadow covers my face and it allows me to look up at the poolboy, and I can hear from the portable stereo, 'Our love's in jeopardy,' and the poolboy opens his mouth, the lips full, the teeth white and clean and even, and I overwhelmingly need him to ask me to get into the white pick-up truck parked at the bottom of the driveway and have him instruct me to go out to the desert with him. His hands, perfumed by chlorine, would rub oil over my back, across my stomach, my neck. As he looks down at me, with the rock music coming from the cassette deck and the palm trees shifting in a hot desert wind and the glare of the sun shining up off the surface of the blue water in the pool, I tense up and wait for him to say something, anything, a sigh, a moan. I breathe in, stare up into the poolboy's eyes, through my sun-glasses, trembling.

'You have two dead rats in your drain.'

I don't say anything.

'Rats. Two dead ones. They got caught in the drain or maybe they fell in, who knows.' He looks at me blankly.

'Why . . . are you . . . telling me this?' I ask.

He stands there, expecting me to say something else. I lower my sun-glasses and look over at the gray bundle near the Jacuzzi.

'Take . . . them, away,' I manage to say, looking down.

'Yeah. OK,' the poolboy says, hands in his pockets. 'I just don't know how they got trapped in there?'

The statement, really a question, is phrased in such a languid

378

way that though it doesn't warrant an answer, I tell him, 'I guess
. . . we'll never know.'

I am looking at the cover of an issue of *Los Angeles*
magazine. A huge arc of water reaches for the sky, a fountain,
blue and green and white, spraying upward.

'Rats are afraid of water,' the poolboy is telling me.

'Yes,' I say. 'I've heard. I know.'

The poolboy walks back to the two drowned rats and picks
them up by their tails which should be pink but even from where
I'm sitting I can see are now pale blue, and he puts them into
what I thought was his toolbox, and then to erase the notion of
the poolboy keeping the rats, I open the *Los Angeles* magazine
and search for the article about the fountain on the cover.

I am sitting in a restaurant on Melrose with Anne and Eve and
Faith. I am drinking my second Bloody Mary, and Anne and
Eve have had too many kirs, and Faith orders what I believe to
be a fourth vodka gimlet. I light a cigarette. Faith is talking about
how her son, Dirk, had his driver's license revoked for speeding
down Pacific Coast Highway, drunk. Faith is driving his Porsche
now. I wonder if Faith knows that Dirk sells cocaine to tenth-
graders at Beverly Hills High. Graham told me this one afternoon
last week in the kitchen, even though I had asked for no
information about Dirk. Faith's Audi is in the shop for the third
time this year. She wants to sell it but she's confused about which
kind of car to buy. Anne tells her that ever since the new engine
replaced the old engine in the XJ6, it has been running well. Anne
turns to me and asks me about my car, about William's. On the
verge of weeping, I tell her that it is running smoothly.

Eve does not say too much. Her daughter is in a psychiatric
hospital in Camarillo. Eve's daughter tried to kill herself with a gun
by shooting herself in the stomach. I cannot understand why Eve's
daughter did not shoot herself in the head. I cannot understand why
she lay down on the floor of her mother's walk-in closet and
pointed her stepfather's gun at her stomach. I try to imagine the
sequence of events that afternoon leading up to the shooting. But
Faith begins to talk about how her daughter's therapy is
progressing. Sheila is an anorexic. My own daughter has met
Sheila and may also be anorexic.

Finally, an uneasy silence falls across the table in the restaurant on Melrose, and I stare at Anne who has forgotten to cover the outline of scars from the face-lift she had in Palm Springs three months ago by the same surgeon as did mine and William's. I consider telling them about the rats in the drain, or the way the poolboy floated into my eyes before turning away, but instead I light another cigarette, and the sound of Anne's voice breaking the silence startles me and I burn a finger.

On Wednesday morning, after William gets out of bed and asks where the Valium is, and after I stumble out of bed to retrieve it from my purse, and after he reminds me that the family has reservations at Spago at eight, and after I hear the wheels on the Mercedes screech out of the driveway, and after Susan tells me that she is going to Westwood with Alana and Blair after school and will meet us at Spago, and after I fall back asleep and dream of rats drowning, crawling desperately over each other in a steaming, bubbling Jacuzzi, and dozens of poolboys, nude, standing over the Jacuzzi, laughing, pointing at the drowning rats, their heads nodding in unison to the beat of the music coming from the portable stereos they hold in their golden arms, I wake up and walk downstairs and take a Tab out of the refrigerator and find twenty milligrams of Valium in a pillbox in another purse in the alcove by the refrigerator, and take two milligrams. From the kitchen I can hear the maid vacuuming in the living-room and it moves me to get dressed, and I drive to a Thrifty drugstore in Beverly Hills and walk towards the pharmacy, the empty bottle that used to be filled with black-and-green capsules clenched tightly in my fist. But the store is air-conditioned and cool, and the glare from the fluorescent lighting and the Muzak playing somewhere above me as background noise have a pronounced anesthetic effect, and my grip on the brown plastic bottle relaxes, loosens.

At the counter I hand the empty bottle to the pharmacist. He puts glasses on and looks at the plastic container. I study my fingernails and uselessly try to remember the name of the song that is floating through the store's sound system.

'Miss?' the pharmacist begins awkwardly.

'Yes?' I lower my sun-glasses.

'It says here "no refills".'

'What?' I ask, startled. 'Where?'

The pharmacist points to two typed words at the bottom of the piece of paper taped to the bottle next to my psychiatrist's name and next to that, the date, 10/10/83.

'I think Dr Nova made some kind of . . . mistake,' I say slowly, lamely, glancing at the bottle again.

'Well.' The pharmacist sighs. 'There's nothing I can do.'

I look at my fingernails again and try to think of something to say, which, finally, is, 'But I . . . need it refilled.'

'I'm sorry,' the pharmacist says, clearly embarrassed, shifting from one foot to the other, nervously. He hands me back the bottle, and when I try to hand it back to him, he shrugs.

'There are reasons why your doctor did not want the prescription refilled,' he offers kindly, as if speaking to a child.

I try to laugh, wiping my face, and gaily say, 'Oh, he's always playing jokes on me.'

I think about the way the pharmacist looked at me after I said this as I drive home.

I walk past the maid, the smell of marijuana drifting past me for an instant. Up in the bedroom I lock the door and close the shades and take off my clothes and put a tape of a movie in the Betamax and get under washed, cool sheets and cry for an hour and try to watch the movie. I take some more Valium and then I ransack the bathroom looking for an old prescription of Nembutal and then I rearrange my shoes in the closet and then I put another movie in the Betamax and then I open the windows, and the smell of bougainvillaea drifts through the partially closed shades, and I smoke a cigarette and wash my face.

I call Martin.

'Hello?' Another boy answers.

'Martin?' I ask anyway.

'Uh, no.'

I pause. 'Is Martin there?'

'Uh, let me check.'

I can hear the phone being set down and I want to laugh at the idea of someone, some boy, probably tanned, young, blond, like Martin, standing in Martin's apartment, putting the phone down and going to look for him, for anyone, in the small three-room studio, but it does not seem funny after a while. The boy comes back on the line.

'I think he's at the, um, beach.' The boy doesn't seem too sure.

I say nothing.

'Would you like to leave a message?' he asks, slyly for some reason, and then, after a pause, 'Wait a minute, is this Julie? The girl Mike and I met at 385 North? With the Rabbit?'

I don't say anything.

'You guys had about three grams on you and a white VW Rabbit.'

I do not say anything.

'Like, hello?'

'No.'

'You don't have a VW Rabbit?'

'I'll call back.'

'Whatever.'

I hang up, wondering who the boy is, if he knows about me and Martin, and I wonder if Martin is lying on the sand, drinking a beer, smoking a clove cigarette beneath a striped umbrella at the beach club, wearing Wayfarer sun-glasses, his hair slicked back, staring out to where the land ends and merges with water, or if instead he is actually on his bed in his room, lying beneath a poster of the Go-Gos, studying for a chemistry exam and at the same time looking through car advertisements for a new BMW. I'm sleeping until the tape in the Betamax ends and there's static.

I am sitting with my son and daughter at a table in a restaurant on Sunset. Susan is wearing a miniskirt that she bought at a store called Flip on Melrose, a store situated not too far from where I burned my finger at lunch with Eve and Faith and Anne. Susan is also wearing a white T-shirt with the words LOS ANGELES written on it in red handwriting that looks like blood that hasn't quite dried, dripping. Susan is also wearing an old Levi's jacket with a Stray Cats button pinned to one of the faded lapels, and Wayfarer sun-glasses. She takes the slice of lemon from her glass of water and chews on it, biting at the rind. I cannot even remember if we have ordered or not. I wonder what a Stray Cat is.

Graham is sitting next to Susan, and I am fairly sure that he is stoned. He gazes out past the windows and into the headlights of passing cars. William is making a phone call to the studio. He is in the process of tying up a deal which is not a bad thing. William has not been specific about the movie or the people in it or who is financing it. In the trades I have read rumors that it is a sequel to a very successful movie that came out during the summer of 1982, about a wisecracking Martian who looks like a big, sad grape. William has been to the phone in the back of the restaurant four times since we arrived; I have the feeling that he leaves the table and just stands in the back of the restaurant because at the table next to ours is an actress who is sitting with a very young surfer, and the actress keeps glaring at William whenever he is at the table, and I know that she has slept with him, and she knows I know, and when our eyes meet for a moment, by accident, we both turn away abruptly.

Susan begins to hum some song to herself as she drums her fingers on the table. Graham lights a cigarette, not caring if we say anything about it, and his eyes, red and half closed, water for a moment.

'There's this, like, funny sound in my car,' Susan says. 'I think I better take it in.' She fingers the rim of her sun-glasses.

'If it's making a funny noise, you should,' I say.

'Well, like, I need it. I'm seeing the Psychedelic Furs at the Civic on Friday and I totally have to take my car.' Susan looks at Graham. 'That's if Graham got my tickets.'

'Yeah, I got your tickets,' Graham says with what sounds like great effort. 'And stop saying totally.'

'Who did you get them from?' Susan asks, fingers drumming.

'Julian.'

'Not Julian.'

'Yeah. Why?' Graham tries to sound annoyed but seems tired.

'He's such a stoner. Probably got crappy seats. He's such a stoner,' Susan says again. She stops drumming, looks at Graham straight on. 'Just like you.'

Graham nods his head slowly and does not say anything. Before I can ask him to dispute his sister, he says, 'Yeah, just like me.'

'He sells heroin,' Susan says casually.

I glance over at the actress whose hand is gripping the surfer's thigh while he eats pizza.

'He's also a male prostitute,' Susan adds.

A long pause. 'Was that . . . statement directed at me?' I ask softly.

'That is, like, such a total lie,' Graham manages to say. 'Who told you that? That Valley bitch Sharon Wheeler?'

'Not quite. I know that the owner of the Seven Seas slept with him, and now Julian has a free pass and all the coke he wants.' Susan sighs, mock wearily. 'Besides, it's just too ironic that they both have herpes.'

This makes Graham laugh for some reason and he takes a drag from his cigarette and says, 'Julian does not have herpes and he did not get it from the owner of the Seven Seas.' Pause, exhale, then, 'He got VD from Dominique Dentrel.'

William sits down. 'Christ, my own kids are talking about Quaaludes and faggots, Jesus—oh take your goddamned sunglasses off, Susan. We're at Spago, not the goddamned beach club.' William gulps down half a white-wine spritzer that I watched go flat twenty minutes ago. He glances over at the actress and then at me, and says, 'We're going to the Schrawtzes' party Friday night.'

I finger my napkin, then I light a cigarette. 'I don't want to go to the Schrawtzes' party Friday night,' I say softly, exhaling.

William looks at me and lights a cigarette and says, just as softly, looking directly at me, 'What do you want to do instead? Sleep? Lie out by the pool? Count your shoes?'

Graham looks down, giggling.

Susan sips her water, glances at the surfer.

After a while, I ask Susan and Graham how school is.

Graham doesn't answer.

Susan says, 'OK. Belinda Laurel has herpes.'

I'm wondering if Belinda Laurel got it from Julian or the owner of the Seven Seas. I am also having a hard time restraining myself from asking Susan what a Stray Cat is.

Graham speaks up, barely, 'She got it from Vince Parker whose parents bought him a 928 even though they know he is completely into animal tranquillizers.'

'That is really . . . ' Susan pauses, searching for the right word.

I close my eyes and think about the boy who answered the phone at Martin's apartment.

'Grody . . . ' Susan finishes.

Graham says, 'Yeah, totally grody.'

William looks over at the actress groping the surfer and, grimacing, says, 'Jesus, you kids are sick. I've gotta make another call.'

Graham, looking wary and hungover, stares out the windows and over at Tower Records across the street with a longing that surprises me, and then I close my eyes and think about the color of water, a lemon tree, a scar.

On Thursday morning my mother calls. The maid comes into my room at eleven and wakes me by saying, 'Telephone, *su madre, su madre, señora*,' and I say, '*No estoy aquí*, Rosa, *no estoy aquí . . . * ' and drift back to sleep. After I wake up at one and wander out by the pool, smoking a cigarette and drinking a Perrier, the phone rings in the pool house and I realize that I will have to talk to my mother in order to get it over with. Rosa answers the phone, which is my cue to move back up to the main house.

'Yes, it's me.' My mother sounds lonely, irritated. 'Were you out? I called earlier.'

'Yes.' I sigh. 'Shopping.'

'Oh.' Pause. 'For what?'

'Well, for . . . dogs,' I say, then, 'shopping,' and then, 'for dogs.' And then, 'How do you feel?'

'How do you think?'

I sigh, lie back on the bed. 'I don't know. The same?' And then, after a minute, 'Don't cry,' I'm saying. 'Please, please, don't cry.'

'It's all so useless. I still see Dr Scott every day and there's the therapy, and he keeps saying, "It's coming along, it's coming along," and I keep asking, "*What's* coming along, *what* is coming along?" and then . . . ' My mother stops, out of breath.

'Does he still have you on the Demerol?'

'Yes.' She sighs. 'I'm still on the Demerol.'

'Well, this is . . . good.'

My mother's voice breaks again. 'I don't know if I can take this any more. My skin, it's all . . . my skin . . . '

'Please.'

' . . . is yellow. It's all yellow.'

I light a cigarette.

'Please.' I close my eyes. 'Everything is all right.'

'Where are Susan and Graham?'

'They're at . . . school,' I say, trying not to sound too doubtful.

'I would have liked to talk to them,' she says. 'I miss them sometimes, you know.'

I put the cigarette out. 'Yes. Well. They . . . miss you too, you know. Yes . . . '

'I know.'

Trying to make conversation, I ask, 'So, what have you been doing with yourself?'

'I just got back from the clinic and I'm in the process of cleaning out the attic and I found those photographs we took that Christmas in New York. The ones I've been looking for. When you were twelve. When we stayed at the Carlyle.'

For the past two weeks now my mother always seems to be cleaning out the attic and finding the same photographs from that Christmas in New York. I remember the Christmas vaguely. The hours that passed as she chose a dress for me on Christmas Eve, then brushing my hair in long, light strokes. A Christmas show at Radio City Music Hall, and the candy cane I ate during the show which resembled a thin, scared-looking Santa Claus. There was the night my father got drunk at the Plaza, and the fight between my parents in the taxi on the way back to the Carlyle, and later that night I could hear them arguing, the predictable sound of glass breaking in the room next to mine. A Christmas dinner at La Grenouille where my father tried to kiss my mother and she turned away. But the thing I remember most, the thing I remember with a clarity that makes me cringe, is that there were no photographs taken on that trip.

'How's William?' my mother asks when she gets no reply from me about the pictures.

'What?' I ask, startled, slipping back into the conversation.

'William. Your husband,' and then, with an edge, 'my son-in-law. William.'

'He's fine. Fine. He's fine.' The actress at the table next to ours last night in Spago kissed the surfer on the mouth as he scraped caviar off a pizza, and when I got up to leave, she smiled at me. My mother, her skin yellow, her body thin and frail from lack of food, is dying in a large, empty house that overlooks a bay in San Francisco. The poolboy has set traps smudged with peanut butter around the edges of the pool. Randomness, surrender.

'That's good.'

Nothing is said for close to two minutes. I keep count and I can hear a clock ticking and the maid humming to herself while cleaning the windows in Susan's room down the hall, and I light another cigarette and hope that my mother will hang up soon. My mother finally clears her throat and says something.

'My hair is falling out.'

I have to hang up.

The psychiatrist I see, Dr Nova, is young and tanned and drives a Peugeot and wears Giorgio Armani suits and has a house in Malibu and often complains about the service at Trumps. His practice lies off Wilshire and it's in a large white stucco complex across from Neiman Marcus, and on the days I see him I usually park my car at Neiman Marcus and wander around the store until I buy something and then walk across the street. Today, high in his office on the tenth floor, Dr Nova is telling me that at a party out in the Colony last night someone 'tried to drown'. I ask him if it was one of his patients. Dr Nova says it was the wife of a rock star whose single has been number two on the *Billboard* charts for the past three weeks. He begins to tell me who else was at the party when I have to interrupt him.

'I need the Librium refilled.'

He lights a thin, Italian cigarette and asks, 'Why?'

'Don't ask me why.' I yawn. 'Just do it.'

Dr Nova exhales, then asks, 'Why shouldn't I ask you?'

I'm looking out the window. 'Because I asked you not to?' I say softly. 'Because I pay you one hundred and thirty-five dollars an hour?'

Dr Nova takes a drag from his cigarette, then looks out the

window. After a while, he asks, tiredly, 'What are you thinking?'

I keep staring out the window, stupefied, transfixed by palm trees swaying in a hot wind, highlighted against an orange sky, and, below that, a billboard for Forest Lawn.

Dr Nova is clearing his throat.

Slightly irritated, I say, 'Just refill the prescription and . . . ' I sigh. 'All right?'

'I'm only looking out for your best interests.'

I smile gratefully, incredulous. He looks at the smile weirdly, uncertain, not understanding where it comes from.

I spot Graham's small, old Porsche on Wilshire Boulevard and follow him, surprised at how careful a driver he seems to be, at how he flashes his signals when he wants to change lanes, at how he slows and begins to brake at yellow lights and then comes to a complete stop at red lights, at how cautiously he seems to move the car across the road. I assume that Graham is driving home, but when he passes Robertson, I follow him.

Graham drives along Wilshire until he makes a right on to a side-street, after crossing Santa Monica. I pull into a Mobil station and watch as he pulls into the driveway of a large, white apartment complex. He parks the Porsche behind a red Ferrari and then gets out, looks around. I put on my sun-glasses, roll up my window. Graham knocks on the door of one of the apartments facing the street, and the boy who was over earlier in the week, in the kitchen, staring out into the pool, opens the door, and Graham walks in, and the door closes. Graham walks out of the house twenty minutes later with the boy, who is only wearing shorts, and they shake hands. Graham stumbles back to his car, dropping his keys. He stoops down to pick them up and after three tries, finally grabs them. He gets into the Porsche, closes the door and looks down at his lap. Then he brings his finger to his mouth and tastes it, lightly. Satisfied, he looks back down in his lap, puts something in the glove compartment and pulls out from behind the red Ferrari and drives back on to Wilshire.

There is a sudden rapping on the passenger window, and I look up, startled. It's a handsome gas-station attendant who asks me to move my car, and as I start the engine an image that I'm uneasy about the validity of comes into my line of vision: Graham at his sixth birthday party, wearing gray shorts, an expensive tie-dyed shirt, penny loafers, blowing out all the candles on a Flintstones birthday cake, and William bringing a Big Wheel tricycle out of the trunk of a silver Cadillac, and a photographer taking pictures of Graham riding the Big Wheel around the driveway, on the lawn and eventually into the pool. Driving on to Wilshire, I lose track of the memory, and when I get back home, Graham's car is not there.

I am lying in bed in Martin's apartment in Westwood. Martin has turned on MTV and he is lip-synching to Prince and he has his sun-glasses on and is nude and pretends to be playing the guitar. The air-conditioner is on and I can almost hear its hum which I try to focus on instead of Martin who begins to dance in front of the bed, an unlit cigarette hanging from his mouth. I turn over on my side. Martin turns the sound on the television off and puts on an old Beach Boys album. He lights the cigarette. I pull the covers up over my body. Martin jumps on the bed, lies next to me, doing leg lifts. I can feel him raising his legs slowly. He stops doing this and then looks at me. He reaches down below the covers and grins.

'Your legs are really smooth.'

'I had them waxed.'

'Awesome.'

'I had to drink a small bottle of Absolut to endure the process.'

Martin jumps up suddenly, straddling me, growling, imitating a tiger or a lion or actually just a very large cat. The Beach Boys are singing 'Wouldn't it be nice'. I take a drag from Martin's cigarette and look up at him. He is very tanned and strong and young, with blue eyes that are so vague and blank they are impossible not to fall into. On the television screen there is a piece of popcorn in black and white and beneath the popcorn are the words: VERY IMPORTANT.

'Were you at the beach yesterday?' I ask.

'No.' He grins. 'Why? Thought you saw me there?'

'No. Just wondered.'

'I'm the tannest one in my family.'

He has half an erection and he takes my hand and places it

around the shaft, winking at me sarcastically. I take my hand from it and run my fingers up his stomach and chest, and then touch his lips, and he flinches.

'I wonder what your parents would think if they knew a friend of theirs was sleeping with their son,' I murmur.

'You're not friends with my parents,' Martin says, his grin faltering slightly.

'No, I only play tennis with your mother twice a week.'

'Boy, I wonder who wins those matches.' He rolls his eyes. 'I don't want to talk about my mother.' He tries to kiss me. I push him off and he lies there and touches himself and mumbles the lyrics to another Beach Boys song. I interrupt him.

'Do you know that I have a hairdresser named Lance, and Lance is a homosexual. I believe you would use the term "a total homosexual". He wears make-up and jewellery, and has a very bad, affected lisp and he is constantly telling me about his young boyfriends and he is just extremely effeminate. Anyway, I went to his salon today because I have to go to the Schrawtzes' party tonight, and so I walked into the salon and I told Lillian, the woman who takes the appointments down, that I had an appointment with Lance, and Lillian said that Lance had had to take a week off, and I was very upset, and I said, "Where is he? On a cruise somewhere?" and Lillian looked at me and said, "No, he's not on a cruise somewhere. His son died in a car accident near Las Vegas last night," and I rescheduled my appointment and walked out of the salon.' I look over at Martin. 'Don't you find that remarkable?'

Martin is looking up at the ceiling and then he looks over at me and says, 'Yeah, totally remarkable.' He gets up off the bed.

'Where are you going?' I ask.

He pulls on his underwear. 'I have a class at four.'

'One you actually go to?'

Martin pulls on faded jeans and a Polo pullover, and slips his Topsiders on, and as I sit on the edge of the bed, brushing my hair, he sits next to me and, with a boyish smile spread wide across his face, asks, 'Baby, could I please borrow sixty bucks? I gotta pay this guy for these Billy Idol tickets and I forgot to go to the Instateller and it's just really a hassle . . . ' His voice trails off.

'Yeah.' I reach into my purse and hand Martin four twenties, and he kisses my neck and says perfunctorily, 'Thanks baby, I'll pay you back.'

'Yes you will. Don't call me baby.'

'You can let yourself out,' he calls as he walks out the door.

The Jaguar breaks down on Wilshire. I am driving and the sun-roof is open and the radio is on and suddenly the car jerks and begins to pull to the right. I step on the gas pedal and press it to the floor and the car jerks again and pulls to the right. I park the car, crookedly, next to the curb, near the corner of Wilshire and Le Cienega, and after a couple of minutes of trying to start it again, I pull the keys out of the ignition and sit in the stalled Jaguar with the sun-roof open and listen to the traffic passing. I finally get out of the car and find a phone booth at the Mobil station on the corner of La Cienega, and I call Martin, but another voice, this time a girl's, answers and tells me that Martin is at the beach, and I hang up and call the studio but I am told by an assistant that William is at the Polo Lounge with the director of his next film, and even though I know the number of the Polo Lounge I don't call. I try the house, but Graham and Susan are not there either, and the maid doesn't even seem to recognize my voice when I ask her where they are, and I hang up the phone before Rosa can say anything else. I stand in the phone booth for close to twenty minutes and think about Martin pushing me off the balcony of his apartment in Westwood. I finally leave the phone booth and I have someone at the gas station call the auto club, and they arrive and tow the Jaguar to a dealership in Santa Monica where I have a humbling conversation with a Persian named Normandie, and they drive me back to my house where I lie on the bed and try to sleep, but William comes home and wakes me up, and I tell him what happened, and he mutters 'typical' and says that we have a party to go to and that things will get bad if I don't start getting ready.

I am brushing my hair. William is standing at the sink, shaving. He has only a pair of white slacks on, unzipped. I am wearing a skirt and a bra, and I stop brushing my hair out and put on a blouse, and then resume brushing my hair. William washes his face, then towels it dry.

'I got a call at the studio yesterday,' he says. 'A very interesting call.' Pause. 'It was from your mother, which is a strange thing. First of all because your mother has never called the studio before, and second of all because your mother doesn't particularly like me.'

'That's not true,' I say, realizing it's better to pretend not to listen.

'You know what she told me?'

I don't say anything.

'Oh come on, guess,' he says, smiling. 'Can't you guess?'

I do not say anything.

'She told me that you hung up on her.' William pauses. 'Could this be true?'

'What if it could?' I put the brush down and put more lipstick on, but my hands are shaking and I stop trying and then I pick the brush up and begin brushing my hair again. Finally, I look up at William, who is staring at me in the mirror across from mine, and say, simply, 'Yes.'

William walks to the closet and picks out a shirt. 'I really thought you hadn't. I thought maybe the Demerol was getting to her or something,' he says drily. I start to brush my hair in fast short strokes.

'Why?' he asks, curious.

'I don't know,' I say. 'I don't think I can talk about that.'

'You hung up on your own fucking mother?' He laughs.

'Yes.' I put the brush down. 'Why are you concerned?' I ask, suddenly depressed by the fact that the Jaguar might be in the shop for close to a week. William just stands there.

'Don't you love your mother?' he asks, zipping his pants, then buckling a Gucci belt. 'I mean, my God, she's dying of cancer for Christ's sake.'

'I'm tired. Please. William. Don't,' I say.

'What about me?' he asks.

He moves to the closet again and finds a jacket.

'No. I don't think so.' These words come out clearly and I shrug. 'Not any more.'

'What about your goddamned children?' He sighs.

'Our goddamned children.'

'Our goddamned children. Don't be so boring.'

392

'I don't think so,' I say.

'Why not?' he asks, sitting on the bed, slipping on loafers.

'Because I . . . ' I look over at William. 'I don't know . . . them.'

'Come on baby, that's a cop-out,' he says derisively. 'I thought you were the one who said strangers are too easy to like.'

'No,' I say. 'You were, and it was in reference to fucking.'

'Well, since you don't seem to be too attached to anyone you're not fucking, I'd think we'd be in accordance on that score.' He knots a tie.

'I'm shaking,' I say, confused by William's last comment, wondering if I missed a phrase, part of a sentence.

'Oh Christ, I need a shot,' he says. 'Could you get the syringe—the insulin's over there.' He sighs, pointing. He removes his jacket, unbuttons his shirt.

As I fill a plastic syringe with insulin, I have to fight off the impulse to fill it with air and then plunge it into a vein and watch his face contort, his body fall to the floor. He bares his upper arm. As I stick the needle in, I say, 'You fucker,' and William looks at the floor and says, 'I don't want to talk any more,' and we finish dressing, in silence, then leave for the party.

And driving on Sunset with William at the wheel, a glass of vodka nestled between his legs, and the top down, and a warm wind blowing, and an orange sun setting in the distance, I touch his hand that is on the wheel, and he moves it to lift the glass of vodka up to his mouth, and as I turn away and we pass Westwood, up, above it, I can actually see Martin's apartment flash by.

After we drive up through the hills and find the house, and after William gives the car to the valet, and before we walk towards the front entrance, a crowded bank of photographers lined up behind a rope, William tells me to smile.

'Smile,' he hisses. 'Or at least try to. I don't want another picture like that last one in the *Hollywood Reporter* where you just stared off somewhere else with this moronic gaze on your face.'

'I'm tired, William. I'm tired of you. I'm tired of these parties. I'm tired.'

'The tone of your voice could have fooled me,' he says,

taking my arm roughly. 'Just smile, OK? Just until we get past the photographers, then I don't give a fuck what you do.'

'You . . . are . . . awful,' I say.

'You're not much better,' he says, pulling me along.

William talks to an actor who has a new movie opening next week and we are standing next to a pool, and there is a very young, tanned boy with the actor, who is not listening to the conversation. He stares into the pool, his hands in his pockets. A warm wind comes down through the canyons, and the blond boy's hair stays perfectly still. From where I'm standing I can see the billboards, tiny lit rectangles, on Sunset, illuminated by neon streetlights. I sip my drink and look back at the boy, who is still staring into the lit water. There is a band playing, and the soft, lilting music and the light coming from the pool, tendrils of steam rising from it, and the beautiful blond boy and the yellow-and-white striped tents that stand on a long, spacious lawn, and the warm winds cooling the palm trees, the moon outlining their fronds, act as an anesthetic. William and the actor are talking about the rock star's wife who tried to drown herself in Malibu, and the blond boy I'm staring at turns his head away from the pool and finally begins to listen.